# WITH WELLINGTON'S HUSSARS
## in the
# PENINSULA AND WATERLOO
### The Journal of Lieutenant George Woodberry, 18th Hussars

# WITH WELLINGTON'S HUSSARS in the PENINSULA AND WATERLOO

## The Journal of Lieutenant George Woodberry, 18th Hussars

Edited by

## Gareth Glover

and

## Colin Yorke

Frontline Books

## WITH WELLINGTON'S HUSSARS IN THE PENINSULA AND AT WATERLOO
### The Journal of Lieutenant George Woodberry, 18th Hussars

First published in 2018 by Frontline Books,
an imprint of Pen & Sword Books Ltd,
47 Church Street, Barnsley, S. Yorkshire, S70 2AS.

ISBN: 978-1-47389-397-9

CIP data records for this title are available from the British Library

Printed and bound by TJ International Ltd, Padstow, Cornwall
Typeset in 10.5/12.5 Palatino

For more information on our books, please email: info@frontline-books.com,
write to us at the above address, or visit:
**www.frontline-books.com**

# Contents

# Foreword

My interest in the journals of Lieutenant George Woodberry of the 18th Hussars was initially pricked by contact from a good friend of mine, Colin Yorke, who had previously worked with me on the publication of the Journal of Ensign John Drummond of the Coldstream Guards. He informed me that he had obtained a copy of Woodberry's journal held by the National Army Museum in Chelsea, which covers the period from January to September 1813 only[1]. I was already aware that excerpts of Woodberry's journal had been previously used by Eric Hunt in his book *Charging Against Napoleon*[2] but on further investigation I became really intrigued when I realised that the journals of George Woodberry had only ever been published fully in 1896 by Georges Helie in French! The French version also interestingly covered a much greater expanse of time, covering George's service from January 1813 right up until July 1815. Even more extraordinary was the discovery that the French version of early 1813, which covered the same period as the handwritten journal held by the National Army Museum, differed significantly in their content; not in the basic facts thankfully, but in the finer detail, each making mention of certain aspects which were not duplicated in the other with some dates also omitted in the French version. These idiosyncrasies had also been noted by Peter Hicks, a British professor who works with the Fondation Napoleon, who republished Woodberry's account, having added in the missing

---

[1]  Reference NAM 1968-07-26.
[2]  Published in 2001, Eric Hunt had used snippets from the diaries of three hussars to tell the story of the 18th Hussars during the Napoleonic Wars, one of which was George Woodberry's.

dates from the British version, but again only published in French. The handwriting in the English journal has been compared with the image of the one page we have of the notebook containing Woodberry's account as used in the French version by Helie. It is certainly identical, so why were there two versions of the same journal?

By now, my interest was definitely piqued and I decided to work with Colin on publishing the entire Woodberry journals for the very first time in English. This is the result, which I trust that the reader will find is an invaluable primary source on the life of a young hussar officer in Wellington's army, one which has for far too long been largely ignored in the Anglo-Saxon world simply because it was only available in the French language. Unfortunately, all records of the whereabouts of the journals Georges Helie was able to view and translate are now lost, but clearly, they were in France and with that country having suffered much in two world wars, it has to be presumed that the original journals no longer exist.

George's handwriting style is very fluid and quite neat in comparison with many of the scrawls the editor has had to grapple with previously. It is written by someone who was not only highly educated, but Woodberry was clearly a gifted writer and story teller and although he starts writing the daily journal reluctantly, it is clear that it soon became a source of comfort to him and was no longer a chore. There is some possibility that George may have preserved the journals with a view to publication, but if so it never came to fruition in his lifetime and there is thankfully no real evidence of wholesale amendments at a later period. The journal entries are fresh and uncluttered with the dreaded hindsight; humorous but also devastatingly blunt and honest at times; often providing the unvarnished truth as he saw it and he was also an incorrigible rumour monger.

In all, his journals are fascinating, scandalous and entertaining all at once, whilst the editor has found evidence to back up every statement he makes, even down to the British officers accused of cowardice at Waterloo, who were quietly persuaded to resign their commissions instead of causing great embarrassment by having to hold Court Martials weeks after the greatest victory of the British Army.

It must also be said, that George Woodberry is throughout, an enigmatic figure, his family, even his birth and death are still shrouded with some mystery, but a great deal of investigation work carried out by Colin, myself and the contacts we have managed to develop in Venezuela, have now answered most of the questions about his life, although frustratingly a number of gaps do still remain. If the publication of his journals leads to any further discoveries regarding the life and death of George Woodberry, the editor would gratefully receive such information via the publishers.

George Woodberry states that he was born on 13 April 1792[3] and he makes it clear that he viewed Worcester as his home. Utilising these few scraps of information at our disposal, it is almost certain that he hailed from the Woodberry family which resided in the ecclesiastical parish[4] of Claines. His grandfather (also a George) was baptised at Pershore near Worcester and married Hannah Mills at Claines on 22 January 1760. Our George was the son of the next generation of George Woodberrys who married his mother Maria (nee Pitman), in Claines on 18 July 1786. Two baptisms can be found in Claines for their children, William on 1 May 1787 and Elizabeth on 25 January 1791, there are however no records of a baptism for our George in 1792.

It is also unclear how the family made its money, as there are no records of commercial enterprises, deeds or wills to indicate their occupations; however the fact that his father was apparently a close friend of Lieutenant General Sir John James Hamilton, 1st Baronet (1755–1835) of Woodbrook near Strabane in Ireland, who was a highly respected and experienced officer of the Honourable East India Company, the British and Portuguese Army, there is more than a suspicion that his father made his money as a merchant, trading with the far east, but he probably was not a member of the East India Company himself, as he cannot be found in their records and he was settled in Worcester and fathering a number of children before he was beyond the age of thirty. The idea of the family trading is further backed up, by George's own statement that his elder brother William had died in Surinam in South America on 19 August 1809, because he does not appear to have served with the Royal Navy and therefore was almost certainly there carrying out mercantile operations of some kind.

George Woodberry joined the Army slightly late for somebody starting out on a military career, being twenty years old when he was gazetted as an Ensign in the 10th (North Lincolnshire) Regiment of Foot on 16 January 1812 vice (replacing) Ensign E.H. Bulkeley who had resigned his commission. Why George began his military career later than usual for this era, or why he chose a Lincolnshire regiment are still a mystery, although it may well have had something to do with the fact that a Lieutenant Colonel John Potter Hamilton, possibly a relative of

---

[3] He celebrated his twenty-first birthday on 13 April 1813, he must therefore have been born in 1792.

[4] Claines is not and never has been a village in its own right, but simply an ecclesiastical parish which encompassed a number of small villages to the north-west of Worcester.

General Hamilton, was then serving as a major in the 2nd Battalion of this regiment. George had purchased this rank, the regulation price then being £400[5], which was no small amount at the time[6] and shows that he clearly came from a moneyed background.

It is questionable if George ever actually joined the depot of the 10th Foot, both battalions of the regiment then serving abroad in the Mediterranean; because having gained this first rung on the ladder, George was not slow to exchange into the eminently more fashionable 18th Light Dragoons (Hussars) as a cornet. He exchanged into this regiment after only four months, on 9 April 1812 vice R. Greville who had been promoted. George again purchased this position, the regulation price for a cornet in a line cavalry regiment being no less than £735[7], although he would have got £400 back by the sale of his ensigncy in the infantry. George's record on joining the 18th Hussars confirm that he was from Worcester, that he was 21 years old and that he was 5 foot 9 inches (1.75 metres) tall. But George did not stop there in his meteoric rise, because having only served eight months in the hussars, barely time to complete his riding training, he purchased a lieutenancy[8] on 10 December 1812, in the regiment vice Lieutenant Samuel Greathead who had retired. This purchase[9] would have cost a very handsome £997 and 10 Shillings,[9] although he would have received £735 back by the sale of his cornetcy.

Purchasing rank, was by no means the only costs incurred in becoming a young hussar officer. The costs of becoming a cavalry officer were astronomical, providing a charger, a second horse and pack horse, saddlery, dress and undress uniforms, a curved 1796 pattern light cavalry sabre and accoutrements as well as a camp equipment suitable for a young gentleman to go on campaign with. Indeed, a board of officers was assembled in 1806 to enquire into the 'expense attending the equipment of a subaltern officer' which calculated that it cost a precise sum of £458[10] to kit a junior officer out appropriately, on top of his purchase costs, and that did not include the costs of hiring servants which were deemed 'almost absolutely necessary'. Therefore George, or more certainly his father, had laid out no less than £55,000 in modern terms to gain his lieutenancy in the cavalry that year.

[5] Figures from *The British Army Against Napoleon*, page 152.
[6] Equivalent to about £18,000 today.
[7] Equivalent to approximately £29,000 today.
[8] Malet in his history of the regiment does get confused regarding George Woodberry's rank in 1813, often referring to him as a Cornet.
[9] Equivalent to approximately £36,000 today.
[10] Equivalent today to around £19,000.

That was not all however. A cornet received pay of £146[11] per annum and a lieutenant £164 and 5 shillings[12] per annum, this was not adequate to live on comfortably in such an affluent regiment's mess, indeed it was calculated that an officer required an allowance from his father of no less than £500 a year simply to maintain the standards expected of a subaltern officer.

We unfortunately have no statement from George regarding his training, but on 1 January 1813, he began, somewhat reluctantly it would seem, a journal as the regiment began their march from Brighton en route for Portsmouth, having been ordered out to join the army in Portugal. Why was he writing a daily journal? The obvious answer would be, that it was the norm for an officer to retain a journal, almost certainly for their own and their family's edification in later years rather than with any idea of ever publishing such. However, in George's case there is the unusual fact that there have existed two versions (with some differences) of the first volume running from January to September 1813, although the one used for the French translation now appears to have been unfortunately lost forever along with the journals which continued on until 1815. Georges Helie does not appear to have known of the second version of the earliest journal, however Peter Hicks has incorporated passages from this second account to fill in the blanks in his revised French version, especially from around the time of the Battle of Vitoria.

There has been some confusion as to why two versions of his journals have existed at all, indeed to my knowledge, this is rather unique. Often roughly written daily journals were tidied up and expanded with a view to publication much later in Victorian times, when there became a national craving to read the journals of the soldiers who had fought in 'The Great War'.[13] However, George's journal was not re-written many years later; indeed it can be definitely established, that this 'fine copy' was actually transferred from his undoubtedly battered and scruffy daily journal on an almost daily basis, either last thing that evening, or more often, early the following morning before his regiment marched. Why? It can only be because he had promised to send a copy of his journal home, almost certainly this was done at the request of his parents, possibly in lieu of writing letters home, as there is little

---

[11] Equivalent to approximately £6,000 per annum.
[12] Equivalent to approximately £7,500 per annum.
[13] Until 1918 the British public had referred to the Napoleonic Wars as 'The Great War', when in that year an even more terrible and costly war ended, which was then given that sobriquet, which it retains to this day.

evidence in his journal that he ever wrote to them, although he often mentions writing to his sweethearts back in England and of course his accountant. The subtle differences in the texts of the two versions are undoubtedly often caused by a little self-censorship, (not repeating some of the colourful encounters he had with various women or easing back on descriptions of some of his antics), but he also sometimes changes his statements slightly, presumably based on a fuller knowledge of an incident at a later time. He headed the 'fine copy' *The Idle Companion of a Young Hussar During the Year 1813.*

However, what often gives away the different times of writing the two journals are the fact that the French version will say that they are about to march somewhere and then describe what happened on the march on the following day's entry; whilst the English version will often state that they have made the march and often record what happened on the march on the same day's entry. Because of this, much in the English journal on one date is often stated on the next day's entry in the French version. It is also clear that at times of extremes, particularly around the time of the Battle of Vitoria, George simply did not have the time to keep up his rough daily journal, hence the French version is silent on these days. As George had to find time to catch up writing his diary, possibly a few days after these events, he only wrote into his 'fine copy' and that is why these dates only have an entry in the English version. Occasionally, however, as I have previously said, George says more in the rough journal than went into the fine copy which was to be seen by other eyes. Luckily, we do have the alternative version of this first journal and we are able to enjoy his complete, unedited record of these events by comparing the two versions.

It should also be mentioned, that the fine copy of the journal held by the National Army Museum in inscribed within with the Blount family crest. The Blount family had two branches, one based at Mawley Hall in Shropshire and one at Sodington Hall, Mamble which lies only eight miles north west of Worcester. It is undoubtedly this second branch that knew the Woodberrys. Walter Blount the 7th Bart had died at the age of only thirty-five in 1803, his son Edward Blount, who was then only eight years old, becoming the 8th Bart and running the estate from his coming of age until his death in 1881. Edward Blount is almost certainly the man who either would have supplied the book to George to record his adventures in, or the book was given to him by the Woodberry family after George sent it home from Spain, and the crest added later. Either way, the Woodberrys being closely connected to the Blounts is another proof of the high social standing of the family.

In summary, in this first ever complete English version of George

Woodberry's journals I have chosen for the January to September period of 1813 to use the more expansive, fine copy, English version of his journal, but where the French version of these journal entries does contain different or fuller descriptions of events I have added this additional information into the text using italics to identify that it is from the alternate source. After September 1813, we unfortunately do not have fine copies of the journal and everything produced is a direct translation of the Helie version of his journal. However, having been able to directly compare the English and French versions of the first journal has allowed me to confirm that they are intrinsically the same account (with minor amendments as detailed above) and that gives me confidence that the remainder of the French account has been faithfully and correctly translated and published by Georges Helie. Obviously, it is far from ideal that this first English version is so heavily reliant on having to translate back from French, a text which has already been translated from the original English. Such double translation is guaranteed to mean that the words George actually wrote in 1814-15 cannot be exactly identical to the words we have produced here and it would be foolish to pretend that it ever could be; but what we can be sure of is that we have maintained the *meaning* of George's writing and this happily can be attested to by a close scrutiny of the two versions of the first journal, which actually translated back into very similar language to that he originally used and that the meanings were found to be identical. The reader can therefore feel comfortable that in reading this book, they are able to get a very honest picture of the adventures and scenes that George Woodberry endured in his three years of campaigning on foreign fields.

The only changes the editor has made to George Woodberry's text is some amendment of the punctuation to help the reader follow his meaning and the removal of much unnecessary capitalisation of words which is frankly simply irritating and in no way, alters the meaning. The only other change made is to alter, where known with absolute certainty, the names of places and people to conform with the official spelling to aid the reader in their identification. Where uncertain of a name I have indicated this either by a footnote or simply by [?] and if part of a word/name is omitted I have added the missing letters in and annotated these in [brackets] to indicate them as my additions for clarity. I have also inserted a great number of footnotes to help explain what or to whom George is referring, these can either be referred to as the reader progresses or ignored to allow George's story to flow. I have only occasionally given brief statements to guide the reader through the issues/occurrences George occasionally passes by without comment in the text, these additions have been kept to a minimum and are clearly delineated from George's own text.

There are however, two further questions to answer regarding these journals.

To the question as to whether George actually continued with the practise of writing up a 'fine copy' of the other later journals; the answer is almost certainly, yes, or at least he began to do so. George recounts that he was pleased to send home safely the first 'fine copy' of the journal which was now full, with his servant John Ipper in the autumn of 1813. He also mentions that he has another book ready to act as his 'fine copy' book for the next period of campaigning, but later he recounts having lost much of his baggage, which undoubtedly would have included this second copy of the journal. At this point, with little opportunity to procure another book to replace this lost 'fine copy' of the journal and with George probably not really fancying the chore of re-writing all of the lost section even if he could procure another suitable book, the idea of keeping the second journal going seems to have been shelved permanently and is never mentioned again. So, this explains why there is only one journal in the National Army Museum and why it only covers the first nine months of his campaigns.

The other obvious question is why did the full set of rough journals seemingly remained in France, when George left the country when he resigned in 1818, and whereby Georges Helie came to publish them in Paris nearly eighty years later? Unfortunately, George's journal ends in July 1815, probably because the fighting was then over and the boredom of garrison duties, even though in a delightful part of France, led to George to simply lose interest in recording the mundane. However, it is patently clear from George's journal, that he was a very young man, virile and adventurous, with a roving eye, but also liable to lose his heart to some attractive young lady on a regular basis, whilst still able to move on to another love, quickly forgetting the former, each time the regiment moved its quarters.

During his later years, which will be fully described at the end of his journals, he actually attested in court in 1824 that he had formally converted to Catholicism whilst in France in 1818. It is not too much of a leap into the dark therefore, to suggest that George converted with the aim of marrying some French girl he had met during this period and that the journals were left with her, when the romance fell through and George finally left France, never to return. In fact, it is virtually the only plausible explanation.

Having explained the strange and convoluted circumstances regarding George's various journals, it is with relief that we can now turn to George Woodberry's service with the 18th Hussars in Spain, France and Belgium. The 18th was basically an Irish regiment, raised in Ireland in 1759, with the Earl of Drogheda as its colonel and many of the men enlisting from that island, but it had no official nomenclature at this time. In early 1813 George embarked with six troops[14] of the 18th Hussars for Portugal and having arrived in Lisbon, where the regiment was brigaded with two further hussar regiments, everything was prepared for their advance to join the Duke of Wellington's army, which then lay in their winter cantonments along the Portuguese border, waiting impatiently for spring to arrive when the Anglo/Portuguese army could march into Spain once again and attempt to finally drive the French army out of Spain. The previous year, the Duke of Wellington had wrested – at great human cost - the major border fortresses of Ciudad Rodrigo and Badajoz and had then smashed the French Army in the field at a stunning victory just outside Salamanca. Following up this success, Madrid had been captured and the French had been forced to abandon southern Spain in its entirety. Unfortunately, the year had not ended so happily for the allies, with Wellington failing to capture the minor fortress at Burgos and being chased back out of Spain by superior French forces. This retreat was made infinitely worse by the complete breakdown of the supply system, leaving the soldiers to virtually starve, living only on acorns and the occasional stolen livestock – despite the threat of hanging if caught in the act – desperate times requiring desperate measures to survive.

Despite this disastrous end to the year's campaigning, the new year augured in the promise of a great advance, with luck, they would drive the French over the Pyrenees and completely free Spain from their tyranny. The reason there was such optimism in Wellington's army was primarily based on the fact that news of Napoleon's Grand Army having perished almost to a man in the snows of Russia was now filtering through to the troops, and that the French were rapidly reducing their numbers in Spain to make good their losses in Germany. George and his fellow hussars therefore arrived in Portugal at the perfect time to be fully involved in this new and, quite possibly, pivotal campaign.

It is now time to let George tell his own story.

---

[14] Cavalry regiments at this time usually consisted of five squadrons, each of two troops numbering in practise around sixty men per troop, each commanded by a captain or senior lieutenant.

about 2 OClock a Prussian ADC of Bluchers arrived from the Left &
enquired for Wellington and told us that 30,000 Prussians were advancing
to our Assistance soon afterwards we saw them coming but at a great distance
Nothing could equal the grandour of the sight the attack on our Centre.
the Enemy opposed a horrible fire of Artillery from more than 200
peices under cover of the Smoke of which Buonaparte made a General
attack with Cavalry & Infantry in such numbers that it required
all the Skill of Wellington to post his Troops & all the good qualities
of the latter to resist the Attack:— General Picton who was on the
high Road from Brussels to Charleroi advanced with the Bayonet
to receive them but was unfortunately killed at the moment when
the Enemy appalled by the attitude of the Division fled & fled thus fell
one of the finest Characters in the British Army — — Picton —

    Thy name — our charging Posts along
    Shall be the Battle word —
    Thy fall — the theme of choral song.
    From Virgin voices poured.
    To Weep — would do thy glory wrong.
    Thou shalt not be deplored: —

The Life Guards & Blues then Charged with the greatest vigour.
and the 29th & 105th French Regiments lost their Eagles in this charge
together with from 2 to 3000 Prisoners.— a Column of French Cavalry
at whose head were the Cuirassiers charged but were not successful
After this the Prussians came up & commenced skirmishing & pettering in
the rear of the Enemy. the French Cavalry charged them in Style. but
nothing could save the fate of the Day — the French army was Defeated —

# Acknowledgements

As always with a work of such complexity, there are many people who contribute along the way and deserve my very grateful thanks. I must of course start by thanking Colin Yorke for bringing these journals to my notice and ably supporting me in the seemingly interminable problems we encountered in establishing much of the life of George Woodberry. It is my heartfelt hope that this is not the last time we work together.

I must offer my thanks to Martin Mace and John Grehan at Frontline Books for supporting my aim of publishing as much as possible of this Napoleonic material. As always, I have to offer my thanks to the Napoleonic community in general who have helped me solve a number of thorny questions raised in George's journals, but I must single out Ron McGuigan for particular thanks, a man who has an ability to discover information that often simply astounds me. In our great quest to learn of George Woodberry's later life in Venezuela Colin and I would like to thank Luisa Henriquez, Esther Nouel, Francisco Guerra Hernández, Milhone Tosta, Edgardo Mondolfi Gudat and Rosalind Roystone for the help and enthusiastic support that they willingly offered on what is a difficult, complex story, not helped by the seriously dangerous state of Venezuela at present.

Finally, I must as always reserve my final words of thanks for my wonderful wife, Mary, who has as always unquestioningly supported me entirely in my pursuit of my great (other) passion.

Gareth Glover
Cardiff April 2017

# Chapter 1

# Ordered to Join the Army

Porchester Castle, Friday 1 January 1813
The Eighteenth Regiment of Hussars marched this day from
Brighton[1] on their route to Portsmouth to embark for Portugal. I was
commanding a detachment of twenty men here[2], when I heard the
orders for embarkation had arrived, Lieutenant Morris[3] was
immediately despatched to relieve me, and I posted off to Brighton,
to take leave of my friends Mrs Perkins and Amelia[4]. I met the first
division of the regiment at Arundel[5].

Brighton, Saturday 2nd Jan Saturday.
I dined with my friends here and took my leave about 11 o'clock.
Slept at the castle (Arundel), and left Brighton about 4 o'clock Sunday
morning, met the regiment at Havant, orders having arrived for them
to remain there till the transports are ready to take us on board.
Smith[6] and his wife with Mrs Moseley[7] were at Emsworth, dined
with them, when Mrs M[oseley] gave me a small parcel, containing

---

[1]  The regiment had been in Preston Barracks, Lewes Road, Brighton.
[2]  Porchester Castle was then being used as a Prisoner of War depot and George Woodberry's detachment
    would have been there, to act rapidly in the event of an escape and to convey messages.
[3]  James Morris had joined the regiment as a cornet on 2 April 1812 and had gained the rank of lieutenant
    on 22 October 1812. He was captured at the Action of Moralles on 1 June 1813 but was released after two
    days.
[4]  This would appear to be a Miss Amelia Perkins, the child of Charles and Mary Perkins who was baptised
    at Southwark on 14 February 1802. This would make her only just over eleven years old. I have not found
    any record of her marrying and it would appear that she was buried at Mile End Town in late 1879.
[5]  George was attached to Captain Bolton's Troop.
[6]  Lieutenant Enos Smith, 18th Hussars.
[7]  I have been unable to establish any family contact with the Moseley's, however he later calls Mrs Moseley
    'Aunt', presumably meaning that she was a close friend of the family rather than an official aunt. Miss
    Moseley her daughter was therefore a close friend rather than related to George.

a note and a seal from Amelia, and a gold pencil case and a pen from Mrs Perkins; how kind they have always been to me, what return can I make equal to it. The feelings I entertain of respect and friendship for them will never be effaced – no this will never decay.

Havant, 7 January 1813.
So much pleased this morning by the arrival of my friend Mr Vanboorst[8], who came to see me before I left the kingdom.
The six troops were split over nine transport ships, the *Belona, Majestic, Lutona, William, Richard, Eeres, London, Lord St Helens* and *Bulman*.

Saturday 9 January.
This evening I went to Brighton to see Miss Amelia, once more before I go, was with her and Mrs Perkins till Wednesday the 13th. When I returned to Havant and found the order for embarkation had arrived and the first division of the regiment marched into Portsmouth to embark. I found Mr Vanboorst waiting very impatiently for my return, we went together to Portsmouth, got there just as my horses were put on board the *London* No. 287 viz bay horse, pony, and grey horse – [named] Crafty, and God send they may go safe.

Portsmouth; remained here till Sunday evening 17th when I went on board the *London* No. 287 with Lieutenant Hesse[9] to take my passage, during the time I remained in Portsmouth I went several times to the theatre, and saw Mr Betty[10] perform several of his most favourite pieces, dined with Smiths and Mrs Moseley several times.

Laid in sea stock:
12 Live fowls
Lemons [*for the punch*] and Oranges
2 Hams
2 Cases Portable Soup
3 Dried Tongues
3 Quarts of *Oats for Porridge*
6 Half quarters of Loaves

[8]    I have been unable to identify this Mr Vanboorst [or Van Voorst], however it is clear that he was George's accountant.
[9]    Charles Hesse had joined the regiment as a Cornet on 1 December 1808 and had gained the rank of lieutenant on 4 May 1809.
[10]   Mr William Henry Betty, was a famous child actor performing around 1800, who had quit the stage in 1808 to attend Christ's College Oxford. Having graduated, he tried to relaunch his career, with a return to Covent Garden in 1812, but he was unable to find the magic he had shown as a child actor and had therefore sought work outside of London.

3 Dozen *Sour* Herrings
3 Pound Butter
3 Dozen *Bottle of* Porter
3[11] Pound Tea
3 Bottles Brandy
1 Pound Coffee
2 Bushel Potatoes
9 Pound Sugar
2 Pound Cheese
3 *Pound of* Wax Candles
*30 Pounds of Fresh meat*
*3 Jars of Pickles*
*Milk*
6 Pounds of Rice *for pudding*

The regimental history records that six troops[12] of the 18th Hussars embarked on 13th and 14th of January for Portugal, under the command of Lieutenant Colonel the Honourable Henry Murray. The passage to Portugal was enlivened, not just by the weather, but also by the real threat of capture by American privateers, America having declared war on Britain in 1812.

Ryde, Monday 18 January.
Went on board the *Majestic*[13] in the *London's* boat, saw Deane, Bolton and *Quincey*[14], *and found them very sick in their hammocks. After we had mocked them, we* then went to Ryde *to order a good breakfast,* where Hesse and myself dined; it's a very pretty village, lays close to the sea having Spithead opposite to it. After dinner we returned to the ship. *Walk to the village, chat with the girls and dinner, orgy complete and retire on board –  fifteen shillings for one mile for the boatman!* The commodore's ship, the *Aboukir* 74 guns[15] lies very near us; *and the sloop, the Spitfire*[16] *form our convoy;* he hoisted the Blue Ensign this evening for all officers and men

---

[11] Incorrectly shown as 2 in the French version.
[12] Cavalry regiments at this time were usually formed of four or five squadrons, each squadron being split into two troops, each of which were commanded by captains.
[13] HMS *Majestic* was a 74-gun warship built at Deptford in 1785 and which had taken part in Nelson's Battle of the Nile in 1798.
[14] This refers to Paymaster William Deane, Captain Robert Dawson Bolton and Assistant Surgeon John Quincey, all of the 18th Hussars.
[15] HMS *Aboukir* had been launched on 18 December 1807 at Frindsbury in the Medway.
[16] HMS *Spitfire* had originally been built as a fireship in 1782, but was re-designated as a 14-gun sloop during the Napoleonic wars.

to repair on board their respective ships. The wind this evening remained very fair, *we'll probably sail early tomorrow*. This being her Majesties birthday[17], all 'the men of war' in Portsmouth harbour and Spithead fired a royal salute in honour of it, it had a beautiful effect and gave me some idea of a naval engagement. Slept in a hammock or cot last night *for the first time*, like the berth very well, may [I] never lay in a worse place or sleep less comfortably than I did in it.

Tuesday 19 January.
About ½ past 9 o'clock this morning we set sail from Spithead, the whole convoy got under weigh and had a very pleasing effect, about 98 sail, [for the] most part transports, having our regiment, the 15th Hussars and detachments of several *infantry regiments*. During the day we spoke with Smith, Dolbel and Kennedy[18] on board the *Latonia* No. 363, Smith informed me that he left Mrs S[mith] And Miss Moseley in very good health and spirits in the care of his brother at Portsmouth, strong breeze blowing all day, *and as long as gay England was in sight, the bridges [decks?] were filled with the world and many anxious eyes were turned towards this side.* Have lost sight of land this afternoon *about four o'clock. Almost all the passengers very sick. For the moment, I feel good, but my servant Ipper[19] made all the necessary preparations for when I'll be sick; I suppose therefore that I will be. Poor Hesse already looks like a corpse.*

Wednesday 20 January.
This morning found the fleet off Plymouth, saw land again, thank God. Had a beautiful view of the Eddystone Lighthouse and the convoy for miles round. *We have on board eleven infantry officers, mostly of the 42nd[20]. Around four o'clock* this afternoon we laid to, agreeable to signal from the commodore Captain Parker[21] of *Aboukir* and the *Spitfire* sloop of war for the fleet in Falmouth to join the convoy. The sea very rough all night, Hesse and most of the people on board were sea sick this night, *except the crew and me.* Saw the Lizard light very plain and land most of the night, was walking on deck till about 2 o'clock a.m.

---

[17] I can find no royal personage in the family of King George III with a birthday on 18 January, nor any other event to warrant such a salute.
[18] Lieutenant Enos Smith, Cornet John Dolbel and Captain Arthur Kennedy of the 18th Hussars.
[19] Private John Ipper, who did receive a Waterloo Medal.
[20] The 42nd Foot had lost heavily during the 1812 campaign in Spain, including four officers killed at the Siege of Burgos. This cadre of officers was obviously being sent out to make up the shortfall.
[21] Captain George Parker R.N.

Thursday 21 January.

The sea very rough, the wind blowing very hard, yet we were obliged to lay before the wind waiting for the ships out of Falmouth harbour. The Lizard is a bold looking land, and may in fair weather be seen a long way off, near it are the *Shag*[22] rocks, Eddystone Lighthouse I saw yesterday, stands on a bed of rocks, sunken and can be seen 20 miles off, we hove to within a few miles of it, during the night it had a beautiful effect. Some years back a French frigate destroyed this lighthouse, but upon it being represented to Louis XV, the captain was immediately dismissed the service[23]. This day last year I was gazetted in the army, ensign in the 10th Regiment of Foot[24]. Soon after three p.m. the commodore and the Falmouth fleet appeared in sight, about 12 sail. We now set sail again with a south-east wind, went all night about 7 knots an hour. Hesse, *was so sick that I did not expect him to last the night.* Likewise, my servant, *in the same state and all the good things he has prepared for me he serves to himself.* the Lizard lighthouse[25] we saw very plain this evening.

Friday 22 January.

Wind remains still very fair, *the captain promises* if it continues, we shall be there, Lisbon, about Sunday night next *or Monday.* Lost all sight of land, entered the Bay of Biscay about 12 this day, and rather disappointed the sea not more blusterous than in the channel.

Saturday [23rd]

Wind still continues very fair, saw the Lisbon packet[26] sail through the fleet. An owl was found roosting on one of the masts this morning, but was frightened away before a gun could be loaded. Two women aboard very ill, one brought on deck in a very fainting state, gave her some brandy *and my oatmeal. One of them tried tonight to throw themselves over the edge. Great tumult!* This night an American privateer chased us *and we to windward of the fleet,* but we sailed too fast for her, we saw large shoals of porpoises jumping out of the sea,

---

[22] George wrote Stag, but it is actually named Shag Rock off the Lizard.

[23] George is slightly in error here, during the construction of the first lighthouse in 1696, a French privateer took the builder Henry Winstanley prisoner and destroyed the work done so far on the foundations, causing Louis XIV to order Winstanley's release with the words 'France is at war with England, not with humanity'.

[24] George had joined the 10th Foot as an Ensign by purchase vice Bulkeley who retired. Ref. *The London Gazette* 16564.

[25] The current lighthouse at the Lizard was built in 1751 and manned by Trinity House from 1771.

[26] A regular mail service ran from England to Lisbon during the war.

round the vessel. Some on board who wished to be considered knowing, said it predestinates hard weather, but the weather still remains as it did. During the night, we passed Cape Ortegal on the coast of Spain. The fleet is very much dispersed. Hope to God, none of our transports are taken by the French or the Yankies, several suspicious vessels have been seen this evening.

Cape Finisterre, Sunday 24 January
Found the fleet this morning off Cape Finisterre, out of the Bay of Biscay, God be thanked. About 10 a.m. we hove to waiting for the commodore and the fleet to windward to come up. The convoy very much dispersed this morning, some of the ships appeared twenty miles off us. Set sail again about 12, the wind very much abated and getting more to the south. The climate very much altered, the weather more like June or July than January, it had a surprising effect on all those on board. The women [were] found walking on deck for the first time, *all joyous and all the world seems content.* Hesse much better, so was my servant Ipper, about 3 p.m. was completely becalmed, the sea as serene and smooth as the Thames. This was a new sight to me and brought many pleasing thoughts to my recollection as I sat on deck, had I the pen of a Gray, Goldsmith or Falconer[27], I might describe the calm.

Whose least wave stood tremulous, uncertain where to turn![28] The view now became particularly grand. The convoy carrying all the canvas they were able, had a beautiful effect, but it was all of no avail, we could not proceed, the ships were their own masters, going where they pleased, we made about one knot an hour all night. *We are almost there but must wait throughout the night.*

Monday 25 January.
Found the calm continued all night and much the same all day. The sea if possible more smooth than yesterday, all on board recovered of their sickness. Very surprising I have not been sea sick myself, never having been to sea before in my whole life. The captain lent me some fishing tackle, but after several hours of fruitless attention and fatigue, gave it up as a bad job. Still off Cape Finisterre, saw *a*

---

[27] He refers to Thomas Gray a well-known poet (1717-1771) made famous by his *Elegy Written in a Country Churchyard*, Oliver Goldsmith the Irish novelist and playwright (1728-1774) famous for *The Vicar of Wakefield* and *She Stoops to Conquer* and William Falconer (1744-1824), a physician, but also a prolific writer of very miscellaneous essays.

[28] From a poem entitled *Rambles in Autumn* by James Thompson (1700-1748).

*host of these sea creatures* which the sailors call Portuguese Men of War, and likewise many birds called 'Mother Carey's Chickens'[29]. About 8 p.m. a slight breeze sprung up, we sailed about 4 knots an hour all night. This day I dined with Hesse on board the *Thomas, and* Captain Williams *his friend,* bound for the coast of Africa. The captain *gave a good dinner and* made us both pretty well tipsy, and then we returned to the *London*; Hesse very ill after this frolic. *At eight hours, a light breeze blew up.*

Tuesday 26 January.
This morning it became calm again, *and from the top of the mast,* we saw land for a short time, supposed to be Vigo. Two strange sail amongst the fleet this morning, but owing to the calm, the commodore could not make sail after them; they looked very much like American privateers. Hope none of our convoy are captured, am very fearful for some, only sixty-two in sight this morning, out of near one hundred and *twenty*[30]. This evening a breeze sprang up from the south, was therefore, obliged to haul to against the wind *and to shorten the sails.* Took an observation today at Meridian[31]; found ourselves [in] latitude 41 degrees 20 minutes, Atlantic Ocean.

Wednesday 27 January.
The wind very much against us, kept tacking about in hopes of getting on. The commodore made signals to the fleet which our captain did not perceive; he fired a shot at our vessel which had very nearly gone into the cabin (*the ball glanced the cabin window*). Hesse and self were sitting at dinner when we heard the shot whiz [by]. A Spanish corvette, suppose from the coast passed through our fleet, the commodore fired a shot at her and she hauled to, he then made signals for her to come close to him and signals to the convoy to lay to till he had examined her papers, and he detained the fleet about two hours. The hold in an uproar this morning, arising from a man – i.e. a brute, breaking a bottle on his wife's head, we had the fellow confined in the forecastle and stopped his grog and upon our making enquiry respecting the woman and quarrel, found the fault on her side, allowing the black cook to kiss her, therefore her grog was stopped likewise. Latitude 40 deg. 35 min., the more I see of the world, the more I am disgusted with [both] man and woman of the

---

[29] Storm petrels.
[30] He previously stated ninety-eight vessels, but of course further ships had joined off Falmouth.
[31] The height of the sun at midday.

lower order. Fancy a brute such as the one mentioned, striking a woman on the head with a wine bottle, and then the woman to so far degenerate herself, as to allow the black cook, the ugliest man I ever saw, take liberties with her person and that, under the eyes of her husband. I cannot form an idea which of the two deserves most blame.

Thursday 28 January.
The wind very much against us all day making very little progress in our voyage, most of our provision gone, only 3 fowls left. One I gave to Mrs Sweeney *wife of Sergeant Sweeney*[32], poor woman she is still very ill. I am rather unwell, have a very bad cold, begin to get low spirited, being kept here so long *and so tossed about*, latitude 39 deg. 25min.

Friday 29 January.
In very low spirits, wind very much against us *but flitting, we did a little tack*, about 1 p.m, saw land which afterwards proved to be the Rock of Lisbon[33] *but we soon lost view*; very happy in the knowledge we are so near our journeys end. Kept sight of it all afternoon, the wind very much against us, can never get in with this wind. *Everyone fears a storm, simply because a few porpoises innocently made their antics around the ship and Falconer*[34] *makes them appear before a storm. We have already seen however it had not been a major issue, on this ship. I have always seen superstitious people as odd, I had fun whistling and the captain requested me to stop for fear that the sailors do not do me some violence. I saw that despite my kindness to the women on board, I was dealt as if I was crazy or worse, as I had whistled.* Latitude 38 deg. 35 min., we kept tacking about all day and night.

Saturday 30 January.
This morning the Rock of Lisbon appeared very plain, suppose about 9 leagues off. The wind remained in the same quarter, blowing fresh off the Tagus. The sea as rough as in the Bay of Biscay, owing to the wind and tide, very few of the convoy to be seen, all much scattered *and it is believed that none has yet entered into the river. I don't like all this renewed life: now all of them are cheerful and healthy and I feel*

---

[32] This is Sergeant William Sweeney or Swiney.
[33] The Cabo da Roca, a sight of this promontory indicated that they were near Lisbon.
[34] William Falconer, Scottish poet, died in a shipwreck in 1770. Woodberry is here referring to his descriptive poem in three songs *The Shipwreck* written in 1762.

*disgusted with everything. I lost my appetite and I am then expected to share the joy of my companions.*

Sunday 31 January.
Our vessel much further from the rock this morning, than it was last night, blowing a strong breeze from the east all day. *Read the prayer for the troops on board. Our horses are starting to be sick.*

Monday 1 February 1813.
This morning the captain called me up soon after six of the clock to see the eclipse of the sun, which appeared as the sun arose about 7 a.m. and remained partially eclipsed till 10 minutes to 8 o'clock. It was a most beautiful sight and I was much gratified with the sight, not having seen an eclipse of the sun for 8 years before. Still beating about, the wind remaining in the same quarter. A thief on board, two of the men lost things, one a clock, the other a pair of boots. I made complaints to the captain and he ordered his sailors on deck, during which time my sergeant and the mate went into the forecastle and searched it over, when at last they discovered both articles hid under some sails and it was afterwards ascertained that a sailor named Scott had stole them. The captain wished to have the fellow punished by running the gauntlet[35], but I persuaded him not, as the fellow appeared very sorry for his offence. *Otherwise it will be like a vessel of war.* The wind changed two points this afternoon and we were able to make more sail and got very near the Tagus during the night.

Tuesday 2 February.
Was much pleased this morning on finding we lay so near the mouth of the Tagus, Lisbon Rock on our left and Cape Espichel on our right, we got into the Tagus about 2 o'clock *the mouth of the river is several miles wide and we can just see the city of Lisbon at a distance of 20 miles,* when a complete calm came on. The scenery here appeared very grand. Fort Saint Julian and the distant view of Belem and Lisbon, which appeared placed on so many hills, and forms to the eye one of the most grand and pleasing sights that can be conceived. The Rock whose gigantic members hideous to our view being too near, had a very romantic and grand appearance when contemplated

---

[35] The gauntlet entailed the crew standing in two lines, armed with ropes ends or wooden batons, the man to be punished having to pass between the two lines, receiving their blows as he progressed.

from a distance of a few leagues, thank God we got past the bar before 9 o'clock this evening, and can cast anchor. I then went to bed happier than I had been for many day's past. Spoke this evening to Smith on board the *Latonia* 363, all well, I was very happy to hear his voice again; it being night could not see him. Hesse and I had fun with our journals because Hesse kept a diary, and it is through his persuasion that I started mine; will I be in the mood to continue? We were even now worried we would be stopped by a calm and if there is a current in the river or the wind changes we could be caught in the open sea. We are all upset by the lack of fresh meat. I now hate eating fish!

# Chapter 2

# Preparing for Campaign

Having finally arrived at Lisbon following a tedious passage, George was eager to get himself ashore and explore this novel new world. It would not be long before George viewed Lisbon without his rose-tinted glasses on and saw the real city. The troops were quickly disembarked and were soon organising their equipment and fattening their horses ready for the trying campaign that was only a few months away.

Lisbon, Wednesday 3 February.
The tolling of the bells woke me this morning about six o'clock, I was awakened by a view of Lisbon which appeared fully as if by magic. Many boats brought us fruit, bread and edibles. The strange aspect of the Portuguese, their dress and their ways, meant that for a while I couldn't believe my senses. Thank God landed safe at last after 14 days being tossed about. I had every eye on me as I came on shore at eleven o'clock at Black Horse Square[1]. I then kept walking on not knowing where to go, at last I met Hesse who had soon followed me on shore, our uniforms did bring many curious looks[2] and we then took a turn through all the principal streets and so on

---

[1] Officially known as the Pracio do Comercio, this fine square in Lisbon has the statue of King Jose I on horseback prominently at its centre. The statue has turned more green now with verdigree but was black then. It therefore became known colloquially as 'Black Horse Square'.
[2] The army had been in Portugal for over four years by this time, so this comment may at first appear strange. However, the hussars had only previously been on the peninsula for a short spell in 1808 up until the Battle of Corunna and in that campaign, they had landed at Corunna and returned to England from that port, never actually setting foot in Portugal. Therefore, their appearance in hussar uniform at Lisbon in early 1813 was a complete novelty.

until a time when fatigue made us think of our comfort. Seeing a name written at a hotel and hoping to find a compatriot there, we went in and we were not disappointed in our expectation and afterwards went to a hotel kept by a Mrs Benson, an Irish woman, got a good dinner. Afterwards went with some infantry officers to the opera being Madam Bernadette Benefit.

The house is tolerably good, considering that the actors repeat verbally what the prompter reads, and that often louder than the actor, they get through their parts with much spirit. The music is pleasing and they dance a sort of 'pas de deux' with castanets called a bolero and a fandango with much exertion, but with very little grace. The women are not active; they make more pleasing action with their arms and legs, occasioned by the castanets. The bolero music is simple and pretty. We slept at Mrs Benson's this evening, very bad beds indeed feather beds being unknown in this city, a Lieutenant Wallis (Henry) 52nd Regiment[3], who dined in the cafe in a large company, refused this day after dinner to drink Lord Wellington's health. What an ass! I would thrash him with pleasure!

I find he[4] is very much disliked by all the officers who have come from the army; he was at Lisbon last week. He made a grand entry into the town, and nothing but 'Viva de Grande Lord' was heard from every Portuguese. He lodged at the Regent's Palace in Buenos Aires; orders were issued out by the Regency to receive him as the saviour of the country, and he visited the opera, boxes 20 dollars each. General illuminations for three nights, a Portuguese frigate laying in the Tagus was illuminated in a very superb style, having three, small variegated lamps about the sails.

My *two* horses both well and comfortably housed at Belem. Last Sunday night a.m., sorry for one of our transports, G[5], is reported to be captured by the Americans[6], has 45 men and 60 horses on board belonging to Captain Turing's[7] Troop, his horses likewise Lieutenant Jones'[8] are on board, a very severe loss in this country, horses are so very dear. Got the men landed on Friday from on

---

[3] Lieutenant Henry Wallis, 52nd Foot, remained in Portugal with the army until September 1813, he transferred to the 2nd Garrison Battalion in May 1814.

[4] He here talks of the Duke of Wellington, who had angered many in his army with his harsh criticism of the state of the troops during the retreat which ended the campaign of 1812.

[5] *The Transport letter 'G'*.

[6] An American privateer captured the *Canada* Transport, but released it, the captain having signed a bond for a ransom of £3,000. The ship arrived safely a few days later, see George's journal for the 10 February.

[7] Captain William Turing was later killed at the Battle of Vitoria.

[8] Captain Turing, Lieutenant Valentine Jones, 40 dragoons and 60 horses were captured by the American privateer. By March 1813 Jones had transferred to the 3rd Dragoons as a captain.

board the *London*, all well, then marched them to Belem barracks, dined with Smith and Kennedy. Called and delivered my letter of introduction to Messrs McMahon & Co., and Charles Kruse Esq., (Merchants) got an invitation to dinner at each place, but I am afraid I cannot go.

Belem, Saturday 6 February.
I saw the Queen's palace[9] and gardens this morning, the palace is in ruins. It was used, I think, for barracks by the French when they occupied Lisbon. There remains little furniture and a few old tables which did not deserve to be taken, otherwise Junot[10] would have not left them. I have often heard those gardens spoke very highly of, but in my opinion they are very far from being laid out with anything like good taste, several beautiful fish ponds well stocked with gold and silver fish, and an aviary containing a horned owl and two hawk like looking birds. Lisbon is not so fine a city as you are led to expect on viewing it from the Tagus. The streets are narrow, but there are some very good streets – viz Silver and Gold Street[11] and those adjoining them. The statue in Black Horse Square is the finest piece of workmanship I ever saw. In the square, near three thousand souls perished owing to the water rising in the Tagus, during the earthquake in1760[12], it's about the size of Golden Square[13]. The churches are good buildings, but the altar pieces gaudy. The Virgin Mary and Infant are in most churches represented by figures three feet high, draped with much heavy ornaments and rich lace and are preserved in glass cases.

The poorer class of Portugal appear to think of nothing but religion and whisky, which is carried about all day, like sprats or mutton pieces in London. I saw the city illuminated last night, so great is the number of candles that burn before the images fixed above the doors and on the walls of churches. They cry out in the streets a species of eau de vie as we offer lamb and sprat in the streets of London, and I noticed that the people were drinking and indulge in [it] a large part of the afternoon.

---

9   The Palace of Ajuda was begun in 1796 to replace a wooden structure hastily built to house the royal family after the 1755 earthquake; but hampered by design issues, lack of money and French destruction. It did not begin to be used as a Royal palace until 1825.
10  General Jean Andoche Junot, Duc d'Abrantes.
11  Prata Street and Ouro Street are now the hub of Lisbon's shopping area known as Baxia.
12  George is again mistaken. The terrible earthquake and consequent tsunami which devastated most of Lisbon occurred in 1755. It was only following this disaster that the Praca do Comercio square was built.
13  Golden Square in Soho, London.

The regiment received orders to march to Luz this afternoon; we got away from Belem about 3 o'clock. The country is very fine, the views are beautiful, the roads very bad, we got into Luz about 5 p.m., received a billet to an empty house where I took up my abode for the night.

The regiment moved to the outskirts of Lisbon where the horses could graze, but by now George was less enamoured by the Portuguese and there were worrying signs of ill-discipline amongst the men.

Luz[14], Sunday 7 February.
I slept in an empty house, on the ground, rats and mice running over me all night. There were no locks or handles on the doors, and with the horrific information I have been given on these scoundrels of inhabitants, I slept very little. This morning I began to examine the village which is a poor miserable little place. I obtained another billet to a second empty house nearer the barracks where I removed to, a palace with a garden, but not a single piece of furniture, without fireplaces, except in the kitchen. A very fortunate fellow I am, last night in the bustle some of the rascally Portuguese stole my cloak; the very thing I shall most want up the country, to wear on a night picquet. The village is surrounded by gardens, all most enchanting and romantic, planted with oranges, olives and vines, delightful walks through avenues of orange trees flourishing in all their beauty of southern luxuriance, irrigated and cooled by intersections of fresh water streams in all abundance and directions. The whole country appears hilly and has therefore, many descending streams.

The barracks from appearance was originally a monastery, there is a very handsome church standing at the left angle of it, part in ruins, suppose owing to an earthquake. Four men belonging to the 'Oxford Blues'[15] who were quartered here about a month ago were stabbed by some of the villagers, but none was materially hurt; I am informed by a Portuguese farmer who lent me two chairs and a table, that every Portuguese carry a knife about them, and is always considered a part of their dress. Colonel Murray[16] gave orders for no officer to be without his sword on and constantly to be regimentally dressed. I wish he would give the example.

---

[14] Luz is now a suburb of Lisbon.
[15] The Oxford Blues, or the Royal Horse Guards, known as such because of its traditional blue jacket.
[16] Lieutenant Colonel the Honourable Sir Henry Murray commanded the 18th Hussars in Portugal.

The lower order of Portuguese are a poor miserable set; comfort has not yet passed into the middle class in a country like this, where the climate is very serene and bright and the verdure of the fields invite the inhabitants abroad at all times, is the less temptation and the less necessity for this domestic elegance. The prevalence of their religious enthusiasm and observances are great obstructions to their industry. There are so many Saints days and holidays, so many priests and churchmen that little room is left for exertion.

Luz, Monday 8 February.
Sat on a Court Martial this morning for the first time, on two men for un-soldier like behaviour to their officers, they were both punished this afternoon before the regiment. No one can detest corporal punishment more than I do, but subordination must be kept up or we shall all soon go to the dogs. I am very much afraid some of our men will get themselves into serious trouble when we join Lord Wellington's army, for if they go on with any of their drunken tricks there, Lord Wellington may perhaps shoot some of them, which I should be extremely sorry for.

I look forward with pleasure for the regiment to go into action, [&] am confident they will not disgrace themselves and return home, whenever we may; it will be with laurels. Yesterday I was to have dined with The envoy of His Britannic Majesty, Mr. Stuart[17], and was likewise invited by C. Kruse esq., but being very much fatigued I declined going to either.

Luz, Tuesday 9 February.
This morning I rode to Lisbon. Lisbon is built on seven hills and is seen to great effect when seen from the opposite bank of the Tagus. There are forty churches, twenty convents of monks and eighteen of nuns. The streets are generally narrow, houses of people very poor, with small windows and tiles. Among those of the nobility, they are elegant, built in stone with extensive gardens. I was today at the fair to buy a mule, but could not get one to suit me, what few that were in the market they asked exorbitant prices for, none under one hundred and eighty dollars.

When the regiment was in Portugal and Spain four years back[18], mules then sold for twenty-five dollars. Dined at the Golden Lion

---

[17] Sir Charles Stuart was Envoy Extraordinary to Portugal and the Brazils from 1810-14.
[18] During the short Corunna campaign, where they performed well.

with Captain White[19] and Mr Struth a volunteer in our regiment[20], we afterwards went to the theatre St. Carlo[21], saw performed a comedy called Adelasia[22], and a very grand spectacle called Andromeda and Perseus[23], the only thing worth seeing was the dancing and Perseus on his flying horse, which was very well executed, the first dancer in this theatre is Madam Norah.

Luz, Wednesday 10 February.
Heard this morning, that the transport missing had arrived in the Tagus and that it was captured by an American privateer, who allowed them to proceed after making the captain sign a bond for three thousand pounds to be paid for her ransom. They likewise disarmed the whole of our men and took a part of their appointments; uncommonly lucky they were not captured by us as Frenchmen. I returned to Luz again this morning to attend parade; Smith came and stayed with me all day. I gave him for dinner two woodcocks, beef, potatoes and two bottles of bad wine.

Luz, Thursday 11 February.
Smith came and breakfasted with me, he received a letter from Mrs Smith a few days back, he informed me a thing I was very anxious and happy to hear, of the health of my dear friends, Mrs Perkins, Amelia, and Miss Moseley, employed myself all day writing to them. Lost only six horses, since we embarked at Portsmouth, the 15th Hussars have lost a great many. Hesse's pony died a few days after it was disembarked at Lisbon, am very sorry for poor Hesse as it's a very severe loss here. He cannot purchase one here for less than sixty guineas.

Luz, Friday 12 February.
Wrote this day a long letter to Amelia and one to Miss Moseley, and put them in the post office myself this morning. I drew on a bill on Greenwood Cox & Co[24]., for £50.00 sterling, for which I received 205

---

[19] Probably Captain George White of the 3rd Dragoon Guards.
[20] Volunteers were young educated men, who were unable to afford to purchase a commission. They would accompany the regiment, fighting as a ranker, but allowed to 'mess' with the officers. Their sole aim was to distinguish themselves in battle and 'get noticed' by a senior officer in the hope of gaining a commission on the death of another officer.
[21] The Teatro Nacional de Sao Carlos, Lisbon's opera house.
[22] The only opera named Adelasia I can discover is actually called *Adelasia and Aleramo* first performed at La Scala in Milan in 1806, but this is described as a serious opera.
[23] The opera was first performed in 1781.
[24] Greenwood, Cox & co. Army Agents were established at Craigs Court, London.

dollars and 8 real, Portuguese money. The rainy season I suppose is not yet over, all last night it rained dreadful hard, and again this day, got very wet on my return from Lisbon. This day I dined for the first time with the mess formed by the following officers, am now a member of it, may we be always able to keep it up in all parts of the country the campaign may lead us to: Colonel Murray, Captains Bolton and Burke[25], [Paymaster] Deane, Lieutenants Rowlls[26], Woodberry and Doctor Quincey. I found everything very comfortable and eat [sic] a very good dinner.

This evening was entertained with a fine concert of vocal music by my old friends the frogs, lizards, and cricket birds[27]. I have not heard their music since I left Hounslow Barracks[28], but I think they are more noisy here than in England. The three churches in the village of Luz have been pulled to pieces; there is however, plenty of gilding remaining, and some quantity of pictures, which would disgrace a sign post in England. They have however, had the goodness to write over the different saints who they are. I have daily strolled into one of the churches and I either mistake religion myself, or many in this country do. I think the best evidence of our sincerity and of our being partakers of grace, lies in subduing our tempers and those sins which most easily beset us. But I see many, place their religion in strict opinions in fiery temper and forward practice conformed thereto. It grieves me to see so much profession of strict religion while other things are not conformable with it.

Some rascally Portuguese has stolen my cloak since I have been here. The ingratitude of the villain, it cost me 8 guineas in London; well I hope I shall not lose anything more valuable. I dislike the lower orders of Portuguese very much; it may be illiberal, but those of them with whom I have any dealing have proved very deceitful; except my servant Roderick[29].

Luz, Saturday 13 February.
The Hussar Brigade[30] were inspected this morning on Inquisition

---

[25] Captain Edward Burke.
[26] Lieutenant Charles Rowlls.
[27] More commonly known as a Grasshopper Warbler.
[28] Hounslow Cavalry Barracks was built in 1793.
[29] This is the first mention of this Portuguese servant Roderick, whom he presumably hired whilst at Lisbon.
[30] The newly-established Hussar Brigade commanded by Colquhoun Grant would consist of 10th, 15th and 18th Hussars, although Oman claims that the brigade was only formally established in April 1813.

Square Lisbon[31], by Generals Leith[32], Peacocke[33] and staffs, who expressed themselves pleased with our appearance, the 15th looked very well, they wore the pelisse slung on the shoulder[34]. Our regiment; 6 troops marched from Luz and met the 15th Regiment there soon after forming the line. The generals came and inspected us; we afterwards marched back to our old quarters, our band playing the whole way. The 10th Hussars are expected shortly.

On the way to Lisbon, the aqueduct a work which former grandeur and magnificence, raised more for utility than ornament caught my astonished sight as I passed its stupendous height and strength riveted my admiration. Some of our men have been thieving again, a house and garden was robbed last night in the village. Colonel Murray issued very severe orders respecting it this evening, and ordered a patrol of twenty men during the night to go round the cantonments. I am Orderly officer this day, for the first time since I left England. The following are the present prices of different articles here, and at Lisbon.

Eggs each 1½ Vintems[35]
Port Wine per bottle ½ Dollar.
Butter lb 16 Vintems.
Porter English, a bottle, 12 Vintems.
Cheese very bad lb 14½ Vintems.
Tea best lb 1 Dollar.
Sugar soft lb 6 Vintems.
Coffee lb ½ Dollar.
Chickens couple 1 Doll. 6 Vintems.
English Ham lb 12 Vintems.
Pork 1lb, 10 vintems
A brace of Wood Cocks 1 Dollar.
Brandy per quart ½ Dollar,
A brace Partridges 1 Dollar, 6 Vintems.
Genièvre Gin per quart ½ Dollar.
Rabbit each 16 Vintems.

---

[31] Praca do Rossio or Praca do Don Pedro IV, one side of which is lined by the Estaus Palace, which was then home to the Inquisition.
[32] Major General Sir James Leith.
[33] Major General Warren Marmaduke Peacocke, Commandant at Lisbon.
[34] This would appear to indicate that the 18th had yet to copy this foppish style of wearing the pelisse on one arm only.
[35] The Portuguese dollar was worth 40 vintems; each vintem being worth 25 Reis. The Portuguese dollar was worth about 4s 6d sterling.

Block of Salt 18 Vintems.
Brace of Hares 1 Dollar.
Oranges 8 large 1 Vintem.

Luz, Sunday 14 February.
Raining very hard the whole day, a church parade ordered, but no parson came. Last night the house wherein Kennedy, Smith and Dolbel sleeps at in Benfica was attempted to be broken open by a banditti of 9 fellows, those Portuguese scoundrels. Dolbel fired a pistol at one and Smith discharged the content of a pistol at another, they then made off. The country about Lisbon bears evident marks of some violent convulsions of nature, deep rents and hollow ravines run in parallel direction to the coast, while the side towards the sea and river consists of remarkable bold and steep cliffs. Valentine's Day it was, I know in dear England, instead of this raining place, how happy I should be, perhaps at this moment reading a valentine from my dear girl.

Luz, Monday 15 February.
Rode to Belem to look over 12 mules belonging to General Leith, but none of them suited me. Much dispute amongst our officers disputing the money allowed for mules and the embarkation money, the captains wish to have it all, I have not troubled myself about it. The 10th Hussars were disembarking all yesterday and this day. The 15th have reported themselves ready for immediate service, we are nearly ready ourselves, and have only a few of the horses to shoe up. This evening I went with Lieutenant Smith, to the English Envoy's Ball at Buenos Aries[36]. The company very great and mostly Portuguese, there saw some charming women, but very short, Smith owned he had formed an erroneous idea of them, before the evening. Met my friend Kruse, who seems to be a very fashionable young man at Lisbon, he introduced me to several very nice girls, but I declined dancing. Lord Worcester[37] danced the whole evening, country dances, but about an hour before the ball broke up, waltzing commenced. Hesse attempted – Worcester and an officer of the Portuguese waltzed very well. We had plenty of refreshments of the English kind and ended after about three o'clock. I slept at the Paris Hotel with Smith, met Captain Webber Smith[38] at the ball.

---

[36] A suburb of Lisbon.
[37] Lieutenant Henry Somerset, Marquess of Worcester, 10th Hussars, was aide de camp to the Duke of Wellington.
[38] Captain James Webber Smith Royal Artillery.

Luz, Tuesday 16 February.

After breakfasting with Smith at the Paris, we walked to Lisbon to the mule fair, bought none, all being high priced. I went to Belem this day, first day for Brigade Orders – Lieutenant Smith put under arrest this day by Colonel Murray, for 'Wilful Neglect of Duty', and coming out to Portugal in a different ship to what he was appointed, by which means many of the men's necessaries were lost, and the colonel intends making him pay for everything lost on board the vessel, he ought to have come out in. After he has done that, I suppose he will be released from arrest. Captain Burke spoke to me this day, about [me] coming into his troop; believe I will get appointed to it.

Luz, Wednesday 17 February.

Rode over to Benfica, where Turing, Kennedy and Carew's[39] troops are quartered, saw Smith who seems very indignant at Colonel Murray's proceedings in putting him under arrest. Benfica a small village 2 miles from Belem, the aqueduct runs very near it and has a very noble appearance[40]. An immense number of aloes border the road about the villages of Luz and Benfica, and in some spots are seen the Indian Fig trees[41], both of these are easily planted and form hedges impenetrable to cattle, but which men can easily destroy. There is also another objection to them, namely the great difficulty to keep them within bounds, because they spread so very rapidly in a short time.

In July and August I am informed the aloes are in bloom, the high stems covered with flowers form a very beautiful object. Now I am speaking of aloes, it may not be improper to observe, that it is propagated very easily from the roots of young plants, it may therefore, be planted without trouble, and thus quick hedges are rapidly formed, but unfortunately it spreads too far, in Algeria, I am told, that thread is made from it, by a very simple process. The largest and best leaves which are free from spot or decay are cut, the labourer then presses a square board obliquely between his breast and the ground, lays the leaf upon it and scrapes it with a square iron bar which he holds in both hands by which all the juices and pulp are pressed out, and only the nerves (fibres) of the

---

[39] Captain Robert Carew, he died of his wounds suffered at the Battle of Vitoria.
[40] The Aguas Livres acqueduct, completed in 1744, brought clean drinking water to the city from the mountains 18 km away.
[41] Commonly known as Banyan trees.

leaves remains, which, by this means suffer themselves to be divided into very fine threads, that are then hung over a thin card to dry. This thread is not strong, and as it rots in water the utility is limited. Last night some of our men broke open a house and robbed it of many valuable pictures and candlesticks, very bad beginning indeed.

Nineteen of our men very ill and many horses sick, the climate I suppose disagrees with them. There are doubtless, vagabonds, who disgrace the name of soldier; but is judgement to be passed on a whole profession, because individuals are dishonest? Who would destroy the whole body, if one or more of the members were diseased, would not amputation be first resorted to? So also, must in every station every degree of punishment follow guilt, and as the progress of the decay is stemmed by the loss of a limb and the body is restored to its pristine vigour, so is the infection of vice averted from the 'Body Military' by severe and striking examples, and discipline maintains its legitimate sway. Every profession, every trade, have their delinquents and though the soldier occasionally transgresses the rules of orders, what class of civilians have not also rioters amongst them. A miserable dull place this Luz.

Luz, Thursday 18 February.
General Stewart's[42] horses are arrived, likewise an excellent pack of foxhounds, 18 couples. It is reported General the Earl of Uxbridge[43] is coming out to command the whole of the cavalry here. I wish it may prove true. There is some good news from the army, some say the French are leaving Spain, and that King Joseph (Napoleon's brother) is gone and Marshal Jourdan[44] is being appointed Regent. The regiment parades twice most days, always watering or marching order every morning. Much pleased with the perusal of two English newspapers; belonging to Kennedy, of the 25th and 26th January. Smith was released from arrest this morning by Colonel Murray after giving him a very severe lecture, he appears very

---

[42] Lieutenant General Sir Charles Stewart had been ordered to join Wellington's army, but Wellington refused him, stating that he could not give him command of a cavalry division as he wished or even a brigade. He also had severe reservations regarding his suitability to command cavalry because of his poor eyesight. He eventually served in Germany instead. He was known later as Charles Vane, 3rd Marquess of Londonderry. Reference *Supplementary Dispatches* Vol. VII, pages 586-8.

[43] Lieutenant General Henry Paget, The Earl of Uxbridge, famous for his Waterloo exploits, was an able cavalry commander, but was unlikely to serve with the Duke of Wellington, having eloped with his sister-in-law.

[44] Marshal Jean Baptiste Jourdan.

indignant at Kennedy because he told the truth, and the colonel because of his mercurial manner, and I dare say will leave the regiment sooner through this affair. Man is a short sighted creature, with whatever liberty he may direct his actions, he can never answer for the results, nor foresee to what they may lead in time to come.

Our daily rations arrive every morning from Lisbon and are delivered out to the regiment about midday; my rations are as follows, one pound of bread, rather brown but very good, ¾ lb of beef, generally killed a few hours before, a pint of sour wine, 6 pounds of hay, 8 pounds of corn, and 9 pounds of wood for which I am charged three pence[45]. An officer may live very well indeed in Portugal on his pay, particularly after he gets up country. An ill constructed cart is employed, drawn by two bullocks, driven or rather led by a stout fellow who walks in front of the animals; he has a stick with a small spike at the extremity to goad them occasionally. This vehicle being extremely long, narrow and clumsy will carry from six to eight hundredweight, and as the Portuguese have no idea of greasing the axletree, when loaded they send forth a horrible noise[46]. Twenty or thirty of these carts bring our rations daily. Went to Lisbon this day in the hope of buying a mule, but without success, offered 200 dollars for a fine one, but would not take less than 250 and that price I think is high.

Luz, Friday 19 February.
Smith breakfasted with me this morning; I afterwards looked at several mules and at last have bought one which I think will carry my baggage very well. I paid 150 dollars for him. Most of our men are guilty of bad conduct, they are discovered to have sold their horses' corn daily; and ransack the houses, pretty goings on this; some example must immediately be made. The Portuguese live very frugally and their happy climate almost exempts them from every want, but that of food; who would remain in the house, when there is so much beauty to invite them abroad? The name of an Englishman is very much respected and the women look upon us with compassion. What a pity that such brave men should be such heretics! When will religion appear what in its own nature it really is; the first blessing of man, that which should link us to one another, as we are linked to one common parent. The time may be distant, but it will arrive. I rode to Thomar this afternoon to inspect the arms of

---

[45] Incorrectly shown as 4½ d in the French version.
[46] The superstitious carters believed that the noise kept evil spirits away.

the detachment quartered there, distance from Luz about two miles. The country along the road, very beautiful being rich and variegated by nature and very highly cultivated. This country as to climate is a paradise; even the worst parts of it are charming.

Luz, Saturday 20 February.
The regiment out in review order this morning went through a few manoeuvres, preparatory to being reviewed next Wednesday by General Peacocke. My servant Ipper very much scalded this day; brings the soup to table at our mess, his foot slipped and he fell, soup and all. Cornet Dolbel very ill of a fever, yesterday his life was despaired of, and afraid his mind, like mine roves to that dear island England where he has left his heart. Smith looked very poorly today and I notice there are many sufferers, the climate, fruit and wine don't agree with them, thank God I am in excellent health, and hope to remain so; may all my absent friends be so likewise is my constant prayer.

Luz, Sunday 21 February.
Dined with Smith, Kennedy and Dolbel at Benfica, afterwards rode with them to Lisbon and went to the theatre, St. Carlos, saw an Italian opera and ballet with plenty of dancing. I have a much higher opinion of the Italian actors than I had when I first saw them here, several songs were rapturously applauded, and so were several dancers, particularly Madam Norah. I never wish to see a better dancer in one point of view, and a more indecent one in another, she quite shocked my modesty. The house was very crowded, so much so that we were obliged to put up with a seat in the front of the pit, for which we paid a dollar each. A few choice friends who will be allowed to browse these notes laugh no doubt at this sentence: but it is a fact for last night. On my return to Luz, then about 12 o'clock a.m., found my servant Ipper and Portuguese Roderick locked up in the Guard House; went then and relieved them. They were taken up by the patrol who found them in the village after 9[47] o'clock.

Luz, Monday 22 February.
The regiment paraded in watering order this morning, when we received our orders respecting the review tomorrow. The 10th and 15th I understand, brought out the whole of their review furniture, we have none, therefore shall not equal them in appearance,

---

[47] Incorrectly shown as 10 o'clock in the French version.

however there is one comfort, our dress will be more becoming a regiment on service than either of the others. Most of this day employed myself arranging and packing up my clothes, preparatory to our marching up country, to join the army under Lord Wellington. Had the whole of my baggage on the mule and find he can carry it well.

I take the following articles with me.

2 Pelisse's
1 Jacket
1 Dress Waistcoat
4 Regimental Pantaloons
3 [Prs] White Pantaloons
1 Leather Pantaloons
2 Blue Waistcoats
2 White Waistcoats
Cotton Drawers
2 Flannel Drawers
3 Flannel Waistcoats
12 Hose
12 Shirts
4 Black Handkerchiefs
6 Pocket ditto
2 Foraging Caps
1 Hussar ditto with oil skin cover
1 Cap liner
1 Sash
1 Pelisse Liner
3 pr. Gloves
2 Night Caps
Canteen, Breakfast & Dining
Service complete
1 Leather Trunk

Double Saddle Bags
Basket with Locks
Spy Glass
Great Coat
Flannel Jacket

Leather Bucket
15 Cakes of Soap

1 Dressing Gown
2 Blankets
1 Rug
1 Bear Skin Bed
Dressing Case
Writing Case
10 Books
1 pair Hussar Pistols
1 Pocket Pistol
1 Powder Flask
1 Pinch Belt Plain
1 Pistol Belt and Pouch
Dress Sword
Dress Sabretache
Plain Sword
Plain Sabretache
Sword Knots
Racing Jacket
2 Feathers
6 pair Boots
1 pair Shoe
2 pair Slippers
1 Hussar Pipe
Complete
Hussar Horse Accoutrements Complete
2 Horse Cloths
2 Horse Blankets
1 Plain Saddle
2 Plain Bridles
Pack Saddle Bridle etc., Complete
3 Shoe Brushes and Blacking
2 Clothes Brushes

Boot Jack                                     Oil skins and straps to go over
                                              the baggage

Copy of the orders respecting the dress of the officer's tomorrow for
the review by order of Colonel Murray:
'The regiment will assemble at Luz in review order tomorrow morning
at half past 8. Neither officers nor men are to wear their cloaks which
are to be left at home. As the officers have not their horse review
furniture; only the plain blue shabraque and regiment sheepskin to be
worn, and leather horse collars, and plain hussar bridles.
'The officers will wear white leather pantaloons, white leather sword
and pouch belts. Regimental forage caps, cap line and feathers,
regimental jacket, hussar sash, with three rows of gold knots in front
according to order. The regimental silver sabretache, and the officers
as well as the men must wear their pelisse's slung.
'The orders on the subject of the officer's dress being thus fully
detailed, no excuse will be taken from any officer appearing dressed
in any other manner. The Lieutenant Colonel trusts that both officers
and men will turn out in a manner creditable to the regiment. If the
men turn out ill, they have no excuse whatever for they have
everything requisite for their appearance in review order, though
the officers have not their review furniture. Still if they make their
servants turn out their plain bridles and furniture well cleaned, they
will have quite as soldier-like appearance, as the more splendid
review furniture of the two other regiments of hussars.'

Luz, Tuesday 23 February 1813
The regiment marched to Campo Pequeno[48] about 9 o'clock this
morning, to be reviewed with the 10th and 15th Regiments of
Hussars by General Peacocke. Soon after 11[49] o'clock he with his staff
and about fifty officers, mounted some on horses, others on mules
and asses, they entered the ground and were received by the brigade
with a general salute, we then marched past in open column of
divisions, filed off by three, and trotted past in divisions. After the
10th and 18th were ordered off the ground to their quarters, the 15th
then went through the whole manoeuvre of a field day, and were
much admired and praised by the General Colonel Grant who
commanded the brigade[50]. The ground much about the size of St.

---

[48] This is now a northern suburb of Lisbon.
[49] Incorrectly shown as 10 o'clock in the French version.
[50] Brevet Colonel Colquhoun Grant 15th Hussars, he is often referred to as the 'Black Giant'.

James's Square, was not large enough for the whole brigade to manoeuvre upon; very few people [came] from Lisbon, to what I expected. The 10th Regiment was dressed in complete marching order. The 15th in complete review order, shabraques, bridles, etc. I think we looked as well as either; we were the strongest of the three. We only talk about our departure next for the interior.

Cintra: Immediately after the review, I mounted my mule and rode to Cintra, distant from Luz about 3 leagues, it was evening by the time I arrived there, therefore, saw nothing of the place this day. I met several officers at the hotel, a very good one kept by an Irish woman, Mrs Daisy whom I dined with. One a very gentlemanlike man, Captain Oglander of the 47th Regiment[51], who lost his left arm at the storming of Badajoz, he informed me of many useful things I should want with the army, with hints and anecdotes that will be of service to me there; in all, I liked this Captain Oglander very much, and hope I shall meet him again.

After dinner, I was much amused by a young man who had in his pocket a recommendation for Marshal Beresford; he spoke of the benefits that he will draw. His first commission is for the 30th infantry, then he talks of the probability of an advancement in the Portuguese service, thanks to the Marshal. Oglander asked him what was his relationship to the Marshal or what great personages were interested in him: none of this, his uncle was the doctor of the mother of the Marshal! I passed through Benfica, Quelus and two other villages on my way here, all miserable places.

Cintra, Wednesday 24 February.
I was up this morning soon after 6 o'clock and after obtaining a guide, proceeded to the convent on top of the mountain[52], which is remarkably high, rough and intricate, the winding walks overlooked by craggy rocks and hilly heights skirted by ravines and hollow ways, no one can conceive how beautiful; the never ceasing novelty of the charming prospects which everywhere gratify the eye of a stranger. The picturesque form of the rock is truly enchanting. The monks were very polite to me; saw every part of the convent and a most beautiful altar piece of alabaster, supposed to be four hundred years old was particularly striking. I should think the convent is not less than two miles from the village, it stands on the very top of the

---

[51] Captain Henry Oglander 47th Foot, despite losing his left arm, continued to serve with the battalion in Spain until 1814 when he went on half-pay.
[52] Convento de Santa Cruz da Serra da Sintra, built in 1560. It is open to the public today.

highest rock and a Moorish castle[53] stands on another point of it and is in a very high state of preservation. The view of the sea, furrowed by numerous boats, is wonderful, so is a beautiful house where Mrs Murray was born, now in ruins. Of all the places in this world, I think none can boast of so fine a prospect as this charming Cintra.

Marshal Beresford[54] was walking in the garden of the New Palace[55] with General Hamilton[56], whom my father knew well[57] who I was some years ago introduced to. As he saw me often, he immediately recognised me and introduced me to the marshal, who after asking me several questions respecting the regiment invited me to dine with him at 6 o' clock. I went there and met Admiral Martin[58], Generals Hamilton, and Brisbane[59], two Portuguese Marquises, Colonel Wall, Major Wynne[60] and several Portuguese officers I knew not. Sixteen sat down to a most elegant dinner, which I very plentifully partook off; likewise, I had little compassion for the wine. After taking coffee, I sat down to a whist party with the admiral, General Brisbane and Colonel Wall. I lost 3[61] dollars and left there with Mrs. O'Daisy about 11 o' clock. We dined in the room where the famous or infamous Convention of Cintra was signed by Junot[62] and Dalrymple[63] after the battle of Vimieiro[64]. General Brisbane came over to Cintra, like myself, purposely to see the beauties of the place, he appeared quite enraptured with it and 'said' he would ride any day twenty miles to see a view equal to the one he there saw from the palace garden. The marshal was most superbly dressed for dinner, in a marshal's uniform in the Portuguese service, with a very rich star on his breast. The Portuguese Marquises sported stars likewise. General Hamilton was particularly attentive to me the whole evening, gave me a deal of advice and information. Asked me if I would like to be on his staff,

---

[53]  The Moorish castle is still there today and is indeed a fine example.
[54]  British General William Carr Beresford had been appointed to reform and command the Portuguese Army and was made a Field Marshal in the Portuguese service.
[55]  The 'New' Palace refers to the Seteais Palace, built in 1787.
[56]  Lieutenant General John Hamilton served with the Portuguese Army.
[57]  General Hamilton served much of his early army life in India, where it is likely that he encountered George's father.
[58]  Admiral Sir George Martin was Commander in Chief of the Tagus from 1812-14.
[59]  Brigadier General Sir Thomas Brisbane.
[60]  The identities of Colonel Wall and Major Wynne have proved to be problematical as no officer with these ranks are listed as serving in Portugal at this time.
[61]  Incorrectly shown as 5 dollars in the French version.
[62]  General Jean Andoche Junot, Duc d' Abrantes.
[63]  General Sir Hew Whitefoord Dalrymple.
[64]  The Convention was actually signed at the Palace of Queluz.

I intend asking Colonel Murray, as I should like it of all things. He was dressed in a Portuguese general's uniform, blue and gold; he is here for his health which is very infirmed.

The village of Bucellas, where the wine is made of that name lies on the left of Cintra at the foot of the rock, it is seen in the midst of orange and olive groves, I had not time to go there, though not more than a league distant. The plains of Vimeiro are seen from the convent on the rock very plain. I likewise discovered on a hill a few miles from Cintra a great many human bones lying about, suppose of soldiers who were killed during the time, the armies were in the neighbourhood about 4 years ago. I saw the Old Palace in Cintra, a room was shown one, where one of the kings of Portugal was imprisoned and died after many years of captivity. The print of his feet walking backwards and forward on one side of the room, where he was chained are distinctly seen, there are several very beautiful rooms and in very high perfection. One called the swan room[65]; the ceiling most beautifully painted with swans, another room of the same size with the ceiling painted in the same manner, only of magpies. Another room, more grand than either of the former, with the arms of all the nobility of Spain painted on the walls and ceiling, I saw so many curious sights here, that it would fill my book, were I to mention all; therefore must leave Cintra with the hope of once more having an opportunity of visiting this heavenly place.

Luz, Thursday 25 February.
Got home this morning from Cintra about 11 o'clock, first thing I heard was that Mr Dolbel and Captain Kennedy had been quarrelling last night and were expected to meet this morning on the affair, but soon after heard that Dolbel had apologised to Kennedy. Canary birds are in abundance in every garden about Luz and Benfica. I have likewise seen the kingfisher a beautiful bird, about the lakes near Cintra. Game of all kind are very plentiful in the country, there are likewise many wolves about Cintra, a few weeks back, one followed a man and seemed several times determined to attack him, however, the wolf was killed the following day by dogs, and proved to be the largest wolf ever caught in this country.

The palace at Cintra, where Marshal Beresford resides is very extensive, and boasts of great beauty in the architecture. The domains of the great Marquess of Pombal[66], joins the gardens of this

---

[65]  The Swan room at the Palace of Sintra/Cintra is still a major tourist sight.
[66]  José Francisco Xavier Maria de Carvalho Melo e Daun (1753–1821), 3rd Marquess of Pombal.

palace. I saw a great many beautiful prints in the rooms, very few paintings of notice. Nothing, as I have repeatedly said, can be more picturesque and beautiful than the interior of this country. A traveller of any fancy cannot help amusing himself with the fairy dream as he passes through those lovely vales and summer fields. Perhaps the proverb 'I built castles in Spain', owned its origin to the setting of this kind. The country is sometimes like a park. How delightfully thought, I might an Englishman of small fortune cultivate a small estate in a country like this. The purchase of agricultural land at a distance from cities and towns is a mere trifle, and the land wants nothing but that ordinary skill which everyone possesses in England, to reward the husbandman thirty-fold.

Luz, Friday 26 February.[67]
Received off Captain Deane[68] this day £4 2s 6d for bat forage[69], an allowance made to the officers in the service. Rode to Belem for Brigade Orders, from thence came through Lisbon. All very anxious for the arrival of the packets, three due, trust I shall receive a letter from Amelia. It is reported Lord Wellington is unwell and that the French are still at Salamanca.

Luz, Saturday 27 February.
Smith breakfasted with me this morning, when we enjoyed ourselves talking of absent friend's we love. Went with Rowlls to see [the] senior divisions casa at Benfica, was very much pleased with the sight, it being by far the best furnished house I have seen in this country. A great many very fine paintings and curious china and ivory figures, a very good library and a museum of natural curiosities, in one of the rooms a Turkish throne has a very pleasing effect, and to me a novel sight. The gardens claim likewise particular notice being the handsomest I have seen, laid out with much more taste than usual in this country, several fountains and a grotto, and which attracted my admiration. The trees all covered with bright green leaves, with golden fruit and with white blossoms, perfuming the air with their fragrance.

I begin to like this country more and more daily, for I think it a paradise to England with regard to the climate. This house was originally kept by Mrs Murray's father, whose name it still goes by.

---

[67] Incorrectly printed in the French version as 6 February.
[68] The position of Paymaster always carried the equivalent rank of the most junior captain in the regiment.
[69] An allowance was paid for the feeding of officer's horses, known as bât.

Lizards and snakes are here in abundance about this village, cannot walk out without meeting them on every path, particularly if near an old wall and ruins, in which they live. At this time, every tree except orange are in blossom, the hedges and gardens look quite enchanting; perhaps in England all my friends are enjoying themselves round a roaring fire, while I am here sitting in the shade writing this, sweltering to death with the heat of the sun.

The climate agrees very well with me at present, though so very hot. My friend Smith, speaking of his wife this morning, said 'he anticipated the pleasure of beholding in the arms of his Jemima on his return', if he remained abroad a few months, a pledge of affection which would be the greatest happiness of his life. Oh poor Smith, alas poor Enos[70], surely you are mad, poor fellow he has already too great a plague, what would she be, if surrounded with a family? I sincerely pity him, so does my friend Donna Maria. I wish she was here, and I with her. I think we should laugh at poor Smith's experience. Whenever any of us ride out, every Portuguese cries out 'viva senhor', at the same time takes off their hats and bows. The following lines from the Subalterns Complaint, gives a just description of the natives.

> Viva senhor - They compliment to all,
> To English, French, the Pope, or even the Devil.
> With hat in hand they lowly cringing bawl.
> Vastly polite, tho' not sincere, yet civil.

Luz, Sunday 28 February.
I know not whence it happens that the people of England, who seem of all men most strongly inclined by nature to cultivate the soft arts of peace and social life, have less enjoyed these blessings, than almost any nation of the world, at least in modern times. They rather indeed have been, as the poet Euripides expresses it. 'Vied with perpetual toils and ceaseless War'.

The course, however, to which the evil fortune must be ascribed, may be found also in their nature. For being passionately fond of freedom, and eager to retain the supreme command, they choose to have recourse continually to arms, rather than yield a step to any rival power. Went this afternoon to Lisbon and was at the Saliteres Theatre, the house was much crowded. I attempted to get a box, but

---

[70]  First name of Smith.

was asked 4 dollars for one; I found a good seat in the pit for 3 shillings. It answered my purpose as well, for I saw everything I wished, but was occasionally annoyed by the prompter reading much louder than the actor repeats. The dances, I went to see, went off with great elan, particularly a bolero, by a Spaniard and a little woman with thick legs. I shall never forget her, the more she showed her shapes, the more applause till at last I can say I've seen everything I wanted to see and more. The scenery and transformations at this theatre are the best I ever saw. If they had a few of those I saw last night, at Covent Garden Theatre in a Pantomime, it would be a serious rival to Mother Goose, and produce many golden eggs.

Luz, Monday 1 March.
Rode with Smith to Lisbon, the people all mad, throwing water, oranges, flowers, nuts and every kind of nuisance at each other, we got a pail of water over us, and Smith turned to insult the people who had made the attack, when a suave damsel threw the contents of a certain vase at him which unfortunately missed. I got him to understand that he looked like nothing on earth, and we sneaked out of town as quickly as possible, but not before having served as a target for ripe oranges, coffee and peas: and were covered with so much flour that we looked like two millers. many I saw sporting masks and curious dresses, I think they say their carnival commences this day. I was very glad when I got out of the town.

I laid in a good stock of tea, sugar, coffee, hams and tongues, to take up the country, so did Smith. It is rumoured that our regiment will march in a few days. Went with Rowlls this evening, to the Ministers Ball, Sir C. Stuart, met most of my brother officers there, almost all the officers of the 10th and 15th Hussars and Mr. Kruse who invited me to dine with him on Sunday next. Immediately after the ball, several of the ladies threw a white powder over many of the gentlemen which they had brought with them for that purpose and we went into a lot of niches: they were all of them, as a reward, embraced and kissed. It created great mirth; some of the gentlemen were rather displeased, and were therefore laughed at, as they deserved. I don't think there were more females present than at the last ball, but by far the greater share of beauty. Received of Mr Deane Esq., (William Deane, Paymaster), 14 Dollars.

Luz, Tuesday 2 March.
Shrovetide. Colonel Murray, went this morning to Cintra, so did

Hesse and Curtis; Clements[71] lost his mule last night, supposed to have been stolen by some of the natives. I much enjoyed myself this morning with my delicious neighbours; I made them little affairs, I kissed them, etc: they took everything with an appearance of good humour. Lots of fun this morning with my servant; neighbours throwing water, flowers and oranges at each other. Smith and Lieutenant Cottin[72] of the 10th Hussars dined with me at the mess, we have referred them, Smith and he were so abominably drunk that I fear that neither one nor the other will ever return. Captain Clements mule that was supposed to have been stolen was taken by mistake by Lord Arthur Hill[73] on his return from the Minister's Ball.

The weather grew much warmer, but still the army could not march; tempers frayed and ill-discipline increased.

Luz, Wednesday 3 March.
Sat on a Court Martial most of this day, trying four prisoners, two acquitted, the others guilty, one was sentenced to receive 300 lashes in the usual manner, the other to a fortnight's imprisonment. Very much annoyed all day with a confounded headache, fancy I must have been a little groggy last night, Smith and Cottin were dead drunk, so was Rowlls. Cottin in going home, fell off his mule, and it strayed away, was obliged to walk nearly 3 miles with the assistance of a Portuguese who luckily passed by; he has heard nothing of the mule since, hope he will find the creature again, but think if the Portuguese get hold of her, he never will.

The Portuguese ladies dress according to my observations very much like the English, particularly at the opera and balls, but in their houses they are constantly in black and in the mornings they wear gowns of English manufacture, generally cotton, but very coarse and in the afternoon of black silk. Their clothing is remarkably neat about the feet and ankle, but the symmetry of their legs and feet are not beautiful. Their persons being in general short, it follows that their legs and feet are thick, yet many walk very elegantly. In manners the ladies are remarkably affable and attractive. The hair which is allowed to grow very long is twisted and tied up very tight at the back of the head. The lower order is similar to the lower order of the

---

[71] Captain John Clements, who soon after this became an aide de camp to Marshal Beresford.
[72] George mistakenly spells his name Cotton, but it was Lieutenant John Cottin, 10th Hussars, who was killed at the Action of Morales on 2 June 1813.
[73] Lieutenant Lord Arthur Hill, 10th Hussars.

English, and equally as noisy, quarrelsome and violent. There is evidently an insolence of disposition prevalent amongst them, which amounts to a disgrace, men and women sit in the sun for hours during the day, amusing themselves with their thoughts, or else occupied with their fingers in the heads of their neighbours, reclined either on their lap or on a stone for convenience. They are certainly not very clean, either in their external or internal clothing, and generally are barefooted as well as bear headed.

Colonel Murray returned from Cintra this afternoon and dined at the mess, he saw my friend General Hamilton who is much better than he was last week and informed me that it is only the lack of officers in the regiment at present that prevents him from letting me go on his staff. The wind very high blowing a gale at sea, I am afraid!

Luz, Thursday 4 March.
Sergeant Major Sweeney of Captain Bolton's Troop was put under arrest for drunkenness and disrespectful behaviour to his officers; the day before yesterday. It is the first case of its kind since I am in the army, he begged to be allowed to lose his stripes, instead of being brought to a Court Martial. A packet arrived at last; expect to get some letters tomorrow. This afternoon was punished McCrealley[74] of Captain Burke's Troop for selling his necessaries; he received 300 lashes; one of the men tried by the Court Martial I sat on yesterday.

Luz, Friday 5 March.
The regiment out in marching order this morning, and I think looked uncommonly well. Our mess broke up on account of Colonel Murray and Rowlls' refusal to pay that attention to it they ought. We have formed a new one with Deane, Bolton, and Burke. Very much disappointed today in not receiving any letters from England by the packet, there are still two packets due; hope my friends have not quite forgotten me.

Made a present of the following things to poor Russell[75], who is still very ill; am afraid he will never be able to stand the campaign; 4 shirts, 2 white overalls and several trifling things.

A soldier of the 32nd Regiment[76] was hung this morning at Belem, for stabbing the mate of the transport he was on, and attempting to murder his officer, he looked a very fine fellow and behaved with a

---

[74] The nearest name to this in the Regimental Muster is Private Michael Crielly.
[75] Lieutenant Robert Russell.
[76] The 32nd (Cornwall) Regiment of Foot.

deal of fortitude and exhorted his hearers not to be guilty of the like offence, acknowledging the justice of his punishment. The 10th and 15th Hussars were out with the whole of the Lisbon garrison for the occasion, he suffered on the banks before Belem Castle.

Luz, Saturday 6 March.
Rode to the Campo Pequeno, and saw the race between Captain Close's horse[77] and Captain Johnson's[78], the latter won very easily indeed. Close had a marquee on the ground with plenty of refreshments, which proved a desirable accommodation from the heat of the weather. This morning's sport reminded me of Brighton, seeing Smith, Saunders[79], and several others of the artillery, who were present there when I rode the grey mare. Lieutenant Russell came and sat with me this evening, when he informed me [of] all the circumstances respecting Major Hayes'[80] case, which was to be tried by Court Martial; my opinion is, that he will be dismissed from the service. I daily spend an hour or two learning the language of the beautiful Hannah, my Portuguese neighbour.

Luz, Sunday 7March.
The inhabitants of this village are very religious, or they appear so, they generally resort to every church in the neighbourhood, beginning at the most distant and rich, each repeating certain prayers with much seeming devotion in all of them, and on the way, keep praying their way home; much better I think if they would employ themselves [in] other ways than they do, to clean their homes.
A list of officers who came out with the Eighteenth Hussars, and are now still with the regiment in health:

Colonel, Hon. Henry Murray.
Major James Hughes.

| Captains | Bolton | Lieutenants | Russell | Cornets | Curtis |
|---|---|---|---|---|---|
| | Turing | | Conolly[81] | | Dolbel |
| | Clements | | Jones | | Curtis D |

---

[77] Captain Henry Close 5th Dragoon Guards.
[78] This would appear to be Captain John Johnstone, 3rd Dragoons.
[79] 1st Lieutenant William Saunders, Royal Artillery.
[80] He means Major Philip Hay of the 18th Hussars who had remained in England. The Court Martial went ahead and he was acquitted, it did not hamper his ongoing military career, becoming a Lieutenant Colonel in June 1814.
[81] Lieutenant James Conolly retired in September 1813.

| Kennedy | Smith | Foster[82] |
|---------|-------|------------|
| Carew | Hesse | Woodberry |
| Burke | Rowlls | Blackett |

Adjutant Waldie[83]
510 Rank and File
528 Horses
Doctors, Chambers[84], Pulsford[85], Quincey.

Dined with Bolton and Deane, an excellent dinner; divine service was performed by the Brigade Chaplain to the regiment on the parade this afternoon. The scorching heat of the sun was very annoying. My grey horse Crafty very unwell, God only knows how I shall manage if he dies. Poor Smith very much vexed, he received no letter by the last packet; he wrote home yesterday a scalding letter on the subject.

Luz, Monday 8 March.
Received from the Commissary; a pack saddle, canteen, haversack, and blanket, for my private servant. Smith breakfasted with me; afterwards I rode to Lisbon and bought 2 silver forks [for] 6 dollars and a stand of cruets for my canteen, rather unwell with a swelled throat. Just heard that the Life Guards are going on rather queer, many have mutinied, and the colonel was obliged to call in the assistance of the Blues[86]. Great talk of us going up country this week, God send we may. The Portuguese are very much pleased with the brigade, and speak of us in high terms. The mode of conveyance for travellers is by post [chaise]. Which is exactly the same kind of vehicle as represented in Gil Blas[87]– viz a carriage similar to a one-horse chaise covered in, it is drawn by two mules or horses. The trappings and harness are chiefly made of cords, with leather ornaments and belts. This machine proceeds about four miles per hour; this country is at least a century behind England in everything. Deane, Bolton, Chambers and Pulsford came to my casa this evening and had some grog tonight.

Luz, Tuesday 9 March.
General Stewart's pack of hounds came over to Luz this morning. I took them round the neighbourhood, but had no sport; they are to

---

[82] Cornet William Foster.
[83] Lieutenant James Waldie, Adjutant.
[84] Surgeon William Chambers.
[85] Assistant Surgeon Lucas Pulford.
[86] I have not discovered any evidence for a mutiny within the Life Guards at this time.
[87] *L'Histoire de Gil Blas de Santillane* is a novel written by Alain Rene Lesage and published in 1735.

be over here again on Thursday, when I hope to have sport. I dined with Deane, Bolton and Burke; poor Rowlls that we had forced from the mess, now lives in the most miserable way. He cannot get anyone to mess with him. The peasants here use a heavy cart pulled by oxen and guided by a big fellow who walks before the tow bar with a stick with a small point at one end to prod as the occasion requires. These vehicles are low, enclosed and solid, they can carry six to eight hundred pounds in weight, and as the axle is never greased, it makes a horrible noise. Twenty of these carts give us each day our rations.

Luz, Wednesday 10 March.
Marched to the Campo Grande[88] and was inspected by Colonel Grant, we had the whole of the regimental as well as private baggage of the regiment with us; rode over and dined with Smith and Kennedy at Benfica. Troop Sergeant Major Duncan[89], of Captain Kennedy's Troop, I am sorry to hear, has defrauded him of a large sum, near eighty pounds, it's a very serious loss to him here where money is so scarce. I hope to God he will make an example of him, as Davison[01] did of Sergeant Major Everett[91], who was broke for the same thing. Though, Everett died broken hearted a few weeks after he was reduced. Bought a regimental cloak off Smith, I am to give him £5.0.0 for it. Last night Lieutenant Waldie met with a severe accident, was thrown off his mule and nearly broke his leg; was unable to attend the inspection this morning.

Luz, Thursday 11 March.
Love is the most delightful of all passions known to the human breast, it carries a man through all misfortunes, supports him under every care and trouble in life, and supported by love I have braved winter chills and summer heat. Love makes my homely meal comfortable, a dinner of my rations, 1lb of meat and a 1lb brown bread, with contented cheerfulness I enjoy it, and am thankful for such food, and ate it with relish. In health and cheerfulness, I arise from the mean repast and retire to a bed, many would think hard, but in which I sleep as soundly as ever a prince in his palace. It is

---

[88] Now a suburb of Lisbon.
[99] Troop Sergeant Major James Duncan.
[90] Captain Hugh Davison who then transferred to the 17 Light Dragoons in December 1812.
[91] This must have occurred prior to the end of 1812 as he does not appear in the Regimental Muster of December 1812.

love for any [woman?] and an honest heart, that causes all my happiness, it is the root whence happiness springs, the link that connects everything together and the prop that supports the whole. May [Amelia?] be as happy, what a blessing I should feel if confident of it. Rode to Lisbon with Smith, and bought many trifles to add to my travelling stock; another Court Martial today on a Farrier McMahon[92] for stealing iron. Another packet arrived, but no letters for me. Nothing like the chivalrous dispositions of both Curtis and Dolbel. They talk about the number of the French that they have killed. I recommended that Dan Curtis bears the motto: 'Do tell'.

Luz, Friday 12 March.
Reconciliation between Colonel Murray and Captain Clements, brought about by Colonel Palmer of the 10th[93], I am extremely glad of it, and may they always be friends. Smith dined with me, Bolton thrown from his horse on the parade and very much bruised, unable to stand and give evidence at a Court Martial. I was a member and gave one of the prisoners, Redmond[94], a character reference. A brutal outrage committed on one of the troop horses last night, had its tongue cut out. I was on the court of enquiry, but no proof to incriminate any of our dragoons, hope it was a Portuguese.

Finally, orders began to arrive for the cavalry to march up country to join the army. Everybody was anxious to move.

Luz, Saturday 13 March.
  Graham[95] of Kennedy's Troop punished this morning for theft, received 250 lashes. The packet arrived this morning, the letters to be delivered some time tonight, hope I have some to receive. The 15th Hussars have received their route to march up the country, next Monday; suppose our regiment will follow about Wednesday or Thursday. I am very anxious to be gone from here. Wrote to Mr Vanboorst, Captain Wheeler[96] and to Browne Hall & Co. Deane and

---

[92] There are four McMahon's in the regimental muster, none of which have any annotation to indicate that they were the farrier. They are Arthur, James, Patrick and Richard.
[93] Lieutenant Colonel Charles Palmer, 10th Light Dragoons.
[94] George calls him Redman, but the only man with a name like this in the regimental muster is Private William Redmond.
[95] Private William Graham.
[96] The only Captain in the Army with this name was Captain Samuel Wheeler of the 80th Foot, who transferred into the Ceylon Regiment in June 1813.

Burke[97] came and sat with me this evening. Oh my barrel of brandy, it goes very fast, if the regiment don't move very soon, I must lay in a fresh stock. Yesterday being a particular day amongst the Portuguese; the Host was paraded in grand style round Lisbon. Colonel Grant of the 15th Hussars, whom everyone knows to be a great 'Blood'[98], on riding past the procession of yesterday and saluting it, unfortunately his wig came off with his hat as the sacrament passed, which caused great laughter, even to the monks and friars etc.

Luz, Sunday 14 March.
Received a letter from my friend Mr. Vanboorst who informs me of his health, and that the bill for £60 I drew on Greenwoods[99] is provided for, his letter is dated the 2nd inst. Divine service was performed by the brigade clergyman, before the regiment on parade, this afternoon. Had the pleasure of reading several English newspapers, a very great treat to us here. The only thing interesting in them are the letters and communications respecting the Prince of Wales. Sir Ralph Abercrombie[100] and Marques Wellington[101] with many other distinguished generals, commenced their military careers in the 18th Hussars; then light dragoons. Cornet Dolbel was so confident of being gazetted lieutenant, the following gazette after we left England, that he had all his baggage marked accordingly. How astonished he must have been when he read the name of Lieutenant Lynch[102] from the 17th Light Dragoons, gazetted in our regiment, some say he was raving all night and swearing he would send in his resignation the next morning; second thoughts are best, and he still remains a cornet, Colonel Murray will not recommend him[103].

Deane informed me this afternoon of our mess plate left at Brighton, being stolen, a serious loss that, to the regiment. No fresh meat to be got, besides our rations for love nor money in Lisbon their religion

---

97 Incorrectly shown as Bolton in the French version.
98 A swaggering dandy.
99 The Army Agents, Greenwood, Cox & Hammersley of Craigs Court, London.
100 George is mistaken, General Sir Ralph Abercromby who was killed at the Battle of Alexandria in 1801, was in the 3rd Dragoon Guards.
101 Arthur Wellesley, the future Duke of Wellington did serve in the 18th Light Dragoons from 1791-3.
102 Henry Edward Lynch transferred into the 18th on 30 January 1813 from the 17th Light Dragoons and exchanged again to the 5th West India Regiment, remaining as a lieutenant by 19 June 1813.
103 Dolbel did get his lieutenancy on 22 April 1813, vice Lieutenant George Ball. Ball was superseded being absent without leave.

not allowing the Portuguese to kill in recent days. What a strange set of beings the Portuguese are, but much more so their religion.

Luz, Monday 15 March.
All very anxious for the arrival of General Stewart to take the command of the brigade because we do not like Colonel Grant, our regiment I think are looking better than ever they did. The 15th Regiment of Hussars did not march as reported they would this morning. Conolly, whose brother lately died, speaks of going home on that account, his brother has left him £4,000 per year and 8 fine horses in the stable, a lucky fellow this Conolly. Many of my brother officers are very poor, Hesse and Curtis are particularly so, I am afraid I shall soon be like them if our paymaster doesn't soon issue out more stuff, only 3 dollars left. Dolbel who paid few if any of his debts in England, sports plenty of money here.

Luz, Tuesday 16 March.
Sent my large trunk to the regimental stores, it contains the following articles:
4 Leather Pantaloons 4 Pantaloon Hose
1 ditto Breeches 1 Pair Flannel Drawers
2 Cloth ditto 1 Cotton ditto
3 Cotton Pantaloons 2 Coats
1 Dress White ditto 2 Silk Handkerchiefs
1 Dress Blue ditto 1 Pantaloons
7 Waistcoats 1 Dress Belt
1 Dress Pelisse 1 Pair Pumps
1 ditto Jacket 3 Sheets
Dress Cap Linen 1 Pair Boots
1 Blue Overalls 1 Set of Horse Clothes
5 White Neck Handkerchiefs 3 Shirts
1 Black Silk Stocking 2 Cotton ditto
2 White 1 Sabretache
1Great Coat Account Book, Ledger
1 Whip Hat Brush
Pistol Case 2 Pipe Tubes
1 Dress Sash 1 Ladies Picture
2 Books, Syntax, & Sword Exercises
McMahon of Captain Burke's Troop punished this morning for drunkenness, received 150 lashes. The regiment held itself in readiness to turn out in marching order all this morning, but for what purpose it was ordered, I know not. Lord Hutchinson entered

the army in our regiment, 18th Hussars, from whence he passed to the 67th Foot[104]. Lieutenant Dunkin[105] wrote to Colonel Murray from Brighton that he felt himself much hurt; when he heard I was to come out with the regiment over his head, that his greatest wish was to go on service with the regiment, and was now ready to come immediately. All very fine talking, he knew I was coming out near a fortnight before we sailed, yet never troubled himself till near two months after; so much for Dunkin and the white feather; dined with Bolton, Deane and Burke.

Luz, Wednesday 17 March.
St.Patrick's Day. About 3 o'clock this morning was serenaded by our band with the tune of 'St.Patrick's Day in the morning', under my bedroom window. Finding that the custom in the regiment on this day is that the English officers should treat, I asked Bolton, Burke, Deane, Chambers, Rowlls and Pulsford, who did me the honour of their company. I made them pretty groggy and they departed in peace about 12 o'clock. The Portuguese keep this day as strict as the Irish. Many broken heads in the regiment this evening; one man carried into the hospital more dead than alive. The following Regimental Orders were given out by Colonel Murray.

Regimental Orders. Saint Patrick's Day.
The retreat will not sound tonight till 10 o'clock, at which hour every man must return quietly home. Ireland looks to the 18th as particularly her own, to uphold her name by their good conduct abroad, and she has reasons to be proud that they did belong to her. But on the long list of crimes discreditable and mean, which of late have prevailed in the regiment their country can look with no feelings, but those of humiliation and regret. It is hoped however, that the occurrence of the festival of their Patron Saint will recall to the recollection of every Irish soldier, that a high sense of honour above every mean or dishonest action, is equally characteristic with undaunted courage and nature, if a fine born Irishman. Murray.

---

[104] He refers here to General Sir John Hely Hutchinson, the 2nd Lord Droughmore, who had joined the 18th Light Dragoons as a Cornet in 1774, but was promoted to the 67th Foot as a captain in 1776.

[105] Lieutenant Thomas Dunkin had originally been a cornet in the 1st Dragoons, but had joined the 18th as a lieutenant on 19 September 1811. He seems to have taken an inordinately long time to join the regiment on campaign.

On the morning of the feast of Saint Luz, Luz, Thursday 18 March. Rode with Smith to Queluz, and saw the palace[106]. The apartments are very beautiful, particularly those painted and decorated under the directions of Marshal Junot when here in 1808. The paintings are remarkably fine, executed by the first Italian masters, a set representing the exploits of Don Quixote, and four large pictures, representing five of the Royal family of Portugal taking refreshments after the sports of the field, claimed my particular notice. Two court rooms, the Queen's, and one furnished by orders of Junot for Buonaparte, are very elegant, likewise the music room. The gardens are laid out with more taste than any I have seen in this country, and the formations are superior to any I ever saw in my life. Like all the palaces and beautiful buildings, I have seen in this country, this charming place is going fast to die; every part of it neglected. The beautiful painted ceilings stained, the tapestry and walls disfigured, a miserable picture of war in Portugal.

A large fleet arrived in the Tagus from England with two thousand horses to remount the cavalry, and about two thousand of the Foot Guards with numerous detachments for other regiments[107]; we are to march up the country immediately thank God. In what circumstance, can the Portuguese nation display more opportunity, and all its energy; let it show itself worthy and determined on freedom, its liberty and its existence are at stake. The decisive moment has nearly arrived, in which it will be called on to rouse all its ancient valour; dined with Deane, Bolton and Burke.

Luz, Friday 19 March.
Received off William Deane; paymaster, 56 dollars; one month's subsistence to the 24th Inst. Rode to Lisbon and bought myself a bedstead and several other things to take up the country, met with Mc Mahon who informed me of the arrival of General Stewart at Oporto, all hurry and bustle, expecting to receive our route immediately. Generals Graham and Picton[108] arrived this morning

---

[106] Built in 1747, the palace was originally the summer residence of Dom Pedro of Braganza, but after the destruction of the Ajuda palace in a fire in 1794, it became the official residence of the Prince Regent and the Royal family until they were forced to escape to Brazil in 1807.

[107] The memorandum dated Horseguards, 31 March 1813, showed that 1,965 horses had been sent or were then departing to bolster the artillery. *Supplementary Dispatches* Vol. VII, page 592.

[108] Both had returned home to recuperate. General Sir Thomas Graham was to serve as Wellington's deputy for much of the war in Spain but had been forced to go home during the winter of 1812/13 with a serious eye complaint. It had improved by March 1813 and he returned to the Peninsula. Lieutenant Sir General Thomas Picton had been wounded the previous year at the storming of Badajoz and suffered from a fever, he now returned to command the 3rd Division in the new campaign.

from England in a frigate, 10 days from Portsmouth, by her we are informed of the glorious success of the Russians over the French and the surrender of Danzig[109]. Being the Festival of St. Joseph, most shops shut up, with very little business going on in Lisbon. This day two months ago the regiment sailed from Portsmouth.

Luz, Saturday 20 March.
Rowlls asked me yesterday to dine with him today, but his servant got drunk, and no dinner was provided. I then went and dined with Smith at Benfica, Kennedy, Dolbel and Foster dined there too. Soon after dinner Smith, Foster and Dolbel began a conversation on riding, which ended in very high [and] abusive language from each to the others. Kennedy interfered and told Dolbel who was certainly much in the wrong, the impropriety of his conduct; at one time I expected nothing less than a duel would be the consequence between Smith and Dolbel but neither one nor the other seems man enough to fight and everything is arranged. I remained neutral as I always intend [to do] on similar occasions. Sat on a Court Martial this morning at Benfica; on John Foy[110] of Turing's Troop, for stealing corn and striking a corporal on duty, the court was adjourned till Monday, when it will sit here.

The delay in moving north was irritating, as the troops were fit and ready to go; but the lack of forage, until the crops began to grow prevented it.

Luz, Sunday 21 March.
Divine service performed to the regiment on parade. This day I joined the old mess again, formed by the following officers, Captains Bolton, Deane, Burke and myself; Lieutenant Cottin of the 10th Hussars dined with us. I wrote yesterday to Mr. Vanboorst and to Miss Spooner[111] and Lord Worcester both very long letters. The dress of the country people is truly laughable, their ragged jackets slung[112], a monstrous large cocked hat with ridiculously made boots, and large pigtail and a stick in their hands about 8 feet long, fifty to

---

[109] These were false rumours, as the Russian and Prussian troops besieging Danzig found it a tough nut to crack; they did not actually capture it until 29 December 1813.
[110] Private John Foy.
[111] This would appear to be Miss Lydia Spooner, born at Worcester to John and Sarah Spooner on 23 November 1798. If so, she had an elder brother James who was born on 6 September 1795.
[112] He means worn on the shoulder like an hussar.

sixty[113] such figures are seen in groups at the end of every street in the villages, a devilish good thing if the laws of this country would allow a part of them to be pressed for the army.

The reason we don't march tomorrow as was expected is owing to the great scarcity of forage up the country, we shall, therefore, remain here a few weeks longer. Nothing can be luckier for us; for by this delay our horses will get in excellent condition. The regiment has not lost more than 8 horses since we left England; and at this moment not more than 7 men [are] sick, and none of them dangerous.

Luz, Monday 22 March.
How beautiful the scenery of this country [is], I am quite enraptured by it. This morning I rode on the Lisbon road to Queluz where hedges of geraniums line each side of the road, now in blossom. I think the hedges must extend near 3 miles. This country might be made a perfect paradise. Every pond I have seen, either in garden or meadow is stocked with beautiful gold and silver fish. English straw hats and bonnets of all shapes and sizes are worn by the women here. The dress of the Portuguese at Lisbon is very much altered since the English first came; both male and female, particularly the head dress. The straw hat or bonnet is a substitute for a lace handkerchief. The round hat for an unwieldy cocked hat; gowns of English cottons are worn by all descriptions. I sat all day on the Court Martial that adjourned in Benfica, Foy's trial we got through, and commenced Sergeant Anderson's[114] for selling meat, the court adjourned until tomorrow morning at 10 o'clock.

All mad this afternoon, nothing but the talk of peace and of the brigade going home in three months[115]. Colonel Murray caught the infection, he told me seriously, in his opinion that the regiment would be in England in that time. I would rather stay here a year or two and see a little service, before I should like the regiment to go home, and it is my opinion that we shall see plenty of that fun.

These reports are very well to keep the married men with Mr Dolbel and a few others in countenance. Thank God I think I am as much beloved by my brother officers as anyone can be, on the contrary; there's Mr Dolbel, the whole have cut [him], and [I] shall not be surprised to hear of his leaving the regiment. Colonel Murray

---

[113] Incorrectly shown as 20-30 in the French version.
[114] Sergeant Robert Anderson.
[115] Another wild rumour.

a few days back, refused to sign a recommendation in his favour, to get him made lieutenant. The unmanly manner in which he boasts of the amour with Lady Charlotte Howard at Brighton, will long draw on him, the disgust of every man of honour, and if General Howard should by chance hear of his boasting, it is likely a horse whipping might be his reward[116].

Luz, Tuesday 23 March.
On a Court Martial the whole day, Sergeant Anderson's trial closed, we found him guilty of selling the squadrons' meat, which being a breach of the Articles of War, sentenced him to be reduced to the rank of Sentinel (dismounted) Dragoon, but the court strongly recommended him to the clemency of the commanding officer, afterwards proceeded to the trial of Mahony of Captain Clements Troop for drunkenness. Tomorrow the court will resume its sittings and proceed to enquire into the abuses in Captain Turing's Troop, when I hope we shall be released, for I am heartily tired of sitting on this court. Rode to Lisbon with Bolton and Deane; heard that the Life Guards and Blues, who are on the road to the army, are in a bad condition, it is supposed they will not muster 200 each regiment when they get there. Six of the Life Guardsmen are sentenced to be shot for mutiny, a few days back at Thomar, but I have not heard that the sentence was put into execution[117].

Luz, Wednesday 24 March.
Statement of officers, men and horses, of the Eighteenth Hussars now at Benfica and Luz, 25 officers, 514 men, 509 horses, 28 private mules, 9 sick men in hospital, and 8 sick horses.
The Court of Enquiry to investigate the abuses in Captain Turing's Troop sat this morning, afterwards I went to Lisbon and bought 4 silver forks, 1 dozen silver buttons and 4 pairs of bespoke Lisbon shoes for Amelia. I got quite tipsy this evening at the doctors, Deane, Bolton, and Clements were in the same way. The city is bleak, the inhabitants starve during Lent and pray without meaning. I was unhappy tonight with Deane. Cottin of the 10th was apprehensive this evening.

---

[116] Lady Charlotte, the daughter of General Kenneth Alexander Howard, 11th Baron Howard of Effingham, was only ten years old in 1813!
[117] I have been unable to discover any evidence to support this claim.

Luz, Thursday 25 March.
Received from the paymaster, William Deane Esq., 38 dollars and 4 shillings being 200 days Bat money from 25 March to 25 September, (payment for a military servant). Colonel Palmer received orders to proceed to Thomar and take up quarters for the brigade, we shall, therefore, march in a few days. Thomar is 6 day's march from Luz, and about 7 from the army, I dare say it's the intention of Lord Wellington to keep us near the supplies as long as possible. It was with regret I heard yesterday of the loss of the frigate Java, and the death of that brave officer Captain Lambert[118]. This is the third frigate the Americans have taken, fault must attach somewhere; oh, that the ever to be lamented hero Nelson was now alive; he would soon be revenged for this national disgrace[119].

The Portuguese girls are lively creatures, I tease Hannah and Louisa my pretty neighbours to death about their religion and many other things equally disagreeable to me. I observed to them, that their sex be dirty devils to be eternally lousy themselves, when Louisa coolly observed, then how much more dirty you are who never de-louse yourselves at all.

The last time I was at the opera in Lisbon, returning home I received the content of a certain pot over me, it is the custom of the country to throw every kind of nuisance out of the window. Smith [is] seriously afraid he must call Dolbel out and fight him, before he can bring the fellow to a true sense of honour and good behaviour. Living in the same house with Dolbel, Smith is expected to put up with a great deal of insolence and he is forced to hear a number of insults about the army, and its more than Kennedy and Smith can do to keep him at all in bounds. What fools they both are to not be provoked!

The Court Martial ordered to reassemble this morning and to reconsider the crime we found Sergeant Anderson guilty of, and the punishment we awarded him being too lenient. The court confirmed their former opinion and returned the proceedings. The court then proceeded to the trial of Sergeant Sheridan[120], armourer for absenting himself without leave and for drunkenness.

---

[118] HMS Java was originally the French ship Renommee which was captured by the British in 1811 and renamed. The Java was captured by the USS Constitution on 13 December 1812, her Captain, Henry Lambert, was mortally wounded and died seven days later. The wreck of the Java was burnt by the Americans as being beyond saving.

[119] The Royal Navy discovered that the American frigates were better built and more heavily armed than their own frigates and suffered the consequences during the early phases of the War of 1812. The other two losses mentioned were HMS Guerriere and HMS Macedonian.

[120] Sergeant James Sheridan.

He was found guilty of the first charge and sentenced to be reduced, the court then broke up.

Luz, Friday 26 March.

The regiment paraded this morning at 7 o'clock when the stripes were cut off Sergeant Anderson's jacket; Foy received 200 lashes, Sergeant Sheridan and Mahony, paraded by the colonel. The proceedings of the General Court Martial's, on Adjutant Lieutenant G. Towell, of the 3rd Dragoon Guards[121], and Major Hay of our regiment, both most honourably acquitted. Towell was originally a sergeant in the 18th Hussars, his good behaviour caused General Jones[122] to recommend him for promotion and he was appointed Adjutant to the 3rd Dragoons, soon after his appointment there was some dispute between the widow of a major; then Captain Hays, a Sergeant Major and others respecting a balance due from Hay, to her, which he refused to pay. Upon the widow and her friends, examining her husband's papers, they found a receipt from Major Hay acknowledging to have received £20part payment of £100 from Towell, for recommending him to the Adjutancy of the 3rd Dragoons. This receipt was shown to several, and at last General Stewart heard of it and brought Toole and Hay to a General Court Martial. It became the interest of each to defend the other and by good fortune, both were honourably acquitted.

The proceedings of the Court Martial on officers of the 85th[123] Regiment were read. The sentences were as follows: two officers of the regiment broke, and all the officers in the regiment to be drafted to other regiments immediately[124]. The reading of these cases detained us for three hours during the parade. I received a letter from Donna Maria this morning, who informed me the pleasing news of the health of all my dear friends, particularly of Amelia's, who will write to me in April. Found a most beautiful dog this morning, cream colour, if I am lucky enough to preserve him during the campaign, and take him home with me, what a handsome present he will be to Amelia.

---

[121] George incorrectly calls him Toole. Lieutenant George Towell had originally been a quartermaster sergeant in the 18th Hussars and had become a cornet in the 3rd Dragoon Guards in August 1810. He arrived in Portugal in the April of 1813 and served throughout the remainder of the war.

[122] Major General Oliver Jones of the 18th Hussars.

[123] Incorrectly shown as 83rd in the French version.

[124] The 85th Foot had all its officers changed in January 1813 following a period of bitter in-fighting and duelling.

Luz, Saturday 27 March.
The oranges and lemons being all gathered. The husbandman is now employed in the vineyards.
Smith breakfasted with me this morning, when I read a part of Donna Maria's letter to him; he received no letter from Mrs S[mith] by the last packet.

Luz, Sunday 28 March.
By the packet before the last, we heard of all our mess plate being stolen out of the barracks at Brighton, we are now informed that T. Vines the man[125], I had some thoughts of bringing out with me as servant did steal it, and he and his wife are now in Horsham gaol for it. I am taking lessons to learn the German flute off a McKenny[126] master of the band but I make little progress. The waltz composed by McKenny and called by him after my name has become a very great favourite here. It was called for first by one of the officers at the Ministers Ball, and was danced for nearly an hour and has ever since been a very great favourite, particularly with the Portuguese ladies. Being officer for General Orders, I rode to Belem: no time fixed for our march from here. All that is necessary for the movement of our army is moved into the interior as soon as shipments arrive from England. We all hope for a vigorous and successful campaign.

Luz, Monday 29 March.
Morris[127] one of my batmen confined last night, by order of Lieutenant Hesse and the Adjutant for mutinous behaviour to the Sergeant Major, and [I] spoke to the officers and got him released, after great trouble; if ever he is guilty of anything again, he shall be punished.

Luz, Tuesday 30 March.
What monkeys the Portuguese make [of] their children, fancy a boy of eight years old dressed as follows:- round hat, frilled shirt, and neck cloth, a long shirted coat and waistcoat, pantaloons and hessian boots, generally with a walking stick. The women wear a kind of boot made very like our hussar boots, these are usually worn by those who have thick legs. Bought a pony this day at the mule fair in Lisbon, price 40 dollars, I have now everything complete, don't

---

[125] This Vine does not appear on any muster roll of the 18th and must have been a civilian.
[126] Private William McKenny.
[127] Private Thomas Morris.

care how soon the route for our marching arrives. Lieutenant Jones gazetted to a troop in the 3rd Dragoons[128]. For my part I'd prefer to be an active lieutenant in a regiment of hussars than a captain in a heavy dragoon regiment. The packet arrived this morning and brought this news and likewise two letters, one from Mr Vanboorst, the other from a dunn[129].

Luz, Wednesday 31 March.
Read 6 English newspapers, all full of the proceedings against the Princess of Wales[130]; God send she may overcome all her enemies. And that is the wish of the Army.

Luz, Thursday 1 April.
My brother William's birthday[131]; I left today, against my consent and that of Bolton, my troop for Burke's; Hesse and the two Curtis are placed in Bolton's. Huzza! The route for the march of the regiment tomorrow, arrived this morning, it is as follows: April 2nd, Sacavem, 3rd, Villa Franca [de Xira], 4th, Azambuja, 5th Cartaxo. Received; from Captain [Paymaster] Deane one month's pay up to 25th inst.

---

[128] Lieutenant Valentine Jones was gazetted a captain in the 3rd Dragoons.

[129] A dun or dunn was a letter demanding payment of an outstanding bill.

[130] The Prince Regent (the future George IV) was married to Caroline of Brunswick, who was rumoured to have carried on a number of affairs. In 1806 a commission made up of the Prime Minister, Lord Grenville and a few senior ministers were appointed to conduct a 'Delicate Investigation' into the truth of the rumours. No evidence was uncovered, but Caroline was excluded from all royal events and was shunned by much of society. Caroline exiled herself from 1814 onwards in Italy. She did attempt to attend the King's coronation in 1821 but was barred from entry by armed guards and died soon afterwards possibly of cancer. She was buried in Brunswick Cathedral.

[131] This would make sense, with William being baptised at one month old on 1 May 1787.

# Chapter 3

# Joining Wellington's Army

Finally, the Duke of Wellington judged that the crop growth was nearly sufficient to allow the mass of horses accompanying his army, to be supplied with feed and the hussars were ordered to move forward to join it. George was clearly very pleased to start campaigning, although it was not long before he suffered the privations that accompanied it.

Luz, Friday 2 April.
At eight o'clock this morning the right wing of the regiment[1] marched to Sacavem. I'm leaving tomorrow. I was sitting on a Court Martial all this day, tried 4 men at Benfica, Corporal Thompson[2], punished this morning, received 100 lashes and reduced, this man was particularly well recommended, as to character, few in the regiment bore a better. All the officers interceded for him, yet Colonel Murray would not pardon him. His poor wife was within hearing of her husband's sufferings, and [I] must say, I was never so much affected, more by her sobs than her husband's cries; I wanted to be one hundred miles away. His crime was drunkenness and striking Sergeant Williams[3]. Hesse paid me and Dolben a part of what I lent him. William Woodberry had he lived would have been 24 years old on this day.[4]

---

[1] Sometimes, it was necessary to split the regiment into two wings to march separately, to ease the demands on the supply system.
[2] Corporal John Thompson.
[3] Sergeant Thomas Williams, Trumpet Major.
[4] This would appear to be an afterthought from the previous day when he mentions his brother's birthday as 1 April. However, if he was the William Woodberry born in 1787 he would have been 26 this birthday.

Sacavem, Saturday 3 April.

The left wing of the regiment marched into town around noon. The road to it from Luz is very pleasant. This is a poor wretched very dirty town, and its inhabitants are also very miserable, nothing worthy of notice in it. Surgeon Chambers and I walked round the town and on the neighbouring heights had a beautiful view of the Tagus. Senor Pauls of Lisbon has a beautiful villa on a hill near the town. We walked round the garden and saw part of a rock that was mined, blow up. I stood behind a tree when it exploded. Captain Webber Smith's Troop of artillery is quartered here, he asked me to dine with their mess, but I declined having invited Chambers to take pot-luck at my billet, which is better than I expected to find, after leaving Luz; stabling here for about 300 horses. Chambers dined with me and we drank so many toasts that at the end both of us could just about see.

Villa Franca [de Xira], Sunday 4 April.

The regiment marched from Sacavem soon after six this morning and arrived at this place completely drenched with rain. I never before saw it rain so hard. We passed the famous lines[5] where Wellington made his stand against Massena[6], what with nature and art they appear impregnable. The weather being so unfavourable, I had no opportunity of observing the beautiful scenery this road abounds with. Villa Franca, originally the headquarters of Marshal Massena, Alhandra being Lord Wellington's, is a small dirty place containing about 800 houses and stands on the bank of the River Tagus, and forms a considerable landing place. There is a very good inn in the town where 8 of us dined, and took our leave of comfort for some time, an infantry officer told us that from this day we may date our misery. I hope what I have heard of the country may not prove true. I had a very good billet here, and very much enjoyed myself. It is Palm Sunday a great day among the Portuguese; who make the noise of the devil in the streets. Stabling for 400 horses.

Azambuja, Monday 5 April.

The road at first leads over a hill, we then came to an extremely well cultivated and extensive plain, shaded with olives, which

---

[5] The Lines of Torres Vedras.
[6] Marshal Andre Massena, Duc d'Rivoli.

accompanied the Tagus for a considerable distance, and afforded a prospect which after having long seen nothing but hills and mountains, was uncommonly pleasing. The Portuguese are too much accustomed to rocks and mountains, whenever they had occasion to describe a charming country, [they] always begin by saying 'it is a large plain'. The town has nothing in it to recommend it to notice. The hills and mountains behind it are beautiful; I went on them with Chambers, part of a line of defence, crosses them, which appears very strong from nature. Torres Vedras is distinctly seen, so is the important pass of Rolica, where the British Army obtained a distinguished victory in the campaign of 1808[7]. They stormed the pass and hills in a grand style, though defended with great valour by General Delaborde[8]. The ground seems to consist of steep hills, covered with woods. There are a variety of charming views from those heights, Santarem, Cartaxo, Muge, Escaroupim, and Lamarosa are distinctly seen. I got a very good billet here.

My hostess a young woman of great family and fortune paid every attention to my comforts, ordered her servants to cook and wait on me. Chambers dined with me, we had an excellent dinner, and we joked with the widow and her handmaidens. The Portuguese dress here according to the old custom of the country, which I think becomes them much better than the English dress, which has become so much the rage in Lisbon and its neighbourhood. On our march today, we met the Fourth Dragoon Guards, returning from the army to Lisbon, to embark for England, dismounted. This regiment has been out about a year and a half, [but] have never drawn their swords on the enemy, the horses, due to lack of proper care, are exhausted and [it] is now obliged to be sent home dismounted, not being able to obtain a remount[9]. One of the officers of the 4th had his baggage stolen yesterday by a bandit between this town and Villa Franca, his servant was leading a mule with the baggage, when several fellows came and tied his arms behind him, and tied an oil sack[10] round his head, then they took the mule and all away. Stabling, in this town and its neighbourhood for 600 horses.

---

7  The Battle of Roliça opened the Peninsular war on 17 August 1808.
8  General Henri Delaborde.
9  This would appear to be a little unfair as the 4th or Royal Irish Dragoon Guards along with the 9th and 11th Light Dragoons had been ordered home and were ordered to hand all their fit horses over to the regiments remaining in Portugal.
10  A hessian sack.

Cartaxo, Tuesday 6 April.

We arrived here soon after 10, met Burke on the road who had provided a billet at two quintas for half [of] his troop 2 miles before we came to the town. Partook of an excellent breakfast with him and Hesse, I am again in debt to Skinny[11] thanks to him for an excellent billet in the same casa, with himself, we mess together; and shall find it very comfortable I am sure.

The road from Azambuja to Cartaxo is remarkably pleasant, the variety of scenery truly enchanting, the road lies across very high hills and the higher we ascend the more lovely and cultivated and pleasant the country appeared. Cartaxo looks very pretty from the hills, the immense plain on our right, properly a wide flat valley enclosed on one side by the forerunner of the Serra da Estrella, the largest highest mountain in Portugal, and on the other by that range itself, which on this side appears a high but gently declining mountain, its forerunners lose themselves in hills. The plain is extremely well cultivated containing fields of maize and rye, vineyards and small woods of pine and chestnut trees, a number of villages also surround it, there are also many meadows, where countless herds of cattle graze.

We arrived at Cartaxo from across country and my horse Dick got me over a wide ditch, to the astonishment of Murray and Burke, who believed that he could not jump and who took their horses to be famous jumpers. They had however, to dismount and cross the gap with great care. There is nothing in the town to recommend it to notice, but its name which is well known in England, being the headquarters of Lord Wellington during the time that French Massena lay in the neighbourhood of Santarem and Thomar and likewise being the place where that brave man the Marques de la Romana died on the 23 January 1811[12]. Lord Wellington has so justly appreciated his merit and virtues, and a whole eulogy will serve to mark the loss which Spain has suffered by his death, as well as the common cause of the allies. I had every reason to believe my horses would not answer any purpose when obliged to march, yet I find them in better condition than any other officers. Stabling might be found in this town and its neighbourhood for 1,000 horses.

Cartaxo, Wednesday 7 April.

Wrote a very long letter to my dear friend, Amelia; rode out with

---

[11] A nickname for Burke.

[12] Pedro Caro, 3rd Marquis of Romana, died at Cartaxo on 23 January 1811.

Colonel Grant, Murray and Burke called at the quinta[13] where the men of our troop are billeted, saw they were all comfortable. Burke received four newspapers this morning; the only news in them is the proceedings against the Princess of Wales and an account of the death of the Duchess of Brunswick[14], who died at Blackheath on the 23 March, and the official account of the taking of the Java frigate by the Americans.

Cartaxo, Thursday 8 April.

I rode with Chambers this morning to Santarem; saw the strong lines occupied by the Marquess of Wellington, opposite the bridge, during the time Marshal Massena was in Santarem. The country around seems all laid waste, and many years of peace must pass before it will gain its former flourishing state; three parts of the houses in Santarem are completely gutted. I never beheld such a noble place in such ruins. The remains of the old Roman wall and citadel now a venerable ruin, no people in the world built in the manner of that extraordinary race. On the top of one of the church towers, are 7 skulls hanging up, I made some enquiry respecting them, and was informed they were of traitors who had plundered the churches and assisted the French. All the monuments of importance are transformed into hospitals for sick soldiers.

It is incredible how many strong posts may be found in this country, depend upon it, that Portugal is invincible. It is impossible that with such natural advantages and such stout forms and hearts; for they undoubtedly possess them both, they can be subdued; France must exhaust itself in the attack before they will weary of the defence. Bolton dined with Deane, Burke and self, who mess together, when we made him quite tipsy, before we let him go, he had then two miles to ride, how he will curse us tomorrow.

Cartaxo, Friday 9 April.

Colonel Murray is billeted in the same house as the Marquess of Wellington used. I am in the same house Romana died in, which I did not learn of until this morning; what a small town to find quarters for the generals and staff of the British Army, which it did. Each man receives a ration of very good country wine, besides the other rations;

---

[13] From its location near the Tagus River, this may well refer to Quinta do Pedroso.

[14] Princess Augusta Frederica was King George III's elder sister, she had married Charles Duke of Brunswick in 1764. Her husband was killed at the Battle of Auerstadt in 1806 and she retired to England in 1807 and died at Blackheath on 23 March 1813.

wine is sold here much cheaper and better, than at any other place I have been at; 3 vintems a quart. The people here are extremely civil, but like all the lower class throughout the country I have seen, excessively dirty; one of their greatest amusements is combing one another[15]. Chambers and Pulsford dined with me this day.

Cartaxo, Saturday 10 April.
Dined with Smith at the quinta where he and Captain Kennedy and troop are billeted. It is near the Tagus River. It was a very unpleasant return and I had great difficulty in finding my way back.

Cartaxo, Sunday 11 April.
One of my troop horses fell down a precipice and was nearly killed; I rode over and saw him, and soon got the creature out, who is now doing well. Tomorrow Burke and self will remove to the quinta on the left, where 46 of the troop are quartered.

Cartaxo, Monday 12 April.
My neck very bad, find it a general complaint amongst all the English in this country, owing I suppose to the heat of the climate. Colonel Murray has ordered Lieutenant Dunkin to join the regiment here immediately, this will astonish him a little, Burke and myself removed from Cartaxo this morning to the quinta belonging to Senor Baynes who has likewise 46 of our men and horses quartered on him. Chambers came over and dined with us, we likewise had the honour of Colonel Azerbendice of the 2nd Cacadores to dine with us, we all got so, so (pissed I think is the expression). The day is excessively hot, I got my tent pitched at the back of the quinta, on a most commanding situation, from which we enjoy the most delightful scenery. I left Jossa and Legon[16] in Cartaxo with my horses, and only brought Ipper and the Highlander pony with me. In the end we are very happy. I don't know why Burke wanted to withdraw to this quinta, he is rather sad and dejected, and I suspect some malice, because he is quite a sneaky character. It is likely that we will soon return to the place where we came from.

Quinta near Cartaxo, Tuesday 13 April.
My birthday, I got up very early this morning and bathed in a brook very near the quinta, and feel myself very much refreshed. I began

---

[15] For lice.
[16] Two Portuguese servants he had hired.

to look worse than I did last week or any time since I left England; must therefore take care of myself, will try to leave off drinking so much wine. I doubt it's that which affects my neck. A strange fellow this Senor Baynes, I took very little notice of his daughter, yet the old buck walked her off to Santarem this morning, wife and all, dammed suspicious people these Portuguese. Colonel Azerbendice who dined with me yesterday was promoted for his valiant conduct at Badajoz. I am now 21[17] years old and I invited Smith, Chambers and Pulsford to dinner.

This being my birthday I was determined to be merry, God only knows if I shall survive another. How happy perhaps, is my dear friend Amelia, who will return to Camberwell this day, to meet her friends and keep my birthday, heaven send that she may be in health, perhaps at the moment reading my letter. I cannot forebear wishing myself with her; I am surely in love, for I feel it and can say it now.

Chambers and Pulsford came and dined with me. I asked Smith, but owing to the great distance and bad roads, [he] sent an excuse. Soon after Pulsford arrived we sat talking in the tent, when a most tremendous storm of thunder and lightning came on, which seemed to shake the bases of the mountains, the lightning was incessant and streamed like a meteor to the troubled air. The rain fell in torrents, which rolled in cataracts down the sides of the mountain with great velocity, while the loud warning peal, communicating their arrival in the brook at the water mill below our house lingered on the ear, and for the inhabitants of this climate the scene executed no visible alteration, but in an Englishman, it will never fail to inspire awe and veneration for that being whose power and guidance are thus made so conspicuously manifest. The storm lasted about an hour, after which we took a delightful walk on the hills and mountain. Found the breeze very refreshing after the excessive sultry heat, during the time the storm had lasted. I sent the doctors home quite fresh, we had an excellent dinner today, fish, soup, fowl, beef steaks, omelette and rice pudding. The crone of Villa Franca who predicted for us a famine is no doubt amused to tell such jokes.

Quinta near Cartaxo, Wednesday 14 April.
I got up early this morning and I bathed in the stream: I am feeling very refreshed. All my comrades say I am very bad, for they drink

---

[17] The French account shows 22, but this must be an error as he confirms later that he was born in 1792.

wine and I have renounced it for the future. Went out a coursing with the captain of militia, my padrone's son, had very little sport, the Portuguese dogs are good for nothing. As I expected, during my absence, Burke packed up all his moveable's and returned to Cartaxo, where he intends to remain, till the regiment receives its route. Webber Smith's Troop of Horse Artillery marched through Cartaxo this morning to Santarem. The road is covered with detachments who join their corps. The situation this quinta stands on is very picturesque; the Tagus is seen on one side, an extraordinary high mountain overlooks it on another. The plains of Santarem, the Estrella Mountains and several woods of firs, make it one of the most delightful situations [a] pen can describe. This neighbourhood abounds in game of all sorts, particularly partridges and wild ducks, the partridge is much larger than in England.

The cottages are very indifferent, having no chimneys, the smoke when they do light a fire, penetrates through all parts of the roof, they have little or no furniture and pigs which are certainly of the largest and best portioned kind, are their inmates. I often think within myself what a beautiful site for a cottage, or with how much ease some of the dwellings of the inhabitants might be turned into an English house; the quinta I am now writing in for instance. Sergeant Taylor[18] was tried by a Court Martial yesterday, for disobedience of orders and was acquitted. Burke and the four senior subalterns formed the court. I was gazetted cornet in the 18th Hussars this day one year, from the 10th Regiment of Infantry, it is now over one year.

Quinta near Cartaxo, Thursday 15 April.
Venda [Vale] da Pinta, a village at the foot of a mountain called the Serra de Montejunto has a most charming appearance from my window, the white steeple of the church, with part of the village itself, surrounded by gentle rising hills covered with corn fields scattered over with clumps of olive trees, with Montejunto in the background apparently touching the clouds, forms a most beautiful landscape. I breakfasted with the two sons of the padrone, one a very handsome lad from Lisbon college, they prepared plenty of eggs and watercress, beef fried in oil, and tea. It is incredible how soon we conciliate ourselves to their customs, as even oil becomes as tolerable as the English butter. Wrote to Mr Vanboorst this day; rode into Cartaxo this morning when Burke informed me, that General Stewart is not

---

[18] Sergeant John Taylor.

coming out to Portugal, but has gone to Hanover, there is likewise news from the Marquess of Wellington. The French are preparing to move, whether to advance or retreat he does not know. I think this news will be the means of us being sent forward immediately. I hope we shall, for I am heartily tired of this place already, it is so very dull. Paid Egan[19] 12 shillings for tailor's work done for me.

Quinta near Cartaxo, Good Friday, 16 April.
Went out a coursing this morning and killed a few rabbits. I never spent a Good Friday so dull before, in England I always had a party of friends, or was out dining at some feast, whereas today I was compelled to eat my dinner alone, no fish, but plenty of good soup and beef. I am plagued to death with the troop; the men are going on very bad. Two men were punished this morning by their comrades, and I was compelled to send another, George Carr[20] to Cartaxo to be tried by Court Martial. I am now determined to work them right and left, till I bring the fellows to a true sense of duty.

I am never out of danger, the militia captain, he spoke to one of the sergeants last night saying that he threatened to stab me or cut my throat on account of his sister, who he said I came on purpose to seduce; what a villain, he is worse than his father, who took the poor girl to Santarem, he went there himself this morning, and when he returns I will teach him to threaten an English Hussar's life.

The mountains have their tops in the clouds, and variegated landscapes deck the distant lawns. The orange trees are now coming into blossom. The fruit was picked off the trees since I have been in this country, of course there must be more than one crop yearly. A most beautiful fox came out of the rocks yesterday; I should have killed him, had not my gun misfired. I killed a most beautiful coloured lizard this morning, nearly 18 inches in length. I have seen no crows or rooks in this country, there are plenty of vultures continually to be seen soaring in the air. Smith and Kennedy have obliged Mr Dolbel to leave their quarters and to turn him out of their mess; this fellow must be very uncomfortable, being universally cut by all his brother officers.

Quinta near Cartaxo, Saturday 17 April.
The regiment was out on a field day order this morning, and marched quarter part of the way to Azambuja to meet the 15th

---

[19] Private Patrick Egan.
[20] Private George Carr.

[Hussar] Regiment, then formed a brigade and went through a few manoeuvres on a piece of ground near the road side. The charges were made on a terribly rough terrain and many horses were exhausted. Sergeant Fletcher[21] died this morning, his death owed in a great measure to a kick from his horse, and this is the first man of our regiment we have lost since it left England. The women do nearly the whole of the labour of the fields and vineyards; they may be seen by the dozens, driving ploughs, and using the hoe: but there is usually one of the kings of creation to prevent chat and arguments.

Quinta near Cartaxo, Easter Sunday, 18 April.
Received three English newspapers, Evening Mail[22] I think. I am indebted to Mrs. Perkins for them, my gratitude can never keep pace with her kindness to me, and may I have it in my power to return it tenfold. The priest of the parish paid me a visit this morning, I think he imagines me a Papist, thank God I am not; Mass was performed in this quinta, immediately after all the rustics came on the green side of my tent, a guitar was procured and played by a very nice girl. A fandango was danced by four, very much in the Bolero style, snapping their fingers and it commenced to raining which soon ended all their sport. I intended to ride as far as Santarem, but the rain prevented me, the Portuguese keep this day with much spirit, no one would imagine it was a Sunday, to see the beastly state the men, women and children were in, all intoxicated not with a religious zeal, but with wine and spirited liqueurs. Rowlls is very much quizzed at present. I don't know how it will be when they get near the enemy. The morning we left Luz, he made the following soliloquy. 'It rains – this augers ill – damn – I am low spirited'. Hesse dined with me today, Rowlls sent an excuse.

Quinta near Cartaxo, Monday 19 April.
Sitting on a Court Martial all day at the Marquise Quintila's Quinta at Campo Verde, Bolton's quarters. I saw Robert Curtis poor fellow, he must be left behind through illness, and perhaps he will never join us again. I never saw a young man so much altered, he is unrecognizable. It is said that he is tormented by the idea of dying and the possibility of fighting, but I still follow the charitable rule to believe only half of what is said by the world, and yet the half!... In

---

[21] Sergeant George Fletcher.
[22] Evening Mail was published in London from 1802-1867.

any case the doctors offer to leave him at Santarem. Lieutenant Hesse removed this day to Captain Turing's Troop; I have now the entire command of Burke's Troop. Our route of march arrived this day; we march towards Thomar on Wednesday. The Fifteenth Regiment takes the lead, and will pass through Cartaxo tomorrow morning on their way to Santarem, by this means they will be a day's march in advance. The 10th will follow our regiment on Thursday. I dined with the doctors today at Cartaxo, one of Burke's mules very much hurt.

Quinta near Cartaxo, Tuesday 20 April.
Received a newspaper and letter from Mr Vanboorst; sat on the Court Martial held at Captain Bolton's quarters at Campo Verde, which finished this day. Colonel Azerbendice, of the 2nd Regiment Cacadores, supped with me, so did my padrone Senor Baynes; received a present of a live fox from a gentleman in the neighbourhood.

Santarem, Wednesday 21 April.
A rainy day, a very uncomfortable march, I was up soon after 2 o'clock, and left the quinta about four, it never ceased raining the whole way to Santarem. I got a very good billet, but not good stabling, Burke who was sent forward to take up the quarters, never got a billet for the regiment, we were therefore, obliged to put up the troop horses how and where we could. Smith was sent forward to Golega this afternoon, to insure us billets tomorrow. I had a good stroll around the town; it cannot be contemplated without regret to seeing so many beautiful buildings falling into decay. Santarem is built in the form of a crescent on the Tagus, and is about fifty miles from Lisbon, overlooking a noble plain, Campo Verde, its former southern walls are ancient with six gates and an old citadel, to which I hear King Alphonso 6th ordered a hornework, which is now in very high preservation, it has after been the residence of Kings, and is now very rich. The French have certainly committed some wanton ravages and disorders in this town. The Host (religious), was paraded in very grand style through the town soon after our arrival. Foster and Quincey dined with me, I afterwards went to the coffee house and saw Rowlls and Pulsford play at billiards, Webber Smith and the flying artillery battery arrived in the town soon after us, and not finding very good stabling, passed through the city; and bivouacked with their horses in a field near the town, pitched tents and in a very short time, this looked very much like service. The

poor fox after having travelled from Cartaxo in a bag was doomed to fall in the streets of Santarem, when I ordered him to be turned loose; he occasioned much sport to all for several hours, the Santarém rabble chasing it from house to house. The last I saw of him was in a parlour where he had frightened all the women in it.

[Vila Nova da] Barquinha, Thursday 22 April.
The troop that was billeted near the town was marched with the whole regiment at 6 o'clock this morning, we got to Golega about 12 noon, where the 10th and part of the 15th have their quarters. Saw Burke who had provided billets for the troop in a convent, saw the men put up, then went to my own billet at a quinta half a mile from Barquinha[23], hereto I have been very lucky and have always got good quarters, thanks to Captain Burke. The country between Santarem and this place is remarkably varied and skirts a deep valley covered with corn, vineyards and orchards all glowing with the best prospects of rewarding the husbandman's toils. This day's march was a very long and fatiguing one, six long leagues, about 27[24] English miles, the day excessively hot. There are in the house two very pretty girls whose mischievous glances have made me blush.

Barquinha, Friday 23 April.
Captain Clement's Troop with the whole of the staff of the regiment marched in here this morning, the remaining troops are quartered as follows, Bolton's squadron at Atalaia, and Turing's at Thomar, the 15th Regiment at Thomar, the 10th at Golega, the artillery at Santarem. Murray and Deane breakfasted with me, Murray and Chambers dined with Burke and self. I walked to Tancos a very pretty village on the banks of the Tagus, but very much destroyed by the French, not a sixth part of the houses inhabited, on the opposite side of the Tagus is the village [of] Arrepiado. I crossed over to it with Chambers and found it as much destroyed by the English, who lay in it while the French were in Tancos. The 2nd Regiment of Life Guards was here, just marched in from Chamusca, the[y] march tomorrow for Sernado. I got a boat and went and examined the famous old Moorish castle of Almourol which stands on a rock in the middle of the Tagus, saw several inscriptions on the stones, but could not make them out. The Tagus, the finest river I ever saw, and all the country about it is most beautiful and romantic, even the

---

[23]  Almost certainly Quinta de Cardiga.
[24]  Incorrectly shown as 20 in the French version.

spoilations of war cannot deface its beauties. It is exactly the scenery in one of the woods of which Petrarch[25] would have had his nightingales to sing their wild melody to the listening woods, and to the moon shining mildly on the clear face of the water.

The woods of pines and olives are particularly beautiful. My billet Quinta de [Cardiga?], stands in the midst of a wood of olives, we have a most magnificent view of the Tagus and the hills and mountains on the opposite banks. The town of Chamusca on the top of one of the hills has a very pleasing effect.

Barquinha, Saturday 24 April.
I rode with Burke to Atalaia, where I saw Smith and Kennedy; on our return we passed through a very pretty village called Moita. Lost one of the men of Kennedy's Troop, supposed murdered and thrown into the Tagus at Cartaxo[26]. This village like most of the others, where the French have visited, has been completely Frenchified, that is to say, reduced to mere walls. I shall never forget the kind treatment Chambers and self, received from one of the friars at the convent near the Moors castle beyond Tancos, who after showing us every curiosity in the place, regaled us with plenty of good wine and cake, and made me accept a dozen oranges. As I still have the handkerchief he lent me to take his gift, I hope that he will come here.

Commissary August Schaumann was far from impressed when he was ordered to join the 18th Hussars. He noted in his journal 'As I had had some experience of troops freshly landed from home, who were unfamiliar both with the country itself and with war conditions, and as I was also aware of the ridiculous pretentions of English cavalry regiments in general, and cordially detested them, my disgust may well be imagined'. [27] His experience of the regiment did not improve his humour however, 'I did not get the smallest help from the regiment, The whole crowd were like fledglings; they only knew how to open their mouths to be fed. If anything was lacking, the officers knew no other remedy than to exclaim to one's face in a cold and stately fashion 'I shall report it!'

Barquinha, Sunday 25 April.
Received three newspapers from England dated 7th to 14th. Burke

---

[25]  The Italian scholar and poet Francesco Petrarch (1304-1374).
[26]  This man was not murdered but AWOL and he returned a few days later.
[27]  Schaumann, page 363.

introduced me to Lieutenant Wilbraham of the Royal Navy[28], he is naval commander here of the naval vessels to safeguard communications between Lisbon and the army and to monitor the replenishment of our troops. I was delighted to meet this old sea wolf and I invited him to dinner. He swore vengeance against the Yankees and expressed his impatience to be put in front of them; from him I have learnt many curious and strange acts committed since the war began. The inhabitants of this village by his account, are in the French interest who used to bring them supplies for their army and who paid them well. Rowlls dined with me, Burke dined out with Colonel Murray.

Barquinha, Monday 26 April.
Our troop at Quinta de Cardiga broke open a wine house and plundered it of near a pipe of wine[29], before it was discovered. I rode over with Burke and saw nearly the whole troop in a beastly state of intoxication, Sergeant Eyres[30], Corporal Boughtflower[31] and the whole guard are the principals in this transaction, and they are all confined. The Deputy Commissary General Schaumann[32] dined with Burke and self, this man was at the siege of Badajoz, the account he gave of the town during the first two days after it was taken is beyond anything I have heard before and froze my blood[33]. General Stewart's horses are ordered to be sold at Lisbon, so there are no hopes of him coming out to command the Hussar Brigade. The English newspapers state his destination to be Germany instead of this country.

Barquinha, Tuesday 27 April.
It is surprising with what contempt the Portuguese treat the name of a Spaniard, they never mention their names but with contempt, and without adding that they are 'Muito falaca' [very false], very treacherous; they are as irreconcilable as oil and water. A great fall of rain and hail last night and a great part of the day, I received from William Deane Esq. paymaster, 3 doubloons[34] on account of pay.

---

[28] Lieutenant Richard Wilbraham, Royal Navy.
[29] A pipe or butt contains 1,008 pints!
[30] George spells his name Ayres, but it is Sergeant John Eyres in the regimental musters.
[31] George spells his name Barflour, but it is Corporal John Boughtflower in the regimental musters.
[32] Deputy Assistant Commissary General August Schaumann, who joined the 18th on 24 April, has left us a very entertaining journal. He was not impressed with the regiment, being in his view full of greenhorns.
[33] Schaumann was obviously a great story teller, as he was not there during the siege. In fact his own journal states that he did not pass through the city until six months after the siege.
[34] A Spanish doubloon was a gold coin worth two escudos or 32 reals.

During the halt the regiment made at Luz, every officer provided himself with mules, asses and ponies, and these animals, therefore, soon rose in value, and every one the Portuguese could spare was readily bought, no matter how extravagant the price, for many of our heroes wished to carry forward luggage, cooking utensils and every necessary for comfort, which the rations did not supply. I think no regiment ever moved up the country with a greater train of baggage than the Hussar Brigade and the Life Guards. The consequence now is that almost everyone is anxious to dispose of part of those comforts, which were thought indispensible.

An officer of the 2nd Life-Guards, who had built a tandem purposely for this country's service, sold it with harness complete, yesterday at Arrepiado for four dollars, the lowest sum it must have cost him, is one hundred guineas. My mule at the lowest price, cost me one hundred guineas. The portable beds and tents have been given away on the march or sold for very inconsiderable sums; those very articles are now found an indispensible necessary. Thank God I have all my baggage safe and though it weighs near 400lb, yet my mule and pony carries it well, and withal some unforeseen accident occurs, will I hope always do the same. With wheat plains, I contemplate the delightful scenery around me, the winding of the Tagus, the olives, the orange and the cypress which abounds in this district, add further variety to the landscape, and indeed the aspect of the wooded heights and the picturesque forms of the hills themselves, are truly enchanting.

Received a letter from the Brighton Union Bank[35], informing me of William Chambers Esq. bill[36] being dishonoured, and enclosing me their account. A balance is due to me of £22. 9s. 7d, the bankers have requested me to inform Captain Deane that if Lieutenant Rowlls did not immediately order the bill to be taken up, which they hold in their hands, they could proceed against him; Captain Deane for the same, being endorser of them, their amount I believe is about four hundred pounds.

Barquinha, Wednesday 28 April.
I bought 16 yards of coarse cloth and trim to make a tent for my servants, cost 5 dollars 10 vintem. I have now got 70 dollars and 19 vintem, which I hope will carry me through the campaign, for it's

---

[35] The Brighton Union Bank was established in 1805 and taken over in 1894 by the forerunner of modern day Barclays.
[36] A cheque.

very unlikely we shall get any pay again for a long time. Rode to Golega this morning with the quartermaster of the 10th Hussars[37], it is the headquarters of the 10th Hussars. Golega is but a small dirty place, and like every other in this part of Portugal, completely ransacked. The horrors of war seem to have been severely inflicted; nor do I believe the cruelties of the French, of which I have heard much off, to have been overrated.

It is with infinite regret I am compelled to write matters in this my idle companion, against the Portuguese so often. But last night two of our men were robbed and cruelly treated on their way to Atalaia, by a party of Portuguese militia men, whom a generous nation has transported to your shores to combat with an enemy ready and resolved to overwhelm. Was it for you to implant in their breasts by your cruel and inhospitable conduct, hatred to your country and contempt for yourselves. Is it from you that the brave English soldier is to receive insolence and scorn, robbery and murder; can we comment, can we pity such a set of men; if rapacity, if the ravages of war haunt your monastic walls, stored with every luxury that can be enacted from the half-starved, bigoted peasantry; reflect deceitful Portuguese, shrink within yourselves and beseech that omnipotent father of all to grant you that blessed reflection that the 'Good Samaritan' so happily felt.

Barquinha, Thursday 29 April.
A great fall of rain during last night, and this morning; the Tagus very much swollen, the agriculture is apparently as bad as it can be, but a minute human labour perhaps more than compensates for the awkwardness of the instruments. The ploughs are drawn by 6 and often 10 oxen, and driven by a man or woman with a long pole.

Stone walls and aloes are the common fences in this district. The walls being composed of rough fragments of stone piled on each other, cemented with mortar. I rode over to Thomar this morning, the road leads over an extremely well cultivated plain, shaded with olives. This town is situated on a plain which is almost everywhere enclosed by hills or the River Nabao, which gives it at a distance a monotonous appearance; though on a nearer approach it is much enlivened by the gardens on the banks of the river.

Thomar was formally a considerable place, but now much in ruin, the streets are tolerably regular, well paved and have a gay and

---

[37] Quartermaster James Rogers.

cheerful appearance. On the south side is a handsome open square alongside the river, enclosed with a stone wall, built on the orders of King Sebastian, so says an inscription. On the hills that surround this square, is a remarkable edifice, the chief monastery of the Order of Christ. It is a very large compound pile, constructed in many varied tastes, and is said to have begun, by Gulder Paes[38], Master of the order of Knights Templars in 1145. I saw many inscriptions some of very ancient date, one 1312. I saw several of my brother officers there, being Captain Turing's squadron's quarters; it is likewise the headquarters of the 15th Regiment of Hussars. The Portuguese women manufacture through every stage of its progress, a quarter part of the linen used in the country, the spindle and distaff is in much more use than the wheel. The former, I believe, are nearly as ancient as Homer, Ulysses is said to have been the founder of the Portuguese Kingdom, in the same manner, and much upon the same authority, as Adam himself was the founder of the Welsh princes. Into what absurdities may writers be led by a resemblance of names, yet there are still Portuguese historians who insist that Lisbon was so called from its founder Ulysses. They might as well derive Paris from the son of Priam[39].

What a villainous troop I belong to; one of the men confesses he was accessory to a murder, which has never been found out, for want of an informer; and then was caught in the act of a crime, which nature shudders at in Cartaxo. The whole troop have broken open several wine houses since we have been here, and committed numberless depradations. However, the punishment inflicted upon Sergeant Eyres and Corporal Boughtflower and three privates tomorrow morning, for breaking open the wine house at Quinta de Cardiga will, I sincerely hope, deter the troop from committing the like again. Captain [Commander] Wilbraham, Royal Navy, dined with me.

Barquinha, Friday 30 April.
The sentence of the Court Martial on Sergeant Eyres and the men for breaking open the wine house at Quinta de Cardiga was carried into execution this morning about a mile from this place, Sergeant Eyres reduced in rank and received 200 lashes, Corporal Boughtflower and a private, received each 300 lashes, I was sorry

---

[38] Actually, it was Gualdim Pais who laid the first stone in 1160.
[39] In Greek Mythology, Priam was the King of Troy during the Trojan Wars.

for the sergeant who before this act, bore a very good character, privates White and Turner[40] were pardoned.

Finally the route arrived for the march further north to Galizes.

Barquinha, Saturday 1 May.
This day we received our route to Galizes, our march is as follows:
    Sunday 2nd Thomar, (draw forage)
    Monday 3rd Cabacos
    Tuesday 4th Espinhal
    Wednesday 5th Lousa and adjacent villages
    Thursday 6th halt to refresh at above

Friday 7th Cortizes
Saturday 8th Galizes and adjacent villages

Burke was sent forward by Colonel Murray to take up cantonments for the regiment in the valley of the Mondego. I got my tent finished today, it cost me 20 dollars and 29 vintems, several of the officers came to see it, and one offered me 60 dollars for it. I have the vanity to think my tent is better than any in the regiment, I shall therefore keep it.

A very rainy day, but a most delightful evening; our line of march having been altered from Portalegre to Galizes. I could not withstand the temptation of going to Punhete[41]; I had heard so much talk about the place, and only delayed going under the idea of marching through it to Abrantes, I found the road in many parts very delightful. The air is absolutely perfumed with aromatic plants; there are an infinite variety of the Erica[42] and whole commons of great extent covered with myrtle in full blossom. The green cistus grows here spontaneously, Punhete is most delightfully situated at the confluence of the Zezere with the Tagus, it was here the English Army under [the] Marquis; and then Sir Arthur Wellesley, assembled before they marched into Spain and fought the Battle of Talavera[43].

Old Wilbraham rode here with me, and I am beholden to him for information, and I left a sword in charge of him to send to Belem stores. I made a long walk in the evening with two young girls, and I improve in their language, very rapidly.

---

[40] These would be Privates John White and John Turner.
[41] Punhete is modern day Constantia.
[42] Commonly known in Britain as heather.
[43] Fought on the 28 July 1809.

Thomar, Sunday 2 May.

The road passes through a well cultivated, shaded olive plain. I arrived here with the troop by 10 o'clock; got a tolerable good billet over the bridge, the troop I got quartered on the river side at Nabao[44], soon after our arrival. I was appointed to sit on a Court Martial on the Farrier Major[45]; found him guilty and sentenced him to be reduced.

Smith and self was walking about the town all the afternoon, we both bought several articles to add to our campaigning stocks. Thomar is certainly the best country town I have seen in Portugal, the River Nabao, owing to the heavy fall of rain this morning, which by the bye, I have reason to remember, had a very pretty effect from the bridge where it runs over a ridge, called in England the weir, and appeared like a natural waterfall. This town was in the past a considerable place, now it is ruined, but was never in the hands of the French for any length of time. Lord Wellington pursued them and our cavalry drove them through the town pell-mell, and it was in this neighbourhood, our cavalry got a severe check from the rear guard of the enemy.

I am extremely sorry to find a report of our cavalry behaving very ill during the last campaign, which I first heard at Belem, confirmed up country by eye witnesses. I went inside a convent on the left entering the town[46], and where Captain Turing's Troop is quartered. The French seeking treasure, broke open all the coffins, and as they have left them, they remain and will remain until the peace. They showed me a subterraneous passage which I entered and found it led to a burial vault of the monastic nuns and nobility. I there saw a corpse, apparently a few years there, others that had been preserved several hundred, it struck me with horror on taking off a shroud on discovering the face of a beautiful nun, but more so on attempting to raise up the head it fell off leaving me holding a handful of hair! Every ornament in the chapel has been stripped off, and burnt.

I likewise saw another sight not pleasing to me, about eight nuns looking through the grating before their window from a nunnery at the foot of the bridge; after standing, contemplating and pitying their condition; they made many signs to me, and one poor thing lifted up her hands and shook her head and showed by her looks, more than she could have said with her tongue, about her

---

[44] The River here is actually called the Nabao.
[45] Nothing in the regimental returns indicates who this man was.
[46] The Convento de Cristo.

abhorrence to her present station. This day last year I joined the 18th Hussars, then at Hounslow Barracks, every man in the regiment, I mean officers, were mad for driving a barouche[47] and mail coaches, a year has made a great difference, we are all now mad to have a drive at the French.

Cabacos, Monday 3 May 1813.
A wretched day's march this, we left Thomar very early, at the time it was raining excessively hard, the country along our march was most delightful, our road lay across very high hills, but such roads I think there cannot be worse, we passed through the villages, Pintado, [Chao de] Eiras, and Pereiro and several little places.

This village I should suppose contains 30 inhabitants and about 20 houses. The situation delightful, I should have bivouacked, but owing to the precarious state of the weather, was afraid to. I was billeted in a house, but no windows or beds and one room contained Deane, Chambers, Quincey, Rowlls, Pulsford and self, I slept on a table. Last night 14 officers of the 59th Regiment[48] slept in it, the 59th thirteen hundred strong and the 15th Hussars, contrived to stay last night in this wretched village.

Espinhal, Tuesday 4 May.
At 4 this morning I arose from my bed which was a table I had passed the night on, and commenced our march across the Serra da Estrella Mountains, for this place. We rode slowly, and had time to contemplate the scenery of the country. The morning was delightfully fresh and warm, nature glittered in the vestment of spring, and we left the province of Estremadura, and entered Beira.

This morning's march reminded me of one of Shakespeare's woods, so recluse, so distant from the hum of men; every side gratified the eye with heavenly views, many spots were the exact scene for a 'Midsummer Night's Dream', a serpentine brook here and there crossed the road. Espinhal is a very pretty market town, the mountains crowd together from all sides, and the town is not seen until you are nearly in it. The country here greatly improves, hills and valleys succeed to each other, and on both sides of the road are cork, oak, elms and other trees, delightfully interspersed. Hesse who was sent on from Thomar to take up billets for us at Cabacos,

---

[47] An open topped four seater coach popular for summer usage.
[48] The 2nd Battalion of the 59th (2nd Nottinghamshire) Regiment.

lost his way and got into a wood and was forced to stay with his men, a part of the night, without tent or fire, obliged to lay under a tree all night, not being able to find his way out, it unfortunately rained all night. From the appearance of this morning, I think the rainy season is nearly over.

The fair sex in this town are more prepossessing than any I have seen before, many uncommonly pretty. At the door of every house a woman or two may be seen spinning with a distaff[49]. The French, I understand rampaged them as well as their houses and property. So great was the distress of the enemy when in this neighbourhood, they eat [sic] all the asses and goats. I walked on a mount near the town where I saw Castanheira [de Pera], where the right squadron is quartered, and a most extensive view of the country; on the summits of two of the highest mountains are chapels, called St. John's and St. Stephen's, the bold picturesque form of the rocks, gives them a very pleasing effect.

The roads were much better this march than yesterday's, owing to them being across hills, and having never been paved; we passed over a wooden road about a mile in length, the first I have seen, it was made with mountain pine, a very straight tree, laid very close together. Only one church in this town, and that very much destroyed. We passed through the villages, Arega, a dirty little place, and St. Simeon [Casal de Sao Simeo], saw Figueiro [dos Vinhos] on our left between the above places.

Lugar De Ribeira, Wednesday 5 May
After losing sight of Espinhal, I was struck with the appearance of the surrounding country, nothing could be more delightful than the road now became. The base of the lofty mountains, the hills and long valleys, and plains were green with vegetation, and varied with spots of flowering shrubs in full blossom. The whole march this morning was up one hill or mountain and down another. The regiment is in cantonments, the headquarters at Lousa[50]; a troop in each village, we halt tomorrow for rest and proceed on Friday for the valley of the Mondego, this is a very small village and very scantily inhabited, all are dreadfully afraid of the French advancing. In the

---

[49] A distaff is a tool used in spinning. It is designed to hold the unspun fibres, keeping them untangled. It was most commonly used for flax, and sometimes wool. Fibre is wrapped around the distaff, and tied in place with a piece of ribbon or string. The word comes from *dis* which in Low German, means a bunch of flax, connected with staff.

[50] Incorrectly shown as Martin in the French version.

event of them doing so, they intend to take shelter in the Estrella Mountains.

The highest part called Serra da Estrella is directly opposite to my quinta, it has not so pleasing an aspect, for the view partakes more of the terrific than of the agreeable, and the landscape is generally more awful than picturesque. My horses and mules thank God, are very well and I have them in excellent quarters, I have a good quarter myself, everything much better than I expected. Hickey[51] of Captain Bolton's Troop was taken ill last night at Castanheira, and died two hours afterwards, the doctors cannot account for it. Mr Dolbel is likewise so unwell as to be left behind at the above place. I am very sorry for poor Hickey; he was a great favourite of mine, while I was in Captain Bolton's Troop. How uncertain is life, how awful is the thought. Let me pause, if I must write, it must be in my own character. I am a young man and know that the hour approaches with a silent but irresistible rapidity when I shall perceive the world gradually to fade from my sight and close my eyes in perpetual darkness.

The country towns and villages in Portugal have all one appearance, they are most delightfully situated, and an Englishman with a hundred or even fifty pounds a year might live in them as in paradise. Nothing is wanting, but suitable ideas of comfort, which the Portuguese have not.

Lugar Da Ribeira/ [Foz] de Arouce, Thursday 6 May.
A fresh route received for the regiment, we halt on Sunday at Cortizes, and proceed direct to Freixedas where we will halt until further notice. Serra da Estrella. The mountains are covered with pines towards their base, but soon become very bare, and nothing is seen but short grass. The inhabitants are not in this country reputed polite, which in comparison with the rest of the nation is perhaps true.

The Serra da Estrella which is the Montes Herminios of the ancients, is indisputably the most extensive and highest range of mountains in Portugal, for I understand in winter it is covered with snow frequently, during four months and longer, and rises from a mountain plain; which itself is considered high, it lies north east and south west. The northern part is lower, the mountain rising there gently, and being less rocky, for which reason it is called Serra Mansa. But the southern part which is the highest, and in many

---

[51] Private John Hickey.

parts very steep and rocky is called Serra Brava. At Zaragoza [Sabugueiro?], a small village, the Serra presents its highest wildest steepest side and its majestic appearance seems to place it in a class of Alpine Mountains. I rode to Lousa, found it a much larger village than Ribeira, its situation is remarkably pleasant being at the very foot of the mountains, there is a very pretty church, and several uncommonly good houses, and on the whole, do not appear to have suffered so much as other villages I have seen.

Cortizes [Sao Martinho da Cortica?], Friday 7 May.
Never did troops march in worse weather; a very rainy morning and a most uncomfortable march I had; it never ceased raining until after we arrived at this place, which has suffered most severely. I am billeted in an empty house, no windows or any comfort belonging to it. We made a good fire and suspended our canvasses over the front windows and the door. My servants were lying down stairs. It was once a very fine house and well furnished, it was honoured so the padrone informed me with Marshal Massena [for] six nights and Lord Wellington for three. The whole village presents a complete skeleton.

I am now in the valley of the Mondego, in this valley many severe skirmishes have taken place between the French and English, on our march this morning we passed over two bridges, part of each was blown up by the enemy, one over the River Alva, they were so hard pressed by the English cavalry that they blew up the bridge before they had got their own men over, and actually blew up near one hundred of their own men not counting the prisoners. The ground becomes very interesting as we advance. Not a day passes that we discover the sad remains of many brave men, who have fallen in their countries' cause, but whose bones from neglect are still where they fell.

[Vila Nova de] Oliveirinha, Saturday 8 May.
Another wretched day's march raining all the way, we passed over a wild and cultivated heath. Both sides of the road were thickly interspersed with olive trees, and occasionally saw a few oaks which strongly reminded me of my own country. This village which stands on rocky ground in a valley completely hid at a quarter mile distance by olive and orange trees is considered pretty, its church which is now a complete ruin presents a most beautiful picture of antiquity.

This is without doubt as charming a country as in the world. The valley of the Mondego is in some places, steep and abrupt, and

71

inaccessible, with the river of the name foaming over great masses of stone of very singular conformation, apparently caused by the course of the water, it is not here however managed, I should think the decent to the valley to be a league, and the ascent to the opposite mountain to be at least a league and a half.

On the banks of the river stand a number of villages all most romantically situated, I think it the sweetest romantic seclusion I ever beheld, a valley of prodigious extent on either side, bounded by mountains and abounding in every luxury, the oak, chestnut, and most other forest trees, and the orange, the pine, the arbutus[52] and an infinity of others in full foliage and luxuriance of fruit. I cannot help observing how happily I could rest for the remainder of my days in this haven of peace, if I could ever forget my native country. No; here all the riches and all the luxuries of the world could not produce that happiness which at home I feel, though poor of friendships. Only my troop quartered in this village, and I was in hopes of having tomorrow allowed us as a resting day, but a fresh route has just arrived, and we march tomorrow for Fornos de Maceira Dao.

My padrone gave me a chicken for dinner and behaved in every respect like a true gentleman. This is a Portuguese of choice! I rubbed me eyes seeing such food, I thought I was dreaming.

Oliveirinha, Sunday 9 May.
The troop was turned out and ready to march, when orders arrived from headquarters, Bobadela, countermanding the order of march this morning. The reason, headquarters is not at Galizes [as] according to our original route, is owing to a bad fever in the town, which carries off 20 to 30 a day. The Hussar Brigade is now in advance of all the cavalry in this country, all is on the move; we march tomorrow morning and go by forced marches till we arrive on the frontier.

We passed through a village called Moita [da Serra], and a poor miserable place it appeared, a complete ruin, it has suffered from the French and English severely, our men have commenced rampaging every place they stay in, at Cortizes they broke open a cellar and robbed it of oil, and what they could not take, they allowed to run to waste in the cellar. Last night they got into a poor man's house and broke open a box and stole two shirts. I must own

---

[52] A temperate species of plant with berries.

the very last act, very much vexed me, the whole village having shown us so much respect. I soon ascertained the thieves and had them confined.

Nothing but mistakes in this regiment, my God, what an unfit person Colonel Murray is to command the regiment; errors are common in the regiment when a duffer commands us! I am of the opinion of the famous Lord Bacon[53]: 'a very great man is like a high house, where rooms at the top are usually more badly furnished.' I had just written the above and was enjoying myself, and thinking the great benefit the troops would receive from this days' rest, when an orderly came in with orders to turn out and march to Seia immediately. Colonel Grant was at Maceira waiting to see us pass, unfortunately the un-soldier like state of our march, owing to the short notice and we had to hurry, caused him to make some very severe remarks on Colonel Murray's conduct, who had made a mistake and thought we were to halt there, instead of which the orders were for the 10th Hussars to halt and our men to march into cantonments at Seia and halt a day.

The 10th were actively marching into Bobadela, when we left it, then about 12 o'clock. We came through Torrozello, a small village of huts; Maceira which we passed, appeared much like it, Santa Martina [Sao Martinho] on the left of it, is situated on the brow of a hill and has a pretty appearance. I got into this town about five, which stands on a hill; which overlooks an extensive plain on the north side, on all the other sides the mountains overlook it.

Seia, Monday 10 May.
This is [a] neat, tolerably large and populous town, having a market, pretty well supplied with fowls and vegetables, for we found new potatoes, green peas, cauliflowers in abundance, though the place is crowded with military, as one of the divisions of the army being in town and the neighbourhood. I have experienced a very friendly and hospitable reception at my billet. I have no doubt but that this town was formerly more thickly inhabited than it is, for many respectable families who deserted it during the period that the French garrisoned it, have never returned, notwithstanding the expulsion of the enemy from the kingdom. Indeed, many persons told me that the conduct of the French was so cruel, rapacious and tyrannical that numbers felt a horror at the idea of living on a spot

---

[53] Lord Francis Bacon, Lord Chancellor (1561-1626).

which could not fail of recalling to memory those wretched times when, Massena, Junot and General Loison[54], lorded it over all. I am now nearly in the centre of Lord Wellington's army, they are all in cantonments for leagues round this town.

Our march yesterday was for the greater part, through a forest of fine oak, cork and pine trees, the face of the country was extremely beautiful, Seia was seen near a league off. The ruins of a large handsome house which the French burnt on leaving this place, gives the house at a distance an uncommon[ly] pleasing appearance, the road to it a complete zigzag. Galizes is a long straggling place without anything particular, there are some vineyards in its vicinity and large woods of well grown fir, which is here used as firewood, Lieutenant Russell, was nearly shot here, the day before yesterday by a Portuguese, who afterwards made off. Bobadela, the headquarters of our regiment yesterday; originally must have been a very pretty place, it likewise contained more inhabitants than most of the villages we have past [sic], the ruin of an old Roman building gives it a very romantic look. An arch of Roman construction in very high preservation caught my astonished sight, the workmanship of which was exquisite. The olive, the Portuguese substitute for butter, they eat it with everything, and often so excessively rancid as to perfume a whole street, it likewise serves their lamps. They have little or no butter made in the country, but import English and Irish salt butter which sells at 3 or 3/6d per lb. The chestnuts too are a great article of food. They eat them roasted, but chiefly boiled, some they dry and use all the year round, they eat them as we do potatoes, with meat and on all occasions; and it is singular, they call potatoes, castaneos d'india, or the chestnuts of India.

Oliveira do Hospital, a village near Galizes is a place of no great extent, but of great antiquity, it is a dependency of the Knights of Malta, one of whom, I understand resided here until his palace was unroofed by the French. There is not a good house in the town that has not been gutted. At this place is one of the most singular paintings this country possibly exhibits, it is in the church against a white wall, and done with raddle[55] or red chalk; the subject, the passage of the Red Sea, but has nothing of the divine tints of Titian, or the sublime efforts of Michaelangelo, or Rubens, which inspire a melancholy and religious enthusiasm. This picture consists of one

---

[54] General Louis Henri Loison.
[55] An iron ore compound used in dyeing.

solitary ill contrived figure, horridly disproportioned, about 14 feet high, a long raw boned felon, like an inhabitant of the Dog Star[56], and lo and behold, the Red Sea is about 3 feet in length, and two in breadth, over which this colossus of Oliveira do Hospital is straddling. I should not have had the sanguinity to have discovered this to have been the Red Sea, but from the red chalk with which it is painted, and presuming that it must be salt water, from there being two fishes painted in it. This neighbourhood abounds in wolves, I am informed it is not unusual for them to attack men, oxen or horses [even] at midday. An instance occurred lately of one attacking three men of the Guards, and lacerated the arm of one very much, though they succeeded in stunning and afterwards killing him.

A man of Captain Clement's Troop was punished this afternoon for theft. General Packenham's[57] Brigade is quartered in this neighbourhood. I received with the others an invitation to dine with him today, but we all declined it on account of marching early on the morrow morning.

Vila Cortes [da Serra], Tuesday 11 May.
Thank God, fine weather has come at last; we had a dry morning to march here. The road lay over a barren rocky heath, apparently never cultivated. The Estrella Mountains on our right, which are not near so high as those we have seen daily, they were covered with snow this morning, yet the heat of the weather has been since yesterday, excessive. This village is nothing more than a heap of ruins, soon after we arrived there, finding there was not sufficient room for the squadron, the troop was ordered to proceed to Vila Ruiva, where we arrived about 12 o'clock.

There has been a deal of fighting in this neighbourhood since the war commenced, at present the 7th Division of the army is in cantonments in the vicinity, the division was out in field day order, in a field near [Sao] Paio, which town we marched through. We likewise came through Linhares and crossed a bridge over the River Mondego, in the latter place I saw a regiment of Portuguese Cacadores. Vila Ruiva, a village at about 2 miles from Vila Cortes on the left side of the road. The church is a neat edifice, much too good for the appearance of the village which is composed of about fifty huts, built with stone without using any mortar or cement between

---

[56] The Star *Sirius* in the constellation Canis Major (Great Dog).
[57] Lieutenant General Sir Edward Pakenham, brother-in-law of the Duke of Wellington, commanded a brigade in the 3rd Division, which he led when General Picton was absent.

the stone. I was quartered on the priest of the parish, whose casa is in a bad plight, I found him kind and friendly, pious without bigotry, generous without ostentation and desirous of rendering my residence with him as comfortable and happy as his feeble means allowed him, I never slept more sound in bed in England than I did at this good man's home.

We are now drawing near the front line, and begin to find every article much more expensive, indeed there appears scarcity of many of the necessaries of life. The inhabitants are all poor and miserable, what little wheat they had in store or in cultivation, we have seized upon, I pity the poor souls from my heart, and feel the greater abhorrence to the monster, who has long been the scourge of nations.

Baracal, Wednesday 12 May.
We arrived in the town about 12 o'clock after a very long and fatiguing march, this place has nothing in it particularly and much like all the villages we have entered, very much rampaged by the French. We marched through Celorico [da Beira], which is considered a strong position. The fort has been a place of strength and built on solid rock, but evidently before the use of cannon, like most others in this part of the world, of Moorish origin, though some parts appear to have been more modern. The whole town has the appearance of antiquity, a large depot is formed here and a hospital, I saw a great many sick, all seem clean and neatly dressed in flannel. We met them on the road going to Lisbon, to embark for England, nearly fifty carts loaded with sick from the army. This looks very like the advance of the army; I saw today several 'Logan Stones'[58] of a very large size and curiosity. We likewise passed through the village of Cortisal [Cortico da Serra?], and passed over the River Mondego, across a very handsome bridge, which the French attempted to blow up in their retreat, but they only succeeded in part.

Freixedas, Thursday 13 May.
The country more mountainous and difficult; especially towards the end of the march, the road over broken rocks and precipices in some parts, extremely bold and picturesque, which was not a little heightened by the winding line of march of the regiment with the mules, baggage, and bullocks accompanying us. The headquarters

---

[58] Megalithic stones.

of the regiment is at Alverca [da Beira]; the headquarters of the brigade is also here, the whole of the 15th Regiment and our centre squadron is quartered in the town, four squadrons, so it may easily be supposed to be a large place, it contains very few inhabitants, perhaps not forty, it stands on a high hill and overlooks the country for miles.

I saw the 15th out in watering order this afternoon; they have put me out of conceit of our regiment. I saw a great number of dead animals on the road, more indeed than usually mark the advance of an army. On these occasions the wolves and vultures appear as necessary evils, or contagion would be more frequent. This town has received a French visitation, and like others under such circumstances is as well as can be expected.

# Chapter 4

# Manouevring the French out of Position

Having now closed up with the army, the regiment settled into its billets and the men sought to refresh their mounts after the long march, before the advance into Spain began. The weather, however, was unseasonably bad. George was also concerned that the 18th Hussars were not viewed as a well organised or disciplined regiment by the senior officers, which did not augur well for the coming campaign.

Freixedas, Friday 14 May.

Lord Wellington intends reviewing the Hussar Brigade in a few days, when it is expected he will set the whole army in motion and advance into Spain. I procured after great trouble a very good quarter, though without a fire place or glass to the windows; fortunately, I'm not picky. No letters from England, indeed I shall cease to think I have a friend alive, I am afraid the packets for our regiment have been lost, for not one has received letters except Colonel Murray, by another conveyance. Freineda, the headquarters of the British Army is within three leagues of this place, it is much such another village as this, and the Marquess of Wellington is quartered in a wretched house, his room of audience is so low that Colonel Grant could hardly stand upright in it. He hunts every other morning, his dress yesterday was blue frock coat, white waistcoat, white neck tie and grey overalls with a round hat, he is an extraordinary man, for the following morning after the famous retreat from the neighbourhood of Burgos to his present cantonments, he ordered the hounds out and was actively hunting himself. His dress is always very plain and he swears like a trooper at anything that does not please him, he is remarkably fond of the Portuguese and listens to any complaints made to him against the English, but never any made by the English against them.

Freixedas, Saturday 15 May.
The 10th Hussars marched into Alverca yesterday. The 7th Division of the army marched to Celorico yesterday; the army is now on the move. It would take very little trouble to render the roads impassable to an enemy's army. The ground of itself is a fortification, and it would require very little effort to break it up, so as to preclude the possibility of the advance of artillery. These mountain roads are the best defence of the country. The letters so long missing, are now discovered to have been sent to Oporto, the headquarters of the cavalry, instead of Freineda where they were ordered. I have now hopes of receiving some in a few days. The nearer we draw to the frontier, the more distressed are the inhabitants, the wretched state of misery and starvation they are subject to, beggars all description. The longer we stay in our present quarters, the worse it will be for them, we are now actively obliged to send near two leagues for green forage, the whole produce of the fields near us had been consumed by the 15th May, and as those very fields of corn, barley was their principal support for the summer, we are daily accosted by the women and children with tears and moans, begging us to leave them a little to subsist upon.

Galicians: The natives of the province of that name in Spain, are the chief labourers in this country, it is thought there are not less than 8,000 employed in Oporto, and more in Lisbon, and throughout the kingdom of Portugal, political economists suppose no less than a number of forty thousand of these industrious men are to be found. It is a common thing to see four of them carrying a pipe of wine. I had a 'grog and beggar party' this evening, Clements, Conolly, Burke. Last night I was at Lieutenant Mansfield's (15th Regiment)[1], and played three rubbers of whist. Very uneasy about the regiment, Colonel Grant threatened to report us unfit for service, owing to the cursed bad interior management of the regiment and the great neglect discovered in the shoeing department and in the personal equipment of the men. Adjutant Waldie requested by Colonel Murray to resign[2] and Cornet Foster was yesterday appointed acting

---

[1] Lieutenant Ralph Mansfield, 15th Hussars.
[2] The Adjutant bore the blame for the lack of internal structure in the regiment.

Adjutant in his place until the office holder reaches us from England,[3] this must annoy the senior lieutenants.

Freixedas, Sunday 16 May.
A lady of quality and her retinue, travelling I suppose to headquarters, passed through this town, it was the most curious sight I have seen in the country, being dressed in original costumes. Two servants on mules gaily caparisoned, a serving woman mounted on a mule, next came a litter between two mules just large enough to hold the mistress, then followed a woman and two lackeys, then was likewise a man on foot to drive the animals, who carried the litter and the females. All wore the costume of the country. The lady appeared very handsome, and I suspect her to be Madame Linair.

Freixedas, Monday 17 May.
In a field near the town, I discovered the burial ground where I suppose the killed were interred who fell in the numerous skirmishes in this neighbourhood. The dogs of the village having scratched the earth in the cemetery, the remains of many brave fellows are exposed. In no part of the country are there so many Logan stones as there are close to this town, they have a very pretty effect from the chapel at the front of the town. Alverca, is seen, likewise the Estrella Mountains covered with snow. Alverca da Beira has been a pretty place, its situation is truly enchanting, but being so near the frontier of the kingdom has, therefore, suffered severely. I have formed an acquaintance with most of the officers of the King's Hussars[4], should like very much to exchange into that regiment, for I really suspect our regiment will disgrace itself, before long, it will not be the fault of the dragoons, but the ignorance of our Colonel. Lord Wellington reviews us tomorrow, with the brigade.

Freixedas, Tuesday 18 May.
The brigade consisting of the 10th, 15th, and 18th Hussars[5] march from this place soon after 7 o'clock, and after proceeding about six miles on the Freineda road, was formed on a huge heath, the place appointed for the review, where we awaited the arrival of the Duke

---

[3]  Cornet Henry Duperier was appointed to be the new Adjutant and he arrived with the regiment from England in August 1813.
[4]  The 15th Hussars.
[5]  According to Captain Edwin Griffiths of the 15th Hussars (page 136), each regiment had on review the following numbers of men mounted. 10th 494; 15th 496 and 18th 456.

of Wellington and his Staff. After forming line, the 18th in the centre being the junior regiment, [the] Marquess Wellington, general officers and their staff, arrived at noon, they came galloping on the ground. After a general salute he passed in front and inspected the line, we afterwards marched past by half squadron and he expressed himself highly pleased at our appearance, what he said will never be forgotten by anyone belonging to the brigade; and I have the vanity to think he did not flatter us, when he said, 'The brigade is the finest body of cavalry I ever saw in my life, and I feel no hesitation in saying I think it not equalled in Europe'.

Lord Wellington wore the uniform of a general officer with a star and a few orders. There were not so many officers present as I expected to see with the Marquess, the generals were Graham, Brisbane, and Vandeleur[6]. I wanted to see the Prince of Orange[7], but he was ill at Freineda of an ague. The day was remarkably fine, and the appearance of our regiment was much superior to what it was expected. The men of the 18th turned out in very high style and upon the whole astonished the two Royal regiments[8] in all our manoeuvres. Lord Wellington gave the command of the brigade to Colonel Grant and appointed Lieutenant and Adjutant Jones of the 15th, Brigade Major[9]; he likewise gave us the route of march of the brigade, which leaves this place tomorrow morning and commences a march of ten days to the banks of the Douro, where we shall find the enemy strongly posted. Campaigning is now commenced, I received orders to take 56 men to Alverca da Beira for rations, and Conolly [was] ordered to go forward for quarters, these orders did not arrive till near 8 o'clock in the evening. We very plainly saw the mountains in Spain today, shall very soon be bivouacked on them, and I must own, I don't care how soon, for while I am away from England, I wish to see all I can of the world.

Mondego - We have now left this beautiful valley, the most charming seclusion in the world. The river takes its rise near Guarda, from the Estrella Mountains. The Portuguese speak a language peculiar to themselves, made up of French and Castilian, pleasant to the ear and elegant.

---

[6] Major General John Ormsby Vandeleur.
[7] William the Prince of Orange was serving at Wellington's headquarters as an aide de camp.
[8] The 10th Hussars were the 'Prince of Wales' and the 15th 'The King's' and thus Royal regiments.
[9] Lieutenant Charles Jones, 15th Hussars, once paired up with Grant (the 'Black Giant') was commonly known as the 'Red Dwarf'. Grant was a tall man with jet black whiskers, whilst Jones apparently was a small man, with red hair and moustache and wearing a red shako on his head.

Wellington was aware that he possessed greater numbers than the French could bring against him in Spain, the latter having been forced to send thousands of troops back over the Pyrenees to bolster Napoleon's broken forces in Germany after the dreadful losses suffered in the Russian winter. The French army under King Joseph Bonaparte and Marshal Jourdan, was therefore concentrated around Salamanca and placed to defend the line of the Tormes River. Wellington was aware that a direct attack on such a prepared defensive position would be very expensive and may not be successful. Therefore, whilst a force of three divisions under Wellington and Lord Hill, made a demonstration of marching from Portugal towards Salamanca, General Thomas Graham was marching the great majority of the army, totalling some six divisions, further northwards into the mountains. They crossed the border into Spain here and drove back the weak French forces and thus turning the flank of the main French defences. The French were forced to abandon Salamanca and to retire behind other river lines in their rear; only to find each turned successively by this grand flanking movement. The Hussar Brigade led this push and was constantly in contact with the French as they slowly retired.

> Ozzors [Erverdosa], Wednesday 19 May.
> Before I left Freixedas, I received four newspapers and a letter from Worcester, no tidings of the packets said to have been sent to Oporto.
>
> This morning's march, by the bye a very long one, has brought us into a very delightful country. We crossed two very high mountains. I was often struck with the appearance of the country, which presented rich fields of green corn, scattered here and there without the vestige of a human habitation near them, or indeed in sight in any direction, one might almost have been tempted to regard them as the spontaneous productions of the ground.
>
> We met on the road the famous bridges and flat bottomed boats on a kind of wagon[10], there were 18 wagons, each drawn by 14 horses or mules under the care of the Royal Artillery. I hope we shall have the honour of crossing the Ebro over them. This is a small village, but by far the best quarter, I have been in for some time, the inhabitants so kind and obliging. The campaign of 1813 commences this day, the army was this morning put in motion; Frenchmen beware, for we shall soon be at your heels. The weather is now excessively hot, we all begin to experience the effects, usually felt

---

[10] This was the 'Pontoon Train' for building bridges.

by Englishmen in this country. The headquarters of the regiment is at a village called Erverdosa.

[In] very low spirits, I long to receive a letter from my friend Amelia; surely she has not forgotten me. Erverdosa, is a small place, containing a large house, church and about 50 huts. The 10th were quartered at Carapita [Cotimos?], which we saw on our left[11], the 15th at Coriscada. I should have liked to have seen this village, for the appearance was particularly striking. A building very like in appearance a Roman or Moors castle, overlooks it, we marched this day 5 leagues.

Sevillada [Sebadelhe], Thursday 20 May.
We marched this day 7 leagues, man and horse, completely knocked up, we did not arrive at this town till near 2 o'clock having been on the road nine hours, tomorrow we cross the Douro in boats, we crossed the River Lamego and Coa. Small streams in this country receive the name of rivers. We were as much annoyed by the dust today as we ever were with the rain, out of the two, I would prefer the latter.

The further we advance, the more kind and obliging are the natives, though I cannot boast of being in an excellent house yet, I can say I never received more civility in this country and it makes it more agreeable, I have at this moment a charming young woman, knitting a stocking sitting aside of me at the table. I am not able to talk much to her, but we understand each other very well and I would like to stay a month at Sevillada. I wish I could master the language which I am afraid I never shall. The French unfortunately for this town, which from appearance was a good one, was quartered in it three months; it lies in a valley and the ground round it, more cultivated than usually seen about this neighbourhood. The mulberry tree is here planted in groves, like the olive in other parts we have passed; from this I would presume silk is manufactured. The headquarters of the brigade was at Freixo de Numao.

Bivouacked near Pocinho, banks of the Douro, Friday 21 May.
We did not march from Sevillada, till about 12 o'clock, and after rising, crossing several very steep rocks, we descended to the banks of the River Douro and found part of the 15th Hussars being ferried over in three large boats, we were of course obliged to bivouac, I

---

[11] Incorrectly shown as right in the French version.

pitched my tent in a grove of cork trees and took some rest, being very unwell. Villa Nova de Fozcoa we saw on our left, in appearance a village of huts. What a strange unaccountable being is man, the same fire that warmed me, warms me today, my clothes remain each day a defence against the rude attacks of the elements, whilst those things and objects which used to impact to my senses the highest delight and gratification are now [to me] indifferent and disgusting, meals give one no pleasurable sensation, they impact neither on strength or spirit to my system, company, mirth and music which used to mount my spirits have lost their charms, I cannot bear either.

Slept in my tent this night for the first time, service is now begun and we shall have enough of it. Captain Fane[12], A.D.C. to Colonel Skerrett[13], rode over to our camp and informed us of the present situation of the French Army, they have about ninety thousand men to oppose us, and they are making every possible exertion to defend the bridge over the River Duero at Zamora, Captain Fane was originally in the 18th Hussars[14]. I hired this morning a Portuguese boy in Sevillada, he was recommended to me by my friend and hostess.

Torre de Moncorvo, Saturday 22 May.
We marched to the ferry at Pocinho and crossed the Douro in boats during this day, on this side of the river, immense high mountains present themselves, and which we climb with a deal of labour and fatigue, though a very good road, but so steep that several of the cannon belonging to the artillery were upset yesterday getting up, and two men were killed. The road across these heights to this town was narrow and uneven, and through the mountains the country was in a state of wild cultivation, presenting as we descended some delightful prospects. It is necessary to travel the road very slowly, a circumstance which gave us an opportunity of a leisurely view of the country. This town presents a sight very unusual in this country, a neat well-built town, a most noble church in the centre in excellent presentation, a castle, apparently of Roman construction gives the place a consequential look.

Thank God I am getting quite well in health again, and [my] spirits began to flow this morning as usual. The heat and fatigue of the march from Ozzors nearly knocked me up. Nearly the whole

[12]  Captain Thomas Fane 87th Foot.
[13]  Major General John Skerrett.
[14]  He had been a lieutenant in the 18th in 1809.

army is in advance of us, the 60th Regiment[15] crossed on the ferry at Pocinho last night, several regiments are encamped in the neighbourhood, but [I] have not learnt their numbers. The inhabitants of this town are indebted to the Spanish General Silveira[16], for the brave defence of the mountain pass which frustrated every attempt the French made to get into this town, this accounts for it being in its present flourishing state. The infantry camped nearby.

Torre de Moncorvo, Sunday 23 May.
The church I inspected this morning, and found from an inscription it was built in 1622, from the number of flags and other ensigns of religious parade, I should suppose this to be the see of a bishop, the interior of the church is decorated with a deal of gaudy ill painted and worse carved figures. The castle, which is now a venerable ruin, apparently of Roman construction, stands in the very centre of town, and fully commands the adjacent country. At last I have received the letters and newspapers so long missing, they came from Oporto, where they had been forwarded by mistake. I received a long letter from Captain Wheeler[17], and one from a dunn and two newspapers, [dated] 14th and 19th April.

[The] River Douro, which exceeds 200 yards in width, flows through a channel confined by high rugged and steep rocks, the current is very strong, and the bed deep, the shores on both sides are remarkably elevated and bold. The river has its source in the Serra de Cogulla in Spain near Aquilar de Campoo, a small town in old Castile, it enters Portugal a little eastward by north of Miranda [do Douro], and though it has a course of more than four hundred miles, it is not navigable, except in the rainy season below Lamego, in regard to width and depth, cedes to no other river in Portugal except the Tagus. Near Oporto it winds through a valley enclosed by two immense mountains, and will admit vessels of a considerable tonnage, we shall have to cross this river again in the course of a week or nine days.

In Spain, the enemy a few days since surprised a regiment of Portuguese cavalry near Miranda, and most dreadfully cut them up.

---

[15] The 60th (Royal American) Regiment, had no less than 8 battalions in service, mostly in the West Indies. The 5th Battalion, armed with rifles and dressed in green fought at company level as skirmishers for the army, just as the more famous 95th did.

[16] Actually Portuguese General Francisco da Silveira Pinto da Fonseca Teixeira, Count of Amarante.

[17] This must be Captain Samuel Wheeler of the 80th Foot.

I expected we should have been ordered to march today, instead engaged with a days' rest. The whole brigade is in this town, the 23rd Fusiliers[18] marched out last evening at 4 o'clock towards Miranda do Douro. Twenty thousand pipes of port wine are said to be shipped annually from Portugal to England and it is calculated that the English consumer uses forty thousand pipes per year; so half of what we drink must be harvested here. I am now in the province of Tras os Montes. The character of the people seems more amiable in this province than southwards; at all events, it coincides much better with the ideas and wishes of a Briton. Perhaps, gratitude for the recent victories and delivery from their enemies, inspired warmer affections of regard, and being better acquainted with our national character, and more accustomed to an intercourse with Englishmen, their friendships I think are sincere, and their hospitable reception of us, not prompted merely by interested views. It is but charitable to hope, that the latter is the true motive and that the sentiments they uttered were those of the heart.

Great quantity of silk is manufactured in this town, my padrone has no less a number of silk worms than two million[19], they are kept in a large room on shelves, they are now in growth and several boys and girls are in constant watch and attendance in victualing and keeping the beds clean, this accounts for the number of mulberry trees in and about the neighbourhood. This evening I wrote two letters to England, one to Miss Moseley, and the other to Worcester. This will be the last place I am thinking we shall be housed in for some time, as Colonel Grant intends that the brigade shall always bivouac.

Fornos, Monday 24 May.
Bivouacked in a wood of elms, thank God we are now drawing near those reptiles the French, they are now in sight at Mieza in Spain, which is only 3 miles from this place, but the Douro is between us, or they would not sit in their quarters so quietly. This was a very disagreeable day's march, owing to the heat of the weather, we are all fine figures, our faces very much burnt our lips are so painful that we can barely touch them, and we are now bivouacked on a plain which looks into Spain, the ground, sandy soil, appears more cultivated than we have seen for several days. Woods of pine, elm,

---

[18] The Royal Welch Fusiliers.
[19] Incorrectly shown as twenty million in the French version.

oak and mulberry, gives the face of the country a delightful appearance. Our camp is near Fornos which is a small dirty, ill built village, our camp is within 200 yards of it; we detached picquets out, for the first time.

Villa De Ala, Thursday 25 May.
Bivouacked. How delightful is the enjoyment after a long and fatiguing march through a burning sun, to recline on a portable bed in your tent, under a fine grown shady oak tree, how beautiful the prospect. Then the sight of the camp is beautiful! The troop bivouacked, the horses all picqueted to the neighbouring trees, Spain is seen distinctly; a French camp at the distance of a league, the country round in a flourishing state of cultivation; the distant view of the foraging parties belonging to the brigade, the camp all alive, the men cleaning their horses, and cooking etc. The background is occupied by huge chains of mountains. Our march today was along the frontier, within ½ mile of the Douro, which divides the two kingdoms; we saw the French vedettes on the opposite side. They don't appear to be moving from their present cantonments, a few days more will convince them, they must, or fight us.

Spain, which appears a plain, looks in a forward state of cultivation, plenty of green forage. We had the best roads I have seen in this country, to march over this morning, and though a long march, four leagues, it appeared a short and particularly pleasant one. The enemy was in this village last week and levied contribution, our camp was in a field on the left of the town under a number of fine shady oak and chestnut trees. The village consisting of about 100 houses and a church contains nothing worth of notice. The 10th and 15th bivouacked in a field adjoining to us. A very pretty looking village built on a hill on the right of the road, Miranda, about a mile from this place, in which I think we could have procured quarters, but a raging fever prevailed in it, and it was thought advisable to order the men not to approach near it. Two of our men were punished before the regiment, for disrespect[20] and theft.

Sendim, Wednesday 26 May.
The road continued from Villa de Ala[21], a very fertile and beautiful plain, which smiled in all the freshness of an English May. The view

---

[20] Incorrectly shown as desertion in the French version.
[21] Incorrectly shown as Villa Marie in the French version.

of Fermoselle and Cibanal, two villages in Spain, with the surrounding country requires the pen of Thompson to describe. A dammed bad quarter this, what good houses there are remaining in the town, the 15th officers have got. My casa is a wretched hovel, in England, I would not feed a pig in it, yet I must put up my bed and enjoy myself, for tomorrow we march four leagues and may have a skirmish.

The weather is immoderately hot, and we all feel the ill effects of it. Eatables of all descriptions very dear, they have the conscience to ask 20 vintems for a loaf of bread, which we have always had before for three. The church a shabby looking one stands in a square about the centre of the town. The French a few months back levied a heavy contribution, but did not plunder.

Our right squadron is bivouacked in a field near the town, so is a squadron of each of the other regiments. There is a very good painting in a small chapel, the subject, Christ being taken down from the cross; much of the picture has remained in its present unimpaired state. The chapel which is dedicated to Christ now contains the Commissary and his assistants, stores, and this is completely making the house of God, a den of thieves. How happy I should feel myself in this miserable hole, if I was this moment blest with a letter from my friend Amelia and Miss Moseley, I daily long in vain to see the letter they promised to write me at Easter. Pigskin bags for wine; these people have a way of skinning their pigs when killed, the skin is sown up except the neck part, which is the mouth of the bag, most of the wine that is carried in these bags, receives a taste not at all agreeable to my pallet. Onions and lettuce and all kinds of vegetables may be procured in this place; every inhabitant has a myrtle bow at his door, which indicates a vendor of wine.

In Portugal, the compliments flow in torrents from all mouths, in all classes. A simple peasant who encounters another, draws his hat very low, holds it in his hand for a long time, and is informed about his health, his family and does not fail to add this: 'I am at your orders and am your very humble servant'. [*Eston a seu ordens, seu criado*] This is not a special phrase, I've often seen beggars and people of the same class engage in these demonstrations.

Bivouacked on the banks of the River Estouro, between Brandilanes and Castro [de Alcanices], Thursday 27 May.
This day's march brought us into Spain, we are now bivouacked on the border. We likewise take the outpost duty this evening, being in advance of all the Army, the French are in the neighbourhood. Our

camp is very strong by nature, on the banks of the Estouro, the villages Brandilanes and Castro are situated about ½ league from each other, between them is the valley through which the river runs, we are under a wood of oaks, my tent is pitched on the edge of the river on a rock over shaded by two stately oaks, and though no distant views to gratify the eye, yet the spot is pleasing and particularly romantic our march was a very long one, seven leagues, we started at 2 o'clock, and I think I never felt a morning so very cold in my life.

The country through which we past [sic] was pleasant, the two kingdoms are divided by a plain, I saw no mark or boundary, and only knew we were out of the Kingdom of Portugal by being told Sendim was the last Portuguese village, and from the difference of dress and language of the inhabitants of Brandilanes; which is only two miles from the Portuguese village. I saw the encampment of four divisions of the army, 1st, 4th, 6th and 7th and of the artillery and Wagon Train at Malhadas on rising ground on the left, it looked uncommonly pretty. I likewise saw the 5th Division encamped between that village and this place. The whole English force in this quarter amounts to 25,000 men. Gave Smith a quarter in my tent, we both bathed in the river, a ridiculous accident happened to Smith who having only one clean shirt in the world, put it on immediately on leaving the water, however he wished to wet his feet again, in the act of doing so, his feet slipped and he fell in head over heels and created [for] us great laughter.

Camp near Brandilanes, Friday 28 May.
Was very much surprised this morning in seeing from a hill, at the back of our camp, nearly the whole of our army encamped, they must have come there early this morning, or last night, the camp appears to be three miles in length. Outlying and inlying picquets are sent out daily. The picquets of the Main Guard are constantly out of the camp, under the command of a captain and a lieutenant. There is a post to guard the camp under the command of a second lieutenant. A patrol of 50 men was likewise sent out at 3 o'clock this morning. A large army of Spaniards is expected to join us tomorrow.

Great difference of opinion amongst the officers as to the route the army will take tomorrow. It is reported the French are concentrating their forces in the neighbourhood of Burgos, and that they do not intend to make any stand, other than there; if that is the case we have a long march to make, before we have a brush with them. The mosquitoes are very troublesome and bite us very much, immediately they have stung you an itchy pain takes place, which greatly annoys for two or three days. I wrote a long letter to Captain Wheeler from Sendim, informing him of the state of the country, and in answer to his letter. Our halting today has had a wonderful effect on the horses of the regiment, who wanted a little rest; we shall now go on tomorrow quite fresh.

Bivouacked near Carbajales [de Alba], Saturday 29 May.
This morning at 2 o'clock I was up, and after partaking of a good breakfast, the regiment marched for this place. I had the most gratifying sight I ever beheld, the whole army was in motion, we passed several brigades of infantry, and a distant view of the army marching in this direction, this part of the British Army is now under the command of General Graham, we passed through the villages of Muga [de Alba] and Carbajales, near the former village we crossed a ford over the River Aliste. The 10th Hussars and the infantry crossed a wooden bridge on the right. A beautiful ruin of a Moors castle stands in a village on our left, before we came to the ford. On our passing through Carbajales, the inhabitants received us with warm cordiality and joy, bells ringing, while 'Viva Inglaterra, rompa[22] Buonaparte' resounded from all quarters.

The country through which the road passes was highly cultivated and admirably well-watered, what a difference is already to be perceived between the Spaniards and Portuguese, though so near the frontier, they dress very different. The women and men's clothes are of very gay colours, such as blue petticoats and pink gowns, yellow stockings and handkerchiefs; same variety of colour in the men's, we are now encamped on the side of a hill, amongst thick grown under-wood, about 3 miles from the Almendra ford over the River Esla, where the enemy has a picquet of one hundred dragoons, the vedets are very plainly seen from the heights opposite to the camp, so is the town of Zamora, where the French are in force.

Marquess Wellington makes a move to the right with a part of the army and has entered Salamanca, on 23rd inst. The enemy retreated to Zamora. This part of the army is therefore still on the opposite bank of the Esla; it will start moving tomorrow with us and make its junction at Zamora. Burke laid me a wager, some of our men would have a skirmish with the enemy by tomorrow night, one dollar. After dinner, Smith and myself rode to the Almendra ford and saw the

----

[22] Portuguese – defeat.

French picquet on the opposite side of the river, they have a vedette close to the ford and one of ours is placed directly opposite to him. The enemy picquet consisted of a party of heavy dragoons, apparently well mounted. Our regiment has branches of oak in our bonnets.[23]

Having distracted the French with Hill's advance on Salamanca, Wellington suddenly left this force and rode at speed to join Graham's force as it advanced into Spain.

Camp near Carbajales, Sunday 30 May.
All this morning in anxious expectation of the arrival of Marques Wellington, from Salamanca, we are now in the province of Zamora, in the Kingdom of Leon. I am on picquet for the first time and rode over to the Almendra ford, and saw the Marquess of Wellington and staff there, reconnoitring. The brigade received orders to march tomorrow morning, at one o'clock and force their way over the ford and the defile of Almendra and press on the picquet for the first time. Our Commissary and attendants had a very narrow escape, from being taken prisoner on the Zamora road today.[24]

Finally, the waiting was over and the army drove into Spain.

Yeneste [La Hiniesta], Monday 31 May.
At last I have seen a skirmish and it's a caper of which I have already tasted enough. The brigade passed the ford of Almendra, supported by the 7th and 8th Divisions of the army and Bolton's squadron of flying artillery, we passed [at] about 2 o'clock, then very dark, the enemy did not expect us so early and was taken by surprise, and out of about 60 men that formed the squadron in charge of the heights and ford [most] were captured, not more than ten escaped. The officer in command of the picquet was shaving himself at the time [he] was taken prisoner, some of the men made great resistance, but were most horribly cut and hacked about by the men of the 15th Hussars, who had the honour of passing over first and were thereby obliged to act. Captain Carew, Waldie and the veterinary surgeon[25]

---

[23] To commemorate the Restoration of King Charles II.
[24] Commissary Schaumann states (page 368) that on hearing that the French had abandoned Zamora, he entered it with two colleagues to procure supplies. He was however immediately accosted by General Alava (who was in disguise) who advised them to leave immediately as a French cavalry patrol was sure to come to capture them. On leaving they only just escaped from a dozen French lancers who had attempted to cut off their escape route.
[25] Veterinary Surgeon Daniel Pilcher.

saw a party of the flying enemy enter the village of Almendra; they galloped there immediately and took five men and four horses[26].

I was ordered to return to our camp and bring the baggage of the brigade over the river, by the time I arrived with it, the pontoon bridge had been put across the river which I passed over, it was made with nine boats with boards laid across them and side barriers along its entire length, when the baggage mules had advanced about two miles on the road to this place from the ford, an orderly man from a picquet under Captain Grammont [27]of the 10th Hussars, came galloping past and informed us that two squadrons of the enemy's dragoons were advancing towards us. I halted the whole and desired an officer of the Kings Hussars, Lieutenant Mansfield, who had charge of their baggage to remain with the whole, while I went forward and reconnoitred. On my return, I observed all the baggage mules flying back as fast as they were able. I was just able to stop by the swiftness of my horse, about half of them, and proceed immediately here. The enemy who was really advancing strongly, turned about and retreated immediately on observing our picquet; the alarm was given through this orderly and before I had proceeded half a mile, I heard the bugles sounding in all directions. And the infantry who had taken their cantonments for the day, and all the world remained under arms for several hours.

They were obliged to march near two leagues further. This certainly [was] the most fatiguing march I have experienced since I have been in the army. Lord Wellington employs himself reconnoitring and arranging everything on the march, and appears very confident that we shall drive the enemy out of this country. There were several infantry soldiers drowned while crossing the Esla this morning; the horse of Colonel Murray foundered under him and he received a strong contusion on the knee. We passed through two uncommonly pretty villages, Valdeperdices and (second name is missing [Andavias?]), the churches in each gave them a very picturesque effect. At Valdeperdices, the inhabitants gave us bread and wine.

Bivouacked on the left of the road to Toro at Fresno de la Ribera, Tuesday 1 June 1813.

---

[26] Apparently, when Carew was asked how he had captured so many fine fellows, he replied 'Why, as an Irishman, I believe that I must confess that I surrounded them'. Quote from Eric Hunt's *Charging Against Napoleon*, page 87.

[27] Captain Antoine de Grammont 10th Hussars

At Yeneste [La Hiniesta] the church was very beautiful, the images proved the antiquity of it, on the tower over the bells were two stork's nests. I saw their young ones who were playing round their parents in the nests. The Spaniards hold these birds sacred, and it would be at the hazard of our lives to have touched them, a British soldier who killed one last year was massacred by the people.

We left this place and proceeded here, passing very close to Zamora which was on our right, it is situated on the northern banks of the Douro. There was a very handsome bridge, but the enemy had destroyed it a few days back, it was rebuilt by Ferdinand and Alphonso, after the Moors General Almansur[28] destroyed it in the eleventh century. The position of Zamora is on an eminence which commands the river, and it was formally fortified as a defence against Portugal, the walls are still preserved, the town has the most picturesque effect I ever beheld any[where], except Lisbon from the Tagus, it contains several churches. There are the ruins of a palace, and it contains some large barracks. Our commissary got plenty of provisions here this morning for us; the French had only left it a few hours before. On our march this morning, I counted no less than seven villages on a most delightful plain, the other side of the Douro, Bamba a very pleasant looking village is directly opposite to this.

The enemy are about an hour's march before us, they left this place in such a hurry that their horses had not had time to eat the forage cut for them, which we found ready for our horses. A dreadful thunder and rain storm has just passed over us, not at all pleasant to our poor fellows who are bivouacked in an open field, without a tree for shelter, the 15th King's Hussars are likewise with them, the 10th are in this town and have all the best quarters. The house I am quartered at is a poor wretched hut, my horses are in the parlour, our mules in a kind of sleeping room and myself in the kitchen, which is a receptacle of all kinds of animals, and amongst them the old grandfather of the family, who though not seventy years of age, exhibits 'Shakespeare's' last stage, sans teeth[29]. I am exposed to the hungry appetites of myriads of fleas, and entertained all night with the grunting of pigs, squalling of cats, coughing of the old people, braying of mules, squalling of children; in short it

---

[28] These appear in his statement as if they were contemporaries, but de facto ruler of Muslim Spain, Abu Aamir Muhammad bin Abdullah ibn Abi Aamir, al-Hajib al-Mansur lived from 938-1002. Alphonso III of Portugal reconquered Portugal from the Muslims in 1249, whilst Ferdinand II of Aragon who married Isabella of Castile, played a pivotal role in the Christian 'Reconquest' of Spain in 1492.

[29] Referring to the verse of Jaques in *As you like it*.

beggars all description. The country is sown with wheat and oats; it is not very thickly wooded, but is nice and pleasant.

Morales de Toro, Wednesday 2 June.
I want words to portray the gratitude I feel to my God for this day's protection, though several times exposed to the fire of the enemy's artillery and small arms, yet thanks to the Almighty powers above, I escaped unhurt. We marched from Fresno at day break this morning, and arrived in front of Toro, when we saw a French vedette on the hill near the town, and the signal was given by the inhabitants of the enemy then being in the town. All the inhabitants came out to welcome us and on our near approach, the enemy retreated out of the town, we immediately galloped after them, and after a run of nearly a league, came up with them on the plain between this place and Toro.

Two squadrons of the enemies 16th Dragoons[30] were drawn up and appeared determined to oppose us while a considerable body was posted on the right side of the village of Morales in support. Behind this village extends a plain of three miles. The 10th Hussars and 18th immediately formed up in squadrons and walked towards them; I was out in front commanding the skirmishers and had much trouble in keeping my men from advancing upon this body. The flying artillery[31] now came and I was called in, they immediately fired twice and the enemy then broke and moved towards this place, we now discovered two more squadrons of their dragoons formed on the left of this town. A squadron of the 10th Hussars now charged those retreating, when they turned round and charged them in high style, all was now bustle and confusion. The French tried to make their best way off, whilst the 10th and the 18th were hacking and cutting them about in all directions. The two squadrons in the village who had formed up on the left now retreated, our right squadron moved round the right of the village while the 10th were driving the enemy pell-mell through it, and instantly commenced fighting.

The enemy now had near two miles to retreat across a plain, followed up close by the above mentioned three squadrons, it was impossible to distinguish the enemy from our own hussars, such was the confusion. The whole plain in ten minutes presented a dreadful scene, dead, wounded and prisoners in all directions, for as

---

[30] George writes 15th here, but later, correctly identifies them as the 16th.
[31] The Horse Artillery, were often referred to as the 'The Flying Artillery' as with all of the gunnners mounted, they could manoeuvre at great speed.

94

fast as our men could get up with them they [the French] were cut
down, out of the four squadrons a very few made their escape to the
hills in front of this plain where the enemy had eight squadrons
more and a column of infantry with artillery, these never came from
the hills. But upon our closing upon them, and being in the act of
following them up the hill, they fired their artillery at us, it was here
our centre squadron came up with the remains of their flying force
and commenced the carnage. I had a cut at one man myself, who
made point at me which I parried. I spoilt his beauty, if I did not take
his life, for I gave him a most severe cut across the eyes and cheek
and must have cut them out, however in the scene of confusion
when the enemy fired their first shot, he and many other prisoners
made their escape. The ball from their second fire fell within a foot
of my horse, and nearly smothered me with dust, but as the saying
goes, every bullet has its billet! And there were none for me. We in
our turn were obliged to retreat, back out of the range of their
artillery, which after firing about a dozen times, and throwing two
bombs [shells], they retreated. The country over the hills being so
much in their favour and our horses much blown, we took up our
quarters in the village and trust tomorrow we shall come up with
them [again]. The fruits of this skirmish were three officers, two
hundred and thirty-six men, and one hundred and eighty-one
horses, all prisoners[32].

The 10th Hussars who behaved in a gallant manner, lost my
friend I am sorry to say, Lieutenant Cottin, a most amiable young
man and an excellent officer, and one man killed, and Captain
Lloyd[33] and one man made prisoners, we lost one man killed[34] and
two were taken prisoners. Lloyd and the three men taken by the
enemy were actually on the top of the hill, cutting down all who
opposed them, before they knew their regiments had halted, and
they were taken in their attempt to rejoin us. There are likewise nine
men of ours and the 10th wounded, part of them severely. Out of
the numbers of prisoners we took[35], hardly one was to be perceived
without some dreadful cuts on their head and body. I never saw men

---

[32] Oman states 208 men and ten officers were captured; whereas Major Hughes states that two hundred and
twenty French Chasseurs were captured and another sixty wounded were also made prisoner. Edwin
Griffiths says they made 256 prisoners mostly from the 16th Chasseurs. It would seem that the figure was
most likely between 240 and 260 prisoners.

[33] Captain James Richard Lloyd 10th Hussars, was wounded and made a prisoner, but paroled soon
after.

[34] This was presumably Private Job Upton whose leg was apparently blown off by a cannonball.

[35] The Regimental History states that 3 officers, 236 men and 180 horses were captured.

so mad for action as the hussars were before and after the skirmishing, and all appeared disappointed when ordered to march into this place and take up their quarters.

Lord Wellington with Marshal Beresford and staff arrived here in the afternoon, seeing the prisoners and captured horses, and expressed himself highly pleased with our conduct this morning. Amongst the prisoners a lady was discovered in disguise as a man and wearing civilian clothes, the wife of a French officer who was found dead amongst the others in the field of action. Part of the horses taken were divided amongst the officers of the brigade; I received one, besides the horse I took myself, so have two animals added to my establishment. I made Ipper a present of my pony, which he immediately sold. I was sent with the remainder of the horses to Toro to be sold there by auction for the benefit of the brigade; forty-six in number, I delivered them over to Colonel Sturgeon[36], Quarter Master General. I dined with him and was introduced to Colonel Jackson of the artillery [37], a merry kind of being. I did not leave the town until 11 o'clock, when it was illuminated very superbly, the inhabitants informed me, and in every street was large bonfires, round which men, women and children were dancing fandangos and boleros, bells ringing, guns firing and every demonstration of joy, reigned throughout the town.

Lord Wellington being at the headquarters of the army gave a very grand Ball, in honour of our victory this morning. Introduced this day by Captain Gordon[38] of the 10th Hussars to the Prince of Orange, he is a very thin young man, about my height and age, and is here universally beloved by all who have the honour of knowing him. Our march today was a particularly pleasant one, before we came up to Toro which stands on a hill, which by nature is uncommonly strong; its situation is on the north bank of the Douro. It is walled and has several gates, all of Moorish origin. The town which is now uncommonly pretty has fallen off a great deal from what it formally was, it contains some good parish churches, some handsome streets, a large square, and is still venerable in its decay. The castle was once a work of great strength; it now contains the prisoners taken this morning. The enemy blew up two arches of a

---

[36] Brevet Lieutenant Colonel Henry Sturgeon, Royal Staff Corps, Assistant Quarter Master General.
[37] I believe he is mistaken here; this must be Captain Basil Jackson of the Royal Wagon Train, who also wore a blue uniform like the artillery.
[38] Captain Charles Gordon 10th Hussars.

very handsome bridge over the Douro, and I believe intended to plunder, but we disturbed them, before they expected us.

Pedrosa del Rey, Thursday 3 June.
We left Morales de Toro very early this morning and arrived here before 8 o'clock, we had to pass over the ground where our skirmish with the enemy took place, and we contemplated on the dangers past, it was truly laughable to hear some of our wild Irishmen relating their deeds and pointing out as they passed, the bodies they had killed and the spot where the Frenchmen were taken prisoners, and had whacked over their heads with the flat of their sword. The enemy left this place last night, and left Captain Lloyd of the 10th Hussars, who is severely wounded on his parole of honour, they likewise left my old bat man, Morris, who was taken prisoner and wounded yesterday. This is a small place with two very good churches, but nothing particularly striking about them. I was out on picquet duty, the whole day and night, therefore had very little rest after the fatigue of yesterday.

Tordesillas, one of the most ancient and most celebrated towns of the kingdom of Leon, I had the pleasure of riding through, being on picquet and within a few miles of it, I could not resist the temptation to enter the city. It is handsome, well built, and stands on a great site, all the environs are covered with trees, and fine vineyards. The bridge over the Douro has ten arches, it was built in the time of the gothic Kings of Leon, and in the middle of it is a large tower, with battlements. There is here a large palace in which the Queen mother of Charles the Fifth ended her days most miserably under a derangement of the mind, the apartment occupied by her is shown[39]. The river contributes greatly to render the situation of this town delightful, the southern bank, called La Vega, presents a lovely and fertile plain covered with trees.

On my return from this town to my picquet, I missed my way, night coming on; I was near four hours before I joined them, several times nearly smothered in bogs. Colonel Grant, who led the charge made by the 10th Hussars before Morales, received a trifling wound in his side. The 15th is most devilishly mortified they formed the reserve and had no hand in the late skirmish. The

---

[39] Queen Joanna I, the mother of Charles V, was deemed mentally unwell and confined in the Santa Clara Convent by her father Ferdinand II. When Ferdinand died in 1517, Charles was crowned king, whilst his mother remained nominally as co-monarch. She was forcibly confined at the convent until her death in 1555.

prisoners we took all declare they took us for the Spanish corps called Don Julian's[40] who by the bye are dressed something like hussars, they are principally Portuguese and they were determined to take the shine out of them, but found their mistake immediately the charge was made, when all were anxious to escape. This same regiment the 16th Chasseurs with what truth I know not, [boast] of having beaten every regiment ever before opposed to them, and amongst the numbers, the 11th, 14th, and 16th Light Dragoons are mentioned. Only one hundred and twenty remain of the regiment, and amongst them we are informed by the people of this town, were seventy-nine wounded, another brush at them will annihilate the regiment.

Torrelobaton, Friday 4 June. King's Birthday [41].
Don Julian's corps of lancers joined our brigade this morning, so did the 7th Division[42], light infantry , they will in future always move with us, we have likewise attached to our brigade, four nine pounders and two six pounders under Bolton[43] and Webber Smith. I have got the best billet I have had in this country, and should like much to stay here for a few days; indeed, my health almost requires a halt for that time. The heat of the days does not correspond with the cold damp chilly evenings, and being out all last night I have caught a severe cold. My padrone is a true Spaniard; his behaviour to me convinces me of his sincerity in the true cause of his country. The steeples of the churches of this town shook with the merry peals on our entering the town, the cheers of the inhabitants and the lively countenance of the whole on our arrival, gave us a higher opinion of the Spaniards than we had first formed.
The enemy are only half a league from us, and must have heard the bells plainly. This town is built on the side of a hill and has a commanding view of the country, in the town is an antique castle in excellent preservation, we passed through two very delightful villages, whose names I have forgot, the inhabitants of each greeting our arrival with every demonstration of joy. It is expected the enemy will hazard a general battle at Valladolid.

---

[40] The Spanish irregular leader Don Julian Sanchez who formed a corps of some 1,000 infantry and 600 cavalry.
[41] King George III was 75 years old.
[42] The 7th Division was viewed as a second light infantry division.
[43] Captain Samuel Bolton of F Troop Royal Horse Artillery.

Penaflor de Hornija, Saturday 5 June.

We bivouacked in a field near the town, which stands on a small hill, rising from a valley, overlooked on all sides by the plain, being unwell I did not go into town, but it has a very pretty appearance. The whole British Army in the peninsular is now with us, and in the valley, which I suppose is about a mile in length and breadth, their encampments have a very beautiful effect. The army is about ninety thousand strong. The enemy contrary to all expectations evacuated Valladolid last night, and soon after our arrival here, I was sent there with orders, though very unwell and in want of rest. I am particularly anxious to discharge any duties I may be called upon to perform, and will always do so while I have strength to sit on my horse. My orders were to be handed over to the Mayor, but he had decamped with the King and the citizens were trying to choose a different one.

The city is about six miles from this place, I felt a pleasure in going there, even as it is much more than I should have done, if my health would have allowed me to have seen and examined this charming city. Valladolid was the Pincium of the Romans[44], and is I believe one of the first cities in Spain, it is built between the Rivers Esgueva and Pisuerga, in a large plain, surrounded by hills, its public buildings are numerous and approached by gates of a noble structure, handsome fronts and courts embellished with piazzas. They very much resemble those of Covent Garden, having houses or suites of apartments over them, but they excel them. There are two of the finest public walks I ever beheld, the Campo Grande and the Piazza Major. The latter is very spacious and is surrounded by three rows of balconies; where it is computed that thirty thousand people may sit at their ease. It is embellished likewise with piazzas under the balconies, supported by four hundred marble columns and by a corresponding number of pilasters. This will give some idea of the extent and magnificence of the town. I have a notion the piazzas were copied from the Romans, and then passed into Spain and England. At a short distance from Piazza Major, is the Ochavo, an octagonal area, into which, six large streets open at regular distances[45]. Upon the whole Valladolid is a most charming place, and this book might be filled with a description of it, if everything

---

[44] Valladolid was an inconsequential village in Roman times and I can find no reference to its being called Pincium.

[45] The Plaza Ochavo.

worthy of notice was mentioned. Joseph Buonaparte left it only a few days back, he held his court there for some months, and it has been the headquarters of the French Army, the same time the enemy destroyed what stores they could not take with them. They are now in the neighbourhood of Burgos where our army will soon be with them. It is reported this evening that the German hussars fell in with the enemy in their retreat, and took three hundred prisoners.

Camp near [Santa] Cecilia [del Acor], Sunday 6 June.
Bivouacked on a mountain plain, opposite Villamuriel [de Cerrato][46], this plain is supposed to be eleven hundred feet above the level of the sea. We marched this morning 2 o'clock, the whole army moved off about the same time, after proceeding about two leagues over a delightful plain, we arrived before Villalba de los Alcores, a very ancient town, the greater part of its walls still remain and the ruins of the castle, all in very high preservation, its appearance fully convinces one it is of Moorish origin. The streets are narrow and ill paved, after stopping near an hour to rest, we moved on to this place, on our way our advance guard saw a party of the enemies [sic] hussars, which they were on the point of charging, when the French officer advanced in front and had a flag of truce with a letter to the Marquess Wellington, after delivering which, he was allowed to return with his men, he wore a most splendid uniform with several orders on his breast. On our arriving on this ground the 14th Light Dragoons and the 1st German Hussars arrived and are encamped with us. Introduced to the Marquess of Worcester this morning by Kennedy; who seems to be a pleasant companion: he is a lieutenant in the 10th Hussars.

The English mail arrived the day before yesterday. Lord Wellington only allowed the letters to be delivered to the officers, reserving the newspapers till a future time, thinking if the officers got them now; they would be reading the news instead of attending to their duties and we're so close to the enemy. Alas I have no letters from England; I am quite forgot, I shall be soon tired of this country if I do not hear from my friends, particularly those most dear to me. Spain was not always in the degraded state in which we now find her, it is in the nature of all human things to wear out, but as a certain standard of human reason and excellence is necessary to the ultimate design of providence. A wisdom is always in action to

---

[46] Incorrectly shown as Valladolid in the French version.

counteract the tendency of nature, and by grafting, transplanting, and cherishing, to renew and regenerate the original vigour and constitution.

Let me be allowed to hope, that the ensuing campaign will not be in vain, but that Spain, renewed and in grafted with British valour and liberty, will resume her ancient fame and renown, and will again exhibit an example of those brighter days of her history, when her early ancestors stood forth as the pride and bulwark of Christendom, and by their long enduring valour against their Moorish invaders, preserved and transmitted, the blessings of religion, arts, and knowledge from the wasting ravage of the Saracen's sword.

Villalobon, Monday 7 June.

When we left the camp this morning about 4 o'clock, we expected to have an engagement with the enemy. Before this hour the whole army with Lord Wellington and staff moved in this direction, expecting to find the enemy would make some resistance to our entering Palencia, but [to] our surprise and disappointment, found they had retired about six this morning, and we entered with trumpets sounding about nine. This hamlet is about a mile from Palencia, and contains not a single thing worth notice, the church which is seen at a distance is hard to recognize as one on entering the place.

We bivouacked on the north side in a small field, three troops [of] each regiment of the brigade, with the artillery. The remainder were billeted in the hamlet. The whole army is encamped [in] and about Palencia, which is the headquarters. Palencia is a very ancient town and a bishopric in the diocese of Burgos; it is situated in a valley, being watered by the River Carrion on whose banks it stands. Most of the edifices of the town are in the Gothic style, there is a most remarkable old church, built and dedicated by King Sancho[47], after having escaped some perils in hunting wild boar in the neighbourhood. This town is two hundred miles from Madrid; we entered the town amongst the cheering acclamations of the inhabitants. Lord Wellington entered half an hour before with a reconnoitring party; there are two very handsome bridges over the Carrion, on entering the town. There is likewise a canal, which is the first I have seen in this country, it is in an unfinished state, and may

---

[47]  King Sancho of Navarre resettled the town in the 11th Century.

from all account have been a century or two in this condition. The country about the neighbourhood is laid out in gardens and presents everything that can be wanted for the support of life, they bear wheat and other corn, and are abundant in vineyards, game and fish. What a delightful estate would a thousand pounds English money buy in this district? With this sum with English taste, and with one honest English servant, like Corporal Trim[48], who would act as a gardener, and take a hand at the plough, how happy I might close the remainder of my days. This is one of my dreams when I am employing myself in building castles in Spain. The principal street in Palencia is very handsome; having a regular range of piazzas on both sides, all it wants is for the pavement to be flagged. The Cathedral is a most beautiful building in the Gothic style, and nearly as large as Westminster Abbey, but by far more handsome. Lord Wellington gave a grand ball to the residents and officers.

Villalobon, Tuesday 8 June.
A few minutes before the time appointed to march this morning, we received orders to unbridle our horses, owing to the enemy having blown up a bridge which we were to have passed over. On that account the infantry were pushed forward, the whole army passed us and I had the gratifying sights of several old acquaintances. At about ten the bugle sounded, and the brigade was in line to march when the officer's call directed us round; Colonel Grant and the Brigade Major, i.e. the Black Devil[49] [Giant?] and the Red Dwarf, expecting some compliments on turning out so quickly or something else; But we received on the contrary a severe lecture on account of the conduct of the men who had actually broke open and robbed the church and every house in the village, we were the first with the news. He ordered us immediately to inspect the kit of every man, which was done, and two men of the 18th and one of the 10th were brought out of the ranks, having bacon in their possession, they were immediately tried by a Brigade Court Martial, which consisted of a field officer and four captains, and received instead of the bacon six hundred lashes each.

We then proceeded on our march which was very unpleasant one, and arrived at (name forgotten[50]) where the Household Troops, Life

---

[48] The name of the servant in *The Life and Opinions of Tristram Shandy*, written by Laurence Sterne in nine volumes between 1759 and 1767.

[49] The British version clearly states his nickname as 'Black Devil' although he was always referred by everyone in the Brigade as the 'Black Giant' and is stated as such in the French version.

[50] This would appear to be describing the village of Monzon de Campos.

Guards and Blues were quartered on the right of this village, which stands on the side of a hill, a very stately Moors castle, overlooking the village and the bridge of fourteen arches over the River Arlanzon, we left this place after halting about an hour and marched up the hills at the back of it, and arrived on a mountain plain, which we crossed and descended to the town of Tamara [de Campos].

The Kingdom of Leon, which we are now in, is the country formally inhabited by the Vettones, mentioned by Strabo[51]. The celebrated River Douro divides the country into almost two equal parts. The general face is mountainous, but it contains a great number of beautiful fields, good pastures, and large fertile valleys. The River Carrion on whose banks we marched, reminds me of the Counts of Carrion who play a part in the chronicles of Spain. In this neighbourhood, a famous duel took place between the two sons of Count Gonzales, and both sons in law of the Cid and his daughter. The court was present at the duel. The latter were the conquerors, in consequence of which the vanquished were declared traitors, and the County of Carrion forfeited to the Crown[52]. It was at Torquemada the enemy blew up the bridge, the day before yesterday. General Hill[53] and his army entered it yesterday and are proceeding in the direction of Burgos; we are now going a little to the left of it. The siege will commence immediately the battering train arrives.

Tamara [de Campos] was originally fortified with a mud wall, the church which appears in a distant view, nearly half the size of the town, is an handsome edifice, but owing to the rain, I could not venture out, indeed it was late before we arrived here, and I was in a most miserable billet. Servant, horses and self, stuffed into a mud cabin, the interior of which, with only two rooms, is a picture of misery. The whole brigade was quartered in this town, and the generals and staff of three divisions of the army, which was encamped round the walls. How I dislike a general officer in any place, but the field. One general and staff requires as much room in a town as a regiment of dragoons would occupy, and even when they are settled in quarters, they are always annoying you with some foolish orders or complaints.

---

[51] The Greek Strabo [63BC – 24AD] wrote *Geographica* describing the lands then known.

[52] He refers to the Castilian epic poem *The Poem of the Cid* which is 'based' on historical facts. El Cid had married his daughters to the Princes of Carrion, but having been accused of cowardice, they beat their wives and the King orders that El Cid's dowry is returned and in a subsequent duel the princes are beaten and dishonoured.

[53] Lieutenant General Sir Rowland Hill, who was Wellington's most trusted subordinate general.

Fromista, Wednesday 9 June.

This town is a collection of mud walls, churches, houses, cabins and stables, it contains seven churches, and only four built of stone and two of them are very neat and would be admired in England. We only marched a league and a half today across a low swampy ground, nearly up to the horse's knees in dirt. I prosecuted a man of Captain Bolton's Troop for leaving his picquet at Pedrosa del Rey, and for disrespect and I was very annoyed. This is the first time I ever gave evidence of a fellow creature in my life and felt very nervous. The enemy blew up a bridge yesterday at Torquemada. General Hill and the wing of the army he commands entered yesterday and advanced directly on the road to Burgos, which we now leave a little to our right. Headquarters will move as soon as the artillery equipment comes up. The principle church in this town, the enemy fired last year, it is now a complete ruin, but enough remains to show its former grandeur[54].

Villasandino, Thursday 10 June.

Our road from Fromista ran over a naked plain, where neither trees, bush or shrub are visible, we passed through the village of Santillana [Lantadilla?], the only thing of note is their church, which is a strange building without any uniformity or beauty, yet a stranger cannot well see it without wishing to examine its shape, and make. This town, the enemy left about an hour before we entered it. They have a picquet on the mountains behind us, we crossed the River Pisuerga over a bridge of seven arches, upon the whole a respectable looking one, we likewise crossed the Canal of Castile, over a small but neat bridge. All those bridges the enemy ought to have destroyed, which would have much impeded our march. There are three large churches, built much in the English style, but are of a very ancient appearance. The River Odra, turns on the north side of the town, over which is a very good bridge of five arches. The inhabitants were collected at the entrance of the town to welcome us, which they did with cheering acclamation, and every five minutes would set up dancing the Spanish fandango to the simple, if it might be so called of three tambourines, every dancer singing their national air. We were thus escorted into the city; at the same time the bells rang merrily.

---

[54] George omits to mention it, but Major Hughes records that on 9 June, Pilcher the Veterinary Surgeon, was put under arrest for abusing the major.

Wine is to be got in great abundance in every village we pass, the cellars which are dug on the side of rising ground mostly on the east side of the house or villa, have a wooden door, and on entering you descend several yards, when about twenty pipes are discovered, and at this time most are all full, they sell it at one vintem and a half, a quintilla[55].

Padilla [Olmillos de Sasamon?][56], Friday 11 June.
I wrote a letter to Mr. C. Perkins[57] yesterday, and to Mc Mahon, and Mr. Vanboorst. We marched only a league this morning, across a plain similar to the one we crossed yesterday. The right squadron and 10th Hussars marched to Castrojeriz, which is on the right of us, we are very well put up here, and should like much to stay here a few days, our horses begin to want a little rest. The village has a very picturesque effect, a stately Moorish castle, and a handsome looking church, with groves of walnut trees surrounding the whole, gives it a pleasing look. Your expectations of it are not disappointed, for it contains more good houses than I have seen in a village in this country before. The inhabitants welcomed us with dancing on our arrival.

The enemy are reported to be in great force at Pedrosa [del Paramo], a village within three miles of us, my host and hostess who have never seen Englishmen, asked an assortment of questions and are plaguing me to death with their enquiries examining everything I have, yet cannot satisfy them on any point not knowing their language. I shall find great difficulty in learning Spanish after the Portuguese.

It is really astonishing how much more artificially and substantially the Moors built their cities and castles whilst in Spain, to what they have built in Africa, according to accounts I have always heard and read of them, in Africa they are barbarians, in Spain they had all the arts of life, elegance and even luxury, so much is it in the power of fortune to degrade a people. The Spaniard is a superior looking being to the Portuguese. I very much admire the former, and trust they will be able to drive the enemy, with our

---

[55]  A Spanish Cuartillo was about a pint and a Portuguese Quartilho was about a pint and a half.
[56]  I believe that George has made a mistake (or was misinformed) in the name of this village as to proceed to either Padilla which stand close by, they would be making a retrograde movement and would be many miles further away from the French at Pedrosa. I therefore suggest that they were at Olmillos where there is a significant Moorish castle and proceeded to Isar the next day.
[57]  Mr Charles Perkins, Amelia's father.

assistance out of their country. Their peasantry are numerous, Marquess Wellington looks much to them, and [it] would much assist us if they had bold and resolute leaders, with Goldsmith I think:

A bold peasantry, their country's pride,
When once destroyed can never be supplied[58].

The unfortunate refugees from the villages near Burgos came in by dozens yesterday and this morning to Villasandino, how dreadful to the lot of those poor unfortunates, to be driven from their homes without provisions or any comforts of life. Whilst my servant was getting my dinner, I climbed to the top of the ancient castle, which overlooks the town, I found the foundation is Roman and the superstructure is Moorish. I likewise got a sight of the church which is uncommonly elegant. My guide played a Spanish national air on the organ, which I think is the best sounding one I ever heard. While I was in the church our commissary came in, having heard there was some wheat hid in it, we immediately commenced a search and found four barrels of flour and about three sacks of barley, in a room near the steeple, which was seized for our use[59].

I have just heard the enemy are destroying every village and laying waste, everything within six miles of Burgos, we expect the inhabitants here immediately, and they are now in the fields a few miles off in a most deplorable state.

Isar, Saturday 12 June 1813.
We left Padilla [Olmillos?] this morning at 6 o'clock, fully prepared for a general engagement with the enemy before Burgos, we moved forward about a league and a half, when the enemy were discovered on some heights behind this town. The brigade was dismounted and we remained so near four hours, waiting for the heavy brigade and infantry to come up. When they joined us we moved forward in three divisions, with artillery [firing] upon the enemy, who were formed up on several hills in columns. One on the left, the 15th [Hussar] Regiment attacked and they retreated towards the bridge over the Arlanzon, about three miles from Burgos. The 18th moved

---

[58]  It is from Oliver Goldsmith.
[59]  Commissary Schaumann does not mention the incident, but Major Hughes' diary confirms it.

on the right, upon a column formed there, which likewise immediately retreated for the bridge, a third column of infantry formed a square, and was attacked by the heavy brigade, after the artillery had broke them; they then retreated to the bridge, and we gained the heights, our artillery was now brought to bear on them in the valley. Here was nothing but confusion in the main road from Villasera to the bridge which our artillery had the complete range of.

The heavy brigade (4th Regiment[60]) followed the enemy into the valley, charged and took a gun, but the enemy formed square, and the heavys were obliged to retreat, rather in confusion, but nothing could equal the retreat of the enemy over the bridge, at the time with nearly a dozen[61] guns firing at them. I was at the time on the heights aside the artillery that was playing on the bridge. I had the satisfaction of distinguishing myself this day, having the command of the skirmishers, and being on the right flank, saw a party of baggage in the valley, where the enemy was. I got a few men together and made a dash and took it, I just got it on the side of the hill, when a party was sent out after it, and [I] was obliged to order the men to turn about and charge them, which we did, and they fled leaving us as masters of the baggage, which was taken quietly off. It consisted of ten mules and about a dozen prisoners, after the enemy got over the bridge, they took up a position on the hills behind it, entirely out of our reach; orders were given by Lord Wellington to stop firing, and the brigade sent here except Captain Clement's Troop and myself, first lieutenant of the service squadrons, were ordered to remain and patrol the debris on the road to the bridge. As we were too adventurous and got too close, they sent a volley of musketry.

The infantry were encamped on ground occupied by the enemy this morning, at about 6 o'clock the bridge was blown up, and at the same time, as if it was the signal, several villages to the right and left of Burgos were set on fire. The sight though awful was particularly grand; two arches of the bridge in the explosion were completely destroyed in an instant. Before they left the river side, after the bridge was destroyed, we continued very close to reconnoitre, when they opened a heavy firing of grape shot upon us, but I got the men away before any were hurt, nothing better showed the confusion of the enemy during their retreat, than them

---

[60] 4th Dragoon Guards.
[61] Incorrectly shown as forty in the French version.

leaving their wounded on the road. I could not assist them and left them in the same situation I found them in on my arrival, here I made a report of their deplorable situation, but no attention has been paid to it, so I suppose they will perish, if the inhabitants don't take care of them.

When the cannonading commenced upon the enemy's solid squares of infantry, the French General [Marshal] Jourdan instantly rode off, saying as he left them, 'Get to the bridge the best way you can'. I saw him galloping along the road, and pointed him out as Joseph (Buonaparte), having so large a staff with him, but the intrusive King left Burgos yesterday, on his way to Vitoria. The heavies took a gun and an officer prisoner, during this affair; we lost not a man or horse. The prisoners I took with the baggage, informed us that Buonaparte has sent for one hundred thousand men from Spain to be marched into Germany immediately, and that they are now on their way there, if that is true, the campaign will be a short and decisive one, but they say that when he has beaten the Russians, he intends returning to Spain again. I would lay my life upon them never returning, if they get safely out of this country. They had in the field of action, five[62] regiments of infantry, and three of cavalry; upon the whole, they behaved very cowardly indeed. Lord Wellington led our regiment towards the enemy, I thought he intended to do us the honour of leading us to [the] charge, but the column of the enemy's right caught his attention, and he left us to order the artillery up, to move them, which was soon done.

The French blew up the defences of the Castle of Burgos this day, killing up to four hundred of their own men in the explosion. It was a great relief to many of Wellington's soldiers who still retained painful memories of the desperate siege of the previous autumn.

[Las] Hormazas, Sunday 13 June.
We marched from Isar this morning about 10 o'clock, and after a pleasant ride of three hours arrived here, we are encamped on the left of the road to Villaverde [-Penahorada], five leagues from Burgos. This morning at a quarter past 6 o'clock, I was returning to Isar with the picquet, when we were astonished by the shock occasioned by a dreadful explosion, the ground really appeared to shake for the moment, and we were struck dumb and motionless

---

[62] Incorrectly shown as three in the French version.

with the horrid roar. I immediately suspected what had happened, and this was confirmed by the Prince of Orange, who had brought us orders to march here; that the enemy had blown up Burgos Castle, immediately after they had retreated to Vitoria, which is to suffer the same fate, and the enemy is withdrawing on Vitoria beyond a doubt intends leaving this country.

Their blowing up the castle is convincing proof, this is good news for the infantry, for we could not have taken it without sacrificing at least two thousand men, and it is therefore, as beneficial to us as a general victory gained. The prisoners I took yesterday, gave us some hints of what was intended to be done, but none believed them; with them was a woman, she was mounted on a mule, and must have got out of our reach, but seeing me cut [at] her husband, who wanted to follow her, she immediately began to scream, surrendered and came with us. I spoke to Colonel Grant on her behalf, and he very generously gave her the mule to ride to prison with her husband. I never saw a man so busy in my life as the Prince of Orange was yesterday, he carried the orders to the different troops, and was galloping about the whole day; Lord Wellington is very fond of him, so indeed is everyone, no one can be more beloved.

Burgos to my regret, I only saw at a distance of two miles is the capital of Old Castile, and is said by some writers to be the Bravum of Ptolemy, it was for a long time the seat of the Castilian monarchy, but the Emperor Charles the 5th transferred this dignity to Madrid. Burgos, however, is still regarded as the second city in Spain, in dignity and ancient importance. It is built on the declivity of a hill, from whence it slopes along the plain to the Arlanzon, on whose right bank it stands, and whose stream flows close to its walls. The castle stands on the brow of an adjacent hill, it was considered impregnable. The streets are narrow, but the high street, which leads to the metropolitan church is said to be long, broad and handsome, one of the public squares is the handsomest in Europe, being surrounded by a piazza, like that of Covent Garden, over which are erected houses. It is, however, chiefly celebrated for its suburbs, which are on the other side of the River Arlanzon. Here is a beautiful promenade, whose walks are enlivened by the intermixture of delightful gardens which are constantly refreshed by fountains of running water. The celebrated Carthusian Convent of Miraflores[63]

---

[63]  The Cartuja de Miraflores or Milaflores Charterhouse lies 4km from Burgos centre. King John II of Castile and his wife Isabella of Portugal are buried here, but there was no John III of Castile.

stands very near to our scene of action. I wished very much to have seen the tombs of John the 2nd and 3rd of Castile; they exhibit the state of the arts about 1350. The distant view of Burgos, gave me some idea of its splendour.

Cernegula, Monday 14 June.
The road continued over immense high mountain plains, it became rough and heath like. The weather was excessively hot, and about every two leagues to mount still higher, we were all very much fatigued when we arrived here, having marched at least eight leagues. This village a very pretty one, stands at the foot of a high mountain, though it is on a plain at least 2,000 feet above the level of the sea.

This morning I received a letter from my dear friend Amelia, dated Camberwell 24 April, Mrs Perkins and all friends, I hear are in health.

The pace of the march was so rapid that many of the infantry fell out of the ranks exhausted, it also meant that the supplies had difficulty keeping up and therefore even George did not quibble about stealing a sheep.

Horna, Tuesday 15 June.
Soon after 4 o'clock this morning, we marched towards this place, and found it further than ours of yesterday, being 9 leagues. The road for the first five leagues, lay across a plain, we then came to a tremendous pass formed by lofty mountains, whose frightful summits, for such they are, stretched out in many places almost to meet each other, leaving between them, only a narrow space, this road was I think near two miles in a most wretched rough state.

We now came to Puente de Arenas and crossed a pretty bridge over the Ebro; we now had to go along another pass between which runs the river. It is impossible to match a scene more awfully wild than the narrow avenue between the mountains. The scenery is most beautiful; the rocks appear divided by some dreadful convulsion of nature, how easy might these two passes be defended by a few determined men. After leaving sight of the river we came into a beautiful valley, surrounded by high mountains, which is richly adorned with corn fields, fruit trees and transparent streams.

On our march, we saw the enemy's columns moving along a plain in the direction of Miranda de Ebro, where they crossed the river, and I understand have taken up a position in that neighbourhood, they were eight leagues from the river last night, we only five. I took a sheep from a flock on the roadside, killed him in the hussar style with my sword, and divided him with Mr Barrett of the 15th Hussars.[64] I dined off a part, and think I never enjoyed a dinner more in my life. My heart aches for the unfortunate infantry who I saw today on the march, such numbers laying on the roadside unable to stir a step further, it is impossible for the poor fellows to march 35 to 40 miles two or three days running, but Lord Wellington was anxious to cross the Ebro today; God only knows what may be done tomorrow! This village stands in the centre of the valley, and is surrounded by gardens. Captain Clements went this day to Marshal Beresford, his Aide de Camp, and Lieutenant Conolly will, therefore, take the command of his troop. The whole cavalry of the army is now in this valley.

Torres near Medina de Pomar, Wednesday 16 June.
Marched this morning at 4 o'clock to Medina, where the brigade halted near three hours for orders, and was then sent here, during the time we halted, the whole of the British cavalry arrived and formed in the rear of us. The horses are looking very well, we consisted of (11th[65]) 12th, 14th, and 16th Light Dragoons, 3rd and 4th Dragoon Guards, the two regiments of Life Guards and Blues, 1st German Hussars, and our brigade,10th, 15th and 18th Hussars.

The enemy offered General Hill battle yesterday morning, which he was obliged to decline, having only 15,000 men, their army was forty-five thousand. They are only a few leagues from us, and from all appearance a general battle must take place very soon.

I went into Medina and bought several things to add to my campaigning stock; brandy, bacon, figs, and nuts, it is a very ancient town; it contains three churches and a beautiful Roman castle, which gives a noble appearance to the place. It likewise contains many handsome women, whom I saw at their windows, very nicely dressed in black. The females are very fair in general and much handsomer than the Portuguese, they all appear fond of Englishmen, they are in my opinion very much like my country's women, and I admire them the more for that.

We are bivouacked in a wood of oaks, delightfully situated on the banks of the Trueba within a quarter of a mile of the village. Torres

---

[64]  Lieutenant Edward Barrett 15th Hussars.
[65]  The French version incorrectly includes the 11th Light Dragoons who had been ordered home in March.

[is] a deserted village, it ought to be said, for not a dozen inhabitants remain in it, though at a very short time since, it was inhabited by three hundred and fifty people. At present, it is in a ruinous state, the remains of its former state is plainly seen by the ruins of several most excellent houses. The weather is very unsettled at present; the climate is very much like an English August, excepting occasionally having some very cold showers, and dreadful cold chilling nights.

Smoking is a favourite amusement amongst all order of men in Spain, exclusive of the luxury it affords, they esteem it as a preventer of disease arising out of the cold and damp from the night air in this country.

San Llorente, Thursday 17 June.
The road today was bad, being rough in having no labour employed upon it, being a crops country, the road very much neglected. The country however, vied in beauty for any scene we had yet seen, we marched this day five long leagues. Upwards of seventy thousand men[66] are encamped within four miles of us, we having the outpost.

The enemy is now at Vitoria, very strong; Suchet[67] having joined Joseph yesterday, their army is supposed to consist of one hundred thousand men[68]. They retreated from Burgos, quite at their leisure, thinking they had the whole British Army in their rear following them along the high road, and it was only yesterday we heard the 12th, 14th &16th Dragoons had marched on their flank, and which was discovered by them, through the English not advancing to battle on the 15th, when they had taken up a fine position, they found to their surprise only 15,000; General Hill's army yesterday morning, and heard we were on their flank. They immediately took to flight, and are retreating to Vitoria as fast as they are able; tomorrow I think we shall stop a few on the road perhaps, and cut a great number off. My friend Smith is the dullest young man I ever knew, at this time, being a dangerous one I own, everyone is in spirits or else appears so, as they ought, and [should] show a good example to the men, but he is very sad about something, being absent from Mrs Smith may be the cause of it, if so it is a very frivolous one for an hussar.

Colonel Murray was hurt in the knee, when crossing the ford at Almendra, which he did not notice for several days, it became so

---

[66] Incorrectly shown as twenty thousand in the French version.
[67] Marshal Louis Gabriel Suchet did not join King Joseph at Vitoria, his army remaining on the East Coast of Spain.
[68] Without Suchet, Joseph's army at Vitoria numbered some sixty thousand.

bad when at Morales de Toro, that he was left there, we have heard within the last few days from him, and his leg is so bad now, he thinks he must lose it, owing to a formation of matter near the knee bone. Robert Curtis, now lieutenant, who was left at Santarem ill, still remains so, and there is not the least prospect of his joining the regiment again, or at least not till after the campaign. This is the fruit of bad company, the females have ruined him. Received newspapers 28th April up to 14th May; the peasantry of Spain are in general very stout and their dress is uniformly of a dark brown. The Spanish guerrillas are dressed some in French jackets, boots and caps, others in old English regimentals and cut a very novel appearance.

Camp near Berberana Friday 18 June.
At 6 o'clock this morning we marched from a most pleasant camp under a wood of fine oaks to this place, we expected to have marched nearly to Vitoria, but on arrival opposite to Villalba de Losa, we found General Graham engaging the enemy about a mile and a half in front. The enemy defended a village and pass for near an hour; when they retreated in great disorder towards Vitoria, our infantry following them close. The country being very mountainous about this neighbourhood, we are of no use at all, and are therefore, bringing up the rear today instead of having the outpost duty, after waiting near four hours during which time it rained incessantly.

Orders came for us to bivouac, where we could find water and forage, and having plenty of both near us; we took up our quarters immediately. Our camp is directly under a high mountain in a valley between Villalba and Berberana, the latter being base for headquarters; it is a small straggling village[69] containing about one hundred houses, and a small church. Villalba de Losa on our left, stands on a hill, apparently very strong by nature, an old Moorish castle presents the principal object, and almost entirely conceals the place.

We are now in Biscay, and about sixteen leagues from France, where I hope the enemy will immediately retreat to, but it is my opinion they will retreat towards Pamplona, a very strong place in Navarre.

Saturday 19 June.
Having received an order to march this morning, we are waiting anxiously to know if we halt here today; I hope we shall not, for it's

---

[69] Murita.

a wretched spot we are encamped on, no trees to shade us from the inclemency of the weather. Thank God, I got a good night's rest in spite of it. The Spanish army has been marching past our camp since 2 o'clock this morning, they are [still] now passing, but the rain prevents me leaving my tent to see them; [I] shall see enough of them another day. I saw the Spanish General Ballesteros[70], he is a very fine looking man, apparently about sixty years of age, his staff consisting of about a dozen officers well mounted and dressed. I saw a guerrilla chief dressed as follows, a hussar's pelisse and cap with feather, belonging to our 7th Hussars, a French pair of scarlet plush breeches and a Life Guardsman's boots. Amongst the peasantry his dress is much admired, to us it was truly laughable.

---

[70] General Francisco Ballesteros.

# Chapter 5

# 'The Baton Catchers'

The army now found itself within a march of the plains around Vitoria. Rumours were rife that the French army was determined to stand its ground there, whilst others claimed that they would retreat to the Pyrenees without a fight. The next few days would prove to be very lucrative for some individuals within the 18th; but the regiment's reputation was to receive a severe blow.

Subijana [de Alva], Lord Wellington's headquarters
Contrary to my expectations, orders arrived to march, just as I had written the above at Berberana. I am now encamped on the side of a steep hill, on a zigzag walk which overlooks Subijana de Alva, which is now our headquarters. When the brigade got about half way here, we heard the report of guns, and immediately afterwards was informed an engagement had commenced near two hours before, and that the enemy was then retreating, we ascended a high hill and descended into the valley where we are now, and saw our army following up the enemy. The ground being so mountainous, still we cannot act, [we] was, therefore ordered to bivouac on the right of this town, where Lord Wellington and his staff are at the moment. Where my troop is encamped, we found four dead Frenchmen, a great many[1] prisoners are taken this morning by our brave infantry, and tomorrow we expect to get clear of the mountains, and then the hussars will do a little to rid

---

[1]  In the original French version he states 3,000 prisoners were captured, however, he later learnt that this was a gross exaggeration and he left it out.

the earth of a few more, we are panting to have another touch at them.

Subijana is a straggling place, I suppose about two hundred houses and a church, and our Light Brigade drove the enemy through it, this morning in high style; the skirmishing lasted near four hours today. I am in a most charming valley, bordered on each side by thick and romantic cliffs, the summits and hollows of which are covered with trees, at the bottom are several mills turned by the running stream, and at a mile distant we discover a rock glen, through which foams a mountain torrent which falls into the River Zadorra; in the centre of this valley stands Subijana.

I am persuaded that the Spanish never will be conquered; they very strongly resemble the English, the frame of their bodies, and even in their undaunted minds. They may be defeated a thousand times, but they will never be subdued. The English newspapers and people are wrong when they explain that they have nothing to fight for, and I say give them a constitution, give them liberty. In the first place, they have their country to fight for, their soil, their homes, and against foreigners and invaders, surely this is something. And as to liberty, they have as much as they want, as much as they are really capable of [enjoying]. With respect to constitution, you might as well say, give them English roast beef, they have no idea of it, they know nothing about it, and, therefore, neither knows the want of it, nor desires it. If you were to offer it to them, if you were to tell them of balanced powers, they would decline it. Their cause is their country, and if they chose to put Ferdinand at the head of it, why in the name of wonder should you object. I believe there is a great deal of nonsense in the party[2] refinements at home; they know nothing about these people. They are brave to excess, but of course cannot stand yet veteran and disciplined armies. We will at length remedy this defect. The Spanish armies want organisation. I have just seen about three hundred prisoners brought in, they are well dressed and appointed, many more are taken, and are to be sent in tomorrow morning, they are of infantry regiments. I asked one of them after our old friends the 16th Dragoons whom we brushed up at Morales, he shrugged up his shoulders, and explained 'Ils sont perdus' [they are dead].

Sunday 20 June.
There is every reason to believe we shall halt today, as Lord

[2] Political.

Wellington, intends halting in the village until tomorrow morning or we die of hunger. The language of the people here, in the province of Biscay is very different from the rest of Spain[3]. I am told that they pretend their language as they call it, has continued uninterrupted from the very confusion of Babel; though if I might give my opinion on the matter; I should take it to be the very corruption of all that confusion. Another rhodomontado [boast], they have, is that [no] Romans, Carthaginians, Vandals, Goths, or Moors, ever totally subdued them. And yet any man that has seen their country might cut the knot without a hatchet, by saying that neither Roman, Carthaginian, nor any [other] victorious people [have] thought it worthwhile to make a conquest of a country so mountainous, and in some measure so barren. Their guerrillas, have certainly been likewise successful, and they annoy the French who have never subdued them.

The remainder of the French prisoners taken yesterday were marched into this place a few hours back. Four hundred of them were taken and about one hundred killed. They have taken up a strong position a few miles from us, and appear determined to stand a battle, God send they may, for we feel confident of the issue.

This is an idle day for me, I don't know how to employ myself except with this diary, my idle companion. I have used [forced] myself so regularly to write in it daily, that it has become part of my daily duty, and in fact, [I] don't feel comfortable till I have discharged it.

I have just returned from seeing the Convent of the Carthusian order, which stands on the side of the mountains near this village. The enemy very much rampaged through it, but it is plainly to be seen it was once a delightful place; there has been a curious and well-ordered garden, which led me to observe to Smith, that whatever men pretend, pleasure was not incompatible with the most austere of lives. I have often heard from many, the most unaccountable relations of the severity of their way of life, and the very odd origin of their institution. I was therefore, much pleased in finding the following account of it in a Spanish book.

Bruno the author or founder of the order of Carthusian Friars[4], was not originally of this [order], but of another, he had a holy brother of the same order that was his cell mate or chamber fellow,

---

[3]   He refers of course to the Basque language.
[4]   Saint Bruno began the Carthusian Order in France in 1084.

who was reputed by all who ever saw or knew him, for a person of exalted piety, and of a most exact holy life. This man Bruno had intimately known for many years and agreed of his character, that general consent did him no more than justice, having never observed anything in any of his actions that in his opinion could be offensive to God or man. He was perpetually at the devotions and distinguishably remarkable for never permitting anything but pious ejaculations to proceed out of his mouth. In short, he was reputed a saint upon earth. This man at last dies, and according to custom, is removed into the chapel of the convent, and there placed with a cross fixed into his hands, soon after which, saying the proper masses for his soul, in the middle of their devotion, the dead man lifts up his head, and with an audible voice, cried out 'Vocatus sum', [I am called]. The pious brethren, one will easily imagine were prodigiously surprised at such an incident, and therefore they earnestly redoubled their prayers; when lifting up their head a second time, the dead man cried out 'Judicalus sum' [I am condemned]. Knowing his former piety, the pious fraternity could not then entertain the least doubt of his felicity, when to their great consternation and confusion, he lifted up his head a third time, crying out in a terrible tone 'Damnatus Sum', [Guilty] upon which they incontinently removed the corpse out of the chapel, and threw it on a dung hill. Good Bruno, pondering on the passages, drew this conclusion. That if a person, to all appearances is holy and devout should miss of salvation, it behove a wise man to contrive some way more certain to make his calling and election sure. To that purpose, he instituted this strict and severe order, with an injunction to them, sacred as any part that every professor should always wear hair cloth next to his skin, never eat any flesh nor speak to one another only as passing by, to say, 'Memento Mori', [remember death].

There are very few of this order in the country, the principal convent is near Burgos. I am likewise informed that every friar is obliged every day to get into their place of burial, and take up as much earth as he can hold at a grasp with one hand, in order to prepare his grave. [5]

---

[3] He refers of course to the Basque language.

[4] Saint Bruno began the Carthusian Order in France in 1084.

[5] Research, would suggest that the book from which the Carthusian information is taken, was from the *Military memoirs of Captain George Carleton* (1728). Daniel Defoe also made an erroneous claim to be the author. The memoirs were in the *Military Chronicle*, published in London, 1811.

The Battle of Vitoria, was a superb victory for Wellington and his troops, but the 18th Hussars came out of the battle particularly badly, their reputation in tatters. Joseph's French troops were defending the line of the River Zadorra to the north and west of the town of Vitoria which lays centrally on a wide, flat flood plain, which is surrounded by steep hills; with some sixty-five thousand men with 150 cannon. Wellington attacked with superior numbers, nearing eighty thousand (including eight thousand Spanish troops), but only ninety-one cannon. Wellington needed all his numerical advantage to overcome the strong defensive position taken up by the French.

The battle had commenced with Hill's infantry pushing forward along the hills forming the south-western flank of the great flood plain, whilst the centre of his army probed the bridges along the Zadorra and sought to discover fords at which the troops could cross. Meanwhile, the left of his army under General Graham had continued marching in the hills to the north, turning the French defences and aiming to cut off their escape route north towards Bilbao.

The 18th Hussars were initially held in reserve in the centre, until it was discovered that the bridge at Trespuentes was not broken and even more amazingly was completely undefended. Wellington poured troops over this bridge, beginning with the Light Brigade who secured a bridgehead, with the Hussar Brigade not far behind. Having crossed the river and formed up under the protection of the lee of a small height, Grant then ordered them forward, but they immediately came under the fire from a mass of French artillery situated in front of the great rock of Arinez. Major Hughes claims[6] that Grant mistakenly allowed the left wing of the 18th Hussars to continue to move forward, whilst Grant halted the remainder of the brigade and ordered it back under cover. Turing's squadron therefore continued to advance alone and took casualties from both the artillery and heavy musketry from nearby formations of French infantry. Hughes claims that he ordered out skirmishers, but that Turing recklessly ordered a charge and he and a number of dragoons were killed and wounded, before they were finally forced to retire. Many in the regiment felt that the losses suffered here were due to Grant's ineptitude, but Hughes apportions the blame equally to both Grant and Turing for proceeding unsupported and exceeding his orders.

Graham's troops now launched a serious attack on Vitoria from the north and cut the Bilbao road, which caused the French army to waver

---

[6]   *Charging Against Napoleon*, page 102.

and it began to retire slowly on the only road still open towards the east, heading towards Pamplona. As the French began to retreat, this was the perfect moment for the Hussar Brigade to advance, taking swift advantage of the enemy's confusion and turning defeat into a rout. But this is when things went very wrong for the 18th.

As the Hussar Brigade drove forward in pursuit of the retiring French, they soon approached the walled town of Vitoria itself and an instant decision on how the brigade would navigate around the town was needed. Cavalry charging into a defended town was usually a recipe for disaster; as they could easily be brought to a halt by barricades or formed infantry blocking their path, when the men and horses became vulnerable. The brigade was split, with everyone presuming that Grant would order the two wings to pass either side of the town and to reform on the far side again, before continuing the pursuit. However, Grant ordered no such thing.

The 15th Hussars, on the left of the brigade and the left squadron of the 18th (with which George Woodberry served) were ordered to pass to the left (north) of the town and continued to drive on. However, the two remaining squadrons of the 18th, commanded by Major Hughes were ordered by Grant to charge straight through the town.[7] The 10th Hussars were simply to follow them. Hughes did find barricades in front of the town gates, but managed to push through it and enter the town in one mad rush, soon all order was at an end. Fortunately, the French infantry in the town had no idea of defending it and were hurriedly departing, whilst the Spanish residents caused further confusion as they attempted to cut down the Frenchmen as they fled.

Riding like madmen through the streets, the squadrons were broken up to the point that all discipline was at an end, it was a mere fox hunt! By sheer luck, more than judgement, the hussars reached the gates on the opposite side of the town, where they eventually forced a passage through another barricade, as they continued to charge after the retreating Frenchmen.

But having emerged from the town, what was presented to the hussars, was not a wide plain full of retreating Frenchmen, but a huge park, consisting of hundreds if not thousands of vehicles, crammed with valuables and coinage stolen from across Spain, abandoned but for a light cavalry screen protecting the departure of King Joseph. The French cavalry were soon dispersed but the vulnerable King was apparently

---

[7] Hughes does however admit that Grant blamed him for the attack through the town; was it Grant who ordered it, or did Hughes order it of his own volition?

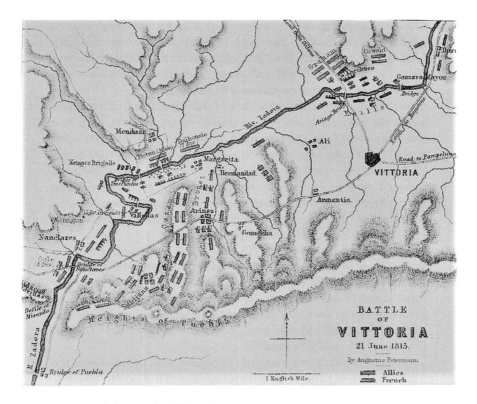

*Above: Map of the Battle of Vitoria*

able to escape capture as these two squadrons, almost to a man, both officers and privates, unilaterally called off the pursuit to rummage through this treasure trove. Hughes states that he refused all offers of plunder, but he no longer had any troops to command and the pursuit of the fleeing French was abandoned. Some of the 10th Hussars, including officers were also implicated in this shameful dereliction of duty and soon the entire army turned to plunder. Wellington believing however that the 18th had been the instigators of this mayhem and the worst culprits, he was livid. George only became aware of what had happened later and he feared the wrath of Wellington and worried about how it would impinge on him and the honour of his regiment.

Field of Battle, Victory of Vitoria
Camp a league from Vitoria, on the Pamplona Road, Monday 21 June 1813.

O God dispose my heart to return, thanks for thy goodness for withholding the sword that was pointed at my existence, from having the effect it was intended; please send this Glorious Victory that it may lead to a general peace, and give happiness to the troubled world, but more particularly England.

We left our camp at daybreak, and marched about two leagues, when we discovered the enemy posted on the heights, their line extending near three miles in front of the town of Vitoria, their left at [Le] Puebla de Arganzon, and centered across the valley of the Zadorra, their army likewise occupied the following villages, Arinez, Gomecha (Abechuco and Gamarra Mayor). In the centre of his position stood an immense high conical hill which commanded the valley of [the] Zadorra, on which I saw Joseph Buonaparte and his staff, very plainly through a glass.

The battle commenced about 9 o'clock this morning, our brigade was in front of the valley, and we saw Sir Rowland Hill's Division obtain possession of the heights of Puebla, the enemy left; it was most strongly disputed, but his brave light infantry, pushed all before them and the Castle of Arganzon[8] was taken; it was here that the brave General Morillo[9] was wounded and Lieutenant Colonel Cadogan[10] was fatally wounded.

The 4th Division and a brigade of cavalry took possession of the villages of Aríñez and Gomecha and advanced in line and columns of brigade on the right of the road from Miranda [de Ebro] to Vitoria. Two brigades of the 3rd Division captured Altura de los Iglesias[11], while the 7th Division and a brigade of the 3rd Division took the villages of Margarita and Zuazo [de Vitoria] and progressed to the left of the road. At this moment, the enemy began to give way in all directions. The brigade of Major-General Skerrett took from the enemy, on an eminence, a few artillery pieces which had been for some time pouring a deadly fire on our centre.[12]

The village of Subijana de Alava was strongly contested for, but we got possession of it, and soon afterwards I saw one of the bridges

---

[8]   Incorrectly named Zalderan in French version.
[9]   Spanish General Pablo Morillo y Morillo, Count of Cartagena and Marquess of La Puerta, also known as El Pacificador (The Pacifier).
[10]  Lieutenant Colonel the Honourable Henry Cadogan 71st Foot commanded a brigade in the 2nd Division at Vitoria.
[11]  I have been unable to identify this place.
[12]  At this point, the French version stops abruptly as his regiment rode into action and does not resume until the following day; this would further indicate that the French version was generally written on the scene and the British version later. when he had more leisure; but clearly not much later, otherwise a great deal of detail would have been forgotten.

over the Zadorra in our possession, and our army is advancing towards the height where Joseph Buonaparte had been. Our brigade and the heavies were moved round by the left and passed over the bridge at Trespuentes, and advanced at a trot, to the front of the said conical hill [Arinez]; it was now very plain to all that a great victory was on the eve of being gained.

I was in exceedingly high spirits, and felt anxious to have a touch at the enemy, it appeared to me at this time, everything was to be gained, and nothing to be lost. I longed to belong to the infantry, the ground was very unfavourable for cavalry, and I began to think it must be so, and that we should be kept in the rear all day. Our troops [drove] upon the enemy towards Vitoria, in admirable order, the enemy retreat broke upon that town, an abundance of cannon was now taken, the cannonading was horrid, three or four hundred pieces of cannon playing on each other. The Portuguese and Spanish troops behaved admirably, and some regiments most conspicuously distinguished themselves. The enemy were driven in the highest style from every position they took; General Sir Thomas Graham, got possession of Gamarra [Mayor] and Abechuco, interrupted the enemies retreat into France, and they were obliged to turn to the road to Pamplona, but they were unable to hold any position for a sufficient time to allow their baggage, treasures, and artillery to be drawn off; the consequences were that it all fell into our hands.

The army of Joseph's, consisted of the whole of the armies of the south and of the centre, and of four divisions, all the cavalry of the army of Portugal, and a part of the army of the north: in all about sixty-five thousand men. They lost six generals and about twenty thousand men in killed, wounded and prisoners. Joseph had a bodyguard of about one hundred hussars, and I think Kennedy's Troop would have taken him, had they kept together, but they ran after a set of fellows and plunder, and did not support their captain, who was very near being taken prisoner, being obliged to dismount off his horse and leap over a ditch to save himself, Captains Bolton and Burke did not give him the support that they ought, and for which I hope they will suffer.

Captain Turing lost his life about 12 o'clock, he was in the act of charging a solid body of infantry, we had galloped from the bridge near the village of Zadorra, and were under cover till the moment he fell, when on the regiment showing themselves on the rising ground before the enemy, who were a few yards only distant, a volley of musketry was immediately fired and Turing and Foster fell, Colonel

Grant immediately gave the order 'threes about', and the brigade retired under cover of a wood of elms.

I was now sent out with a few skirmishers and found poor Cornet Foster lying under a tree where some men had left him, shot through the left leg. I instantly rode towards the infantry lines, and procured two surgeons, and took them to him, it was now the battle became general, we advanced along the Roman paved road towards Vitoria, and we were several times halted, and remained under the range of the enemy's fire. Every position the enemy took up they were driven from, we saw their cannon lying about as we advanced, which they were compelled to leave, at last we came to the town, and when opposite to it, two squadrons of the 18th and the whole of the 10th were ordered to charge through the town; which they did. I was with the left squadron and the 15th, we went to the left of the town, and found there the whole of the enemy's cavalry was formed to protect the retreat of their king, and the infantry. It was here that the Hussar Brigade was dammed forever. Colonel Grant who knew nothing of [the] part of the brigade being ordered into the town, ordered a charge, we advanced upon them, riding over a column of infantry. I know nothing more that occurred till I formed up the squadron, upon the ground we moved from. I saw Carew in the hands of the enemy, and saw the squadron, and the 15th Regiment retreating; I was the last that arrived being pursued (and being wounded), by a whole squadron of the enemy. Poor Captain Carew, the last words I heard him speak, was 'Come along Woodberry and the left'. Whatever could possess the men I know not, they were just preparing to charge us, when two pieces of artillery arrived and put them to the rout; we now advanced, but the brigade never charged again. That part of the brigade who entered the town, charged the enemy through it, but unfortunately for our fame, the men and officers [then] commenced plundering.

Joseph Buonaparte was in the town when our men entered it, he was dressed in plain clothes, and galloped off with an attendant, directing his guard to charge our men, which they did most gallantly, or their King would have been taken prisoner. The roads from the town were stopped up by the immense number of cannon, ammunition wagons, carriages, baggage etc. I understand the inhabitants of Vitoria, commenced plundering the baggage, and murdered all the French prisoners in the town, what wretches.

The enemy was pursued about a league further than the town, when it became so dark, that it necessitated the pursuit being abandoned, we were ordered to bivouac in a wood about a league from Vitoria. I laid myself under a tree, so did Carew's Troop around me, our horses, poor things, fared as bad as us, for we got nothing to eat.

After the battle was over, I saw a mule with baggage on its back, lying in a ditch; I got him out and took it to our camp. The mule was [later] stolen from me, but the content of the boxes I had under my head all night, or I should have lost them. It proved to be a little of Joseph's baggage. One man took a wagon of roast legs of mutton and chickens; we got them in time for breakfast. Turing was buried immediately after the battle by some of the men, near where he was killed; Foster was carried to a village, Carew the enemy took with them, I hope to God he is well.

Vitoria, Tuesday 22 June.
I was sent this morning to this place with the sick and wounded men and horses, I got the men of the brigade comfortably put up in the hospital, where I trust they will recover, there were ten of the 18th only: I also found stables for the horses. I met Blackett, with his party of men on their way to join the regiment, I persuaded him to stay the night here, and return with me tomorrow; we dined together and walked round the town, and saw everything worth seeing.

The capital of the Province of Alava is poorly built and more poorly paved. It is however, a sweet delicious and pleasant town, and is supposed to contain the finest women in the universe. It received the name Vitoria, in memory of a considerable victory then obtained over the Moors[13]; the glorious victory of yesterday will be the means of its name being ever dear to the world. The town was crowded with soldiers, the prisoners and the baggage of the state; all the papers of service of all kinds flying about the street, I picked up a paper which I shall preserve, it is a Commission of Lieutenant General Jourdan, signed by the Emperor Napoleon, Joseph and twelve others, amongst whose names is Talleyrand[14] and Berthier[15].

The hospital, the largest and best I ever saw, is crowded with wounded men. The square is very handsome, though small it has

---

[13] This explanation is the mixing of two stories. It is claimed that the Visigoth King Liugivild founded the city of Victoriacum in celebration of a victory in 581 AD. This new city soon disappears from history until Sancho the Wise, King of Navarre founded the town of Nova Victoria in 1181 as a defensive position on the same site, but not as the site of a battle. Scholars are still not fully convinced by these claims.

[14] Charles Maurice de Talleyrand-Périgord, Prince de Benedente, was a cunning and influential diplomat who served both Napoleon and Louis XVIII.

[15] Marshal Louis Alexandre Berthier, Prince de Wagram, Duc de Valangin, Prince of Neuchâtel.

piazzas all round; there are several very excellent coffee houses, very unusual in this country, and some excellent libraries, of Spanish and French authors. Thank God, I have got some writing paper, pens etc., so I shall write in a few days to my dear friend Amelia and Aunt Moseley. I got an excellent billet in a house about the centre of the town, kept by two ladies, they gave me supper. I dined at the coffee house under the piazzas; bread chopped up with garlic and dressed like a salad, except that water held the place of oil, eggs boiled hard and dressed with oil and garlic, and tomatoes and eggs fried followed the former dish; a very little habit reconciles all these things. Poor Carew, we found at the village of Gomecha, the enemy left him mortally wounded in the neighbourhood. I went to see him with Blackett, but what a sight! Heaven! May I soon forget it!

The Spaniards are brave, but bravery cools quickly. Their rage against the enemy knows no bounds, we saw yesterday the evidence. Upon our arrival in the city, we saw people mistreat the prisoners. They massacred many and when asked why, they answered 'A segurar el prisonero!' [To secure the prisoners!].

Olazagutia, Wednesday 23 June.
I left Vitoria this morning with Lieutenant Russell, at 11 o'clock, Lieutenant Blackett whom I proposed to go with at three; owing to my not being able to obtain the returns correct till after a few minutes before I started, he was obliged to go without me. The first thing Russell and self did was to ride to the village where Captain Carew was, but we found he [had] died last night at half past 8 o'clock, 22 June, and that the doctor, Quincey, buried him in the church; the name of the village is Gomecha.
We now proceeded to Salvatierra, a neat pretty town on a plain, about three leagues from Vitoria, which served yesterday evening as headquarters to Lord Wellington and where the regiment was last night. After halting there about an hour, a man of the 10th Hussars came in from a neighbouring village, and stated that two wounded men of the 18th who had made their escape from the enemy, who had taken them prisoners, with six of the Tenth and Fifteenth Hussars, and himself, had been attacked by a corps of Spanish artillery, and that they had fired on them, and to his belief they were all murdered. I immediately mounted my horse and proceeded towards the village; on our way, we met the artillery, he being with me as a guide, and he pointed out an officer whom he thought was the occasion of it all. I instantly rode up to him and he insisted on him accompanying me to the village to look after the men, he did so

and when we got there, I found they were released by the said officer instead of being detained, and that they were gone to Salvatierra, and I likewise heard [that] they were much to blame. I therefore thanked the officer, and returned to Salvatierra, from whence I had proceeded to this place, and got into a house with my men, eight in number [who] had straggled in, as I had picked up the two wounded men mentioned earlier.

Joseph Buonaparte stopped after the battle in the very house where I am. The woman told me that he appeared to be shot and that he regretted the loss of his baggage: he had not saved even a change of linen. We saw a field of sheep upon which the soldiers seized a sheep, which was immediately killed and [we] had for supper, we were nearly starving having marched near seven leagues we were dying of hunger; I lost Russell on the way. I could get no account of the regiment, they were in advance, but where they are I cannot learn. I hope they will not march tomorrow, or I shall never come up with them, I have to rest this night in a most miserable hole, but I have my belly full, and that is all I desire in this country.

George re-joined the regiment to find that they had been paraded by Major Hughes and ordered to hand over what had been pillaged at Vitoria. Major Hughes records that £2,600 (around £100,000 in modern terms) was collected in cash and there was a great deal of jewellery and other valuables collected as well. It transpired later, that a lot more was not given up this day. It was only discovered later (in December) that Corporal Fox of the 18th had captured Marshal Jourdan's baton at Vitoria, but having removed the solid gold ends, he gave the baton to a friend, Bugler Paddy Shannon in the 87th (The Prince of Wales Irish) Regiment of Foot, who gave it to his colonel and he gave it to Wellington. Wellington promptly sent it home with the despatch to the Prince Regent and the prince famously returned a marshal's baton for Wellington. The gold end pieces were eventually sent to Wellington and subsequently restored to the baton which is now on show at Windsor Castle. The regiment then became unofficially known (at least to themselves), as 'The Baton Catchers'.

Bavomoa [Bakaiku?], Thursday 24 June.
I arrived here about 9 o'clock this morning, having marched about a league, having found the regiment; it has today, so I understand soon after my arrival, been called out to parade, it was for the men to deliver up their plunder and be searched. A great deal was found on them, which of course was taken, to be equally divided amongst

the regiment, on one man was found seven hundred and forty quarter doubloons[16].

There are many most excellent houses in this village, but a most paltry looking church, and very ill paved, the River Arakil, runs very close to it, through the valley, the enemy blew up the bridge at Huarte [Olazti?], which I am informed stopped our army near three hours before they could get it repaired, our brigade found a ford and crossed it. I had some words with Smith this afternoon, and am very sorry for it, as I feel a great friendship for him, more than for any other in the regiment. I am now in the Kingdom of Navarre. On my decease, if I go to heaven and we possess the same knowledge as in this world, the first person I should enquire for and wish to see, would be Henry 4th of France, King of Navarre[17].

The brigade marched to Pamplona, where they rested whilst decisions were made regarding how to deal with the French garrison of Pamplona, to formally besiege or blockade them. The decision was eventually made to use the Spanish troops to blockade Pamplona and to starve the garrison into surrendering.

Aizuain [Asiain], Friday 25 June.
Orders came for marching this morning at 6 o'clock, on our way we passed through two villages, Lakuntza and Irurtzun burnt down by the enemy on their retreat, the poor defenceless inhabitants were cruelly treated, the fires were not out, we crossed the River Huarte [Arakil?] twice, the road was wretched bad, for the first eight miles, after which we came on the regular paved road to Pamplona, the finest and straightest I think I ever saw, on our way we met Captain Fremantle of the Guards[18], who had the despatches in relation to the glorious victory, on his way to England.

About a mile before we got here, Pamplona was seen, it stands in the middle of a delightful picturesque valley, it is about three miles from us. The enemy are in it, tomorrow morning it will be stormed so is the report, it is likewise rumoured that Joseph and a quarter part of the French army are retired to France, which is only four

---

[16] Worth 5,920 reales.

[17] Henry IV (1553 –1610), also known as 'Good King Henry', was King of Navarrr as Henry III from 1572 to 1610 and became King of France from 1589 to 1610. He was the first French king of the House of Bourbon.

[18] Lieutenant & Captain John Fremantle, one of Wellington's aides de camp, was sent home with the Vitoria dispatch, carrying Marshal Jourdan's baton and the colours of the French 100e Regiment. He was made a brevet major by the Prince Regent. Fremantle's own letters have been published by the editor as 'Wellington's Voice'.

leagues distant. Poor Joseph, it is said, looks very sorrowful, and bemoans losing his baggage; some of our officers got a deal of plunder, Burke near two thousand pounds[19], Dolbel as much.

The miseries of war I truly felt yesterday, I never knew the worth of victuals till then, we are all nearly starved, the enemy must have been worse off from the number of dead men on the road who appear to have died through famine and fatigue. The road will not be passable in a few days, several of the bodies lying in the road were reduced to shapeless masses by trampling, and I think I saw at least two hundred dead horses likewise, horrible objects, the country people having skinned most of them. They are left for the vultures and wolves to devour. The brigade is divided into different villages round Pamplona, the infantry are encamped between us and that place. The enemy was forced to abandon in the pursuit, the single cannon they saved at Vitoria to our brave light infantry. I am anxious for tomorrow, to see what will be attempted and done.

Major Hughes informed the officers that Wellington was still in a rage over the regiment's poor showing at Vitoria. He made it clear that if he received any further complaints against the regiment, he would order the regiment to be dismounted and sent home!

Villava Atarrabia left of Pamplona, Saturday 26 June.
Ipper never arrived with my baggage till 6 o'clock this morning, my mule proving obstinate was the cause of the delay. Contrary to all expectations, we marched this morning, Pamplona was regularly invested, we marched on the right and crossed a bridge over the River Arakil, then proceeded to the left and got completely round the town, we see it very plain from this village, being on the direct road to Bayonne.

This is an uninhabited village, most pleasantly situated near the mountains, near it runs a famous aqueduct of one hundred arches[20], it has the appearance of a most beautiful bridge, the highest arch I should think is at least two hundred feet, the distance across the valley cannot be less than half a mile, twice or thrice as long as Westminster Bridge. If I stay here tomorrow I will certainly inspect it.

---

[19]  About £80,000 in modern terms.
[20]  The Noain aqueduct was built in 1790 and ran for 16.5km bringing water to the city from the mountains. Modern roads have unfortunately cut through the aqueduct and it is no longer a continuous structure, but is still stunning to see, running into the city from the south.

Colonel Grant ordered the officers *of the 18th Hussars* before him today, and informed us he has Lord Wellington's authority to inform us that his lordship was very much displeased with the insubordination of the regiment, particularly of the conduct of the men in Vitoria on the 21st inst., numbers of them he saw plundering on the streets, he was likewise very much displeased with several of our officers who were there plundering, instead of being in the field. And to finish he had to inform us that his lordship was determined if he heard any complaint against the regiment, he would immediately dismount us, and march the regiment to the nearest sea port town, and embark us for England, and at the same time send the Commander in Chief (the Duke of York) remarks on the subject. O God has it come to this! I want language to express the grief I feel on this occasion, to think I should have come out with a regiment who have contrary to all expectations, acted so differently.

Pamplona is the capital of Navarre, supposed to have been built by Pompey[21]. It is situated in a pleasant valley, surrounded by lofty hills or mountains. This town, whether famous or infamous, was the cause of the first institution of the order of the Jesuits, for at the siege of this place, Ignatius Loyola[22], being only a private soldier, received a shot in his thigh, which made him incapable of following that profession any longer, upon which he set his brains to work, being a subtle man, and invented the order of the Jesuits, which has been so troublesome to the world ever since.

The brigade was sent in pursuit of a force under General Clausel, which had not been aware of the defeat of the French army at Vitoria. Meanwhile, Dolbel was involved in a scrape near Pamplona, but luckily it does not appear to have got to the ear of Wellington.

Olite, Sunday 27 June.
Orders arrived for us to march about 2 o'clock this morning and we never halted till we arrived at Tafalla, where we found the 10th and 15th, in their quarters since yesterday. We had just got snug in our quarters when the bugle sounded and we immediately turned out

---

[21] The Roman general Gnaeus Pompeius Magnus established Pompaelo in 75-74 BC.

[22] Inigo Lopez of Loyola later changed his name to Ignatius. He was severely wounded during the Battle of Pamplona in 1521, a cannonball striking his legs and breaking the bones in his left leg in multiple places. In an age before removal of the leg was possible, he underwent numerous operations to break and then reset his misshapen leg, but he retained a pronounced limp for the remainder of his life. He underwent a religious conversion during his recovery and formed the Jesuits.

and marched to this place, it was some time before we could account for us being moved, when we learned Lord Wellington arrived this evening at Tafalla and that our quarters would be occupied by his Staff.

Mr Dolbel, who was left in a village near Pamplona to reconnoitre and pick up any stragglers he could find belonging to the regiment; soon as the enemy saw us march off, they sent a detachment of cavalry into the village and had nearly taken him prisoner; but they allowed him to escape, being over anxious to take our former hussar mules and the provisions of our commissaries, many of which were taken.

We are now in pursuit of twelve thousand men under the command of General Clausel[23] who proceeded along this road, instead of going into France. There is every hope; we shall take him and his army. The wound I sustained at Vitoria is healing well; I feel very little uneasiness from it now. One of our scoundrels today gave a false alarm; Lord Wellington on learning this immediately punished this individual by the Provost Marshal. We have no chance: we cannot do anything in the regiment without his lordship being informed. There must be a spy among us and I believe I know who it is.

<u>List of Officers of the 18th Hussars, 24 June in Spain</u>

Major Hughes Commanding

| Captain | Bolton | | | Lieutenant | Hesse |
|---|---|---|---|---|---|
| ditto | Kennedy | | | ditto | Blackett |
| ditto | Burke | | | ditto | Rowlls |
| | | | | ditto | Woodberry |
| Lieutenant | Russell Commanding Troops | | | ditto | Dolbel |
| ditto | Conolly | ditto | ditto | Cornet | Curtis |
| ditto | Smith | ditto | ditto | Lieutenant Waldie Adjutant | |

| <u>Sick</u> | <u>Dead</u> | <u>Wounded</u> |
|---|---|---|
| Colonel Murray | Captain Turing | Cornet Foster |
| | ditto    Carew | |

Being the first English who ever entered Tafalla, we were received with the greatest demonstration of joy, and kindness by all, we got

---

[23] General Bertrand Comte Clausel.

excellent feeds, an abundance of fruit and wine. I showed my good hostess the coat I have of [Joseph] Buonaparte's who immediately brought half of the inhabitants of the town to see it, and I am very much afraid I shall lose it, for if Lord Wellington should hear I have it, I shall surely be obliged to give it up.

Caparroso, Monday 28 June.
We marched this morning at 7 o'clock[24], crossed a wild and uncultivated heath and when we got to the bridge over the River Aragon, I was sent by Colonel Grant with Captain Wodehouse[25] of the 15th. We received orders to ride to reconnoitre Tudela; if the enemy was there, we are to report on strengths; if it had gone, to move forward until we discovered him on the road to Zaragoza. Ordered to make two leagues at a time, the army halting until Lord Wellington had received our report. We followed the highway until at Villa Valtierra, we met an aide de camp of General Mina's[26], who informed us that the French had left Tudela this morning, but hearing that the general and Colonel Waters[27] were in the neighbourhood, we proceeded, but not meeting them, we went on to Tudela. Where, upon entering the gates, near a dozen shots were fired at us by the French sentries as they had seen us coming and we immediately turned about and galloped off, being pursued near two miles by a dozen dragoons who were ready mounted and prepared to dash out after us, if we survived after the fire of the infantry, but the superior metal of our horses, set them at defiance. We after got up on rising ground and saw the enemy withdraw from the town, and it turned out that the French army was actually gone, but had left their rear guard in the town, which upon their leaving, they blew up the bridge.

We now returned to Valtierra which we entered amidst the cheers and acclamations of the inhabitants, who forced us off our horses, into the principle house, where we were regaled with dinner, which by the bye, we could not partake off, owing to the garlic used in the dressing, but we eat heartily of some very nice cake and drank two bottles of champagne. We prefer bread, cheese and wine. The bells rang, the people danced all about the street, the clergy offered up

---

[24] Incorrectly shown as 8 o'clock in the French version.
[25] Captain Philip Wodehouse 15th Hussars.
[26] General Francisco Espoz Mina, was born in Navarre in 1781 and died in 1836. He was a Spanish Guerrilla leader and military general, remaining active in Spanish politics until the end of his life.
[27] Lieutenant Colonel John Waters although a British officer, commanded the 1st Portuguese Line Regiment.

prayers for our success, we were taken to the church by the people who heard their organ, several of their most joyful airs were played, and a Te Deum was sung. We then made moves to leave, but Captain Wodehouse's horse[28] was so tired; he could not proceed further, so I left him at Valtierra in an excellent quarter, they were all anxious to show him kindness.

On my way back I was met by near a hundred men, women and children who came out on purpose to give any English they might meet, wine and cake etc. I was detained near half an hour by them, and was obliged to drink two good bumpers of wine, before they would allow me to depart; at last I got back to Caparroso, completely knocked up, nearly fatigued to death with my poor horse done up as well, and to my astonishment, found the regiment had moved from this place. I was determined, therefore, to remain here through the night; the distance to Tudela is six leagues, twenty-four miles. I have ridden my horse this day 15 leagues, three from Olite here, about 60 miles [in all]. I got the best quarters in the villa, which stands on the side of a rock on the bank of the Aragon, over which is a very handsome stone bridge of seven arches.

Valtierra, is a very neat built village, its church will vie for beauty with many in this kingdom. The inhabitants are obliging and generous, and appear true to the great cause of their country. The River Ebro runs close to it.

Camp near Caseda, Tuesday 29 June.
I came on this morning to this camp, after having informed Colonel Grant what we had seen and gave a description of the country, I then went back to my tent and took a little rest. The 15th[29] are in quarters at Caseda, about a mile from this place. The brigade halt here today, we expect tomorrow to return to the neighbourhood of Pamplona.

The enemy having got into Zaragoza, we shall, therefore leave them to be manoeuvred [out] by the Spaniards under Mina. The plunder and the effects of Captain Turing and Carew were sold[30]. I sat this morning on a Court Martial and tried twelve prisoners, eleven found guilty and sentenced to corporal punishment.

Tafalla, is an ancient town, but very magnificent, the houses built uniformly and high, most five stories, it contains many churches and

---

[28] In the original French version, he claims that Wodehouse was himself too exhausted, not his horse.

[29] Incorrectly shown as 18th in the French version.

[30] The equipment and supplies of officers who were killed were traditionally sold off to clear outstanding debts and any excess transmitted to their family along with a few precious keepsakes.

the remains of a citadel, and wall with turrets, give it the most grand effect, the inhabitants appear rich, they had provided dinner for us, which we were prevented partaking off, and the staff and gentry were also included.

Olite, is likewise a very ancient place, with some remains of a wall, it contained the finest ruin I ever beheld of a castle and a church, together. The French burnt down the latter a few years back, the streets are well paved, the market a very good one, contained plenty of fruit. The weather is very changeable; raining one hour from the next, last night there was a most dreadful thunderstorm, which killed several people. We are encamped in a grove of olives, the first I have seen since I left Portugal, the ground excessively damp and every appearance of a wet night, not very pleasant prospects. Those in front of the camp can see a large convent (order unknown), so large it looks like a village of its own.

# Chapter 6

# Sojourn at Olite

Having failed to corner Clausel, the Hussar Brigade was cantoned around Olite to the south of Pamplona, where the men could rest and the horses could graze happily to regain their best condition. This long-enforced rest period was quite welcome, as the contending armies now faced each other along the Pyrenees mountains, which was no country for cavalry. The young cavalrymen's thoughts began to think of other things, but chasing the local ladies was soon to become a very dangerous game.

Olite, Wednesday 30 June.
This morning we marched back to this town, and very much pleased am I that we are quartered in a town that can maintain us, I believe we halt here a few days. I am very unwell, feel worse than ever I did, all my limbs pain me, and am sure that if I was obliged to march tomorrow and the next day, it would kill me.

No one can have an adequate idea, of what the Moors once were, until they have seen the remains of them in the Kingdom. They were formally a war-like, rich and luxurious people; they are now a nation of gypsies and robbers, burnt up in the sands of Africa. They still remember this country in their daily prayers and supplicate Moor homes, to restore them to the garden of the world. They remind me of that beautiful passage in our scripture, 'By the waters of Babylon, they sat down and wept, when they remembered thee, O Sion.'[1] My friend Miss Newland's brother is here with our brigade, he is a

---

[1]   A slightly corrupt version of Psalm 137.

135

lieutenant in the artillery[2]; I enquired after them today, and was happy to hear all was well, when he last heard from Chichester. Kennedy and Dolbel dined with me today, I had asked Kennedy first and was compelled to ask Dolbel, as he messed with him, which I did not know at first.

Olite, Thursday 1 July.
We had a parade this morning, for the inspection of horses, they are in a very bad state, and only rest will bring them about. I could not get my old quarters in the town, the 15th having it, but I have a very good billet, excellent bed and accommodation, and my host, a civil and obliging old gentleman, who gave me yesterday, my leather bucket full of excellent wine.

Poor Captain Carew's baggage was sold yesterday, it was truly ridiculous to see the prices given for the eatables, two bottles of sauce were sold for 35s/-, cheese of about 7lbs weight sold for 73s/6d[3], two tongues for 27s/-. The principle purchasers were Lord Worcester, General Hill, and Mr Fitzclarence[4], and Somerset[5]. Lord W[orcester] gave 34s/- for a pair of brass spurs. I bought a bridle, which cost me £4, a monstrous price, and cloth for a pair of overalls at £2/14s/0d, which all thought was not sufficient for that purpose, but the tailor of the regiment says it's full enough. Lord Worcester is coming into the 18th Hussars[6], so it is reported he will get a troop, and then exchange with Russell who will get one of the vacant troops.

It seems that Vitoria was to cast a long shadow over the regiment. Wellington was now demanding a full investigation of Mr Dolbel's actions there and calling for his court martial as an example. George does not mention it, but Major Hughes records that Russel was brought to a court martial this day for striking the major, when he interfered as Russel was attacking a woman.

---

[2]   1st Lieutenant Robert Newland of E Troop Royal Horse Artillery was the same Newland who was second in command the Alexander Mercer's G Troop at Waterloo. It is painfully clear that Mercer and Newland did not get on!
[3]   Incorrectly shown as 63/6 in the French version.
[4]   Captain George FitzClarence 10th Hussars (later Earl of Munster) who was then serving with headquarters as Deputy Assistant Adjutant General. He was an illegitimate son of the Duke of Clarence, who later became George IV.
[5]   Major General Lord Robert Edward Somerset who commanded a cavalry brigade. Worcester was just about to become one of his aides de camp.
[6]   This transfer did not happen.

Olite, Friday 2 July.

I had to attend a brigade Court Martial part of this day, but was not called. I wrote a very long letter to my friend Amelia, in answer to hers of the 24th April. I suppose it will find her at Camberwell, she left Mrs. Satis[7], this midsummer for good.

I trust the instructions she has received from that lady may carry her through the world, respected and adored by all who know her.

A subject, that has made a great noise here, amongst the brigade, will cause, *we believe, those involved into forming a Court Martial*[8]. I have brought to notice previously in this journal, the day of the victory of Vitoria, after the 18th and 10th Hussars had charged the enemy through the town, Major Hughes directed Mr Dolbel to take charge of twenty men who were placed sentries over the carriages and baggage of the nobility and French officers, *to protect them from the inhabitants and marauders from the army*. He immediately, so says the report, commenced plundering.

Many of the prisoners and persons of rank belonging to the enemy, dined with Lord Wellington. At dinner in course of conversation, Madam Guize says that if it had not been for a private hussar, an officer of hussars would have plundered her of everything. That after she had delivered up her husband's sword to him and likewise a beautiful double barrelled gun; he took by force off her finger a ring. Lord Wellington was in a great rage and swore he would sacrifice him immediately, *and make him an example to the army*. He sent for Colonel Grant the next morning, and reported it to him, at the same time, desired him to make immediate enquiry, so that he could bring Mr Dolbel, whose name he had learnt to a Court Martial. Mr Dolbel wrote a justification to Lord Wellington, and to the officers of the brigade, and utterly denies the ring business, but owns that he took the gun and sword; here the matter stands at present.

Soon news arrived that the 18th would be moved out of the Hussar Brigade. Their pairing with the hugely experienced and professional soldiers of the 1st King's German Legion Hussars was almost certainly an attempt by Wellington to force the regiment to improve. In his leisure time, George showed a fascination for visiting the local nuns, a favourite distraction it would seem with many of these young officers.

---

[7]  This further confirms Amelia's youthfulness, as she had only now completed her education.
[8]  In the French text, this translates as a Council of War, but clearly means to indicate that the officer would be court-martialled.

Olite, Saturday 3 July.

Gave evidence against a man, at the brigade Court Martial this morning; received four newspapers, 24th May to 2nd June, but no letter. I sent the letter off, I wrote to Amelia, likewise wrote one to Mr Vanderboorst. The Brigade of Hussars, being too strong against the others, will be reorganised: there will be four brigades formed in the future.

I am very happy to understand the Hussar Brigade will be broken up immediately by Lord Wellington, who is not at all pleased with Colonel Grant's manoeuvrings at the Battle of Vitoria, they all allow this officer, to be possessed of courage and resolution, but all say he wants judgement. The 10th and 15th are to be brigaded together and Lord Edward[9] Somerset will command it. The 18th will be brigaded with the 1st German Hussars, under General Bock[10]. The whole of the cavalry brigades will be likewise broken up and formed as follows. 12/13th Light Dragoons and 14/16th Light Dragoons, brigaded together. The 18th will leave this city early to join the 1st Hussars, German Legion, under General Alten[11].

Lord Worcester gave a party a few nights back, to the inhabitants of the town, the heavies gave a Ball tonight at Tafalla, to the inhabitants and they invited all the officers of the brigade, but I believe that nobody will go.

I proposed this morning to our Brigade Major for the officers to give a ball for the ladies of Olite. There is very bad news arrived from General Murray[12], who it is reported embarked the troops under his command at Alicante, in the greatest confusion, leaving his heavy battering [train] and baggage in the hands of the French, under Suchet. We shall move forward immediately, we have more to do than we imagined last week. Lord Wellington intends leaving Pamplona to be besieged by the Spaniards, God knows how they will succeed.

The Spaniards have a curious method of threshing their wheat, a piece of wood about one yard in length and about one [foot] in breadth, is drawn by three mules or horses over it upon a level piece

---

9   The text mistakenly says Fitzroy Somerset, who was Wellington's Military Secretary.
10  Major General Baron Eberhardt Otto George von Bock commanded the KGL Heavy Dragoon Brigade, he died in a shipwreck in 1814.
11  Major General Victor von Alten was to command the brigade.
12  General Sir John Murray had landed a force on the East coast of Spain as a diversion and placed Tarragona under siege. However, at the mere rumour of the approach of a force under Marshal Suchet, he abandoned his siege guns and re-embarked his troops. He was later court-martialled but cleared.

of ground, generally kept for that purpose. In the wood are a number of nails and sharp stones which have been driven in, which pulls the straw to pieces and at the same time completely, threshes wheat from it. It is afterwards sifted and put into bags; the straw is kept for the forage of animals and to make beds etc., all their beds are stuffed with straw, no feather beds in this country.

Opposite to my quarters is a convent and in it are twenty-two nuns. I was talking to several last evening through a thin partition of wood. This morning I was allowed to see them through a grating, there were several young women amongst them, but none handsome, one had been in the convent for thirty-two years, was the most engaging of the whole. She entered it very young, and her countenance bespeaks she was once beautiful. I asked them if they would like to live in a casa, instead of the convent, which was answered immediately by the Lady Abbess in the negative. They appeared particularly happy in the sight of an Englishman, and though I could not talk much to them, I made them comprehend that I was a hussar, and that in England we are the pride of the fair sex, which they were not at all astonished at. They said they liked us better than those they had seen from their windows in red coats.

I am now quite recovered from the fatigue of the march, and am ready to begin again tomorrow morning. What a silly fellow Smith is, he will not be friends with me, though I speak to him every time we meet, which he returns in a very distant way. Let him sulk as long as he pleases, I have nothing to reproach myself of, with regard to this coolness. This country is certainly a paradise to England, in some respects, what a pity it is not inhabited by English! I am just returned from an evening walk round the public gardens, from all sides are wafted the perfumes of the roses, the orange and the narcissus, oh delicious, oh celestial evenings, when all the senses revel in the delights, and the benign goddess sees none but happy mortals serenade her. The natives are very fond of evening walks, they are constantly out.

Olite, Sunday 4 July.
I went this morning to the convent, and heard my friendly nuns sing. I was much gratified; they are hid from your sight, similar to the Magdalene's in Blackfriars Road[13]. Their chapel is very

---

[13] Magdalene Hospital for Penitent Prostitutes moved from Streatham to Blackfriars Road in 1772, when it was renamed simply Magdalene Hospital.

handsome, it contains a delightful organ. After the service was over, I asked to see them, when the Lady Abbess told me, they were going to confession; what in the name of wonders, have they to confess? What very much surprises me to see at this season of the year, the mountains covered with snow.

It is reported, Lord Worcester is coming into the 18th Hussars, and that he will procure a company in the infantry, and exchange with Russell for his troop. My horses are again in excellent condition, it is surprising how much they have improved in a few days. I don't care how soon we move now; I am almost tired of this place, though I am so well put up. If I procure leave of absence, and return to England at Christmas, how glad I shall be. I begin to feel a need to see my native country again; one year is quite long enough to be away from home and friends, if I don't get leave, dammed if I don't resign.

On picquet last night, a confounded cold night; Lieutenant Conolly, gave a ball this evening at his quarters, it was attended by all the respectable and the rag tag and bobtail of the town. Waltzing was on the go nearly all night; Doctor Quincey dines with me.

Olite, Monday 5 July.
What a despicable fellow is our Captain Burke, there is not a grain of gentleman in him, and he is the laughing stock of the brigade. Sergeant Taylor was brought to a Court Martial this morning, mainly to annoy me, and because he thinks I have got too popular in the regiment. He yesterday took away from me my second batman, and offered me the choice of two of the most notorious rascals in the regiment, in his place, but I will have nothing to do with either. Went out this morning at 6 o'clock with the foraging party of the regiment, it was a delightful morning, what a shame it is to lie in bed after that hour. I think I shall get up daily to take a ride at this hour, whilst the regiment halts. Provisions are very cheap in this town, I have just bought a quarter of mutton for a dollar; everything but butter is to be got.

It was not the French who destroyed the castle and church, now a beautiful ruin, but Mina, the French occupying them at the time, he likewise drove the enemy out of Tafalla, and destroyed the castle there. There are four gates to enter this town, Olite, and it is impossible to enter it, but through them, we have sentries at them every night at 10 o'clock, and no-one is allowed to pass either way, without the watchword. Lord Edward Somerset inspects the 3rd

[KGL] Hussar Regiment[14] in a field near this town, in watering order. I understand General Sir Stapleton Cotton[15] will review us in marching order on Wednesday.

I am much pleased this afternoon for Sergeant Taylor, who was acquitted of the charges brought against him, and Major Hughes told Captain Burke to send me the second batman he took from me yesterday. Smith informed me this morning that he received a letter from Mrs Smith by the last packet, that she has seen the Perkins's that they were all well and desired to be remembered to me. They often want rain in this country, to supply the defect of which, I observe in the gardens, an invention not un-useful, there is a well in the middle of the garden, and over that a wheel with many pitchers or buckets, one under another, which with the wheel being turned by an ox, the pitchers scoop up the water on one side, and throw it out on the other side into a trough, that by little channels, conveys it as the gardener directs into every part of the garden. By this means, their flowers and salads are continually refreshed and preserved from the otherwise over parching beams of the sun. Bolton, Kennedy and Dr. Pulsford dined with me.

News now arrived that Colonel Grant was to be superseded in command of the brigade.

Olite, Tuesday 6 July.
Colonel Grant who has had the finest command in the world, the Hussar Brigade, is superseded in the command by Lord Edward Somerset. Grant went to Lord Wellington to remonstrate with him, and Lord Wellington gave him leave to go back to England immediately, which Grant accepted, all his horses and finery are to be disposed of this day, and he sets off for Santander[16] tomorrow. God be thanked we have got rid of the 'Black Giant', but I regret that the 'Red Dwarf' stays with the brigade. A Spanish author gives the following account of the languages in Spain; the Spanish speak and use the same language which is called the Castilian tongue, formed by the union of many languages, particularly the Latin. The affinity with it is so great that one can jointly with the same words, and the same construction, both in verse and prose, speak Latin and

---

[14] Incorrectly shown as Brigade of three regiments in the French version.
[15] Lieutenant General Sir Stapleton Cotton was in overall command of the cavalry.
[16] Incorrectly shown as Bilbao in the French version.

Castilian. The Valencians and the Catalans speak a language of their own, which resembles the Languedocian tongue in France, from whence that nation and people drew their origin. The Biscayan's, have alone until now preserved their rude inelegant and barbarous language, it is very different from the others, and the most ancient of Spain, when it anciently was the only language of the whole country. It is said that that all Spain spoke the Biscayan language before the Romans had entered those provinces, and enforced their language. The Biscayans were a rude, ferocious, and savage people, and the mountains, where they live being inaccessible, it never entirely acquired the yoke of a foreign empire, nor is it improbable that with their ancient liberty, they have preserved the ancient and common tongue of Spain.

I have ascertained that my desk has been robbed of four doubloons within the last few days. I valued my servants for their honesty, don't know whether to blame them or not, however I am much to blame myself for leaving the key of my desk about, and thereby leaving a temptation too great for many in their situations. I hope to God, John Ipper has had no concern in it, for I really respect him and think he is the most faithful servant in the world.

Olite, Wednesday 7 July.
Sir Stapleton Cotton, reviewed the 18th Hussars this morning, the men turned out remarkably clean and neat, and upon the whole, very strong. After inspecting the line, we marched past by half squadrons, and filed past, which finished the review. I have not yet heard what his sentiments are in respect of the regiment. The regiment deserves the praise it has received. He was dressed in a most superb uniform, as a general of hussars, red and gold; likewise his staff were dressed as hussars.

Forage has become so very scarce, owing to the number of cavalry in the neighbourhood, that I believe we must move from this town in a day or two if we cannot procure it. Cornet Curtis, who was sent to a village near Pamplona for stragglers, brought us the intelligence, of the commencement of the siege, he heard the firing, now it has begun, we shall speedily hear of its fall. Lord Wellington and Marshal Beresford are now reconnoitring the passes over the Pyrenees, on his return it is reported, we shall proceed towards Zaragoza.

A grave Spanish writer whose historical work I have been labouring over, says, Tubal son of Japheth, the [third] son of Noah was the first man who came into Spain, that he peopled divers places, possessed and governed Spain, with just and mild laws. Captain Burke got a diamond cross in the plunder he took at Vitoria, this he never gave up, but Major Hughes ordered him to deliver it, to the paymaster. Burke says he sent it as a present to General Charles Stewart, but the officers insist on having it, and therefore, will write to the general for it, some say it is worth two or three thousand pounds, if so, it ought to be divided amongst the regiment. This is very serious for Burke, a sergeant said that he took this object, and threatened to put him in jail if he ever said a word, which did not prevent the sergeant from reporting him to Hughes.

The Spaniards have a great attachment to the stork, in every village, there are some; they build nests on the towers of churches and convents, and are never disturbed by the natives. An English soldier shot one last year in some part of the country, but he lost his life through it; the people murdered him. They soar in the air, like a swallow in fine weather; they are a novel sight to an Englishman. The first I saw flying, I took for wild geese.

Lieutenant Rowlls intends sending in his resignation on account of ill health, this will be a step for me. I hope to get home in December, by hook or by crook. On calculating the distance of our march, since the regiment left Lisbon, I find it as follows, marched fifty-six days, two hundred and twenty-two leagues; in English miles, about nine hundred.

I went this evening to Lord Worcester's Ball; it would beggar all attempts at description. There were all the reputable women, and all of another description in the town present; the same was beyond anything, the surprise of many finding themselves in such company, who left the room in disdain, caused laughter to many of the bucks, who had brought the latter company. Lord Worcester must feel hurt at their conduct, for of course there will be no more balls, fandangos were the rage, the women danced them, and many dressed and behaved in a very immodest manner. I left rather early, not as pleased with the evening's diversion.

The Spanish lady wears her hair platted and tied with a ribbon, very close to the head, it then hangs down her back, but in general in the balls and parties they bring their hair across their left shoulder, and it hangs across their breast, which looks very pretty; so they appeared last night.

I have seen a little girl of six or seven years old, whose hair was at least twenty inches long. I have many times observed mothers, tying their infant's hair, and it is common to see children of a year old with its hair in a ribbon. The general dress is black stuff and muslin, it being wartimes, I believe is the cause of all wearing of that colour. The Spanish women on the whole are very much like the English; I cannot say the same of the males to my countrymen; a few are deserving of that character only.

Olite, Thursday 8 July.
I received four newspapers from England, June 2nd to 11th[17], thanks to my friend Mrs Perkins and Amelia, who I trust are in health. Wrote a letter to my friend, Captain Wheeler; informing him of the glorious victory, and other news from the army. A most dreadful thunder storm this afternoon, I am hardly recovered from the horror it occasioned in my breast, I have experienced several storms in this country, but none as dreadful as the one today. The natives appeared not the least moved or alarmed, on the contrary, my landlord kept working on digging, to sing and talking to his wife and child, while I expected every moment the house would be knocked down upon us.

Nothing but dinner parties now; I dined yesterday, with Captain Bolton: I have a small party again today. Lieutenant Berkeley and Wombwell[18] of the 10th Hussars, and Kennedy, Hesse, and Dolbel were at my quarters, smoking cigars till near 10 o'clock this evening. I think Wombwell to be the most gentlemen like man in the 10th Hussars.

The regimental band were meant to perform that night, but had found other distractions!

Olite, Friday 9 July.
The 10th and 15th Hussars were reviewed this morning, by Sir Stapleton Cotton, on a field between this town and Tafalla; they went through the manoeuvres of a regular field day. Rowlls is still very unwell, and sighs after breathing; and begins to think nothing but his native air will bring him about, he has very much fell away and looks worse than, perhaps than I think he is.

---

[17] Incorrectly shown as 4th in the French version.
[18] Lieutenant the Honourable Augustus Fitzharding Berkeley and Lieutenant George Wombwell 10th Hussars.

It is with extreme sorrow I have to notice a most daring outrage, and murder, committed near the south gate, last night on a private of the 15th Hussars, he was found with his brains knocked out, and his mouth stuffed full of rags, which I presume were put in to stifle his voice[19]. A few days back, two men of the town were stabbed, but by their own townsmen. These were the occasion of jealousy. One died after a few hours afterwards, but no enquiry was made after the murderer. A very laughable affair on the evening of Lord Worcester's Ball, he had engaged our band to play, but at the appointed time, they never came; a non-commissioned officer was sent in search of them and found the whole in a room dancing, completely naked, except having their pelisse's slung across their shoulders. I understand there were some women present, but have not heard whether they were stripped or not.

The general opinion now is, that Lord Wellington, will take his army into France, if so it will be the finest movement in the world, for the cause of the Germans, Russians and allies. Lord Wellington's headquarters, I understand, was in a village in France, the day before yesterday. The inhabitants have fled from all the villages near the Pyrenees. Suchet after frightening General Murray out of the country, immediately marched over the Pyrenees into France leaving garrisons in all the strongholds, so did General Clausel, likewise with his army, this is only the report of the day, but I think it is probable.

A number of shocking attacks now occurred, George actually discovered one of the victims on his travels.

Olite, Saturday 10 July.
I went out this morning after the foragers, but missing my way, got some distance on the left of them, got lost several miles away from them. I was about to return, when I heard a cry of distress at a distance; after looking about some time, I saw a poor fellow on the top of a hill, holding up his hands and begging for help. I likewise saw another running away, I rode up the hill and found him nearly dead, having been stabbed in the back part of his head and neck, it bled profusely, and I assisted him on to his mule, and brought him to this town. The villain was entirely out of sight, by the time I got to the man, I thought it more essential to try and preserve this man's life, than to leave him to perish, for want of assistance, whilst I

---

[19] This was Private Wilks of the 15th Hussars, he is identified by Captain Joseph Thackwell.

should have been making a search, after the assassin. He is a Portuguese commissary of the 10th Hussars, his assassin fled, he is not found. Doctor Quincey dressed him, and I believe the wound will not prove mortal.

Last night the unfortunate man of the 15th Hussars, who was found murdered that morning, was buried in a church yard near the town. The troop he belonged to, attended the funeral, so did most of the officers of the brigade; so did crowds of the inhabitants, one of them a respected character of the town, remarked to me, that he thought it not at all unlikely, that his murderer was present, the priests ought to give him up to public justice; they knew him before this.

All I am afraid of is that the Hussars Brigade, will upon quitting the town, leave some dreadful moments of their revenge, for their murdered comrade. This unfortunate man was seen in the company of a woman, walking outside of the town, the evening before he was discovered murdered, it is therefore likely, he was murdered in a fit of jealousy.

This neighbourhood abounds with vineyards, the vine is differently planted in Spain, to what it is in Portugal, here the vines grow bushy like a current tree, and are planted in regular rows; in Portugal, they are allowed to grow higher, and are, therefore, obliged to be propped up with canes and rods. Wrote a letter to Miss Spooner at Worcester, and sent it off by this day's packet. Last night I bought a horse off the veterinary surgeon of the 10th Hussars[20], a black Andalusian. I gave him one hundred and twenty dollars; he would be worth about six hundred in England. He took him at Vitoria, he had belonged to a French general, who had received him as a present from Joseph Buonaparte, he is six years old, and I have named him Vitoria. A great number of guerrillas passed through this town today, on their way to France, now is their time to butcher the French, which I expect they will; [destroying] many poor families.

George had now rightly become wary of fraternising with the local ladies. With so much spare time on their hands some of the other officers were quarrelling.

Olite, Sunday 11 July.
I went out this morning at half past five, with the foragers of the regiment, we rode over a league before we found any, it was a

---

[20] Veterinary Surgeon Henry Sannerman.

delightful morning, and I entertained myself, in practising my Vitoria, in the nice parry exercise of a charger, and found him well broke.

The gardens are full of fruit; it is now ripe, except the grape, which is still green. I fancy the fruit better here than in England, it may only be a fancy. I received a billet doux, from a lady in the town, who signs her name Isabella Lucinda, inviting me to a party this evening, but finding from enquiry, none of the officers of the brigade have been asked, I have declined the honour, it may be instead of a party a 'tete-a- tete', the consequences of which may be, on my return to my heart, a knife in my side, no - no my 'Dulcineas'[21], no intriguing with any of you. I don't want to be murdered, I have seen what your creatures; assassins I ought to call them, will do. More murders, McNaughton[22], one of the bandsmen, was discovered in a field about a mile from this place, murdered, and a man of the artillery with him. Some men have been sent after them, so I shall see them when they return.

Captain Burke and Lieutenant Dolbel have a dispute of honour, which must be settled in some way, in a few days, I shall, therefore, forebear from saying more upon it now. I saw this morning, an innumerable quantity of vultures, from whence the soldiers inferred there must speedily be another engagement.

Don Julian or Hulian, as the Spaniards call him, is the Captain General of all the guerrillas, he is the terror of the French, and a refugee of his own country, he had his father and sister murdered by the French, and has like Hannibal, sworn eternal hatred to them, whether at peace or war. After being expelled from the patrimony of his ancestors, it was not long before he, in some measure avenged their deaths. Returning with his guerrillas, from the mountains, he found a French colonel, who had been a great aggressor in that part of the country, and upbraiding him, for his numerous cruelties; told him, that he was Don Julian, who had the satisfaction of putting a stop to his villainies, and sending him to another tribunal to account for them. This was in the same house in which his father had been murdered.

Marshal Beresford, and my friend General Hamilton, deserve all that can possibly be said in their praise, to have formed such troops as the Portuguese, from such uninspiring material. I waited to hear

---

[21] Temptress.
[22] George spells it McNorton but it was in fact Private Bartholomew McNaughton.

other officer's opinions of them, before I returned to give mine, in my idle companion [the journal], but find all agree with me, that they are second to the English against the world. They fought most bravely at Vitoria, and are confident Lord Wellington's despatches will inform the world as such. I have just learned another man of the 15th Hussars has been found murdered, in a wood between here and Tafalla; this is the second man the 15th have lost.

Olite, Monday 12 July.
This life of idleness, I certainly dislike very much, if we were but on the move, it would be more pleasant, but to be halted so long in such a murderous place as this, is very annoying. A few English books would make our situation better, as Captain Cochrane[23] was saying; I am known in this town by the inhabitants, by the name, Don Gorges, as the name Woodberry, they cannot pronounce. My fair Portuguese Hannah could never pronounce it likewise.

This morning I received newspapers, June 11th to 14th, but no letters, which rather surprises me. I have just returned from Major Hughes, where the officers of the regiment had assembled, by order, to investigate the dispute between Captain Burke and Mr Dolbel; when after deliberately and maturely weighing the whole affair, came to the unanimous resolution, that they ought to be requested to resign immediately. But Major Hughes recommended a milder course, and proposed that they should be reprimanded in the most strongest manner, before the officers of the regiment, which was accordingly done, by both being instantly called into the meeting. Major Hughes told them of the sentiments of the officers, and though want of courage is not proved against either, yet the language made use of by both, was such, which ought to have gentlemen to have had immediate recourse to arms and that death alone ought to have settled it between them, and that it ought never to have been referred to him. However, as commanding officer, he now strictly forbids them proceeding to any but conciliatory arrangements; they immediately begged each other's pardon. Their dispute began a few days ago: Burke told Dolbel he was the most quarrelsome fellow in the regiment, and if he said anything to him, he would cut him down; this was in front of the squadron. Dolbel, told Burke in answer, to his remarks of being the most quarrelsome, that he Burke was a dammed liar. These proud men spoke first of

---

[23] Captain the Honourable William Erskine Cochrane, 15th Hussars.

fight, but they soon subsided, and they wished that the affair was forgotten when the officer corps seized on it.

I saw a Spaniard this evening put one of his hands to the wheel of a cart, and a very heavy one apparently, and turned it over, it astonished me I must own, I requested him to put it upright, which he likewise did using one arm.[24] Some of our men being present, I requested they try and do it, which they did without effect. Orders given out this evening, that no man leaves his quarters without his side arms.

Olite, Tuesday 13 July.

McNaughton who was found murdered in a wood near here, was buried on the spot, this poor man was an excellent player on the clarinet, this is the first man of our band we have lost, I don't expect a replacement will return, they ought never to have come out, it was one of the first bands in England, and considering the expense each officer was at in supporting them, and bringing the band to the perfection it achieved, I cannot think General Stewart was justified in ordering them out with the regiments.

I have been very unwell the last few days, and feel still worse. Captain Kennedy who is quartered next door to me, is very ill, and I have kept to his room most of yesterday and today – bowel complaints. There is assuredly not a more heavenly and lovely kingdom in the world than this Spain, if the industry and taste of the inhabitants bore any proportion to the bounties of nature. I was dreaming all night of my friends, Mrs Perkins, Amelia and Miss Moseley; I thought I saw Amelia with her arms around the neck of a man, who they all told me was her husband, I was much affected and instantly awoke.

I hope they are well for I have been continually dreaming of them lately, if I recollect right, Mrs Perkins talked about going to Bath this summer if she has not altered her mind, they will leave town about this time. It came out during the investigation into the dispute between Mr Dolbel and Captain Burke, that Captain Kennedy, Lieutenant Hesse and Dr Pulsford, had each refused to be his second or friend in the matter, now those very men have always pretended the greatest of friendship for him, clung to him like leeches, but Dolbel had a large stock of hams, tongues, and he had likewise a private servant, who always cooked good dinners. Of course those

---

[24] Strangely, he repeats this scene on 6 January 1814.

intimate friends, partly lived with him, they appeared inseparable, but when the man wanted their assistance and advice, they had not known him long enough. He was nearly a stranger to them, they therefore declined the honour. The more I see of the world, the more ingratitude I discover in it.

I rode out this afternoon to the mountains, on the left of this town. I had dined, and it being cooler than usual, I was tempted to take the longer ride. In the mountains I found a very pretty cottage, and rode to it, and was met at the door by an old man and his son and daughter, they offered me some wine, which I partook of, and stayed with them near an hour. During which time, the old man recounted, what he had done to distress the enemy of his country, part of his story only, could I understand. On my going away, he took me to a cave near the side of the road I had come along, and there discovered five or seven skeletons of French men, whom he and his son had murdered; many thousand have suffered in that way, in this country victims of the ambition of Napoleon.

The women of Spain are handsome, sprightly, and pleasing. To their natural charms, they know how to add the attractions of dress, and of graceful motions. They are uniformly kind and affable in their manners, and an Englishman can find very few faults in their domestic conduct, and those are often perceived in his own countries women. It has been just ascertained that near ten thousand men of the enemy are at Sanguesa, Navarre, which is about six leagues from this town: where they have come from, I cannot learn, but shall hear more of them tomorrow.

Olite, Wednesday 14 July.
This morning we were out at 5 o'clock, and after punishing several men behind the convent of nuns, a regular change of quarters took place; three troops of the 15th Hussars, having moved from the town to Pedclian [Pitillas?], a village just by. Three of our troops took posession of their old quarters. The reason for this change was on the orders of the inhabitants who wanted the granaries, where our horses were stabled. Lord Edward Somerset did not like to move the 18th, because we were not in his brigade[25].

This day last year, the Prince Regent reviewed us on Hounslow Heath, and gave the regiment great credit for its appearance that

---

[25] Although no longer officially in the same brigade, they did not actually join their new brigade for two months.

day. Good God, how the regiment has fallen off since then, now half the officers are implicated, so I was informed last night, in an unfortunate affair respecting the plunder and remaining in the town of Vitoria, and will be obliged to exchange, resign, or perhaps [before] either can be done, they may be cashiered. Their names are Major Hughes, Captain Bolton, and Burke, Lieutenant Conolly and Dolbel, Adjutant Waldie; these are the men, Lord Wellington has on his blacklist. The whole may not suffer, but I think it likely the whole may leave. That brute of a fellow Dolbel, has charges against Bolton and Burke, which would supersede them, no one yet knows how he will act. The regiment it is plainly to be seen has gone to the devil; God send, I was out of it, but I must now stop and see the end of it. I feel more than happy when I think of that day, and of my not going into town, during the plundering. I dined with Kennedy yesterday, he poor fellow is very unwell, fearful his name may be but in question with the above; I think [this] is the occasion of his illness, reports in the regiment, intimate that he got a [purse?], Burke gave up the diamond cross, which is supposed to be worth about a thousand pounds[26]. One of the men gave me a present today, of a piece of French calico, which I will get made into shirts and sheets, though it is too fine for either, yet it is the only way I can smuggle it home. Russell, Waldie, and Dolbel came to my quarters this evening, and thereby got some brandy and water.

Olite, Thursday 15 July.
Captain Carew's old troop, presented me yesterday with a most beautiful poodle dog that they took at Vitoria, for my conduct with them at that glorious battle. It was a gift from the whole troop, who had kept the dog amongst them, since the victory.

We get everything we want here except butter, and there is none of that. Sugar is the dearest commodity, being 3 to 4 shillings a pound. I have got plenty yet in my hamper. The loaf, Miss Moseley bought for me at Portsmouth, is yet in the stock! Captain Kennedy is dangerously ill, Smith in high spirits, because he is the next for a troop, and thinks Kennedy may die.

Olite, Friday 16 July.
It was true, that the French were at Sanguesa, but only a foraging party. There are, however, about eleven thousand under Clausel at

---

[26] Incorrectly shown as five hundred in the French version.

Verdu, which from the map, I suppose is better than ten leagues from this place, a party of the heavies have been sent to Sanguesa, to remain there and watch their motions. I cannot learn where Lord Wellington is, or exactly where this French force came from, however, after a few days we will know, how they are to be disposed of. Employed myself making a foraging cap, having obtained a piece of embroidered cloth, from part of a coat front, it is a very dashing one, and much admired amongst all the officers.

Lieutenant Smith gave me a flute at Luz, I offered to buy it from him, but said I might have it for nothing, but today he sent Dr Pulsford for the flute; something strikes me [that] this doctor is a dangerous fellow and the principal cause of Pulsford and me being at variance. Time will discover, no more dinners shall the 'Pill' get out of me, till I am satisfied. I cannot help thinking what an immense prize the enemy will get, if they take the baggage of the Hussar and Heavy Brigade, every day I hear of some having rich prizes, which till now they have kept secret. Lieutenant Russell has a quantity of French rich lace, which would be a very handsome present to a female. I offered him fifteen pounds for it, but he will not part with it. They are all anxious to get my coat, they wish me to give it up, that it might be sold and the proceeds divided; no - no, this I will never do. Smith who was with the baggage got very little, he is the principal one who insisted I should give it up to the regiment, but Major Hughes said 'It is the thing which annoys him very much'. I think we can never be friends again, however, I can never think of making him a confidential friend, for he is not deserving of it. I went this afternoon into the convent, and saw the nuns; they gave me a cup of chocolate, and some sweet cakes.

I would give the world to be able to speak the Spanish language, but I am sure I never shall. They informed me that about two years back, a nun escaped with a French officer, but he was obliged after a very short time to give her up to the convent, where she was consecrated, directly to the punishment of immuring[27]. She survived about a fortnight afterwards. What greater punishment can there be on earth, than to be confined between four narrow walls, only open at the top, and thence to be half supported with bread and water, till the offender gradually starves to death, but after all this dreadful account, I have the vanity to think the youngest nun aged about

---

[27] Confinement in a small enclosed space.

twenty-five, would leave the convent and follow the fate of the 18th Hussars, in defiance to her vows.

We get every kind of fruit, of the highest perfection and very cheap, except currants and gooseberries, I have seen none in the country. The grape is nearly ripe; they look very tempting now, but are not yet eatable.

Olite, Saturday 17 July.

Poor Foster is no more, he died a few days back at Vitoria[28], the morning after his leg was amputated. A braver fellow never existed, from the moment he joined the regiment, he seemed only to exist for the profession, which he had chosen. On his arrival in Lisbon, high in spirits, with all the enterprising hope of youth, with all the enthusiasm of his character, bent on honour and military fame. He eagerly grasped at every occasion which presented itself of increasing his knowledge in military art, he was never idle, he was equally beloved by officers and soldiers, such a loss cannot be too highly estimated or too deeply regretted, and he has concluded a career not less brilliant to himself than destructive to the hopes of his family.

There is a large convent of the Dominican order in this town, I have seen many very splendid convents of this order in Portugal, and Spain, they have all, over the gates, the figure of a man in stone, and near it a dog, with a lighted torch in his mouth. The image I rightly enough took for the saint, but on enquiring of one of their order, the meaning of the figures near it he gave me the following relation. 'When the mother of St. Domingo was with the child of the future saint, she had a dream which very much afflicted her. She dreamt that she heard a dog bark in her belly, and enquiring at the oracle what is not said. The meaning of her dream, she was told that the child should bark out the Gospel, which should thence shine out like a lighted torch, and this is the reason, that wherever you see the image of this saint, a dog and a lighted torch is within the group'.

It is likewise a noted order, having had more Popes and Cardinals of the order, than of any, if not of all the others. The whole care and conduct of the Inquisition, was entrusted to them, thank God that the Inquisition, is now abolished. I am most cursedly annoyed, I went as usual to see my nuns, when the old 'Hag of an Abbess' told

---

[28] He died of wounds received at Vitoria on 8 July.

me, she had orders from the Alcalde[29] to deny me admittance, and requested I would go there no more. Hang me, if I am not inclined to annoy the old lass for this; I will too, but as the regiment will go in a few days, it shall be the morning we move.

Olite, Sunday 18 July.
I wrote a long letter to my 'Aunt Moseley'. A part of Don Julian's corps of lancers came into the town today. They are part of a retreating army under Mina, whom the French defeated a few days back at Zaragoza, and took five hundred prisoners, most of the army I understand is near to Caparrosa; the enemy having followed them to Tudela. Went to the convent chapel and heard the nuns sing, they still refuse me admittance, I wonder what can be the reasoning of them, it must be those rascally friars.

Olite, Monday 19 July.
The late Cornet Foster's baggage has just come in, the servants inform us news not at all pleasant to hear, that his master died through neglect. A report circulated today that Mina is still at Zaragoza, and that he has had no engagement with the French.

A most laughable occurrence took place yesterday, at Smith's. He and Blackett had invited Captain Stuart and Lieutenant Seymour of the 10th Hussars[30], to dine with them, and had flattered themselves, in having provided a good dinner and every comfort for their guests, but alas, when the dinner was brought to the table, it was entirely spoiled, a pigeon pie was burnt to a cinder, a quarter of mutton in a like state. When Smith, Blackett and Stuart saw this, they began laughing, but Seymour did not like the joke, and after attempting to eat a little of the pie and pick the mutton bone without success, he got up and walked home; this has given Smith very great umbrage; fortunately, he is not a man to fight, otherwise we might fear the consequences of the case. Lieutenant Arnold of the Life Guards[31] is in General Orders to be put under arrest and detained in any town he may be found in, having left the regiment without leave. Suppose the Vitoria business frightened him; he is to be sent to headquarters as a prisoner[32]. The news of the victory at Vitoria was announced in

---

[29] Mayor.
[30] Lieutenant Horace Seymour and Captain Simeon Stuart, 10th Hussars
[31] Lieutenant George Arnold, 2nd Life Guards, retired from the army in 1814.
[32] This refers to the General Order of 2 July 1813.

England on the 3rd inst., Lord Wellington is reported to have been made a Field Marshal[33].

Olite, Tuesday 20 July.
Captain Bolton, Deane and Kennedy, and Lieutenant Curtis dined with me yesterday, I gave them soup, two roast fowls, two rabbits boiled with onions, beef steak and onions, peas, potatoes and a rice pudding – not a bad set out. Captain Turing's portfolio was opened by Major Hughes, in the presence of Captain Deane, and Kennedy, a will was found, he therein leaves the whole of his property to his sister's son, a young boy. Cornet Foster's baggage was examined, and a will was found, which was opened, he gives a horse to Carew, and then another to the 'Blues'; all his mules and baggage etc., to his servant. I sent the letter by packet today to Miss Moseley, at Camberwell, Surrey. I am very tired of this idle life, I hope to God we shall move soon. I am informed there are near two hundred wounded officers in Vitoria, and that daily one or two die, more from neglect than anything else.

Captain Dundas of the 15th Hussars[34], met with a severe accident near this town a few days back, riding a French horse, it fell with him, and so much hurt him, that he was obliged to be carried home in a blanket, and has remained insensible ever since. There are nearly two thousand injured officers in Vitoria, both English, Portuguese, Spanish and French; several die every day due to a lack of care, as there are so few physicians.

Headquarters is now in France and the siege of San Sebastian commenced several days back, the whole of the army, with the exception of the cavalry and the division before Pamplona are there likewise, it is said that there has been some engagement with the enemy in France. Bayonne is the next place after San Sebastian surrenders, but I understand it is not fortified, therefore, will cause no delay to our movement up the country.

Olite, Wednesday 21 July.
Dreaming all night about Amelia, and my friends at Camberwell; cannot think what makes me dream of them so much. San Sebastian the town, Lord Wellington is besieging is a very clean town and neatly paved, which is no little rarity in Spain. It has a very good

---

[33] The Prince Regent did indeed promote him to Field Marshal for his victory at Vitoria.
[34] Captain Thomas Dundas, 15th Hussars.

wall about it, and pretty citadel, reports say very strong. The harbour is accounted the best in all of the Bay of Biscay. Short tours will not admit of great varieties, yet the country round is extremely pleasant, and abounds with plenty of wild fowl, but we have no guns. I take my daily ride in different directions from the town, but it is poor amusement to people under suspense. I long to move one way or the other, this idle life ill agrees with me, as with my comrades. Bought two Bayonne hams this morning, the finest I have seen in the country. Bayonne hams are to a proverb celebrated all over France. I rode to Tafalla this afternoon, to the annual fair, though unlike in some respects to the English fair, yet from the number of females, I began to fancy myself at Greenwich at Pentecost, upon the whole I had a deal of fun before I returned home. Dined out, Kennedy's with a party.

Olite, Thursday 22 July.
I dined this day with Lieutenant Smith and Blackett, and met there Captain Kennedy, and Hesse, they gave us an excellent dinner; Smith and self are getting better friends, though both rather shy of each other. Cornet Foster's effects sold by auction this morning, I bought one of his double-barrelled pistols, and a tongue, Smith bought the other pistol. Received newspapers from England, dated 14th to 21st July; the account of the skirmish at Morales is mentioned, in a private manner, no official account being available at that date.[35]

Olite, Friday 23 July.
Sir Stapleton Cotton, last night, ordered our band over to Taffalla to play at the Ball given there by the 5th Dragoons Guards with the nickname of 'the Green Horse'[36], in memory of the glorious victory of Salamanca, last year, when they distinguished themselves. From the number of cannonballs and shells I had noticed lying about the fields near the town, I concluded there had been a battle fought near. I found that it had; it was between the brave Palafox and Lefebvre[37]. The patriots were completely routed, they retreated to Tudela, from thence to Zaragoza, famous sure to eternity of letters that shall last so long, for the brave defence it made against the tyrant of the world.

[35] The French version mistakenly omits the 23 July completely, but even more confusingly, what is printed on 22 July in the French version is actually from the 23 July in the English version.
[36] It got this name from the facing colour of its uniform.
[37] Marshal Francois Lefebvre.

Palafox was brought through this town, wounded and a prisoner, on his way to France, but death released him from his sufferings[38], and robbed Spain of her bravest and beloved patriot, and the universe of a superior being. I rode to the hills on the right of the town, a very charming ride. Olite appears far more interesting than when reviewed from any other point, from which I had yet seen it, it appears closer and more compact, its church, houses, and walls, and towers are more happily blended, and from these heights, we look down upon it as if seated at the bottom of a valley, by the side of a noble stream, a branch of the Aragon. The whole surrounded with cultivated fields, good gardens and vineyards.

I got admittance again into the convent, I am informed I may come in as usual, I spoke rather free about it; the Alcalde, therefore, withdrew his order respecting the admittance of officers. Rowlls dined with me today, and in the evening, my friendly Spaniard brought a violin and played several waltzes.

Olite, Saturday 24 July.

During the inspection this morning, Mr Dolbel was playing tricks with his chestnut horse, when the animal became sulky, and in its turn played Mr Dolbel a few tricks; he threw him and kicked him on the forehead, which ended with Mr Dolbel being carried to his quarters, more dead than alive.

News arrived this morning from headquarters that the enemy under Soult[39], are coming down upon us, and intend to relieve Pampelona and San Sebastian. We are likewise informed that Lord William Bentinck[40] and the Alicante Army are advancing on the lines of Zaragoza, now, if this army joins us, we shall be able to defy any forces the French are able to bring against us. Breakfasted with Hesse, a public one; met Kennedy, Rowlls, Pulsford, Burke and Chambers. Captain Dundas, I am happy to hear is getting better, but the surgeons give it as their opinion that he will never be able to ride again, owing to the severe contusion of the brain[41].

About midday, Dean and myself, followed the course of the Aragon, till we found a sequestered [secluded] spot shaded with trees, where we bathed, the day being cloudy, I was astonished to

---

[38] General Jose de Palafox did not die but was taken into France as a prisoner, he lived until 1847.

[39] Marshal Jean-de-Dieu Soult, 1st Duke of Dalmatia.

[40] Lieutenant-General Lord William Henry Cavendish-Bentinck was envoy but also the commander of the troops in Sicily, he landed a force on the East Coast of Spain as a diversion.

[41] He did recover and served in the army throughout the remainder of the campaign.

find the water exceedingly cold at this hour. A traveller must not expect to find feather beds in this country, they will bring him clean straw or maize, or a mattress stuffed with chopped straw, and seems to think the latter a great luxury. The siege of Pamplona is carried on with 'Great Spirit', and I should think, soon will surrender. The enemy possessed themselves of the city by treachery, it was the first stronghold they had in this country; a party of the French having entered the town as friends, and while the Spaniards were getting their rations, they got into the castle, and took possession of it, and immediately had the town under their command, which they have kept ever since, this was affected on February the fifteenth, 1808[42]. Daniel Curtis is very unwell, I don't know who looks worse, him or Rowlls, I am sure this is an unhealthy place; dined with Kennedy, Hesse and Pulsford at Dolbel's.

Olite, Sunday 25 July.
Mr Duperier our new adjutant[43] arrived this morning, he was originally adjutant to the 10th Hussars, and was before that a private and rose through his extraordinary merit. I can only account for the wretched insubordinate state of the regiment, to the want of a good Adjutant; reports speak highly of Mr Duperier.

Last night Kennedy and I met two nice girls walking; we dismounted and walked with them for some time, and then came to their house, we were able to convince them that we would like to have more knowledge of the two women than we should and found we had got acquainted with two of the most respectable ladies in the town. Kennedy who is more brazen than me, walked into the house with them, of course I followed, and was introduced to Mrs Murphy, of Irish origin, who entertained us some time with wine and cake. On our departure we begged very hard to walk with the young ladies tomorrow, but the mother would not consent at all to it, however, I believe we shall have the pleasure of their company today, in spite of mother; we were not such new hands as to believe her, I shall give up the nun, no more my religious fair, shall you see me at your grate.

The Spanish think the work of Cervantes[44], the best and worst romance that ever was written, they say, that it must infallibly please

---

[42] This actually occurred on 16 February 1808, when French troops engineered a snowball fight just outside the gates, they then rushed the guard and secured Pamplona.
[43] Cornet & Adjutant Henry Duperier.
[44] Miguel de Cervantes Saavedra is famous of course for writing Don Quixote.

every man of taste and wit, yet it has had such a fatal effect on the spirit of the Spaniard, before the appearance in the world of that labour of Cervantes, it was next to an impossibility for any man to walk the streets with any delight, or without danger. There were seen so many Cavaleiero's prancing and cavorting before the windows of their mistresses, that a stranger would have imagined the whole nation to have been nothing less than a race of knight errant's, but after the world became a little acquainted with that notable history, a man that was once seen in that notable, was pointed at as a Don Quixote, and found himself the jest of high and low. To this and this only, they say they owe that dampness, that purity of spirit, which has run through all their councils for centuries past, so little agreeable to those nobler actions of their famous ancestors.

I had a dinner party today and flattered myself; the following gentlemen enjoyed themselves, Blackett, Smith, Kennedy, Quincey and Curtis; Smith sent Blackett to me this morning, and on his, Smith's arrival to dinner, we shook hands and are friends again, each saying how sorry he was, that any words had escaped him, that should have led to this disagreement.

News from the East Coast of Spain was very favourable, with the knowledge that Marshal Suchet was withdrawing into France. However, Marshal Soult had taken command of the remnants of the Army of Spain, he would prove a formidable opponent.

Olite, Monday 26 July.
Blackett received letters from Captain Milner[45], dated Valencia 15th inst., informing us that the enemy under Suchet was in full retreat, and the army under Sir William Bentinck, was on their way after them. On Suchet reading the letter from Joseph, informing him of the Battle of Vitoria, he exclaimed that Joseph had lost two armies, but he was determined he should not ruin his, and immediately ordered a retreat into France, and was in such a hurry as actively to forget some of his vedette's, he likewise got a letter from Clements dated headquarters Santesteban 18th inst., he informs us of the arrival of Soult at Bayonne, to take command of the French army, he is in a great rage at finding the army ruined, having been sent from Germany by Buonaparte to take the command. But the victory of

---

[45] Captain Charles Milner 18th Hussars was acting as aide de camp to Lord William Bentinck.

Vitoria has made a great difference, he however, reviewed the remains of the once Grand Army, and made a speech to them, full of threats against the English, and in the name of King Joseph, thanked them for their gallant behaviour at Vitoria. San Sebastian still holds out, the convent was stormed a few days back, the castle it was expected would soon surrender. He likewise informs us that all the letters written since the battle, are still at Vitoria, and that the greater part have been opened. Captain Lloyd of the 10th Hussars, said last night, he thought we should winter in our present quarters, of all the reports, this one is the most annoying, for I am completely sick of this Olite.

Huzza! an order has arrived, and we are to march tomorrow morning, where I don't yet know, I am not particular whether it is towards England or France; so [long] that we are on the march is all I want, for I am heartily tired of this idle life.

# Chapter 7

# The Battle of the Pyrenees

The order to march from Olite had come with such urgency, because Marshal Soult had launched a major surprise attack against the allied forces in the Pyrenees, driving them out of the mountains, as he sought to relieve the garrison of Pamplona. Soult had caught Wellington unprepared, having been at San Sebastian to view the siege operations.

The allied forces were driven back, but Wellington had instantly ordered all of his troops to rendezvous on a position just north of Pamplona, in the vicinity of Sorauren and rode at breakneck speed to join them there. On two occasions Soult sought to break through to Pamplona, but Wellington's line held and eventually the French were forced to retreat once again into France, harried by the allied troops. The hussars, like all the cavalry, were largely spectators during these battles as the ground was unsuitable for horses.

> Battle before Pamplona, Tuesday 27 July.
> Soon after three this morning, the Hussar Brigade left Olite with the artillery, we expected to halt at Tafalla, various are the reports of our movement, and where we were going, however at last we got opposite Pamplona, all very much fatigued, we have met the grand Lord and Sir Stapleton Cotton, and received orders to proceed to Zolva [Unzu?][1], about two leagues further, we now learnt that the object of our movement was to support the army against a attack

---

[1] Having checked out an old map, Zolva/Zolda is shown in the vicinity of modern day Unzu.

161

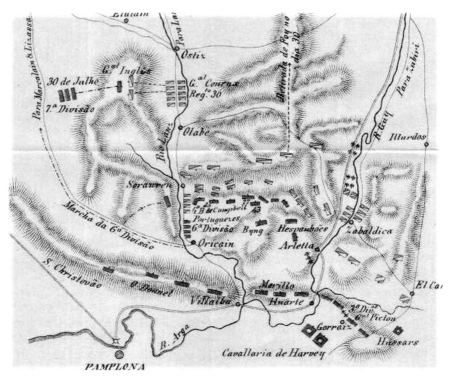

*Above: A Spanish map of Sorauren*

from the enemy,[2] who had driven General Cole[3] and his division from the pass of the Pyrenees called Roncesvalles, with great loss; when we were near the village, we discovered the enemy strongly posted on the mountains in front of Pamplona, which as their principle object, they wished to relieve. The brigade was drawn up opposite them, and remained so till about 4 o'clock in the afternoon, when the French army came down the mountains to force their way into the city, but we advanced with the infantry in front, and drove them to their positions again. I had every reason to believe there would be a deal of bloodshed this evening, had there not come on a

---

2  At this point, just as it did at the Battle of Vitoria, the French version stops abruptly as his regiment rode into action and does not resume again until 1 August; this further confirms that the French version was written on the scene and the British version later when he had more leisure; but clearly not much later, otherwise a great deal of detail would have been forgotten.

3  Lieutenant General Galbraith Lowry Cole.

dreadful storm of thunder, hail and lightning and rain, which lasted till 9 o'clock, when it became dark, we got then into a village, the name I believe is Huarte, we then stopped the night, all prepared and ready to turn out at a minutes' notice. But contrary to the opinion of all, the enemy made no more attempts to return to Pamplona.

During the night the enemy's garrison let off rockets and showed blue lights, several times as signals. The Heavy Brigade likewise was in the neighbourhood. This morning, before we arrived, the garrison made a sortie and killed and routed a great many of the Spaniards who were besieging it. I slept near my horse in a shed, wet to the skin, but drank plenty of brandy, which was the only thing I had tasted since the morning, none of us having any victuals. The two camps had the most beautiful effect, having in every direction large fires, which quite illuminated the country. The infantry position of Lord Wellington's, was in front of the pass up the sides of two immense mountains. The enemy attempted to force his right, but without effect. Early in the evening an order was sent for the whole of our baggage to be sent to the rear, near Vitoria, so that I am left without anything to change my clothing.

The regiment moved across to the right wing of the position at Sorauren although one troop was sent to the left. George led a small detachment forward to reconnoitre but was nearly taken.

Battle before Pamplona, Wednesday 28 July.
Up this morning before day light, in fact, I had not two hours sleep, we advanced to the right of the English position, opposite to the enemy's left, expecting a day of nothing less than broken heads. We were placed by Sir Stapleton Cotton, on a most strong piece of ground by nature, about half a mile distant from the enemy, having a valley in the centre, and a small mountain rivulet between us. Lord Edward Somerset ordered a troop to take a position on the left of the lines; Captain Burke's troop was sent. Major Hughes who came and placed us, sent me with eight men to reconnoitre and patrol a large wood on the side of a high mountain, in which it was expected the enemy had thrown a column, I did so, but found nothing. Captain Burke now sent me to drive in the enemy's picquet and vedette's in front of our position, and to take possession of two villages opposite on their left flank. I crossed a ford with ten picked men, the vedette's and picquets instantly fled, after I had searched the first village [Egues?], and found it deserted

by the enemy, and [un]inhabited, I left two vedette's on the front opposite the enemy's left, and then proceeded to the second village Ibeisua [Ibiricu?], with eight men, which was about a quarter of a mile distant.

On our arrival, I found a party of the enemy's infantry; about fifteen [in number] running away in high style, we galloped after them, one I must have felled or wounded, but for my pistol misfire, they made their escape over a bridge, we galloped through the village, and finding no more, were about to leave two men as vidette's there, when I discovered Captain Burke signal an hussar galloping round in a circle, the signal signified imminent danger. I therefore, trotted with my hussars to the other village, from which I saw a strong column of the enemy's light dragoons galloping down with the intention of cutting me off, but I had not reconnoitred in vain, I had another road to return by. I therefore withdrew the whole of my men that way, and left one end of the village, as the enemy arrived at the other end, and walked quietly over the ford, and arrived at our position in safety. One of my men was wounded over the eye, Sergeant Harrison[4], but very slightly; this was a duty completely to my heart's desire.

The 10th Hussars relieved the 18th about 12 o'clock, we returned in our rear to feed and rest, but were called out about two, and marched back, to assist the 10th Hussars, who would have been cut up, but for our arrival. The enemy and the 10th were skirmishing, they having during our absence, moved the whole of their cavalry, about 3,000 down to the villages, previously mentioned, and threw their skirmishers over the rivulet, they had taken one of the 10th, and wounded Captain Harding[5], and killed a horse under Lieutenant Seymour, when we came up and relieved them, but the skirmishers kept a very respectful distance, they found our men had rifle pieces[6], besides pistols, and they soon wounded a few, and afterwards withdrew. One thing I must not forget to mention; an officer of the enemies [sic] who commanded their skirmishers, all think was an English, or Irishman, he called for the officers of the 10th to come on, 'Why don't these cowardly officers of the tenth come on', and when Kennedy came, and our men drove them over the rivulet, the same officer called out to him, 'Come on you flashy

---

[4]   Sergeant John Harrison.
[5]   Captain Benjamin Harding 10th Hussars.
[6]   He means smooth bore carbines, which were short muskets, not rifles as such.

officer of the 18th, why don't you come over the puddle'. I wish to God they had taken him prisoner.

Lord Worcester was knocked off his horse and severely hurt, this day by a spent ball. The Prince of Orange lost his horse, being shot under him. Captain Gordon of the 10th was wounded in the arm; the staff have suffered severely. There was dreadful skirmishing and fighting on the mountains all this day, some say we have lost two thousand men. After we had relieved the 10th, it was discovered that one of our men had sold his carbine, he was instantly tried by a drum head Court Martial, and punished in front of the enemy, he received seventy-five lashes, and at the same time, which saved him from receiving the whole of his sentence, our attention was taken up by the advance of the enemy in a strong column on the mountains, driving our men before them. When suddenly, we saw a division of ours rise up, who before was held purposely to draw on the enemy after the skirmishers. They first gave them a dreadful volley, being within ten yards of them, nearly half fell, the English then rushed at them with the bayonet, and the carnage was dreadful, near sixteen-hundred men fell, and it was computed that not more than ten escaped. At about seven, the enemy withdrew the whole of their cavalry and infantry, again into the mountains, and we retired to [a] sweet pretty romantic mountain village, called Ratenath[7], where I took about two hours rest in a good house, but with my clothes on, I was obliged to have the door broke open, but when I did get in, the old lady made much of me, and excused herself for barring her door, by saying 'She thought I was Portuguese'.

Battle before Pamplona, Thursday 29 July.
Up again as usual about three and went to our old position, the enemy appeared more quiet, and our army likewise appeared inclined to rest, so there was very little fighting or skirmishing this day, we went to Huarte, and remained in quarters, if such it could be called, for my part I was all day at the door of a barn full of horses, the village was full of general officers and their staff.

General Picton came up today with his division, so did General Hill, the latter was in this village, we are now about equal to the French in point of numbers, tomorrow I think will settle the business. The French headquarters is directly opposite to this village, by appearance it contains about fifty houses; Marshal Soult they say

---

[7] I have been unable to identify this village with any certainty but it must be in the vicinity of Egues.

is in a white house in front of the village, it stands on the edge of the mountains.

Captain Burke was ordered out on picquet, but refused to go, making some trifling excuse. Major Hughes told him, it showed great cowardice, and was ashamed an officer of the 18th should make words about a duty, at the moment when the enemy was near us and ready and determined to annihilate us. Many officers begin to think and say our army must retreat, God forbid, the battle commenced three days back, during which time there has been hard fighting, yet neither have gained much; one hill on the mountain appears to have been the scene of much bloodshed. I trust tomorrow we shall drive them before us. The garrison of Pamplona, made another sortie today and beat back some of the Spaniards, but it caused no movement.

Last evening I saw a sight that pleased me much, while with the regiment on our position, we saw in front of us, near the rivulet, some of the 95th Riflemen, about a dozen, skirmishing with the enemy, they were at it till near dusk, when they left off. Three of the Frenchmen advanced, and next several of the 95th, each without arms, had entered into a conversation, shook hands, and after a short time withdrew to their post; where they are today, looking at each other, but not fighting.

Battle before Pamplona, Friday 30 July.
About midnight, I was called up, an alarm gun having fired from the camp near Pamplona; we immediately after received orders to bridle up, and every man to stand to his horse's head; it was a beautiful night the stars shining very bright. Part of our infantry and artillery were seen moving to the right, many conjectures were formed upon it, most were wrong; all the French fires in their camp were burning very dim, and I told Kennedy, I thought they were off, which afterwards proved true. We received orders to march to our former position, just before day break,

At day break it was discovered they were off, and soon after we heard a cannonading; it was their intention to turn our left, but the Lord Wellington was prepared for them having got near a dozen long nine-pounders upon the mountain, to play on them; we were ordered about eight o'clock to this pretty village Ratenath. At half past twelve o'clock, thank God the enemy are off, they are retreating in the greatest confusion towards France, and several whole regiments are taken. The artillery is now playing on them in all directions.

At six o'clock this evening, we have just received accounts of the enemy, our army has gained a complete victory, after fighting four days, the victory is now certain and glorious, Hurrah. Eight thousand prisoners are now taken[8]. Received newspapers 21st to 30th June from England. I am in my old quarters, the old lady, who before barred her door, sent for me the moment I entered the village, and invited me to her house; not very well today, I took a physic[9] this afternoon.

Battle before Pamplona, Saturday 31 July.
We left Ratenath about nine this morning, and came to this village Ibeisua, the French are still retreating, and our army following them up, a 'Glorious Victory', it is reported ten thousand prisoners are now taken[10]. I was on the mountains this morning, and saw an immense number of muskets and dead bodies left behind with baggage; they are completely routed, they will get through the pass today, and Lord Wellington will again secure it. This village Ibeisua, is the same I mentioned a few days back, having driven the French out of it. It contains about one hundred houses, and stands at the foot of the mountains. The reason we are here is the country the army is now engaged in, being so mountainous we cannot act, and are therefore, useless.

The armies are now on the Pyrenees, fourteen horses were employed to draw each cannon on the mountains. The 10th Hussars have received orders to march at six this evening, towards the armies. As the sun was just about to set, I ascended the mountains near the village with Smith, by a winding path formed by numerous goats, which browse upon it, and enjoyed from the top, a view the most beautiful that can be imagined. The Pyrenees we distinctly saw, but could not discover our army or the retreating French. Pamplona will be stormed in a few days, so it is reported; it is said there are three waggon loads of doubloons in the market place; all our baggage came up today.

Ibeisua, near Pamplona, Sunday 1 August 1813.
All the accounts that have arrived from the army, agree in stating the loss of the enemy to be immense. Their retreat and rout equals

---

[8] This is a gross exaggeration, as 2,700 prisoners were taken during this entire operation.
[9] Medicine.
[10] This is also an exaggeration, Wellington reported about 4,000 French prisoners.

nothing but their retreat from Russia, numbers of the prisoners have only been in the service four months, and are quite lads. General Hill we are informed is in the rear of the enemy, and that they have lost since the 26th inst., fifteen[11] thousand men, this ought to make more noise than the victory of Vitoria did in England and give great pleasure to John Bull. They are now near the pass, I long to hear what was done last night, for from [all] accounts the enemy were in the greatest confusion, throwing away their arms. I hope to God we shall be moved closer to the army today.

I have just learnt there is a likelihood of the brigade being moved to the southward, and that the Grand Lord is much more pleased with this victory than of the Vitoria one. My legs were much swollen, but today they are getting to their original size; it was owing to me sleeping in my boots, and never changing my linen for several days. Lieutenant Waldie is so unwell with swollen legs that he keeps to his bed.

Another Sabbath is past, and instead of praying, I have just returned from a ride, not quite so pleasant a one as many of my friends have enjoyed today in Hyde Park. I have been traversing the field of battle, and contemplating the horrors of war, on the side of one hill, I saw no less a number of slain, than three hundred, and many poor wounded fellows who begged in the name of the Almighty for water and victuals, I am very pleased to say that I had them carried into a village; but on the way, several of these brave souls left this world, but they are removed into the valley, near, or into a world more happy!

The Grand Lord Marshal is still following the flying enemy in France, two thousand-five hundred prisoners were marched through Urdaniz last evening and Lord Wellington continues to harry the enemy with infantry. There are some who think that another battle will take place before Pamplona falls, if so the French must be devilish quick in rallying and raising their forces. The most painful part of the battle I have to describe, the village of Ardanaz, is crowded with wounded British officers, many brave fellows, though who will never see the land of liberty again, that happy region England. O God knows not what my fate is, but I think if ever I live to return to England, nothing shall tempt me to return, except I get the command of a troop, that might make a difference. A

---

[11] Incorrectly shown as ten thousand in the French version. This figure agrees with Wellington's own assessment.

dreadful rainy night, I am in an excellent quarter, thanks to providence.

Ibeisua, near Pamplona, Monday 2 August.
Wrote a long letter to Miss Spooner, Worcester, to enquire after the health of my friends there; General Cole lost his Brigade Major[12] and his Aide de Camp[13] in the late battle, both killed; Marshal Soult's brother has been taken prisoner[14], and when brought before Lord Wellington, he acclaimed most bitterly against his hard fate, 'Saying he was certain he should be tempted to destroy himself', Lord Wellington told him, it was indifferent to him, whether he did or not.

Ibeisua, near Pamplona, Tuesday 3 August.
I took a long ride this afternoon, round the works in front of Pamplona. I had not the least idea that Pamplona was so very strong, as I find it. The infantry and artillery officers near it, all gave it as their opinion, it would capitulate in a few days, the siege is conducted by Don Carlos of Spain[15] and O'Donnel the Spanish General[16]; I dined with Burke yesterday.

Ibeisua, near Pamplona, Wednesday 4 August[17].
I rode to several of the villages in the mountains, and found all most charmingly situated, so romantic and recluse [sic]. I saw some beautiful cascades pour down from the mountains, which turn several mills. The mountains rise in many parts, in majestic grandeur, to nearly the perpendicular height of a mile, which gives a very impressive effect to the scene. I wrote a small note to Amelia and another to Captain Wheeler. Poor Foster's servant takes them to England; he sets out on his way to Bilbao tomorrow. Lieutenant Smith and Blackett dined with me, I gave them an excellent dinner, we afterwards went for a ride round some of the villages, I had seen,

---

[12] He is in error here as Cole did not have a Brigade Major. He actually refers to Captain Christian Avemann 1st K.G.L., who was killed at Sorauren, he was Brigade Major to Major General William Anson.

[13] Major Alexandre de Roverea of the Sicilian Regiment was killed (shot through the head) at Sorauren, 28 July 1813. Cole however says that the remainder of his Staff were all safe in a letter written shortly after to his sister.

[14] This must be a false rumour, as there is no record of his capture and exchange; he was certainly with the French army in early 1814.

[15] General Prince Don Carlos de Bourbon, he and his brother Ferdinand were released from French custody in 1813 on Napoleon's orders.

[16] Spanish General Enrique José O'Donnell y Anatar, Conde de La Bisbal, was actually of Irish descent.

[17] This day's diary is completely missing from the French version.

in the morning. There is a report this evening, that one of our infantry brigades has been surprised, and that they have lost their cannons; I hope to God it is not true.

Ibeisua, near Pamplona, Thursday 5 August.
A dreadful dull life this, we have nothing, but the sound of the cannon before Pamplona to amuse us. The weather is very hot; it is impossible to ride out, except in the evening. The peasantry, who during last week kept close in to the mountains, now begin to venture to their homes, when we first came into the village it was deserted, but now, the inhabitants are all here in safety, it was a distressing sight to see the woman of the house I am writing in, and her daughter, a few days back, on their arrival on finding every article in the house romped[18], the beds and furniture cut and broken to pieces, and everything of value carried off by the French. The church suffered severely, they carried off their priest, an old man, after stripping the church of everything of value, and destroying what they could not take; it is reported they murdered the priest in the mountains.

Hitherto nothing had struck me beyond the ordinary attendants of war, but the villages near the mountains, where the enemies [sic] army was, plainly showed the violent animosity which prevails between the French and Spaniards, indeed the conduct of the enemy, is really painful to think upon. Every house broken open, every piece of furniture destroyed, every cask of wine which they could find, taken away, or staved in, all the fowls, pigs and cattle killed and taken away, and afterwards they set fire to four villages, three of which are completely destroyed. Such were the barbarous and revengeful acts, the French had been guilty of, before they retreated.

Wrote several letters to England; I rode round Pamplona this evening, our batteries having set fire to a house in the suburbs, I think all will fire outside the walls. I met Lieutenant Newland and his lady, not his wife, I don't admire his choice, he might certainly have got a prettier girl to have accompanied him, but what very much surprises me, he appears so fond and attentive to her! Her constancy may deserve it, but if I kept a lady, I would have a handsome one, and run the risk of her being inconstant; sent the letters by Mr. Foster's, servant, to England. The company of a woman, particularly a woman of our country, would be here

---

[18] Destroyed.

delicious and I often wished to have the happiness of a pleasant companion, because I think like Lord Bacon, that in youth, women are our mistresses, in middle age, our companions, in old age, our sick care, and in all ages, our friends.

Ibeisua, near Pamplona, Friday 6 August.
The mirth and pleasantry of the Spaniards very much resembles the English, more than what we usually conceive of, as a Spanish scene. Jesting, loud laughing, pettishness in those who have drunk too freely, and pleasant reproof from their companions; made me many times fancy myself at an English harvest home. The French and English of course, the standing topic of their discourse, every one freely abuse the former, and seem to think that the latter had no other faults, than they were not Spaniards, and were heretics. Mr Dolbel got another dreadful fall, smack into a dirty pond, and never did Sancho Panza[19] on his embassy to Dulcinea[20], make such an out of the way figure as he did, before the parade, afterwards.

This time last year, I was cavorting away at Brighton, much intoxicated with foppery; I think if I should ever live to return, I shall not be the puppy I was when at Brighton, but quite debonair. To be perfect in horsemanship is a necessary part of a gentleman's accomplishments. That a military officer should be an accomplished horseman is a position scarcely necessary to be stated, did not so many John Gilpin's[21] in the uniform of hussars so continually expose themselves. A man who every moment fears to be divorced from his saddle, cannot possibly possess that undisturbed recollection, that cool and undeviating attention, which ought to be given to the troops under his immediate command. I took a long ride this evening with 'Shinny'[22] and Burke, round Pamplona.

Went very near the cathedral, but was not fired upon, as we expected, I think the garrison begins to lag in spirits and will surrender soon, saw several Spanish regiments in huts near the works, before the town, they look very well, but are far different in appearance to Portuguese. Burke for what reason I know not, has altered his behaviour towards me, very much of late; he is very obliging and polite, and appears to court my company, but he is a deceitful knave, and one I must ever despise. It is half past eleven at

---

[19] Don Quixote's page.
[20] Dulcinea del Toboso, Don Quixote's great love.
[21] An allusion to the popular English ballad of John Gilpin, who clings to his horse for dear life.
[22] A nickname for Surgeon William Chambers?

night, and I cannot go to bed until I have written a little in my 'companion'[23]. I am just returned from a neighbouring house, where I was attracted by the sound of music, and have been dancing fandangos with all the women there that looked pretty, and am now as happy as a prince; this is the way to drive cares away, for without some amusement, this village is a horrid dull place.

Ibeisua, Saturday, 7 August [24]
Mina and his army arrived in Pamplona, after taking Zaragosa with four hundred prisoners. The army of Lord William Bentinck must soon make its junction with us.

Ibeisua, near Pamplona, Sunday 8 August.
San Sebastian was to have been stormed last night, or early this morning, God send they may succeed, and take the castle. Zaragosa, memorable for the unparalleled resistance to the French yoke, and being the spot where the immortal Palafox received his death wound[25], when the French stormed the town, on the 21st February 1809; since which time it has remained in the possession of the enemy, till the brave Mina took it on the 30th July. It is the capital of Aragon, and was anciently a Roman colony, the city is very ancient, and contains fourteen great churches, and twelve convents. The famous church visited by pilgrims from all parts of the world, called, 'The Lady of the Pillar'[26], is in this city, the River Ebro runs very near it, the town was called by the Romans, Caesaraugusta[27].

The Spanish women carry everything on their heads; I met one just now carrying a bucket of water. I attempted to lift it, and was much surprised to the weight, but she instantly put it on her head again and walked off, as if she had only a light head dress on. Poor Daniel Curtis, I am afraid, I shall have to write in this book an account of his death before the campaign is over, I never beheld a young man who looked so dreadfully ill, he is wasted away to skin and bone fretting. I am confident it is nothing else; his brother Lieutenant Curtis[28], who was left ill at Santarem, is now at Salamanca, where he intends to remain, for he has written for leave,

---

23   His Journal.
24   There is no entry in the English version, possibly because there was no real news that day.
25   Palafox was not killed, but kept a prisoner at Vincennes.
26   The Cathedral-Basilica of Our Lady of the Pillar.
27   Ceasaraugusta was established by the Romans between 25 and 12 B.C.
28   His brother Robert Curtis had become a lieutenant in the 18th in April 1813.

saying he is unable to proceed further, owing to a rheumatic complaint in his back and arms, (it's all my eye and Betty Martin[29]). He was tired of Santarem, and thought Salamanca a better place to live and enjoy the luxuries of the country, whilst the regiment was in front of the enemy and near danger; I am sorry that the army is disgraced by such beings to study nothing but dress, foppery and debauchery.

The heavy battering train drawn by oxen, will arrive in front of Pamplona this day, we may, therefore expect to hear of that place being knocked about the ears of the French. How dismal is this Ibeisua, another Lord's day and no service performed by the regiment, surely it would be better for an officer to read the church service, by which means many of the men would know that it was Sunday, and might devote part of the day to devotion. Rode this evening with Burke and Chambers towards Pamplona, it was dusk before we got to the videttes, and we went very near the town unperceived, but they discovered us, and commenced firing instantly, fortunately they did not hit us; they certainly took us for a general and his staff, coming to reconnoitre, and I caused them so much alarm by galloping about in front of the town, that their trumpets and drums beat to arms all through the town. On our return to this place we were fired upon several times by the damned Spanish videttes.

---

[29] The phrase 'its all eye' meaning 'complete nonsense' was a common phrase from the 1780s, but at some stage the 'and Betty Martin' was added, but modern experts have no real explanation for this.

# Chapter 8

# Return to Olite

Things having settled back down again and with little prospect of any service for the cavalry, the 18th returned to their old haunt at Olite.

Ibeisua, near Pamplona, Monday 9 August.
A route is come at last, and we leave this place tomorrow for our old quarters at Olite, the 10th and artillery go to Tafalla, the 15th to Artajona, we are disappointed completely, for we made sure of going towards San Sebastian, there is nothing for us to do there, that is plainly the case. General Sir Thomas Picton took up the English position in front of Pamplona on the 27th July, and when Lord Wellington arrived and reconnoitred it, he said 'I am highly pleased Sir Thomas of the position you have taken'. Sir Thomas has since been appointed to command two divisions of the army[1], on account of Picton's Division was always called the fighting one, he is said to be the most determined of fighting officers in this country, except in Marshal Wellington [himself]. Yesterday I wrote to my friends, Mr Vanboorst, and Captain Ellis[2].

Tis not a Frenchman that creates alarm,
Know greater dangers we have here to dread,
When lice and fleas and bugs, a hideous swarm,
From hilt to point, from toe to head.

---

[1]   He is in error, General Picton continued to command the 3rd Division only, when he was in the country.
[2]   Captain Richard Ellis, 18th Hussars, who was then in England on detached service.

Lord Edward Somerset

Ormsby Vandeleur

The Earl of Uxbridge

Sir Hussey Vivian

The only known portrait of George Woodberry in Venezuelan Uniform c.1823

Colonel James Grant

Major James Hughes

Paymaster William Deane

18th Hussar Officer   18th Hussar Musician   18th Hussar

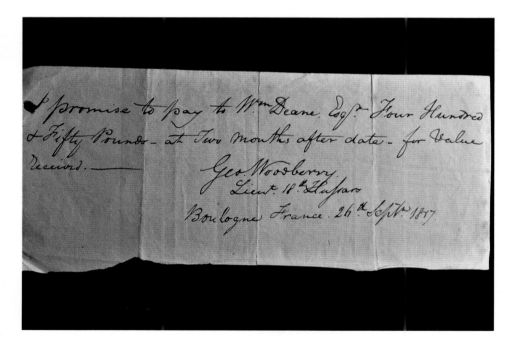

Promissory note from George Woodberry to Paymaster William Deane dated 26th September 1817

18th Hussars by Richard Simpkins

An 18th Hussar by Musician Garside

A Private of the 18th Hussars by Hamilton Smith

St John the Baptist Church Claines where the Woodberrys were baptised

Above: Battle of Vitoria 21 June 1813. Below: 1796 pattern Light Cavalry Sword

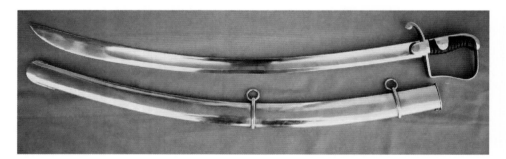

Marshal Jourdan's Baton Captured at the Battle of Vitoria

The Hussars Charge at the End of the Battle of Waterloo by Denis Dighton

Anglesey leads the Hussars forward at Waterloo

Above: Monument of the Heroes, Caracas. Below: George Woodberry's name on the Monument

I dined with Captain Wodehouse[3] of the 15th at a small mountain village near this place; I met their Captain Hancox[4], and Burke, Lieutenant Bellairs[5] and a doctor, of the 20th Foot[6]. The Prince of Orange, set off for England, with the despatches, announcing the late glorious victory of the 6th inst.,[7] the cost to the enemy is calculated at 20,500, killed, wounded and prisoners[8]. Soult was seen on the instant, riding on a beautiful mule, reconnoitring our position, he several times attempted to turn our left, had he succeeded, we must have given up the whole ground in front of Pamplona. The Grand Marshal said 'My friend Soult wants to turn my left, suppose we try and turn his'. The attempt was instantly ordered, and which was as quickly done, which decided the battle, for after we got possession of a[n] immense high hill on their left, the enemy fell back in all directions, and the scene of confusion that followed, can be better conceived than described, it is said nothing but the famous retreat from Moscow, could equal the rout from Pamplona.

General Barnes[9] who commands the Portuguese at Roncesvalles received a slip of paper on the afternoon of the 25th ult., with the following written with a pencil, 'the French will attack you tomorrow morning at three', very little notice was taken of it, but it was true, they did, and were actually in the pass before they were discovered, it was written in English, but no one knows who wrote it. When the Grand Marshal arrived on the afternoon of the 27th, the Third and Fourth Divisions were then closely engaged, it was soon made known his Lordship was come, when the men received him with three cheers, crying out that his arrival was as good as a division, in their favour. His Lordship was in the mountains on the 28th, and saw the charge made by the 40th Foot upon the enemy,

---

[3] Captain Philip Wodehouse, 15th Hussars.

[4] Captain Skinner Hancox 15th Hussars, he had been slightly wounded at Vitoria.

[5] Lieutenant William Bellairs 15th Hussars.

[6] This could be Surgeon Archibald Arnott, who later was surgeon to Napoleon at St Helena; but it could also refer to Assistant Surgeons William Byrtt or David Gordon of the 20th Foot, who were all in Spain at the time.

[7] He refers to the Battle of the Pyrenees which was effectively over by 3 August with the French army back in France.

[8] This would appear to be an over-estimate. Oman's estimate is that French losses totalled around 12,500 killed, wounded and prisoners.

[9] Major General Edward Barnes commanded a brigade in the 7th Division, he was severely wounded during the fighting and was mentioned in dispatches. He commanded a British brigade in the 7th Division, not Portuguese troops. I suspect he meant Major General Thomas Bradford, who commanded the 10th Portuguese Brigade.

and his Lordship instantly cheered them, so did all the staff, the 40th Regiment was led by Captain – (no name given)[10] whom Lord Wellington recommended for a majority. This victory must give pleasure to John Bull, it is so quick upon the last, and it will be so soon, they will hear of it, that I am thinking the people will tire before we have done all we have to do with the Frenchmen. Lord Wellington was very near receiving a bad wound during the battle, a ball struck his sash, and lodged in it, he received no injury heaven be praised[11].

This is not the first time the Grand Lord has defeated Soult, and I think he will be more cautious in future how he advances the French army. I have just learnt of our loss of officers in the different battles, between the, 25th July, and 2nd August; it was one major, ten captains and twelve lieutenants and three ensigns killed; then two general Staff officers, eleven lieutenant colonels, fifteen majors, fifty-one captains, one hundred and four lieutenants, and thirty-one ensigns all wounded;[12] what a butcher's bill this is, so many fine fellows lost to their country and friends.

Lord Wellington is pleased, beyond anything of the conduct of the infantry, and of the Portuguese and Spanish troops on this occasion, and thinks it fifty times more decisive than the victory at Vitoria, and will have the effect of damping the ardour of the enemy's forces. All the stores intended for the use of the garrison (Pamplona) were taken in the retreat by the Portuguese cacadores. Our army have likewise fallen in with the baggage, and taken nearly all of it, mules were selling a few days back in our camps at four dollars each.

On the 26th ult., when our division under General Cole was falling back from the pass, they were compelled to leave all their wounded men, which the enemy took care of, and left in the different villages; since their retreat we have got them again. An officer who was wounded and carried into a house, was visited by several French officers, who told him, that he must be taken care of, and that in a few days, they would have him removed into Pamplona; this shows how confident they were of relieving this place, and of defeating us. Soult was afraid of trusting his artillery

---

[10] I believe this to refer to the senior captain of the 40th Foot, Captain Arthur Heyland, who was made a brevet major after this battle and was killed at Waterloo.

[11] I have not discovered any evidence to back this claim, but a number of Staff were struck by spent balls.

[12] His figures add up to twenty-six officers killed and 214 wounded; whereas Oman shows (for Maya, Roncesvalles and the two Battles of Sorauren) thirty-two killed and 235 wounded (including Portuguese).

in front of his lines, and on the 29th, finding the English were not to be driven from their lines so easily as he first anticipated, fearful of the issue, he sent his artillery into France again, where he was obliged to follow so quickly after, and by which means it was saved. Marshal Soult, addressed a very boasting letter to the French army before he advanced, he therein told them that it was his intention of celebrating the birth of the Emperor Napoleon in Vitoria. Pamplona, I am informed, was most superbly illuminated on the evening of the 27th, I saw myself, many rockets thrown up, but thought they were for signals from the garrison, but they were let off to show the English the joy they felt at the arrival of succour. I have not heard of them illuminating on the following night!

The inhabitants of the town are principally in villages in the mountains, how wretched must be their fate to be driven from their homes and property, plundered and destroyed; the horrors of war, the Spaniards truly feel, my heart bleeds for them.

Ibeisua, near Pamplona, Tuesday 10 August.
We did not march this morning, it was counter ordered, but we do tomorrow morning at five. Out riding with Conolly towards the works near Pamplona, the enemy was firing very much at something on their side of town. I suppose at the heavy artillery that has come up. Lord Wellington, the Grand Marshal is very anxious to get possession of Pamplona, with the works quite intact, and would allow the garrison to leave Spain with the greatest pleasure; to have possession of the whole. Everyone seems anxious for peace; I begin to wish all the fatigues of war over, I wish some of my London friends would inform me how ministries go on, and what the good citizens of London think of the present state of affairs.

Noain, near Pamplona, Wednesday 11 August.
The brigade marched from the villages it occupied on the other side of Pamplona, and arrived in this neighbourhood soon after ten. This village like Ibeisua, is near Pamplona and is on the main road to Olite, it is entirely deserted, and contains not one tenantable house in it, the famous aqueduct, is in the neighbourhood, it contains no water now, it being cut off in the mountains, where the spring is. I dined with Conolly, in a most wretched house, without windows and doors, but had a good dinner, we both had our beds put up, and slept in the same place. Some ungrateful rascal in the troop, during mine and my servant's absence, took the whole of my brandy, near a gallon, out of my keg. I shall find out before long who it was, I

suspect it was Flanagan[13], who I thought the best man in the troop. The trenches are digging in front of Pamplona, near five hundred peasants were pressed from the different villages to work on them.

The news that the vacant captaincies in the regiment were to be filled from outside of the regiment as a punishment for its poor showing at Vitoria, led to much talk of resignations and George considering his own position.

Olite, Thursday 12 August.
The Prince Regent's birthday[14]; the regiment marched this morning at five, and we got here about two, it was a very fatiguing march, about six leagues, and what made it very tiresome, was the burning sun, which nearly overpowered me. On my arrival here, I got fresh quarters, a smaller better one than I had before, and not only that, but the very young lady I had got acquainted with, before I left this town, lives in the house. Kennedy is not so fortunate, for Major Hughes has got into the quarters where the young lady he made acquaintance with lives. I am quite astonished, the troops that were vacant by the deaths of Turing and Carew and which everyone expected Russell and Conolly would succeed to[15], are given out of the regiment, Lieutenant Luard of the 4th Dragoons[16], and Lieutenant Owen, 16th Light Dragoons[17]. Russel and Conolly were there and Conolly sends in his resignation this afternoon. I think I should resign, if my leave of absence does not arrive in November, Smith thinks of resigning his commission too; I am very sorry for poor Russell, he must feel the disappointment very severely indeed, having given up the appointment of Quartermaster, under the idea of him being gazetted to one of the troops. Hesse, I understand is likewise very much disappointed, he wrote to the Duke of York for one of the vacant troops.

The return to Olite seems to have rekindled not only their interest in the young ladies, but also with the nuns.

---

[13] Private John Flanagan.
[14] The Prince Regent, later George IV was born on 12 August 1762.
[15] Russell and Conolly were the two senior lieutenants and would have expected to gain promotion to the vacant captaincies without purchase.
[16] Lieutenant George Luard 4th Dragoons became a captain in the 18th Hussars on 21 June 1813.
[17] Lieutenant Hugh Owen of the 16th Light Dragoons had been serving with the 1st Portuguese Cavalry Regiment since 1810; he was promoted captain in the 18th Hussars, dated 22 June 1813, but he never actually joined and was made a major in the 8th Portuguese Cavalry Regiment in November 1813.

Olite, Friday 13 August.

Poor Russell is in great distress of mind about the troops being out of the regiment, his whole dependence was upon it, in fact the existence of himself, wife and six children depended on his promotion, it was thought he would lay violent hands on himself, last night, so great was his grief.

A nun is to be made tomorrow morning at Tafalla, she takes the vows tomorrow, and I must go and see the ceremonies attendant, which my young Anna Senora, informs me is very grand, and the sight is even novel to them, for there has not been one female take the vows this two years past in this neighbourhood. Burke and our commissary, Schaumann[18], have had a serious dispute, and I understand a Court of Inquiry will be the result of it. I am much surprised that Burke should get into another scrape, so soon after suffering as he did before.

I understand the enemy are entrenching themselves on the other side of the River Nive, which is in France, and have sent eight regiments of cavalry towards Germany, where it is said that war has commenced again. They are certainly acting on the defensive on the Pyrenees; so if the German business is true, we are here for winter quarters for a certainty.

I got my young ladies to waltz with me this evening, when my music master was with me, they seemed much delighted with the English tones. I am thinking of giving a ball to the ladies of Olite, on Monday or Tuesday next. I afterwards took a walk close to an hour in the fields with them and with their mother, I find one is very much in love with Lieutenant Finch of the 15th Hussars[19]. I discovered that one of them is in love with me I think I am also in love with her.

Olite, Saturday 14 August.

I employed myself this morning, translating two songs for my ladies, 'Flowers of the Forest', and 'My Heart with Love is Beating'. I am falling into the error, my dear friend and Aunt Moseley so warned me against, I am getting so desperately in love with Senora Zacarias, but it is not the kind of love that attacks a mortal in England; here it only lasts while in sight of the object, while the English urchin pierces the heart so deeply, that only death erases it, and I actually think nothing

---

[18] Schaumann does not mention it in his memoirs.

[19] Lieutenant the Honourable John Finch 15th Hussars, he transferred to the 37th Foot as a captain in February 1814.

of telling a dozen females here the same tale, and the above translations, shall serve me during my stay in the country. O what fun I have had this evening, Smith came to my quarters and enjoyed himself; my ball to take place tomorrow evening; all the women of the town come there and I invited the officers from Tafalla with all of their favourites that they want to bring.

I went over to Tafalla this afternoon, with a large party of Spanish, amongst the numbers was my padrone and family, to see the nun invested, all the English officers were put into a pew or box near the altar, the nun was of quality, the ceremony was very grand, she was brought into the chapel by her relatives, she was very neatly attired in white with an abundance of lace about her, there was a something I perceived in her looks, that I think plainly told her dislike to her present prospects. The nuns about thirty[20] were in the choir, the strut procession I did not see, though I understand it was very grand, so as soon as she entered the chapel, she kneeled down, and with an appearance of devotion saluted the ground, then rising up and advancing a few steps further, on her knees she repeated the salutes, she then approached the altar, where she remained till the ceremony was over. Then she fell down on her knees, before the altar, and after some short mental orisons[21], she withdrew into an inner room, where she put on her nun's weeds[22], in which making her appearance, she again kneeled and offered up some private devotions, which being over, she was led to the door, on the side of the chapel, which led to the nunnery, where the nuns stood, ready to receive her with open arms. The nuns then conducted her into the choir, where after they had entertained her with singing and playing the organ, the ceremony concluded and we departed; poor miserable creature, I dare say compelled to that life by a cruel father or mother, to enrich a more favourite child. The Cortes has abolished the Inquisition, and I trust it will not be long before they do something to decrease the numerous, monasteries, convents, and nunneries, that serve to impoverish the country.

Olite, Sunday 15 August.
This day was ushered in by the ringing of bells, being the anniversary of the feast of Assumption by the Virgin Mary, kept by the people

---

[20] Incorrectly shown as twenty in the French version.
[21] Divine silent prayers
[22] Garments.

here as a holiday. There was a grand procession paraded round the town, and then to the large church. In the afternoon, I went to Tafalla, and saw the nun take her vows, as described earlier. In the evening I gave a ball to the fair ladies of Olite; I suppose there was about forty-two of the towns people present, the whole of my brother officers were present, but as it was at Lord Worcester's Ball; there were a few of the immodest amongst the numbers. I was not at all pleased with Major Hughes, who brought one of the most notorious of the country round, but she was a beautiful dancer, and everyone admired her, she was a dancer at the theatre in Pamplona, and waltzed with Hesse, delightfully. The band played some of our most favourite English dances, and with very little trouble and instruction. The ladies did their part admirably; we kept it up until till about ten o'clock[23], and finished the ball with [blank - a supper?]. I had provided sandwiches, negus[24], and lemonade with pastry, quite in the English style. Most of the gentlemen appeared [half] cut, and the women all merry, on their leaving for their homes. Smith, left very early indeed, but he danced two dances with very nice girls; I had got my rooms done up in high style for the evening, and it was beyond doubt the best English ball given in Olite, in every respect, but more particular in having more women, it was quite laughable to see Waldie dance, he fell against the different ladies, and kicked one, and knocked another down. I opened the ball with Donna Senora Zacarias Nabasques, with a Spanish Bolero, and received some praise from the females, for its execution. I begin to find I am a favourite in Olite, and I should be very proud of it, were it not for their cursed cut throat husbands.

George suffered a serious theft, but was not alone.

Olite, Monday 16 August.
What a dammed unlucky fellow I am, the rascally servants robbed me last night, my desk was broke open, and sixty-eight pounds taken out of it, not a farthing of it shall I ever touch again, it was in doubloons, seventeen of them, and although there was also valuable jewellery the villains never took a thing but the paper of money; alas I am born to misfortunes.

Lieutenant the Honourable Mr Finch, 15th Hussars, breakfasted with me this morning, he was quartered in this casa, and it was an

---

[23] One o'clock in the French version.
[24] A hot drink of port, sugar, lemon, and spice.

unfortunate one, for his servants or others robbed him of sixteen guineas in gold, missing from his canteen. I do not suspect my servants, but I have my doubts about the honesty of the Spanish domestics. I intended my ball to have taken place this evening, being the anniversary of my acquaintance with my dear friends, Miss Perkins and Miss Moseley, but was persuaded to have it last night, on account of the Spaniards feast. Smith came and sat with me, and we had a deal of conversation, respecting friends, and our affairs in England.

I am particularly anxious to get home again to arrange everything that has been neglected by Mr Vanboorst. I had another dance this evening, the Miss Murphy's, and my patroness, aided by the assistance of a flute; we kept dancing till near eleven o'clock.

Olite, Tuesday 17 August.
We had a Court of Inquiry, respecting the robbery committed upon [me]; Captain Kennedy, Hesse, and myself, after hearing the whole of the evidence, we were firmly of the opinion, McDougal[25] my batman, broke open the desk, and took the money. I have offered ten guineas reward to anyone who will recover the property, but I am almost confident I shall never touch a penny of it [again]. This evening I received a letter from my dear friend Donna Maria and English newspapers dated, 2nd to the 14th July. The letter is particularly gratifying, the information of my friends being in health, and of my dear friend Amelia's intention of writing, a few days after, gives hopes. I long [for it] to be realised, this letter was in answer to the one I wrote from Torre de Moncorvo – Portugal[26]. The little doctor called, Pulsford, and I had another visit from my female acquaintances, six of them, the doctor played the flute, and we danced. The doctor Olly[27] was drunk, and created much mirth, the ladies got him on the ground, and nearly tickled him to death, the little man had a completely black face and I was obliged to drive them away from him.

Spanish ladies have a charm that is dangerous even to describe: as a young Englishman, gracious and polite, full of chivalric considerations, I am wary from the memory of a friend that has since left the country, that he must close his heart against these beautiful

---

[25] Private Thomas McDougal.
[26] Clearly Amelia was not a regular correspondent, he was at Torre de Moncorvo 22/23 May.
[27] A nickname for Pulsford.

repositories of his first oaths, with their perfect oval faces, beautiful light brown hair, big black eyes, mouths full of grace and modest attitudes, with simple clothes that often remind us of the sweet simplicity of Greek beauty, an outfit full of sensitivity and vivacity.

Olite, Wednesday 18 August.

The Spaniards have a custom; to an Englishman it appears a very immodest one, if your back is towards a lady, and she wants to speak with you, she does not gently tap you on the shoulder or winningly pull you round to speak to her; no, they have quite a different method, they give one another most immoderate slaps on the bottom. I was saluted by one of my fair senoras, this morning in the market place, the people all laughed, it was, my confusion and blushing, not her courtesy.

Tafalla was besieged by Mina, the enemy having got possession of it; it was likewise considered a strong place. There are now only the vestiges of the wall and castle to be seen. The governor was killed in the storming of the place, and was buried a few days after.

All the females of the town collected in the market place, and being headed by a most beautiful woman, whose husband had been murdered by the late governor, proceeded to his burial place, and dug his body up; cut his ears and hands off, and then left him for the vultures. The women are devils in this country, but what of that, are they not the same in England[?] I find upon enquiry, there will be another ceremony with the fair nun, the same day next year, when the lady abbess brings her out, and delivers her to her friends. Then again there is a sermon, which being over, she is brought up to the altar in a neat but plain dress, the fine apparel she put off on her initiation, being deposited on one side of the altar, and her nun's weeds on the other. Here the priest in Latin cries out 'utrum horum mavis accipe' (which way do you prefer to take things), to which she answers, as her inclination, or as her instruction directs her. If she, after this year of probation, shows any dislike, she is at liberty to come again into the world, but if awed by fear, as too often is the case, or won by expectation or present real inclination, she makes a choice of a nun's weeds, she is immediately invested and must never expect to appear again in the world, outside the walls of the nunnery. The young lady I saw last Sunday was rather pretty, and appeared about eighteen years old. Mina passed through this town a few days since, and the whole of the inhabitants met him, and he drank two glasses of water during the time they were cheering him with 'viva, viva, and viva'.

Olite, Thursday 19 August.[28]

I begin to wish wanting to get home again, I am not at all well, the weather is excessively hot and sultry, and it quite overcomes me, there is now no likelihood of the enemy coming again. I rode this evening towards the Ebro, which I saw from the top of a hill, the river was heavenly, a most delightful valley, and immense chain of mountains, with the river running beneath. The whole of this grand scene was enriched with all the soft tints, which the sun, just sunk below the horizon, could impart, in this delightful climate. The top of the highest mountains, still glowed with fire, but a purple light reigned in the valley and sober tints were spread over the surface of the river. Spain everywhere abounds with a succession of hills, and ridges and valleys and lawns.

The whole time I have been in Spain, I never yet saw [a] Spaniard in liqueur; they are fonder of water than wine. The Portuguese are as fond of wine as the English. I am very partial to their country's wine, and I seldom get up from dinner, without three pints in me. Received an English newspaper, dated 28th July, I suppose in a few days, I shall receive the others. I had my dog Vitoria sheared today, likewise one of my mules, but looks all the better for it. This day, four years ago, my brother William died at Surinam.

Olite, Friday 20 August.

I have made up my mind, to send in my resignation in the course of a week or fortnight, a letter arrived from Lord Wellington, wherein he informs the regiment, that it was from their conduct at Vitoria, and subsequent behaviour, that was the cause of his recommendations to the Commander in Chief, that two subaltern officers who were out here belonging to other regiments, fill up the troop vacancies, and that Lieutenant Luard of the 4th Dragoons, Lieutenant Owens of the 16th Light Dragoons had been permitted in consequence.

I have just learnt that there is some strange work going on at Tafalla; two of the officers of the Tenth Hussars, I understand are seeing an orderly officer[!]. I employed myself walking round the town, and visited the senora, and had some prime fun at Kennedy's casa.

I have just heard that Lieutenant Fitzclarence[29] was wounded in the thigh at Tafalla yesterday, that he, with others had been playing

---

tricks with some Spaniards, and they stabbed him, it is not a dangerous wound I understand. More fun at my casa this evening, Kennedy, Dolbel, and Pulsford were there, and we were met by Senora Zacarias Aberica and Fermena, and the two Miss Murphy's, the gentlemen were all so and so[30], and the senoras did nothing, but cry out, 'Mucha Drunkies'.

Olite, Saturday 21 August.

Hang the women, they plague me to death, the weather is so excessively hot, I am unable to ride out, and have to stay at home and be plagued by two nice girls, one telling me of my faults, the other accusing me of falseness, 'Voodvurry mucha falsa'. I find they are in love, but it will not do, I say no, no and I see no right way.

The mode of living in Spain is certainly not congenial to that in England, the first order taken in the morning, either in bed, or soon after they rise, chocolate with cakes, or toasted bread, having first drunk some cold water, which is always brought with the chocolate. They dine from 12 until 2 o'clock, seldom later, the tables are about eight feet long and six feet wide, covered with one large table cloth, and a plateau is generally placed in the centre with figures in wax and bottles of wine corked, placed round the brim of it. Bread covered by a napkin, denotes the place of each of the party, the dinners consist of soups and a variety of dishes which encircle the plateau. Each person sitting opposite to a dish, whether of meat, fish, or vegetables, fills his own plate, carves the content, and hands it round, so that during the whole time of dinner, if a large party, they are continually passing and re-passing plates, with something of every sort which passes, the Spaniards always fill their plates, they are moreover very great eaters, some of the dishes are palatable to an Englishman, but their meats are covered with oil and garlic. Their soups are good, the meat is generally boiled in large unshaped chunks, or in pieces and mixed with potatoes, mashed with oil. The Spaniards rarely eat salt or pepper; they seldom use a knife, except in cutting up the contents of the dish next to them, and occasionally stabbing each other. A piece of bread and a fork, answer their purpose, as to what is in their own plates. The pastry is particularly good, the fish is a side dish, generally after the soup are two dishes, one of boiled meat, and boiled fowls together, and the other a sort of stew with sausages, of which garlic is a material ingredient.

---

[30] Sloshed.

Strangers drink and eat as they please, no health drank, and there is not that reserve or respect observed by the servants, who attend the table as in England. They laugh at a joke, set you right where they think you are wrong; both men and women maid servants, are dirty, slovenly and awkward.

Olite, Sunday 22 August.

I received a letter (for my name, but that of a[nother] gentleman); belongs to him, a very rainy day, was employed at home writing. I received two letters, one from Miss Spooner, and the other, Mr Vanboorst, and newspapers from the 14th to the 21st July. I had requested the women of Olite to come to my casa and have a dance this evening, but the sudden news I received of the death of a very close relative[31], prevented it taking place, I likewise received newspapers 23rd July, to the 4th inst.

Olite, Monday 23 August.

Chambers paid me this morning, £17 2s 0d, being the balance due to me for a horse I sold him at Brighton. His bill I paid into my Brighton bankers, and was dishonoured. I asked Chambers to dine with me, which he did, Hesse, Pulsford and Dolbel came up in the evening. I informed Major Hughes of the accounts I had received from England, and that I intended that I should apply for leave of absence to return to England.

Olite, Tuesday 24 August.

I wrote a letter to Mr Vanboorst this morning, and I think from what I have heard he will receive it in nine days. If I had been in London, the last six days, I think it likely I should have been at Camberwell and Peckham fairs, which if I recollect right, are about this time. Corporal Edwards[32], reported yesterday, to Major Hughes that he saw Lieutenant Russell, send three bags of doubloons to his brother, who is a captain of infantry, in the 20th[33] during the action before Vitoria, and the reason he reported it was that he thought an officer ought to have the same punishment for plundering, that had been inflicted on him when he was a sergeant, but reduced, for keeping the monies he had taken at Vitoria in direct disobedience of orders.

---

[31] I cannot discover the death of a Woodberry at this time.
[32] Corporal John Edwards.
[33] Brevet Major William Russell of the 20th Foot.

Major Hughes saw him a few days back, and convened a Court of Inquiry to study the charges presented to him against Russell, but as members of this court are, to my knowledge, guilty of the same mischief, I assume that the case will fall into the water and found that the letter written by Dolbel in justification of himself, respecting the affair of the ring of Madam Guizes, had never been forwarded to Lord Wellington by the Black Giant and the Red Dwarf, to whom we owe much of our disgrace, he has, therefore gone this morning to the Marshal, to explain and vindicate the character of the regiment to him.

Olite, Wednesday 25 August.
A delightful morning, reminds me of England, so cool and refreshing, after a heavy shower of rain. I was surprised this morning during the shower to see most of the females in the street, sweeping and collecting all the dirt, while the boys carried it off. I always considered Olite a very clean town, but was not aware that it was owing to the industry of the fair sex. It so seldom rains in the summer months, in this part of Spain that all the people appeared delighted this morning, and anxious to get wet through by it.

There will be some strange doings in the regiment now. I am sure Burke has made himself despised, by all his brother officers, owing to his crafty methods; he has adopted to get clear of all blame respecting the Vitoria plunder business. All agree his character is noxious; I am to dine with Burke and Chambers today.

I have today sent a petition to Lord Wellington, for a leave of absence for two months to return to England and arrange my family business, and as Major Hughes goes tomorrow to headquarters, he will speak to Lord Wellington in my favour; but I am afraid that this is futile, because his lordship is so angry with the regiment and the conduct of the officers at Vitoria that he will refuse any favour. We have instructed the major, and I hope that when he sees his lordship, he will give him sufficient explanations and defend the good reputation of the regiment.

Olite, Thursday 26 August.
It is very strange that I should have written above some remarks respecting Burke, whose conduct last night, fully proved to me, that any name, but that of a gentleman belongs to him. A very rainy day was employed at home, writing. I had a dinner party today, the following dined with me, Smith, Blackett, Chambers, Russell and Burke, they all stayed rather late. After the meal, the conversation

fell on the subject of a loan. Burke asserted positively that I had made a claim to get it and declared in the most solemn manner that he had seen a letter written by me to Greenwood and Cox on this subject, stating that Mr. Langmore had shown him. I answered that I had never written such a letter. He then renewed his first assertion with so much warmth and also in my opinion so disparagingly for a brother in arms, and especially at my own table, that I let myself give a pretty strong response, in which I positively denied the fact by saying that it was absolutely wrong. On this, Burke stood up in a violent and passionate manner and demanded an immediate apology which I refused, finding that it was rather for him to apologise to me. It was then decided that we would use weapons: I proposed to send word to my home to have my pistols sent, but Burke refused saying: 'I have it, let us toss for who will fire first'. Then he brought out a pistol and a few cartridges with ball and opening his desk, he took out a doubloon which he threw in the air and he said. 'I do not want to shoot you in this room, but you are free to do so if you want'. But he continued to rant and rave and raged so hard that it excited my anger even more. He told Doctor Chambers: 'I will make my report on it tomorrow morning; lets go!' Chambers attempted to reconcile us, which would have succeeded without the grossity [sic] of Burke's language; I told Chambers to load the gun, and surprised him, catching him trying to remove the balls from the cartridges, I cried that things could not be left as they were, and I invited Burke to put them in place. Chambers interposed, declaring that there could be no fighting, and at the same time Burke left the room. I assured them that I would speak of the entire case to the brigade if I was not immediately in receipt of an apology, 'I guarantee that Burke will make you sufficient apology', said Chambers, 'if you leave things where they are'. He went out and a few minutes later he brought Burke back by the hand. He stated that what he had said about the loan was a joke and that he was extremely sorry if any expression he had made had hurt me. On this, Chambers made us shake hands. Burke proposed to keep this secret, and asked me for my word of honour never to speak of this again. I refused outright; then Burke, assisted by Chambers, begged me to receive dinner today. I this morning told all of this to Smith and Pulsford in confidence, and I invited to dinner Smith, Blackett, Chambers, and Russell to meet with Burke, this sad character.

I begin to get reconciled with this country, so do most of my brother officers, the talk of peace is the principle topic, God send it may soon take place. I am very anxious to get to England to arrange my affairs, and I am afraid the Marshal will not grant me leave.

George had heard nothing of his request for home leave, but with rumours of another French attack, he had forgotten about his resignation and was simply eager to re-establish the reputation of the regiment.

Olite, Friday 27 August.
Last night one year ago, I was enjoying myself dancing with my dear friends, Miss Perkins, at her ball in The Crescent, Brighton[34]. I cannot forget the happy days past, a delightful harvest is hope; I [hope I] may pass many happy days in England again. The French are said to be coming again, may my wishes be gratified. I trust the 18th will recover all their former glory, and add new lustre to it. I am determined if I get near them [the French] again, I will fight like a hero, and will sell my life dearly if not supported, anything I will do to regain our former character.

It is plain that the Marshal intends removing many of the officers, I am aware we have a few 'shy cocks', amongst us, and the sooner they [are] turned to the right about, the better. I rode over to Tafalla, and heard from Colonel Roberts[35], that the 7th Hussars in England, who had received orders to embark for the Peninsula, had been countermanded; all agree that peace will certainly take place very soon. About three hundred French prisoners, and two French officers, were marched through this town, yesterday. Blackett spoke to one of the officers, but he was so sulky, that he received no answer. I was informed; they were the garrison of Zaragoza, taken by the brave Mina.

Smith was talking today about my friend Donna Maria; and said Mrs S[mith] had informed him, that she was deeply in love with his brother, and that to keep up the joke, she said all she could to persuade her that Mr Thomas was in love with her. I must take an opportunity of letting my aunt into this secret.

Olite, Saturday 28 August.
Lord Edward Somerset inspected the horses, intended to be sold for

---

[34] The Royal Crescent at Brighton is a beautiful arched terrace of Georgian properties on the sea front.
[35] Brevet Lieutenant Colonel David Roberts, 51st Foot, Brigade Major to Major General Leith; he had lost his right hand at Corunna.

cast[36], likewise the French horses that are to be taken into the regiment, this morning on the Tafalla road. The honourable Mr Finch came to Olite to see me, and he stayed here till Monday morning, we had some fun with the girls, much more we shall have tomorrow, when I think I will give a ball. I spent the afternoon visiting the women and inviting them to my ball tomorrow. The Corporation of Olite wants a throne erected purposely in the square, where the Articles of the New Constitution[37] are to be read. During the evening, bands of music were paraded about the town, with fandangos and boleros in every direction, the alcalde's house was illuminated with a dozen wax candles.

Olite, Sunday 29 August.
All the discourse of the town, was respecting the diversion of bull fighting, to take place this afternoon, every avenue to the square was blocked up with carts, early in the forenoon. At two o'clock, I went to Doctor Quincey's casa in the square, to meet Smith, Blackett, and many others, we took possession of the balconies, and waited near two hours in anxious expectation of the commencement of the sport, during which time we were enjoying looking at the charming women collected at every window. A dozen oxen were at last brought into the square and put into a stable belonging to one of the houses, and they were then released one after the other to be baited by a set of brutes, collected on purpose and the farce began.

There were eight or ten men grossly dressed in sparkles and decorated with countless favours they had received from the ladies. I must own I had not laughed so much before, since I left Lisbon, some of our men who were anxious to see, and more anxious to show the Spaniards, they were not afraid of a wild ox, were hurt, one seriously. One of the oxen jumped into a cart, which was full of spectators, and tossed a few of them into the air. Finally, one of the Spaniards, the most brilliant of all, was caught by a bull and the poor devil was carried home with an open belly. I thought that this accident would put an end to the entertainment, but the joke continued as if nothing had happened. Finally, one of the bulls was killed with much trouble and we return each to our homes. The clothing of the brave-hearted who teased the bull consisted of red

---

[36] 'Cast' horses were those deemed unfit for military service and were to be auctioned off.
[37] The new constitution of the returned King Ferdinand VII.

slippers, with a pretty silk hat decorated with feathers and a red coat. I saw some of the fellows go home rather oddly.

After the bull baiting was over, I returned home to dinner, and entertained my friends, Smith, Kennedy, and Waldie, of our regiment, and Lieutenant Finch and Mansfield of the Kings Hussars, after we had had dinner. The ladies began to collect and my ball commenced about eight o'clock, we kept it up till twelve. I opened it with 'Abereta', with Tekeli, Smith with Senora Murphy, and the second with 'All's well'. I afterwards danced a fandango with Fermina, and attempted to waltz with several others, so did Hesse, but they don't waltz like the English, and their method is not worth learning, and it is unlikely I ever shall attempt to waltz with any Spaniards again; boleros and fandangos, they excel in. We continued then with English country dances, and finished at one o'clock in the morning.

Olite, Monday 30 August.
I was writing letters this morning, after Finch left me for Huerta, one to J. Usher Esq., and one to Miss Moseley. I dined with Kennedy and a large party afterwards, went to Captain Burke's quarters, and was drinking brandy and water, and smoking cigars nearly the whole night. I must leave off two things which have grown on me lately, drinking and swearing.

Olite, Tuesday 31 August.
I rode over to [blank] with Hesse and Pulsford, there being a feast at that village, but the diversion of bull bating did not take place, but plenty of dancing, we met most of the senoras from Olite, and upon the whole, passed a few very agreeable hours, and then hurried home to dinner, but on the road was actually caught in a very heavy shower of rain and thunderstorm, which cooled our flame a little. I dined with Smith, and Blackett, and a party of four, and did not leave their casa, until eleven o'clock. Smith is going to give a music party next week.

Olite, Wednesday 1 September.
How happy was I, last year, on this day, driving to Worthing, and passed the day, most pleasantly, with Mrs S[mith], Amelia, and Enos [Smith], but here I am now, fretting myself about my affairs in England, no amusements, no guns, dogs or partridges, alas poor Georgio! I dined today with Hesse, and Pulsford, met there Smith, and passed the evening most pleasantly.

It is their queen that the Spaniards must blame for all this degradation. To satisfy her unworthy passion, the Prince of Peace, of the Corps of Guards, quickly ascended to the highest honours. He ended up selling his country to the French. The queen had lost the charms of her youth and this miserable wretch treated them with contempt and maintained her despotic power through foreign influence. She recently promoted a young man who was no more than 20 years old and who was in the Guards, but the power of Godoy could not be shaken by the wiles of a woman. He was universally hated, but before her he was one great smile. He had the servants of a king, his palaces were gorgeous, and he was always guarded by a regiment that belonged to him. Godoy is supreme and well dressed; he looks like an Englishman.

Olite, Thursday 2 Sept.
I went over to Tafalla, with Pulsford and Quincey, to play at billiards, I likewise took over my memorial to Lord Wellington, for leave of absence, to go to England; which I hope and trust may be granted me. A very considerable part of the officers of the regiment were staying at headquarters this evening, smoking cigars, and drinking mulled wine. A dreadful stormy night, I never saw or heard one the equal to it. Several officers of the regiment came to my quarters tonight and were occupied in teaching English to the señoras; we had a great time. Learning my friendly senoras English, and lots of laughter it created this evening. I can never think of my doings in Spain, but it must cause instant laughter, in fifty years to come.

Olite, Friday 3 Sept.
San Sebastian, has at last fallen, so I have just heard, it was stormed on the 31 August and that we killed and wounded and took prisoners, upwards of six thousand of the enemy, our losses are likewise, stated to be considerable[38]. I bought a large basket of most delicious fruit, off the gardener, having picked it myself, for 3 shillings. I am confident it could not be got in England, for as many guineas. It consisted of nectarines, peaches, grapes,

---

[38] The French garrison only totalled around 3,200 men and actually lost less than one thousand men killed wounded or prisoners on the 31 August, the remainder of the French garrison continuing to hold out on Mount Orgullo until the final surrender on 8 September. Over the entirety of the siege the British lost around 3,700 men killed, wounded and missing.

black[39] and white pears, apricots, apples and three beautiful melons.

I gave a dinner today to the following; Burke, Hesse, Duperier, Russell, and Pulsford, and gave them a feast, hare and a brace of fine partridges, a present from my padrone. Russell was so-so, and afforded us a deal of amusement. A report this day at Tafalla, that Massena had joined Soult with six thousand men, and that they had made an attempt to relieve San Sebastian, and were driven back with great loss, across the River Nive; from what I have heard of the repulse, it was another victory. Pamplona, it is now calculated will surrender very quietly, the town I am informed is very clean, and pretty, and contains five thousand families. One of the friars, gave me an account of that city, and likewise told me that Zaragosa contains twenty-seven thousand families, Olite four hundred. Pamplona is particularly well paved, and by Spanish monk's calculations, upwards of twenty thousand less shoes are worn [out] yearly, since it has been cleaned and paved, by that I should suppose, it was a pig sty before.

Olite, Saturday 4 Sept.
Sat on a Court Martial this morning, a very hot day, unable to walk out of the town; we have a great many sick in the regiment, owing to the men eating too much fruit. I cannot withstand the temptation myself; they are so beautiful, so ripe, and so sweet, to what grapes are in England.

All very anxious to hear from England, we have had no accounts, later than the 4th August, and Major Hughes, who went to headquarters, some days back, has not yet returned, we are all much annoyed, in not receiving some account from him. All much surprised this morning by the arrival of Captain Croker[40] from England, and not a little astonished, when he informed us that our remounts that we have been expecting for the last fortnight, have not arrived at Santander.

Turner[41] of my troop shot himself this evening, in a drunken fit, the ball went through his belly, and out of his back, and it is

---

[39] The black pear is a very ancient variety of round pear which was cultivated by the Romans, it is easily cultivated and bears a large fruit crop and last longer than the white version. It is currently enjoying a small resurgence.

[40] Captain Richard Hare Croker 18th Hussars.

[41] Private John Turner.

considered a mortal wound. I got him all the assistance I could, and left him in the charge of two men, the surgeon opened a vein in his left arm, and left it open to bleed all night. He appears in great pain, but is so insensibly drunk, as to have no recollection at all, of his dreadful situation. He continually invokes the Almighty. He accuses Burke as the cause of his suicide.

Olite, Sunday 5 Sept.

Turner is still alive; I got him removed into the hospital, where I think he will breathe his last today, he is very sulky and refuses to answer any questions. I got one of the friars to pray for him last night, he arrived with the Host and a wax torch, and after reading some Latin prayers to him, he rubbed oil on the temples, cheeks and feet and hands and departed. I suppose the oil is to assist him through purgatory.

We punished two men yesterday, and afterwards, Turner told several, he would see no more cruelty in the 18th and got drunk purposely to commit suicide, 'how horrid'. Croker brought us some very unpleasant intelligence from England, nothing less than the report of our disgrace having reached England; and that rascal Captain Dundas[42] of the 15th Hussars, who Croker said 'At Vitoria told him the 18th Hussars Regiment ran away at Vitoria, and that the 60th Foot fired at us'. What a villainous liar, a meeting of the officers will take place immediately, and Master Dundas will suffer for his falsehoods.

The worst news I have still to relate; it is nothing less than the desertion of an officer of the regiment, Lieutenant Rowlls, who had been left at Vitoria, where he pretended illness, he was sent to Bilbao, for sea bathing, where he embarked for England, without leave; disgraceful, everything goes against the regiment. I hope to God he may be advertised in the Hue and Cry[43].

The French have collected an army of near one hundred thousand[44] men upon the Pyrenees; we must therefore be on the alert. I think it very likely they will attempt something in the course of a week or fortnight. I have received no answer, to my memorial for leave of absence, I am not at all anxious about going home now I find the regiment has so bad a character in England, the men are

---

[42] Captain Thomas Dundas 15th Hussars; he was the anonymous author of *The British Cavalry on the Peninsula*; printed in the United Services Journal in 1831. He had previously served with the 60th Foot.
[43] A judicial journal.
[44] Incorrectly shown as sixty thousand in the French version, but it is an exaggeration.

good, the fault lies in the officers, had they been well led, they would have done their duty. The storks have left the church towers and steeples, with their young, and gone to the mountains, the inhabitants see nothing of them till about May next, when they return, and take possession of their old nests.

An officer of Don Julian's lancers, the husband of Zacarias, was much hurt at a bull fight a few days back, in a village, near here. He was shining off in high style, when the bull, by an unexpected movement, tossed him up, and ripped all his side open. I believe he is considered now out of danger, but the ladies laughed and cried Viva! As if nothing had happened.

The nuns who I have much neglected lately; I went and saw them this morning, my old favourite, cut me, she would not on any account see me, so much the better, I am very glad of it, but it hurts my vanity. I find they never speak to each other after eight o'clock in the evening, till seven the next morning, when they all attend prayers in the chapel. I asked the reason, and they told me, it was all for God. I told them, I thought he would be more pleased with them if they danced fandangos with the 18th Hussars, than sitting mute for so many hours, during which time their thoughts could be on no good.

Olite, Monday 6 Sept.
Turner died of the wound he had inflicted on himself, yesterday afternoon at half past four; several of the priests came to Bolton, and requested he might not be buried with military honour; [therefore] he was put in a hole, I believe last night without any ceremonies.

Olite was originally surrounded with a wall, and innumerable little watch towers, vestiges of them may be traced, and have the appearance of great antiquity. The castle has been a place of strength, and evidently of Moorish origin, though some parts appear to have been more modern, as there have been embrasures made for guns, but the whole is now a most superb ruin, and has the most picturesque effect, from the Tudela road. The winter I am told, sets in about November, in this part of Spain, and the weather becomes so excessively cold, that the inhabitants seldom leave their houses for weeks together. A great number of wolves lurk about the different villages, and destroy all the cattle that are loose, they come from the Pyrenees.

Colonel Murray has obtained leave and has gone home to England, he is a mere skeleton, he is still very ill and his leg is compromised. The elder Curtis, no one knows what has become of him, perhaps he has followed the example of Rowlls and deserted. I dined with Burke and a select party, consisting of Blackett, Croker, and Smith. All our conversation upon the Field Marshal's official account of the great victory before Pamplona; I am much surprised; it did not make more mention [than that] of the battle of Vitoria.

I understand from all, that there is no likelihood of me obtaining leave to go to England, and I cannot make up my mind to leave the army, and will, therefore, in the event of leave being refused me, stay the campaign out. The 10th and 15th have received their letters and newspapers, but we have got none yet, trust tomorrow we shall receive them in abundance.

Olite, Tuesday 7 Sept.
I rode over to Tafalla with Smith and Blackett, in hopes of obtaining some information, where the bag of letters, newspapers, belonging to our regiment was, but did not see the Brigade Major. It being a beautiful morning, the ride was delightful, we met a large convoy of provisions, going to the Spanish army, and a great many volunteers on their way to Roncesvalles. The Spaniards, according to my opinion, have become soldiers, the enemy will experience a different reception, if they attempt again to cross the Pyrenees, and I think the war will be carried on in the south of France.

I trust the Field Marshal will never attempt to invade France, for I am fully confident of the impracticability of the measure. Every subaltern officer of the regiment, that is out here, seems anxious to leave the service, all disappointed I may say disgusted,[45] having entered the service in a regiment that all England, looked to for something great, by which means we become the envy of the army, but all would have been well, had we had another colonel in the place of that great ass, Colonel Murray, who knows no more how to command a regiment than I do. We are beholding to him for every misfortune or disgrace attached to the regiment. Oh my dear friends in England, you will think all are equally blameable, but my conscience, tells me I have done my duty.

Lieutenant Hesse gave a ball this evening, it was very badly attended, only one respectable girl present, the others all shop keeper's wives', I trust my ball tomorrow night will be the same as my former ones; my padrone would not allow the young senoras to

---

[45]  At this point, the French version cuts abruptly and renews on 1 January 1814.

go. I was there till near twelve o'clock, danced two boleros with Senora Chocolata.

Olite, Wednesday 8 Sept.

A great feast day amongst the Spaniards, all attended mass three times this day, being the Nativity of the Virgin Mary. I received a letter from a chum, and eight English newspapers, 4th to the 18th August. I got likewise two Worcester papers, the first I have received since I left England. My ball this evening went off very well, my room made a very dashing appearance, having obtained some lustres, eight senoras honoured me with their company, and we danced nine sets. Hesse was very great, and danced several fandangos and boleros with them. Dolbel came rather drunk, so did Pulsford. I find I am so great a favourite with the ladies, that they express great regret, when they heard I was going to England, but my leave is not yet arrived, nor do I think it likely I shall get one, for I have received no answer to my application. The band played this evening some of the most favourite tunes, which delighted the Spaniards, and particularly 'Paddy Carey'[46].

Olite, Thursday 9 Sept.

I arose with the sun this morning, and went out coursing, we had two brace of fine grey hounds, but found the hares rather scarce, two only had the misfortune to come in our way, and those we bagged. I feel rather unwell; too much raking[47] lately, is I believe the cause of it, so that it will go off, as usual thank God. Illness has not affected me, since I have been in this country. The climate appears quite changed; it has become excessively cold and bleak.

Major Hughes returned this evening from Headquarters, he saw Lord Wellington, and explained everything respecting the regiment to him, the Marshal told him, he thought the men of the 18th at Vitoria, behaved more like rebels and bandits, than a regiment of hussars, Major Hughes asked him if he had anything to say against their bravery, 'O no, certainly not, I think them very brave, but too impetuous'. Thank God we are not stigmatised with cowardice, as we are with plundering. Colonel Grant of the 15th has behaved towards the 18th, like a father, to him we are indebted for all, he never forwarded Conolly's or Dolbel's statements that they had

---

[46] A well-known jig.
[47] Self-indulgence.

drawn up in vindication of their characters, from the foul insinuations said to have been made to his Lordship, I cannot tell how this will end; I hope well.

I took a long ride this evening, towards the Pyrenees, a traveller of genius, and romantic ideas, would in this country never want employment for his pen; if he only described the enchanting scenery of the country. My road lay north of Olite, and when I had nearly reached the summit of the hills in front, I was presented through a chasm with a most beautiful prospect. The descent below me was through verdant shrubs, mingled with olive trees, below this was seen a most lovely plain, about four miles in extent, with a river meandering through the middle of it, and in the background, ranges of still higher mountains with light clouds lightly hanging on the skirts of them, the highest point of which was either hid in cloud or covered with snow. The small white houses interspersed amongst the vineyards upon the rising ground, were admirably contrasted with the various green tints below, and the brown and red colour of the marble mountains, which towered majestically above.

Olite, Friday 10 Sept.

Lord Edward Somerset inspected the regiment in watering order this afternoon, and expressed himself highly pleased with its appearance. Lieutenant Fitzclarence called on me today, and sat reading the papers for some time; from him I heard all the news from headquarters. I am sorry San Sebastian holds out so long.

His brother the captain returns to Tafalla this day to take the command of the late Captain Windham's Troop, he having been promoted to a majority in the 60th Foot[48].

Pamplona still remains in the hands of the French; the French have risen, a report that there has been a great battle in Germany, that Buonaparte has beaten the allies, with the Austrians who had joined them in a great and decisive battle[49]. No answer to my memorial being with the regiment at H.Q., I give 3 to 1 that I don't get leave, in due course. I have given up all thoughts of it, and therefore, must trust to those friends in England, I have, to do their best for my intentions.

---

[48] Captain Joseph Smyth of the 10th Hussars assumed the surname Windham and is shown in the Army List as remaining in the 10th but detached. He does not appear to have transferred to the 60th Foot.

[49] This refers to the Battle of Dresden fought on 26-27 August 1813, the allies losing 38,000 casualties against some 10,000 French casualties.

Smith and Blackett sent in their resignations this afternoon, Smith and self had a great deal of conversation respecting old friends in England, and I really think I shall be tempted to send in mine, if the Marshal refuses me leave.

Olite, Saturday 11 Sept.
One of my favourite senoras was married this morning at St. Pedro[50]. I went to see the ceremony, but was an hour late; the ceremony took place at six o'clock. San Sebastian has fallen, the castle and all the fortification works were in our possession, the day before yesterday, and the Portuguese have suffered much say the Spaniard's in this town. I offered a Spaniard two guineas for a poodle dog, but the fellow wanted more, I think I will do a copy of my memorial to Field Marshal the Marquis of Wellington:

Sheweth that his personal affairs in England being much deranged … [The next five lines are not legible] … That memorialist had volunteered his service to accompany the regiment to this country in preference to remaining in England and should now feel it painful to solicit your Excellency at the present for the shortest leave of absence, were it not for the above circumstances, which as nothing but his personal attendance would need to adjust, and humbly prays your Excellency for two months leave of absence. This is submitted:

Olite 25 August 1813. Signed: George Woodberry Lieutenant 18th Hussars
I wonder what the answer will be to the above, I am very impatient to know, for all in the regiment, think I will get no leave, and cannot help feeling confident he will grant me the leave prayed for.

Olite, Sunday 12 Sept.
I rode today with Quincey over the camp, and saw immense numbers of game; the view of the surrounding country and the River Ebro was beyond anything I ever saw before. I dined with Burke; we had a church parade this morning.

Following a review of the regiment, they were highly delighted to receive orders to march north and George was sent in advance to organise their billets at the end of each day.

---

[50] I cannot identify this village with any certainty.

Olite, Monday 13 Sept.

Lord Edward Somerset reviewed the regiment this morning, and appeared much satisfied with our manoeuvres. I commanded the left half squadron, and upon the whole, think the regiment conducted itself very well. They certainly turned out as clean as ever I saw them in England.

Mr Finch who came over on purpose, to take me back with him to dinner at Huerta, after the review, I rode with him there, and dined with Lord George Lennox[51], Major Griffiths[52], and their pay master[53], we had a most sumptuous dinner. Lord George is a very pleasant lad, and talks much, while we were at dinner, he received a letter from his brother the Earl of March[54]; from the neighbourhood of San Sebastian, giving him the full account of the siege and capitulation of the castle, it appears the castle contains only a small building, sufficient to hold five hundred men, that was accurately proven that they had upwards of two thousand men in it, and all above the 500, were exposed to a dreadful fire of three hours, from a great number of mortars and guns, and they never fired at us a lot, but showed a flag of truce and surrendered; what fools the fellows were, that they did not fly the flag, before our batteries began. Seventeen hundred and the governor marched out prisoners, and were embarked for England. Poor Dunn, our lieutenant[55], was the subject of much conversation and humour, Lord George amused us with many anecdotes of that officer, when in Portugal with the 9th Light Dragoons. Dolbel did not escape the lash of Major Griffiths, who spoke of him, as the greatest puppy in Christendom.

I slept at Huerta this night, at Captain Wodehouse's quarters, he being at the headquarters of the army, and rode home early most of the morning, where I found a route for the regiment to march to Irurtzun, and an order for me to proceed forward and take up quarters for the regiment at the different villages on the road. There was a great feast and bull fight at Olite on Tuesday, which I could not attend, I likewise intended to have given a dance in the evening, but I am being despatched forward, a day sooner than the regiment, which prevented it.

[51] Lord George Lennox was a Lieutenant in the 9th Light Dragoons but had become an aide de camp to Wellington.
[52] Major Edwin Griffiths, his letters and journals have been published by the editor as 'From Corunna to Waterloo'. He does not mention this dinner.
[53] James Coppin Cocksedge was Paymaster of the 15th Hussars.
[54] Captain Charles Lennox, Earl of March, 52nd Foot, was as extra aide de camp to Wellington.
[55] Lieutenant John William Dunn 18th Hussars. The French printed version mistakenly identifies him as Deane, but it was Dunn who had served previously in the 9th Light Dragoons.

# Chapter 9

# Advancing Again

With Wellington now looking to drive on into Southern France, Somerset's brigade of cavalry were moved forward to support the advance. George had now changed his tune however, and was sorry to leave Olite and his ladies behind.

Mendivil, Tuesday 14 Sept.
After leaving Olite, with great regret, after more than once seeing my favourite senoras and taking leave of them. I marched towards this place, with my men to procure quarters for the regiment, on the march I saw several of my old friends in the 10th Hussars. On passing through Tafalla, I found on my arrival here, it would not do for headquarters, so left it after marking stabling for the centre squadron, there being fourteen houses in the village, which stands on the high road from Pamplona. Very near it was a small mountain river, over which was a very neat bridge, but it had been destroyed by Mina to prevent the French bringing their artillery after him, when he was retreating. I then went to a most pleasant village near the mountains, of about forty houses, and a pretty church called Unzue. I fixed on this place for the headquarters of the regiment, and took quarters for the staff and the left squadron.

All the young senoras are removed to the south, out of the way of danger. I think the French have not paid the village a visit, for in every house, I saw at least fifty to a hundred fowl. The march today was over a road I have before described, and indeed I did not feel inclined to look for more beauties, after leaving Olite. Angaletia wanted much to leave home, and [her] parents to partake of the fortune of Georgio, but it would not do, thank God I can say my conscience is clear. I am not inclined to make myself unhappy, for the momentary pleasure of the situation, no, no. My men robbed for me several fowls, and my poodle Vitoria killed one pretty chicken. I was much surprised in finding large stores of wheat and barley and straw in the village.

Torres, Wednesday 15 Sept.
After seeing the troops put up in headquarters, this morning, I went forward and took up quarters for the regiment in six different villages, this I fixed on for headquarters, being the best, and likewise in the centre of the others, viz. Zizur Mayor, Elorz, Zabalegui, Otano, Ezperun, and Cizur Menor. I am now in a pleasant village, in sight of Pamplona, the roaring of the cannon annoys me at this moment. Was there ever so unlucky a dog as poor me? Lord Wellington refuses me leave to go to England. Well I must either send in my resignation, or run the chance of losing part of my property, besides the disgrace of having many accounts unsettled, which that rascally Mr V[anboorst] will not attend to. I never slept so bad as I did last night, I trusted my poor body to one of the beds belonging to the house, but expected before morning to be half eaten with the bugs and other annoying vermin; my hands and body suffer much from their poisonous stings. The regiment did not go into the above quarters.

Errotz Thursday 16 Sept.
When the regiment arrived at the above quarters I took yesterday, they did not stop, but went on to a different village nearer Pamplona, Major Hughes, wishing to make a short march tomorrow. I then came to this village, which stands at the foot of two immensely high mountains, and it has a rivulet, running close alongside it. I found a village nearby this, full of wounded Portuguese soldiers. This place consists of 24 houses, and stabling for 208 horses. I went further up the pass and found a pretty village of about 12 houses called Errotz, which I took quarters in, for the staff of the regiment. The river here appears very fine, with high towering mountains hanging over it, and the village. The inhabitants appear to much dread the French, received me well, and gave me cake and wine. I slept at Errotz in a very good house, and drank some of the best wine in the country.

Errotz, Friday 17 Sept.
This is certainly the prettiest village I have seen in the country, I got a billet in the pastor's casa, who was most kind and attentive to all

my wants this day, I don't know how it would be if I was to stay here any time. Quincey dined with me, and we got the priest to drink with us after dinner, and he amused us with the account of the conduct of the enemy, and what the village had suffered through them. On my road yesterday to Irurtzun, I passed the spot where the enemy were obliged to leave their only remaining cannon, after the Battle of Vitoria, which increased the numbers taken to one hundred and fifty three.

Major Hughes, Deane and myself bathed together today in the river, which we found was quite saline, it had a surprising effect on us, and I feel quite another being. Lieutenant Dunkin is expected to join the regiment this day, at this village, with the remount from England. On the tops of the mountains, there are ridges of rock that in many instances appear like the ruins of fortifications, and add much to the beauty of the whole. The only expense that I see the Spaniards are at, in living, is the purchase of chocolate, everything else they have in their houses, or on their lands.

Irurtzun is a small village on the high road to Pamplona, very close to the most romantic chain of mountains, through which the road runs. The pass through the mountains is very grand; the mountains are at least two thousand feet above the road, which is only 16 feet wide, and in many places the shrubs and trees growing on the edges of the rocks meet and cause the pass to be obstructed, which gives a grand, but awful appearance. I saw this morning, some very large eagles flying about the mountains, and I am informed there are many wolves. There is a very pleasant hermitage on top of the mountains, and close to the side of it runs a murmuring rivulet, and a very pretty chapel, but it must be a terrible habitation in the winter.

Errotz, Saturday 18 Sept.

The regiment paraded in watering order, and the horses were examined and found to be in excellent order to march immediately if required. Captain Deane who has been to headquarters brought the news back that we are to embark immediately with the Germans[1] for Germany. I wish it may prove true, for I should like much to serve in a campaign in Germany, before I left the army.

The country around us exceeds all powers of description, the village is situated on the declivity of the lofty mountains, the vines

---

[1] The King's German Legion troops, the rumour was false.

on the sides, then the verdure of the gardens, the shady groves on the banks of the river, the lofty elms and chestnuts in the valley, the profusion of fruits, and the transparent streams running from the mountains to the river, render it one of the most enchanting spots in Spain. My host is very kind, I shall never forget him; he appears as much pleased with me as I am with him, I have to ask for nothing, for all my wants he anticipates. This is the second kind priest I have been quartered on, but his hospitality is further enhanced by the gratifying attention of our amiable hostess.

The Spaniards are excessively hardy, the peasantry in this part of Spain have no beds and just sleep in any dry corner on the floor, wrapped up in their cloaks or a blanket in the severest weather. They never take their clothes off, until they are worn out, or until they marry, and invariably wear a broad leather belt round their loins, that would be no inconsiderable inconvenience to any other people. Irurtzun was the headquarters of Lord Wellington, and where he dated his despatches, giving the account of the glorious victory of Vitoria.

Errotz, Sunday, 19 Sept.
The regiment was out in watering order this morning, and four men and a Sergeant Edwards[2] were punished for mutinous conduct yesterday at Irurtzun. A route has arrived, and we march for villages in the Pyrenees mountains, tomorrow morning, and join the 1st Regiment of German Hussars. I received two letters from England and newspapers from 18th to the 30th August.

Muskitz, Monday 20 Sept.
The regiment marched from that delightful village Errotz, at seven this morning. The road was alternately ascending and descending the whole way and became steep and rocky, but as we ascended we were amply repaid by the grandeur of the prospect, which every step offered to our view, this is a poor miserable little village at the foot of some young Pyrenees, which overlook the whole, for we are completely surrounded by mountains, which will prevent me riding much. France is only three leagues from here, and from a very high mountain very near the village, I am informed that Garonne River, may be seen. Conolly intends going to England immediately, having given up all idea of his long talked of tour through the south of

---

[2]  Sergeant John Edwards, he had recently been promoted from Corporal.

Spain, and the court of Palma, and as this book is nearly full of nonsense, I shall send it to England with him. For the perusal of La Donna Maria, and Flora Amelia [Mrs & Miss Perkins]; by the bye I must own I fancy myself much neglected by the latter senora.

I took this morning a grateful leave, and received my host's hearty wishes of success and health, the good priest has been uncommonly kind to me, the five days I was in his casa. I received yesterday from the paymaster, one month's pay for April, and the hussars are now paid two months in advance of the other troops, for they are now getting their February pay. I think I never saw rain so heavily come down, and thunder so loud, as what took place this evening, it was truly dreadful.

Muskitz, Tuesday 21 Sept.
I wrote two letters to Mr Vanboorst and Messrs. MacMahon & Co., at Lisbon, requesting them to dispose of my box of clothes that was left in the stores at Belem, for I think to have them sent to England, where they will be of little or no use, and the expense of travelling (shipping), more than they are worth. I rode over to Oscotz, our headquarters, and saw Captain Kennedy, but heard no news, except that General Alten was expected there to inspect all the quarters of the regiment, it was a very wet and cloudy day. I don't like the Pyrenees as the weather is so changeable. On our march yesterday I saw several olive trees, many appeared to be of great antiquity, their roots and trunks were knotted in the most fantastic forms, and the people believe them to have been planted by the Moors. The battering train is on its way to Pamplona, and I trust it will not be long before we hear of its surrender. Pamplona from a distance appears of Asiatic character, it is situated in the middle of a plain, with clusters of stately palm and olive trees, between which are ancient towers and domes, which have a particular romantic effect.

There is a beautiful monastery, in the mountains near Irurtzun, having a handsome covered way, and gateway; it was called by the Moors 'Idlella', or the house of pleasure, possibly from the pleasure or attractiveness of its site. The Moors appear to have been very sensible of the beauties of nature; their language is full of epistles expressive of this taste. The favourite amusement at the parties in this part of the country including Olite is dancing and singing, the ladies singing agreeably, and by an invitation to do so very readily. The refreshments at these parties are ices, cakes and sweetmeats; the common fault of all the Spanish women is bad teeth, they are inordinately fond of sweetmeats, and ridiculously endeavour to increase their beauty, by covering their faces with patches. The chairs in all the houses are of unequal heights, so as to accommodate persons of different statures.

The principle decoration of the interior of the house in Spain, are similar to Portugal, the floor and sides of the rooms are composed of china tiles, these are at once, cool and handsome, being a white cream ground, painted with flowers in a brilliant and happy style of colouring, highly glazed and shiny like polished steel. The women are remarkably fond of wearing large ear rings, which descend in families, from the make of some I have seen, they were made a century back. I begin to think we shall feel hunger in these mountains, as well as cold. The wine is very bad, and like hungry subalterns, cannot help complaining, when our commissary uses us thus.

I hired Mr Conolly's late servant, Porter[3], this day, I agreed to give him one hundred pounds per annum, he finds himself in clothes, victuals, but when in England, I am to find him a bed; he comes to me in a few days. By my soul I am afraid we shall be starved; Smith has bought a most beautiful little pug dog for his wife, I intend taking home a very handsome pony, at present to a charming young lady of my acquaintance. I don't know who is the greatest favourite with the women of this village, myself or my Portuguese boy. I believe he has learnt his master's trick, for I heard him this evening, praising two girls up to the skies; 'Wapper Chicks'[4] were both. I must ride over to Smith tomorrow morning and get him to give me two sheets of paper to write letters home with this book, to Donna's Flora and Maria. I think much of those women, but they don't think much of me, or they would write to me often, out of friendship, but out of sight, out of mind.

Muskitz, Wednesday 22 Sept.
I rode last evening on the large peak in front of this village, but did not see all I expected from what the inhabitants had led me to expect, the prospect was quite gloomy, nothing but a continuous series of mountains, one above the other; and as for France, I as much saw it as old England, happy England at this moment; however I was gratified with my ride. The beauty of the country, however, remains fresh in my memory and imagination, and produces images which compensate for a narrow room, and a wretched bed.

---

[3]  He was not a soldier.
[4]  The term is unknown, but would indicate large women.

A rainy morning, it is most surprising the change we find in the climate and weather in the mountains. The Spaniards seem unacquainted with the use of tea, except as a medicine, and suppose we are drinking rum and water; when they taste it, however, they reject it with abhorrence. There is a set of people in the country similar to hawkers in England; they carry goods about for sale. I felt rather surprised on examining their articles, to find two thirds were of English manufacture. I went over to headquarters this morning, and am just returned and dined, having been a member of a Court of Inquiry upon Sergeant Major Duncan of Captain Kennedy's Troop; just as I left the village, Smith rode in, having been wandering about the woods and mountains, nearly the whole day, without being able to find his way, he and Chambers are to dine with me tomorrow. I bought four very fine pigeons for six pesetas. Lieutenant Conolly certainly leaves the regiment, on his way to England on the 25th inst. I must write my letters tomorrow, or I shall not get them off with this book with him. There was some very loud thunder and lightning, very vivid, and some heavy rain this afternoon. I saw the mountains very light this evening, which tempted me to take a walk to the top of one of the smaller peaks, I saw the mountains on the opposite side, and just over two small villages on fire, to burn the under wood and drive away the wolves. It had to me, a singular and most magnificent appearance. The curtain of day was drawn, when the gilded blaze, rising from the tops of the mountains, variegated the heavens and added grandeur to the majesty of night.

Muskitz, Thursday 23 Sept.
Lieutenant Dunkin will certainly join the regiment tomorrow, with the remount from England, and Conolly leaves Vitoria tomorrow for Bilbao, to proceed to England. I shall, therefore, send Ipper off with this book and a note to my friend Amelia, for Conolly to take to England with him. Another dreadful rainy morning; I bought three pigeons this morning, all the country people are bringing fowls and pigeons for sale, so I shall not starve.

One of the men tried yesterday at the Court Martial was for stealing a pair of boots, between the soles of which were enclosed eight doubloons, a curious method of keeping money. The garrison of Pamplona expects to be relieved by the 25th inst., which there is now no likelihood of, it is, therefore, anticipated they will surrender and not allow the town to suffer bombardment, it is likewise stated that a quarter pound of horse flesh is sold for three pesetas in the town, and that their stock of provisions is now nearly out. Several

French officers are known to have come out, and satisfied themselves, that there is no chance of relief. Soult dare not attempt it at the present moment. There is great news arrived at headquarters, from Germany, that the whole of the French army has retired behind the Rhine. This comes from General Alten, so that it may be true; Soult was yesterday at Bayonne.

The 18th Hussars are now brigaded with the 1st German Hussars, General Alten's Brigade; he sent a very handsome letter to the regiment yesterday, saying he felt himself highly flattered and honoured by the Commander of the Forces, in having as gallant a regiment as the 18th added to his brigade, and strongly recommended to the officers, not to lapse discipline of the regiment, but to bring punishment to every man, who commits the most trivial crime, that the fate of the whole army is often entrusted to an hussar regiment, and strongly reprobated drunkenness in any hussar, he concluded with the following hints:

The duties of hussars in the field are so various, and require so much practice and experience, that too many opportunities cannot be taken, even in cantonments, to instruct the men in them, and the Major General will find great pleasure in giving that assistance which his experience may enable him to do.

I am ordered upon to lead a patrolling party to Santesteban, and am to go into France. 'Huzza', I am much pleased, because I shall see something of the borders and peasantry of France. I am quite delighted with my duty, for I am to remain and make observations for seven days, and I likewise feel pleased, because it is a post of trust, and I am appointed to it out of my turn. I go on Saturday morning at day break. I have just learnt that Conolly did not leave Vitoria, till Saturday, so that I shall not send the book and letters until tomorrow night. I bought a small pig this evening, and a couple of fowls, to take with me, I am to have twenty men. I should like much to pick up a few straggling prisoners, it would do famously to begin my new book[5] with the account of the capture.

Muskitz, Friday 24 Sept, 1813.

Smith left me this morning on his way to his troop, he dined with me yesterday; I gave him for dinner, soup, pigeon pie, a roast fowl, and a rice pudding, and Dutch cheese, a famous dinner I think for a hungry subaltern. I always like to provide well to entertain Smith, for I actually

---

[5]  This confirms that George had a new book ready with which to continue his 'fine diary'.

think he half starves himself, now he messes alone. We all look dull, more like the present cantonment of the regiment, it's too dismal for all, some seem to envy my duty, many speak of the danger I will be exposed to, but the more danger, the more honour. 'Glory is the word' so says my friend La Donna Maria. I have several times since I have been in the village thought I saw or heard the note of canary birds, this morning I satisfied myself, on seeing near a dozen small birds in an apple tree. I got my gun and shot two of them, one proved to be of the canary breed, only darker than those I saw in Portugal, it is very strange I never saw any since I left that country, before seeing these.

Oscotz is a scattered town on the brow of a young mountain, and is interspersed with gardens and trees, there are two very good streets, containing houses equal to those of Olite, and the general appearance, although irregular is pleasing, conveying the idea of something between a town and village. The church which stands on the highest part of the town has an uncommon pretty appearance. The road from Muskitz, in a valley between the mountains to it, is through an immense large wood. The valleys and mountains are covered in general with stately trees, oak, chestnut and elms.

The main roads of Spain are said to be the finest in Europe, the one from Irurtzun to Pamplona, for three leagues is as straight as an arrow, and looks beautiful. Captain Fitzclarence of the 10th Hussars just left the village, on his way to his regiment, he took a little cold pigeon from me for lunch, he confirmed all the good news I had heard before, respecting the defeat of the enemy in Germany[6]. I don't like this buck, half as much as I do his brother, the lieutenant; this fellow is so uncommonly high and proud, he is one of Lord Wellington's Aide de Camp's, but he prefers doing duty with his regiment, to a life of inactivity at headquarters.

The following Military Notice was discovered stuck against 'Shiny' Burke's door at Oscotz this morning:

Captain Burke having been deprived by the fortunes of war of the 'Society of his dear FRIENDS in the Regent's Hussars, intends graciously to condescend with the 18th fellows'.

Burke was certainly heard to say words nearly to the above effect, I believe only in joke, but the fun is that he threatens vengeance

---

[6] Marshal Ney's force, was defeated by the Prussians, at the Battle of Dennewitz on 6 September 1813. Following this defeat Napoleon drew in his army towards Leipzig.

against the writer who[ever] he [is] and everyone else well knows, but he pretends he does not, and if anyone was to tell him, he would not believe them.

I start for Santesteban tomorrow morning, at day break, I intend taking two horses and John Porter with me, with a few trifling things I may want. This book Ipper takes to Vitoria, this night, which is fourteen leagues from this village, but I am anxious to have it out of my hands, now it is of no more use. I wrote to Worcester today, to enquire respecting some family affairs there.

Santesteban. The road to this place firstly lay across an immense heath everywhere, and there are woods with tracks that would puzzle any stranger to find the right road to a place, our guide however, seemed to be master of his business, and although, he pointed out an immense high mountain, over which he said we must go, still it appears often, as if we are going quite a contrary way to it, but found it a zigzag road of great length, going like two miles to the right and then two miles to the left, until we got to the top.

### List of My Horses, Mules, Servants – September 1813

No. 1 Grey horse, Crafty.
No. 2 Bay horse, Worcester, (my Battle Horse).
No. 3 Black horse, Andalusian, (late King Joseph's).
No. 4 Bay mare Morales, (for baggage).
No. 5 Pye bald mare pony, 2 years old, she is in foal, and stands four feet tall. Named Belisarda, (for the small breakfast canteens).
No. 6 A mule, Doctor, (for baggage).

Fly and Swift, two French greyhounds.

Vitoria, (dog), my French prisoner, a faithful companion.

John Porter, valet and cook.
John Ipper, groom.
Jossa, a Portuguese servant, hired him at Sovillida, very faithful.
Kingston, a mounted Dragoon[7].

---

[7] Private Henry Kingston.

## A List of Officers who came out with the 18th Hussars, from England 13th January 1813

### Remarks

| | |
|---|---|
| Colonel Murray | Left ill at Palencia, and since gone to England. |
| Major Hughes | |
| Captain Bolton | |
| Captain Turing | Killed at Vitoria, 21st June. |
| Captain Clements | Aide de camp to Marshal Beresford. |
| Captain Kennedy | |
| Captain Carew | Killed at Vitoria, 21st June. |
| Captain Burke | |
| Lieutenant Russell | |
| Lieutenant Conolly | Resigned. |
| Lieutenant Jones | Promoted to Troop in 3rd Dragoons. |
| Lieutenant Smith | Resigned. |
| Lieutenant Blackett | Resigned. |
| Lieutenant Hesse | |
| Lieutenant Rowlls | Deserted. |
| Lieutenant Woodberry | Author |
| Cornet Curtis | Promoted to Lieutenant, but left ill at Santarem. |
| Cornet Dolbel | Promoted to Lieutenant. |
| Cornet Curtis | |
| Cornet Foster | Wounded at Vitoria, and has since died. |
| Paymaster Deane | |
| Surgeon Chambers | |
| Surgeon Pulsford | |
| Surgeon Quincey | |
| Adjutant Waldie | Resigned Adjutancy, but permitted to hold rank of Lieutenant. |
| Veterinary Surgeon Pilcher | |

Officers who have joined the 18th Hussars in Spain since the campaign commenced.

Adjutant Duperier
Captain Richard Croker

**Route of the 18th Hussars in Portugal and Spain**
**Embarked at Portsmouth 13th January 1813, and Arrived at Lisbon**
**2nd February**

| 1813 | Portugal-Place | Distance – Leagues |
|------|----------------|--------------------|
| Feb 2 | Lisbon, Belem. | 1 |
| 6 | Luz | 1 ½ |
| Apr 2 | Sacavem | 2 |
| 3 | Vilafranca [de Xira] | 4 |
| 4 | Azambuja | 3 ½ |
| 5 | Cartaxo | 2 ½ |
| 21 | Santarem | 2 ½ |
| 22 | Golega | 4 |
| 23 | Vila Nova da Barquinha | 1 ½ |
| May 2 | Thomar | 3 |
| 3 | Cabacos | 5 |
| 4 | Espinhal | 5 |
| 5 | Lousa | 4 |
| 7 | Cortizes | 4 |
| 8 | Oliveirinha | 5 |
| Bobadela Reg. H.Q. | | |
| 9 | Seia | 3 |
| 11 | Vila Cortes da Sera | 3 ½ |
| 12 | Baracal | 3 ½ |
| 13 | Freixedas | 2 |
| Alverca Reg. H.Q. | | |
| 19 | Ozzors Everdosa | 5 |
| Erredozinho Reg. H.Q. | | |
| 20 | Sevillada | 6 |
| 21 | Pocinho Ferry | 3 |
| 22 | Torre de Moncorvo | 2 |
| | (crossed the Douro in boats) | |
| 24 | Fornos de Algodres | 5 |
| 25 | Villa De Ala | 4 |
| 26 | Sendim | 3 |
| 27 | Brandilanes | 7 |
| 29 | Carbajales de Alba | 4 |
| 31 | La Hiniesta | 5 |
| Crossed the ford of Almendra | | |
| June 1 | Fresno (near Zamora) | 3 ½ |
| 2 | Morales de Toro | 3 |
| 3 | Pedrosa del Rey | 1 ½ |
| 4 | Torrelobaton | 3 |

| | | |
|---|---|---|
| 5 | Penafior de Hornija | 1 ½ |
| | Near Vallodolid | |
| 6 | Santa Cecilia deal Acor | 6 |
| 7 | Villalobon | 3 |
| | Near Palencia | |
| 8 | Tamara de Campos | 4 ½ |
| 9 | Fromista | 1 ½ |
| 10 | Villasandino | 5 |
| 11 | Padilla [Olmillos de Sasamon?] | 1 |
| 12 | Isar | 1 |
| | Skirmishing before Burgos | |
| 13 | Las Hormazas | 3 |
| 14 | Cernegula | 8 |
| 15 | Horna | 7 |
| 16 | Torres | 3 |
| | Near Medina de Pomar | |
| June 17 | San Llorente | 5 |
| 18 | Berberana | 2 |
| 19 | Subijana de Alva | |
| 21 | Vitoria | |
| 22 | Salvatierra | 3 |
| June 23 | Olazagutia | 5 |
| 24 | Bavomoa | |
| 25 | Aisiain | 6 |
| 26 | Pamplona | 3 |
| 27 | Olite Erriberri | 7 |
| 28 | Caseda | 6 |
| 30 | Olite Erriberri | 6 |
| July 27 | Huarte | 10 |
| 28 | Ratenath Battle near Pamplona | |
| 29 | Huarte | |
| 30 | Ratenath | |
| 31 | Ibeisua | |
| Aug 11 | Noain | 2 ½ |
| 12 | Olite Erriberri | 6 |
| Sept 15 | Mendivil | 3 |
| 16 | Torres | 3 ½ |
| | Cigar Menor Reg. H.Q. | |
| 17 | Errotz | 4 ½ |
| | Irurzan Reg. H.Q. | |
| 20 | Muskitz | 2 ½ |
| Oct | Oscotz Reg. H.Q. | |

At this point, George's diary ends abruptly in the 'fine copy' when it was sent home. George states that he did continue in a new book but as he was sent on intelligence patrols into France and then the regiment advanced over the border and George was wounded, he seems to have only kept up his journal in his 'fine copy' as he had done at other periods of frenetic activity. As George had his baggage stolen later, this 'fine copy' was lost forever and we do not therefore have any diary entries from George for the period 24 September to 31 December 1813. Thankfully, George resumed his practise of writing a rough journal on campaign on 1 January 1814 and we therefore do have his rough notes (preserved in the French version only) for 1814 and 1815. However, by referring to the diaries of Major Hughes and the regimental history, we can fill this short void in his story.

Having arrived at Oscotz on the 20 September, the regiment remained there until the 1 October, when it marched to Igurin[?], where they had to halt as the Bidassoa River was swollen by heavy rains.

On 15 October, Sir Stapleton Cotton informed them that he would inspect the regiment at Oscotz on the following day, but it turned out to be a disappointingly wet day. However, upon his arrival at 11.00 hours, Cotton found the regiment strong and well appointed, and he made them a promise to send a good report to Wellington. The regiment appears to have been without pelisses at this time. The men were informed that replacements were on their way, but the weather was so poor, that indoor battledore, shuttlecock and fives provided the only sources of exercise and entertainment. News finally arrived of the surrender of Pamplona on the 31 October.

Orders were then received for the regiment to march to Ilarregui, on the 1 of November, and to Santesteban on the following day; which it achieved despite the sleet and snow. The next day the regiment, reached Etxalar, where it received orders to return to its quarters at Ilarregui, as the poor weather had forced operations to be suspended. On the 6 November, the regiment marched up to Donamaria where it was billeted, whilst the snow continued to fall. It marched on 7 November for Etxalar in the Pyrenees by a bad road which ran alongside the Bidassoa.

The French were now entrenched, about nine miles in front. Moving forward at 04.00 by the Pass of Etxalar, the regiment struggled along a bad road into France passing many dangerous precipices. At last a Provost Marshal was found who guided it down the other side of one of the steepest mountains in the Pyrenees, where there was no road; finally joining the German Hussars at day break. Soon afterwards the infantry made an attack on a series of redoubts in its front. The hussars closely followed supporting the movements of the infantry, but there was no opportunity for them to act. Unfortunately, Wellington also caught a hussar of the 18th chasing a sheep, so the regiment was in trouble with him again. They foraged in the village of St Pee sur Nivelle and returned to Sarre, where they bivouacked, although uncomfortably as the baggage did not arrive.

On 11 October, the French were pursued, but the 18th was eventually ordered to join the 7th Division. It rained violently, and the men were thoroughly soaked. They bivouacked in a wood, the weather eventually clearing and the baggage finally arriving. The following morning extra rations of corn were issued to the horses, and extra rum to the men. Due to the terrible weather conditions, all operations were again suspended, some men and horses were put up in a sheep shed, but most were left exposed to the elements. The regiment then marched to St Pee and with some difficulty found some cover there.

The regiment was on outpost duty near Ustaritz on 18 November, the weather continuing as terrible as ever. On the 30th the brigade was inspected by General Alten in heavy rain. The regiment when on outpost duty was constantly skirmishing with the enemy's outposts from their position near Bayonne.

Captain Kennedy's squadron marched at daybreak on 7 December, crossing the Nive in support of the centre column under Marshal Beresford; the rest of the regiment moving off by squadrons at midday, but they were ordered back on the sound of a heavy cannonading beginning on the right. Orders were now received to march the following morning to join the Germans Hussars, supporting Sir Rowland Hill's troops. Moving off at 07.00 on the morning of the 8th, the regiment crossed the River Nive, at a ford near Halsou, where some of the hussars were drowned. The infantry was engaged all day and slowly advanced, but the rain grew worse, the ground becoming impossible for cavalry action. Drawing lots with the Germans for cantonments the Germans bivouacked, whilst the 18th went into the village of Halsou, and were well received by the inhabitants. Next day, still raining heavily, the brigade was ordered to retire again to St. Pee. It was almost dark when the hussars crossed the ford, which caused great confusion. Nevertheless, Major Hughes, with five troops and the baggage, was able to bivouac, finishing the day supping on bread and wine.

The terrible weather continued and at midnight on the 12th, an order was received to march, towards Cambo, for which the 18th started at 03.00 hours. It was frosty and bitterly cold, with a bright moon. Crossing the Nive again, they joined the 13th and 14th Light Dragoons (Vivian's Brigade), the 14th having suffered some loss, and very much harassed by the cavalry and infantry of the enemy, who had driven them from

Hasparren, Pierre Soult having advanced with all his light cavalry, supported by General Paris. The regiment pushed forward some patrols, which skirmished with the French cavalry at Urcuray, and the following day it went into cantonments at Urcuray.

Two of their pickets were attacked on the 16th, about three miles from Hasparren, by three squadrons of cavalry and one infantry battalion, but the enemy was checked, until the entire regiment and Morillo's Spanish troops arrived and turned the tide. On the 18th, two squadrons commanded by Major Hughes accompanied Morillo to explore the enemy's position towards Mendionde, and to aid his foraging expeditions. On crossing Mendionde bridge, they commenced to skirmish, when Morillo's Spaniards suddenly ran away, obliging the squadrons to fight to cover their flight under intense infantry musketry. All of this took place in narrow hedge-lined lanes and in a short time Major Hughes, Captain Croker and Lieutenant George Woodberry were all wounded, Captain Bolton mortally.

Major Hughes recounts that 'The Cacadores retired, and I was in the process of ordering a retreat when I received a shot under my arm, which lodged in my right breast, and I left the field, the Germans having already retired, I left Captain Bolton to withdraw the Eighteenth. The cacadores already on the road, were charged by the enemy's cavalry, upon which Captain Bolton charged the French with the Eighteenth, driving them back, but in the process getting too close to a wood, from whence their infantry mortally wounded him and took him prisoner. Croker and Woodberry were slightly wounded, with three men; two prisoners and ten horses were taken'. George was wounded in the hand, but he remained with the regiment.

The next day a flag of truce was sent to the enemy, and a letter was received by Major Hughes saying that despite every attention, Captain Bolton was grievously wounded and he requested that one of the regiment's surgeons should be sent. Pulsford and his servant went, saying that they would return if he died, or stay with him until recovered. The following day, Dr. Pulsford returned with the news of Bolton's death.

On the 22nd, the regiment marched to LaBastide Clairence and Hasparren in the lower Pyrenees, and here they remained in winter quarters until the middle of February 1814.

Nov. 1    To Ivercue. Halted on account of the Bidassoa River impassable.

7    Donamaria and Etxalar, halted.

10    Sare, in France. Nivelle.

12-13    Bivouacked near the River Nive.

| | 14 | To St. Pee [sur Nivelle] |
|---|---|---|
| | 22 | At Ustaritz, skirmish. Halt. |
| Dec. 8 | | St. Pee |
| | 9 | Passage of the Nive. |
| | 11 | [St. Nive?] |
| | 12 | Urcuray |
| | 16 | At Hasparren, near Bayonne, skirmish. |
| | 18 | With Morillo, action at Mendionde. |

22      LaBastide [Clairence] and Hasparren, winter quarters, till middle of February 1814.

Copy Certificates of Surgeons for the Medical Commission of London

This is to certify that Lieutenant George Woodberry, of the 18th Hussars, was wounded in the hand by a rifle ball shot by the enemy between Urcuray and Mendionde (middle of France), on the 18th December 1813, during an outpost encounter. This injury has weakened the hand, which will require a period of care and rest to regain its function.

Signed: W. Chambers,
Surgeon 18th Hussars.

This is to certify that Lieutenant George Woodberry, of the 18th Hussars, has had the wound to his hand incurred by ball shot near Mendionde in France, damaging the index finger and weakening his right hand.

Signed: Lucas Pulsford,
Assistant Surgeon 18th Hussars,
March 1815.

English newspaper clipping pasted into the manuscript

We are pleased that this brave young officer, Lieutenant Woodberry, of the 18th Hussars, who had been seriously wounded on December 18, 1813, in an engagement with the French cavalry at Mendionde (France) is sufficiently recuperated to resume his work with his regiment.

Source does not give a date to this notice, but must be early 1814.

# Chapter 10

# Campaign of France 1814

The New Year found the 18th still in the area around Hasparren in winter quarters, desperately waiting for spring to finally come and allow them to start campaigning once again. They did not have to wait as long as they thought for some excitement although it was only affairs between the outposts.

Chapel of Hasparren, Saturday 1st January 1814
I was riding in the town of Hasparren and I saw General Alten, then in Urcuray, where Major Hughes heals quickly from his injuries; my hand is also better and the doctors believe that in a week I will be able to use it. The Basques are very robust, staunch, beautiful, scrupulously honest and surprisingly trustworthy. I am told that they are brave, but they are suspect, because they all abandoned the flag of their own country. They are courteous and polite in their ways, to a degree that exceeds much their state of civilization. In their system, they are of a rare sobriety; for me, their existence is a miracle; with what three Basques eat per day, my dog Vitoria would be a very hungry creature.

Hasparren Chapel, Sunday, January 2
I'm tired of this monotonous life; the poor devils of inhabitants, who currently bless us as their liberators, will soon have just reason to curse us, because we consume all their provisions. Hundreds of young people, deserters from their flags, arrive from the mountains where they were hidden.

Chapel of Hasparren, Monday, January 3
I hunted this morning and I killed two rabbits and a very nice

chicken that had gone astray; I was forced to hide them as the entire neighbourhood is reduced. These people are a cursed race of brawlers, especially the women: they grumble faster and stronger even than an English woman and they are not easily intimidated. The good wife, my hostess, is a true harpie, for her family and to myself, and I am forced to keep Ipper and Sparem Joe[1] on their toes. Deane, the Paymaster, went to Saint-Jean-de-Luz to seek three month's pay. This country is more civilized than that infernal country, Spain.

Chapel of Hasparren, Tuesday January 4
Found near here the ruins of a magnificent castle belonging to the French General Harispe[2]. When Mina came here with his army, his men came in a body to ask him for permission to loot this castle; it was first searched on his behalf, then he abandoned it to the officers and then to the soldiers, who covered the work by setting it on fire. I've rescued several poor farmers from the Spanish ruffians. I don't know why, I hate the entire Spanish nation from the depths of my heart because of their abject cowardice.

Hasparren Chapel, Thursday, January 6
I saw this morning a Basque overthrow a cart that seemed very heavy by lifting it with one hand by the wheel. I asked him to put it back upright, he did it with only a single arm and very easily. Two of our hussars pushed this cart over again with difficulty, and it took three to put it upright.

Hasparren Chapel, Friday, January 7
The enemy concentrated their forces in the vicinity of the Bastide de Clarence; it is likely that they intend to attack us.

Chapel of Hasparren, Saturday, January 8
This morning, at daybreak, the enemy pushed our picquets back at [La] Bastide de Clairence and Bonloc, and advanced on Hasparren, to the great horror of the people, who had received us so well. The sound of the trumpet assembled the brigade, and I was detached with Croker's Troop at the entrance of Hasparren to charge the enemy, if he marched on the town. Our infantry skirmished with

---

[1]  'Sparem Joe' was a nickname for a Portuguese servant George had hired.
[2]  Genaral Jean Isidore Harispe, Chief of Staff to Murât in Spain.

them all day and he made little progress. We expect two infantry divisions this evening. General Picton is with us, and we have our new leader, Colonel Vivian[3], of the 7th Hussars. General Alten has left us yesterday for England.

A squadron of the 18th and the 1st [German] Hussars are, with two guns, on picquet on the heights; the rest have returned to quarters. The men repose near their horses, and are ready to move at the first warning.

Picquet near the Urcuray road to Bayonne, Sunday 9

This night, at midnight, I received the order to go with twenty men three miles forward on this road, in the direction of Bayonne. I installed the picquets and I sent out patrols who soon returned, having recognoitred a camp. I thought it was the enemy who was placed in our rear and along our left flank, but on carrying on in front I found a brigade of Brunswick infantry arriving from Bayonne.

During the night, two army divisions came and camped behind my picquet. At six o'clock, up to a thousand of the enemy made a move along the hills on the left side of the road from Pau, along the Adour; we were then ordered to halt until the arrival of Lord Wellington. About ten o'clock, his lordship passed before my post, and about two hours later, he ordered the attack. Our infantry made a movement forward and the enemy retreated beyond a stream, the Bastide de Clairence. We then re-took possession of our initial positions, and we extended our picquets as before. General Harispe, commanding the French army sent a parley to give the reason for his forward movement; he asked why the English main guard shoot at his people whenever they come to take water. It was agreed that they would remain quiet on both sides as the Bastide de Clairence was occupied on the right bank by the French, and by the English on the left bank. This affair has cost the enemy one man killed and us a corporal injured.

Kennedy was very proud to be the oldest officer present in the regiment; I want to fight and perform some act of audacity, any quick way to gain progress like Kennedy, who is an officer full of merit and a brave man. General Harispe had sent yesterday to the mayor of the chapel of Hasparren an order to prepare a nice dinner for him and his staff of eighteen persons, at five o'clock. Harispe is Basque and much loved by his countrymen.

---

[3] Brevet Lieutenant Colonel Richard Hussey Vivian.

Bernadotte[4], the Prince Royal of Sweden, was born in Pau, capital of this department. I was told that his father is still alive and that he is in the greatest misery, but this seems to me little credible[5].

Chapel of Hasparren, Monday, January 10
My apartment is so miserable I thought already of changing it; but having discovered a good room occupied by the people of the house, I quickly took possession, to the dismay of the poor wretches, but 'need has no laws'. There is a bayonet factory here, the weapon was invented and manufactured for the first time in the city of Bayonne.

Hasparren Chapel, Tuesday, January 11
We placed our picquets on the banks of a stream flowing between the Bastide de Clairence and Bonloc. The enemy retains a portion of the former village; the videttes are almost touching on the bridge, they must give one hours' notice prior to beginning hostilities.

Hasparren, Thursday, January 13
When we move, this country will suffer cruelly, because the Pyrenees crossings will be open to all the guerrillas of Spain and these poor mountain people will be left defenceless. I can anticipate their fate, and my horror redoubles towards the monster that has been so long the scourge of nations.

Hasparren, Friday, January 14
The Spanish army really ill treats the unhappy residents and the complaints made against them to Lord Wellington have decided his lordship to promulgate some severe orders! It is a threat to the camps in the Pyrenees. The Spanish soldiers receive only half of the rations of the English soldiers and they are forced to steal food so as to not die of hunger. The Portuguese had also, in principle, only a half, but Lord Wellington, seeing that they had become such good soldiers and that they fought so well, had them treated as the English troops. They do not have tents, but use very skillfully built shacks; they say that General Picton taught them how. The 2nd Regiment of Cacadores[6] are on picquet near us, it is said that Lord Wellington has great confidence in these troops.

---

[4]  French Marshal Jean-Baptiste Bernadotte had been elected heir presumptive to the childless King Charles XIII of Sweden.
[5]  George was right to be suspicious of this claim, Bernadotte's father having died in 1780.
[6]  The Caçadore battalions formed the light infantry of the Portuguese army and fought in brown uniforms.

Picquet at Bonloc, Saturday, January 15
I relieved a post of the 1st [German] Hussars: the enemy is in our front.
I spent part of the day with three sisters, daughters with a good
nature, but without culture. They played cards with me and they tried
to teach me the Basque language: but I believe that it is impossible for
an Englishman to achieve it. Around 6 o'clock, when it was dark, I
retired my main picquet to a large house, half a mile in the rear,
leaving there a sergeant and six men to monitor the road. My servant
made me a good dinner and I slept well near the kitchen fire.

Picquet at Bonloc, Sunday, January 16
This morning I was at Mass with the villagers; anything to pass the
time. I was relieved at noon by an officer of the 1st [German] Hussars,
and I returned to my lodgings. Hesse dined with me, and at eight
o'clock we dressed to go to the ball given by Sir Stapleton Cotton.
There we met nearly fifty officers and almost as many women, many
remarkably pretty. General Picton danced. After a social, there were a
few waltzes, then a fandango; and finally dinner, with plenty of grog,
which we had no time to eat. It broke up at two o'clock in the
morning. There were several English officers' women, whose figures
and deportment overshadowed all the beauties of the country.

Hasparren, Monday, January 17
Last night's ball has slammed us all; the floor of the room had no
elasticity! I was at the town of Hasparren, to visit many of our
dancers, with Hesse. We found that one of the most beautiful was
the servant of an old chap who appeared to be little charmed by our
presence. Two others were serving in their shops; one of them gave
us each a piece of sugar and she at the same time put one in her
mouth. I think that it was a great honour, in the fashion of her
country, but we could not help bursting out laughing. We changed
quarters today; my troop is better housed and more under my hand.
My house has no fireplace in the kitchen. I've quickly remedied this
by building one, making a hole in the roof and ceiling; I seek
tomorrow for a pipe. The people here are not very happy with my
introduction, but I am in control.

Picquet in Ayherre, Wednesday, January 19
I relieved Lieutenant Bobers, of the 1st [German] Hussars[7]. Here, in

---

[7] Lieutenant Charles von Bobers who was later killed at Waterloo. Beamish No. 777.

the house where the picquet is, is a very pretty girl, whose company is much appreciated by me. She is literate and has some talents; but we cannot expect to find here highly refined women or any who are exercised in the high arts of pleasure.

In the afternoon, I went around La Bastide de Clairence. A pretty bridge separates the two armies; there is accumulated there a mass of material forming an obstacle to prevent surprises by their cavalry. The house which I am in is a farm owned by a rich man who seems, like his whole family, very attached to the English. I told him about the Bourbons and I told him that the white cockade had been raised at St Jean de Luz; but he shook his head and turned away from me with a look of disdain, when I said that that family is better than that of Napoleon's.

Hasparren Chapel, Thursday, January 20
Forage is very scarce; I tried to get my men returned to their old quarters. I am told that there is six months' worth of wheat at St Jean de Luz but the roads are so bad that the mules cannot go back there and return in less than five days. The auxiliary muletiers receive a dollar per day per man and one per mule. They are attached to the commisariat. The daily expenditure is huge and perhaps exceeds that of the army's pay.

Hasparren Chapel, Friday, January 21
I went out with three companies of the regiment to find forage; I searched all the houses of Bonloc, and I only found an insignificant amount. I then threw my piquets forward, chased away the enemy piquet and in ten minutes, my foragers had their fill. I withdrew before the arrival of the French cavalry. I am not afraid of them making a reciprocal movement, as there is no forage on this side. Some of my comrades play cards from sunrise until dinner. Pulsford and Hesse appear to be among the losers, and poor Olly vows daily to stop playing: the next day it is he who starts it up again. Lieutenant Rowlls is a little touched, and if he gets the vacant troop, his brain will be completely deranged. It is believed that he made about 2,000 pounds at the Battle of Vitoria, and since that time, he has never had any clear ideas.

Chapel of Hasparren, Saturday, January 22
All morning, I stared at the moutains and I still view them with admiration. Those who have not seen the Pyrenees, can get no idea of their magnificence. Every night we hear the cannon; the first few

times we thought there was an alert and we put the regiment on alert; but we are now so well accustomed to it, that the noise hardly awakens us; these are our batteries on the banks of the Adour firing on enemy ships carrying supplies to their army in Bayonne.

Piquet at Bonloc, Sunday, January 23

Upon my arrival at Bonloc, I was invited to go to the bridge to speak to an aide de camp of General Pierre Soult. He wished to have some English newspapers, and to discuss other matters, he gave me the latest gazettes that he had received from Paris. I promised to send them back to him tomorrow. I asked several questions which he appeared to avoid answering about his Emperor, finally he said 'You imagine, because we let you remain in this country, that things go badly for us, but you will soon realise your mistake and you will be happy to return over the Pyrenees'. I did not discuss it, knowing that he would never agree with me, and we abandoned the topic. He asked me how we spent our time, I answered that we had dances in Hasparren and that there was one happening precisely then at the house of Sir Stapleton Cotton. He then manifested a strong desire to attend, because of a beautiful lady of Hasparren and her friend, who would be there.

This evening I sent a peasant to the picquet line of the enemy cavalry, to ask the officer to send me some good wine which was for sale in the village: he did and also refused the money that the peasant offered to pay him. French officers take what they please without a thought; I find this very evil is even allowed in their own country, but I would like Lord Wellington to allow us to do the same.

Chapel of Hasparren, Monday, January 24

I was relieved this morning at noon; I had first received the visit of Colonel Vivian, I begin to like him a lot, because he seems to take great pleasure in explaining the outpost service to young officers. Dr. Pulsford is sent to Saint Pee to examine Mr. Morris. The latter had left England with the remount some time ago, and he fell ill at Bilbao where his wife and her child soon joined him. Major Hughes believes that Mr. Morris is perhaps not as seriously ill as he says in his letters.

Hasparren Chapel, Tuesday, January 25

General Picton, Lt. General Sir Stapleton Cotton and General Clinton[8] have their quarters in Hasparren. Picton is much loved in

---

8    Major General Sir Henry Clinton.

the army, despite the strictness of his discipline: he is a man who is never concerned with his own well-being before having ensured that of his men. He searched the other day for the Commissary General of the division and said: 'I see that you have failed repeatedly to provide rations to the division; at this moment, the men have not yet received the ration for yesterday, I have to tell you that if it is not distributed this afternoon, I'll have you bound and whipped before the division'. The other tried to give excuses, but Picton had him put out of the door. The commissary then distributed the rations as soon as possible, but he complained to Lord Wellington. His Lordship listened and said: 'So he threatened to whip you? Well! Go about your business and provide the provisions to the division regularly, or by God, he is a man to keep his word!'.

Chapel of Hasparren, Wednesday, January 26
It is assumed that Bayonne will fall in a month. Its garrison amounts to ten thousand men. The army of Soult, which is about forty thousand men strong, lies on the banks of the Gave de Oloron: the enemy will dispute the crossing of this river, then that of the Gave de Pau and then finally the Adour. The affairs of Buonaparte seem to go very badly; it is said that fifteen thousand men of Soult's best troops were ordered to the banks of the Rhine.

Picquet in Ayherre, Thursday, January 27
I'm again on picquet, there are so few sub-lieutenants with the regiment. I just saw a peasant, from Pau. Marshal Soult and General Clausel have passed their troops in review. He has approximately fifteen thousand conscripts, but their number decreases by ten to twenty men per day by desertion. It happens here in fact daily, and there are thousands of deserters living with the residents within our lines. The enemy wanted to prevent the inhabitants on his side bringing us supplies, but the high prices that everything acquires in the town of Hasparren forces the farmers to take great hazards to get to market, and every night they pass the rivulet with huge baskets of eggs, poultry and bread. I visited all the beds of the house I occupy this morning. The straw-stuffed mattresses have been emptied and I will keep the contents for my poor horses. The woman of the house is angry, but all the officers did the same. The residents gathered in the cemetery, and they swear that they will go to complain to Lord Wellington.

Hasparren Chapel, Friday, January 28
We have now neither hay nor wheat and we are obliged to send

squads out to gather grass along the hedges, the only place where we can find any. Others were used to cut gorse and ferns that we first bash with a mallet and then chop it. The horses are very hungry; this will allow them to live, but will not give them much strength. We pay five shillings for a pound of sugar of low quality; coffee is eighteen pence. We buy from the English sutlers and they have the conscience to let us pay 30 shillings per pound. My former servant Porter, now our sutler, was whipped by order of the Provost in Cambo [les-Bains] for purchasing meat from the inhabitants who were on their way to market, and he then resold it for double the original purchase price.

### Chapel of Hasparren, Saturday, January 29
The priests of this country seem to know the art of living well, you will find in their houses all of the best things possible, while the poor devils of the inhabitants who maintain them, are literally dying of hunger. Sir Stapleton Cotton inspected the quarters of the regiment today. Our cantonment extends for nearly three miles along a row of hills separated by a valley.

### Hasparren, Sunday, January 30
The Spanish army, whose quarters are in the surrounding area, are under the command of General Morillo. They had an engagement all morning with the French in the mountains behind Hélette. I am sure that these scoundrels of Spaniards will receive a good thrashing. I saw an old friend from Olite, the Spanish Captain Murphy; he threw himself into my arms and gave me a great hug. I learned from him that all my friends at Olite are going on well and that Zacarias is now married.

### Mendionde, Monday, January 31
I went out with a party of the regiment to collect, if at all possible, fodder for a day at the expense of the enemy beyond their outposts on the road to Hélette. I am familiar with the field, because it is near the house occupied by the enemy where Bolton[9] received a fatal wound. I arrived on the French picquet out of the blue, who fled at the gallop in the direction of Hélette. I crossed the stream and I occupied the heights opposite; but I made a poor harvest, barely

---

9 Captain Robert Bolton had been severely wounded at the Action of Mendionde (where George Woodberry was also wounded) on 18 December 1813. He was captured and died of his wounds the following day.

enough to feed the officer's horses for a day. We have been engaged with a troop of the 21st Chasseurs, but not a peep to either one side nor the other. As soon as I had recalled my scouts, the enemy retook their position. The Mayor of Mendionde is a kind man with a lot of John Bull in his ways; he came out to view my encounter with a bottle and a cake.

Hasparren Chapel, Tuesday, February 1
The Commissary pays the people for fodder rations, etc., with bills on the Paymaster-General, payable sixty or ninety days from that date. These poor people do not understand these notes and the Commissary returns a few days after and buys them for the twentieth part of their real value. I am sure of the fact[10].

Ustaritz, Thursday, February 3
I came this morning to Ustaritz with Hesse to see some friends in the infantry. I lunched with the Brigade Major Gurwood[11] and I went with him on horseback to Cambo, where there is a hospital full of the sick and wounded of the army. I saw my former servant Bentley[12], who was wounded a few minutes after me, the day when poor Bolton was killed. It was first believed that this unfortunate boy would lose his arm, but there is now nothing to fear.

At the advance posts in Ayherre, Friday, February 4
I enjoyed myself this morning looking at the review of the French troops passing by General Harispe. We saw about three thousand men in fine order, well dressed, with white gaiters. They had three Eagles. I burn to take a French Eagle, and if ever I get in the middle of the enemy infantry during a charge, I shall try to take one or I will lose my life trying. Our horses are starving; two fell from weakness.

Hasparren, Saturday, February 5
Last night, I was abruptly woken from my sleep by my videttes who were under fire; and I remained awake throughout the rest of the night. I never could discover the cause of the shooting. The enemy fired, my men reacted, but nothing was moving, and I'd like to believe that all this fracas was caused by some poltroon of a conscript who had seen the devil or one of his henchmen and who

---

[10] This was a well-known trick by which many commissaries became very rich indeed.
[11] Captain John Gurwood of the 9th Light Dragoons was Brigade Major to a brigade in the 6th Division.
[12] Private Lewis Bentley.

fired on him. Lieutenant Southwell of the 14th Light Dragoons[13], arrived yesterday at Bonloc, at our outposts, he was accompanied by a French officer in parley who he gave into our hands; two lieutenants of French cavalry were sent back to the enemy by Lord Wellington in exchange for Southwell.

Hasparren, Sunday 6 February
Southwell said that immediately after he had been taken prisoner with Captain Brotherton[14], they led them both to Pau, where they took them to dinner with Generals Harispe and Soult. That evening they conducted them to a ball, and that they were kept particularly occupied. The next day, they were transferred to Bayonne by an aide de camp; they dined there with Marshal Soult, and they remained there several days. He then sent them inland, where they remained together until the moment when Southwell was handed over. Brotherton remains a prisoner as Lord Wellington and Marshal Soult cannot agree on his exchange.

Hasparren Chapel, Tuesday, February 8
My poor horses are in a very bad condition; we completely lack forage, and we are obliged to send men up to four miles simply to gather gorse. I walked in the mountains today, but I took my shotgun with two barrels in fear of meeting any Spanish soldiers.

Hasparren, Wednesday, February 9
The Basques walk on stilts quite similar to those that I made myself and wore when I was a child. Our Adjutant, Mr. Dupérier, who is I believe, a native of the Landes Department, has a pair and walks in the village as fast as the peasants. Major Hughes also has a pair, but he is shy and unsure when he uses them.

Hasparren Chapel, Friday, February 11
We left our quarters this morning to go to Ayherre. The infantry was woken at the same time; we warned the enemy of our intended movement three hours in advance. The French were ready to leave at five o'clock in the morning. The Brigade Major gave the signal to our outposts at Bonloc by waving his hat. They [the French] moved out of

---

[13] Lieutenant the honourable Arthur Francis Southwell, 14th Light Dragoons, was captured at Hasparren on 13 December. Being exchanged he could return to his service immediately.
[14] Actually Major Thomas Brotherton 14th Light Dragoons. He was also captured on 13 December 1813 but remained a prisoner of war until the war ended in April 1814.

the village immediately, sounding bugles and with drums beating (119th Infantry Regiment and a squadron of the 2nd Hussars). Marching for an hour after leaving, we could easily have taken them all. If we meet them tomorrow, we will not spare them: from today it would be okay to attack them. We found fodder for a few days, and the horses devoured it all so that I have a great fear that they may get sick.

Ayherre, Saturday, February 12
The poor mare that I had taken in the skirmish at Morales in Spain which, since that time, carried a part of my luggage, fell this morning and I was forced to shoot it with a musket.

George was offered the companionship of one of the local girls, but gave a rather ungallant reply.

La Bastide Clairence, Sunday, February 13
I was walking with Quincey in Ayherre; we had our guns and we were amused with hunting birds. We wanted to see the camp of the two infantry divisions there. The town seems very lively, because of all the officers lodged there; when the army does leave, all the women will accompany them.

I've been at the house at the outposts and I saw the beautiful Maria, who seemed very sad and very abandoned. She asked if she could come with me and follow me during the campaign but I replied 'Marry me? No, Maria. With you I want fun and to play, I really want to embrace you, but hang me, for a wife!'

Ayherre, Monday, February 14
We fought all day in the valley, but no news and no orders.

Ayherre, Tuesday, February 15
Skirmish in the direction of Bidache, where we expect to move every day.

Ayherre, Wednesday, February 16
I was with Burke on the side of Mauléon[15]. A man was brought before a Court Martial for losing his trousers and he would have suffered this morning his punishment if his wife had not come to confess that it was she who had sold them. I have heard of women who wear the trousers, but not yet women who sell them!

---

[15] Mauleon is in the area of Anglet, just south of Bayonne.

# Chapter 11

# Advancing on Orthez

Although Bayonne remained a thorn in Wellington's side and remained under blockade, Soult's army was slowly driven eastward as it tried to hold each successive river line, only to be turned out by Wellington's superior forces. The cavalry largely skirmished and supported the infantry in its advance, but as they moved further eastward the country became more conducive to cavalry attacks.

> Bardos, Thursday, February 17
> Party till two o'clock, we made a march of close to five leagues on a very bad road. I'm in a good house, at the foot of a hill; my hosts are very helpful and have plenty of fodder. The horrible Mrs. M[orris], the wife of the lieutenant, has followed the regiment's long march. I cannot feel for her, when she is a real bitch. I offered to take her child on my horse and to carry it; she refused with an expletive, cursing everyone and the regiment in particular.

The supply of the army remained poor and a blind eye was regularly turned to the men pillaging, disproving the claims that Wellington's troops did not steal from the French.

> Bardos, Friday, February 18
> My luggage only arrived this morning because of the bad roads and the miserable condition of my beasts. Most of the surrounding lands belong to the family of Captain de Grammont, of the 10th Hussars. The enemy is in force three leagues from here, and it is believed that we will pass the river near Guiche on a bridge of boats. There were many complaints against my troop by the inhabitants; my men have

stolen their bacon, but I don't know what to do; our rations have been so bad for some time that I am not surprised to see the poor lads getting food as they can. Need often allows what honour defends.

Bardos, Saturday, February 19
Pulsford came with me this morning to make a visit to the new Captain Russell[1]. During lunch, we drank to his success. Poor boy! This recent promotion has disturbed his brains! A division of our army occupies Bardos.

Bardos, Sunday, February 20
This morning I met Captain de Grammont who went to Guiche[2]. The peasants greeted him eagerly and want his family to be reinstated with possession of his former estates. There has been shooting all morning on the banks of the Adour. Waldie, Russell and Chambers have dined with me and I returned unable to pronounce a syllable.

George was in a very reflective mood and wrote with some pathos.

Bardos, Monday, February 21
I spent the greater part of the day at the Court Martial with Kennedy and Lieutenant M[orris] What a miserable individual he is! He just talks about the brutalities to which he has subjected his wife and God knows she deserves it! But it is still unpleasant to hear of such stories, especially from the mouth of the husband. I bought two lambs for 2 dollars; they are very beautiful and weigh each about nine pounds. Here potatoes are in abundance.

Love is the most delicious of all the passions of the human heart: it supports humans in the face of adversity, guarantees against the worries and problems of life. Assisted by love, I brave the rigours of winter and the heat of summers. Love makes my rations acceptable to me, a dinner composed only of my ration, one pound of meat and a pound of bread. It is with a happy heart that I relish it. I am grateful to have this food and I eat with delight; it is in health and joy that I finish this modest meal and go to a bed that many would

---

[1]   Robert Russell had become a captain on 26 January 1814.
[2]   The Grammont family had come from Chateau Guiche and had been expelled during the Revolution.

find hard, but on which I sleep as deep as that of a prince in a palace. It is my love for [Blank – Amelia?] and an honest heart that cause all my happiness; it is the source from which sprang the bliss, the link that unites all, support which supports all. May all my friends be happy! What happiness for me if I was sure!

Bardos, Tuesday, February 22
I have been with the troop collecting forage on the banks of the Adour. The enemy fired on us. The river is about two hundred yards in width; its current is rapid; we will not pass it without the aid of the pontoons. Our Commissary is very sick, and I'm very concerned; because he is a brave and honest boy, very much loved, and few men of his profession deserve the honour that I give him[3]. The infantry started a movement on Bidache. We will follow them tomorrow morning.

Came, Wednesday, February 23
The brigade had orders to march for Bidache at ten o'clock in the morning. Waldie and I were seconded to prepare the quarters of the regiment; we found the town full of infantrymen. The enemy was at that time in the village of Arancous, which our troops soon attacked. He retired on Oeyregave and crossed the Gave de Oloron in boats positioned there ready to receive them. Our infantry arrived just at the point when they set off in the the last boat and they fired a volley which killed or wounded almost everyone who rode in it. The brigade was deployed in a plain, ready for action, but the enemy fleeing, we went to take our quarters around Came. This town, which has an ancient aspect, is located on a hill on the edge of the Bidouze. Our lodgements are detestable. I did not see my luggage all day. The regiment forded the Bidouze in front of here; our artillery canonnaded the enemy all afternoon across the Gave de Oloron and it is reported that the French intend to oppose our passage.

Labastide de Berne[4], Thursday, February 24
We were pleasantly surprised this morning when entering this town, to find it in all respects similar to an English town: with cafes and

---

[3] Commissary August Schaumann was quite ill at Bardos and being unhappy with the doctors of the 18th Hussars, he visted the French doctor in the village. Part of his cure was to drink whey made by mixing in the slime of snails! No matter how bizarre, it appears to have worked and he slowly regained his health.

[4] I believe he here refers to Labastide-Villefranche and has mixed the name up with Sauveterre de Bearn which lies only 8km away.

shops of all kinds. The infantry and the cavalry were ordered to feign an attack and to try the passage of the Gave de Oloron. We left for Escos by squadrons; the enemy canonnaded us for some time, but we were out of range. The French occupied, across the river, Oraàs and Abitain[5], villages located in the front of the fords. The infantry on our right crossed the river at a ford, but we were unfortunately repulsed and we took serious losses. Piles and farm implements under the water prevented the passage. At three o'clock, we received the order to return to the Bastide de Berne and returned to our quarters. I was sent to the picquets at Saint-Pe [de-Leren] on the banks of the Oloron, relieving Lieutenant Dunkin. I arrived there just in time for dinner and I shared the excellent meal of Dunkin, in the company of the young householder of the house where the post is established.

George was sent on a reconnaissance mission and nearly got into quite a scrape.

At the advance posts in Saint-Pe [de-Leren], Friday, February 25
Having received orders to discover the fords and to probe them, I woke up before daylight and approached the river as close as possible, I saw that the enemy had placed a sentry in front of each ford. I ordered one of my best marksmen to fire on one of them, but he didn't budge nor reply. I was preparing to pass when a peasant came to tell me that the enemy had withdrawn and informed me that the figures I was taking for sentries were only stuffed straw uniforms. I then crossed, but with difficulty, the current being violent and the water deep. I discovered three fords, one in Saint-Pe another at Saint Dos, the third at Auterrive, where I met Lieutenant Hesse. I then sent my report and I came back to dinner.

At three o'clock, I received the order to ride to Auterrive, to find the brigade and to indicate the fords to the commanding officer. I executed this mission. During the passage, I nearly lost my life from drowning rushing to the rescue of a trooper. I am feeling pretty poorly now that I am at my leisure, from having swallowed a gallon of river water and having taken a complete dip. But I do not pity myself; I had no other means to save one of my peers, a brother officer[6]. Indeed, as soon as the regiment saw me in danger, all rushed

---

[5]  He incorrectly refers to Abitain, as this village is on the western bank of the Gave, he probably meant Athos-Aspis which lies on the French bank.
[6]  No memoir of the regiment yet discovered records the name of the officer George saved.

to help me and the man was rescued as well. We made a halt of a few minutes in Castagnede; but the trumpet soon sounded and we received the order to march on Sorde [-l'Abbaye]. We left immediately, and to see the lack of regularity of our line, you would never have believed that we were just a few miles from the enemy. We passed a pretty village named Cassaber and we reached Sorde, where we were put up in mediocre lodgings. It was very difficult to cram the brigade in, and the hotels were all filled by the staffs of the several brigades encamped in the vicinity.

One squadron of the 18th apparently performed well and took some prisoners, although General Vivian's account[7] says that having chased the French cavalry for two miles, when they reached their supports the French turned to fight. The troopers of the 18th, deserted their officers who were nearly captured (Hughes and Burke), but Vivian rallied them and prevented such an embarrassing conclusion, so perhaps it was not such a great performance after all. Bereford's aide de camp was also involved in the charge and used rather a novel weapon.

Puyoô, Saturday, February 26
Left Sorde at eight o'clock in the morning, we marched past the army of Marshal Beresford for over two miles. We passed the Gave de Pau unopposed, the enemy retiring at our approach. We joined the great road to Orthez near the village of Labatut[8]. A squadron of the regiment was then sent to the left to make a reconnaissance and to take possession of a few villages. The remainder moved a league along the road in the direction of Orthez, and there discovered the French outposts near the village of Puyoô. The squadron on advance guard, commanded by Burke, charged, Vivian at their head, and drove the French picquet through the streets of Puyoô and of Ramous in a brilliant manouevre, capturing many men and several horses. Beyond these last villages, the road crosses a high wooded hill; some enemy infantry appeared there, and we abandoned the pursuit, but we placed a picquet at the foot of the hill and the brigade remained in the two villages of Puyoô and Ramous. Captain Sewell, aide-de-camp of Marshal Beresford, charged at the head of the regiment.[9] Having forgotten his sabre, he took a broomstick and

---

[7] Vivian's *Memoir* page 200.
[8] This shows that they passed the Gave de Pau at the bridge of Saint-Cricq-du-Gave.
[9] Captain William Henry Sewell 60th Foot, was serving with the Portuguese Army in 1814, but is not listed officially as an aide de camp to Marshal Beresford.

sprang at the enemy, distributing fearsome whacks all around. The 10th, 7th, & 15th Hussars forced the passage over the river near Puyoô and then returned by the ford at Bellocq. The wine at the auberge at Puyoô is excellent.

The following day, Soult stood his ground at Orthez and a severe battle ensued. The hilly ground was not ideal for cavalry, but once the French began to retire, the hussars were at the forefront of the pursuit, although they were unable to achieve much. The 18th did not suffer a single casualty this day.

Battle of Orthez, Sunday, February 27, 1814
When the regiment began marching this morning, we had little idea that a glorious victory would be won today over the enemy. Thanks be to the Almighty for this blessing! We started this morning by administering the lash to seven men near Ramous, and then we followed the road in the direction of Orthez. We were there joined by

*Below: Map of the Battle of Orthez*

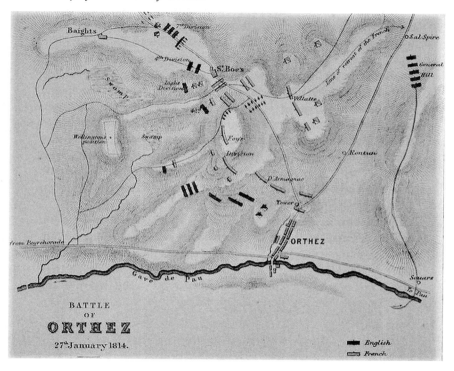

the rest of the English and allied army, and we waited for orders. Nobody would have guessed that we were separated from the enemy only by an insignificant mound. About nine o'clock, the engagement began and our brigade left the main road to occupy a hill on the left. While we climbed it, we heard in the far distance the artillery. It was necessary to cross a very steep ravine walking our horses by the head. We then entered the village of Baigts [de-Bearn], which had been taken and retaken numerous times. We then saw their army in its position, deployed in very impressive style: I regret to say, that this view struck terror into many of my comrades. At this time, Marshal Soult and his Staff passed across the battle front on horseback. The marshal urged his soldiers to fight well, I saw him very clearly with my glass.[10]

We soon came under the fire of the enemy, Vivian wanting to form the regiment more compactly, in case they should attack. But the French did us so much damage with their artillery, that two squadrons of the regiment were sent to the rear, and the right squadron took shelter with their horses in a muddy ditch. I observed how things were going in the valley. Our brave skirmishers continued fighting with varied success. Marshal Beresford and his Staff stood beside us, very exposed, because we were in the centre of the battle line, expecting a division to come to our support. When it finally arrived, we came out of the ditch and we advanced with it. At this time the enemy was withdrawing on all sides; we did not know the cause. It was because General Hill who, after having passed the Gave at Orthez, had turned the left flank of the enemy after a short engagement. The pursuit by the infantry continued until night, no opportunity being presented for our brigade to charge, the 7th Hussars were able to however and brought away approximately seventy prisoners. The road was littered with corpses; there were, I believe, more than at Vitoria; and for the time that the battle lasted, it was one of the deadliest of the entire campaign.

The enemy is in full retreat on St-Sever. It seems that, from the start, Soult realised that he would lose the battle and that knowing the force of our cavalry, he retained his own in their rearguard. They were therefore, several hours ahead of the infantry and completely out of our reach. We occupied the great road in the centre of the position; we were seen very clearly and we expected a hard fight for

---

[10] Telescope or spy glass.

it. We have captured an insignificant number of guns. I don't know how Soult arranged to escape with the rest. Most of our losses were caused during the main attack in the centre. The enemy artillery occupied a strong position next to a mill. It took some time before our guns were able to engage this point, but as soon as they began, some of the French guns were immediately withdrawn. Lord Wellington was hit by a spent bullet, but only slightly injured. His aide de camp, Lord March, was badly wounded[11]. This handsome young man belongs to the 52nd; learning that his regiment was going to advance, he asked Lord Wellington for permission to join his company, saying that he could not bear it if he could not lead it. His request was granted, and we know the result of his bravery. I met his brother, Lord Lennox[12], who was going to see him. His pain was easy to see.

Lord Wellington was never more exposed than in this battle; all his aides-de-camp were away from him and he was seen galloping with a single orderly. He was everywhere where they needed him. My baggage and my servants were, by the result of an error, brought near the regiment during the affair. I received the welcome news when we got the order to bivouac three miles from Saint-Cricq [-Chalose]. I was able to put up my tent and all the other officers came to take refuge in it. I offered them a good supper and almost all slept under its shelter.

The French lost around four thousand men including fourteen hundred prisoners, Wellington's casualties numbering just over two thousand, not too heavy for a direct assault against such a strong defensive position.

---

[11] He was severely wounded in the chest by a musket ball, which could not be removed, he survived until 1860 however.

[12] Lieutenant Lord George Lennox, 9th Light Dragoons, one of Wellington's aides de camp.

## Chapter 12

# The Road to Bordeaux

After Orthez, the French army was in full retreat on Toulouse, but almost daily the cavalry skirmished along the way. The 18th however, were sent northwards towards the city of Bordeaux, which had indicated that it wished to declare for Louis XVIII. George found that the populace here were very frightened of their arrival, but at least they then gave them everything they wanted.

Saint-Aubin, Monday, February 28
This morning, at eight o'clock, the brigade began the pursuit. We passed Saint-Cricq, where the priests and people came to welcome us, Le Mas [Michas?], Doazit, where the bells rang in our honour, before reaching Montaut, a large village on a row of hills as high as those of Saint-Cricq. The enemy left only half an hour previously; it was then five o'clock in the afternoon. Men and horses were harassed after a march of more than forty miles. The order was therefore given to take quarters and we retired to Saint-Aubin, a small village of thirty houses. However, I found a way to accommodate my men.

Montaut is one of the most beautiful towns in the province that I have yet seen in France. I was surprised to observe several carriages, it is a new scene for me these few months. At Saint-Aubin, people took me for a French officer, but when I had denied being so, several women and children threw themselves on their knees and begged me not to kill them. The enemy, during his retreat, have portrayed us as frightening, but maybe this is better, because it is thanks to this reputation that we get all what we want without challenge.

A Chateau near Hagetmau, Tuesday 1 March

I got this morning from Colonel Vivian the order to fetch the rearguard and bring the baggage to Saint-Sever, where I would find the regiment or new orders. I went first to Saint-Cricq, then across the country, up to the road to Sault-de-Navailles and Saint-Sever. Seeing that everyone had gone, I moved on towards the latter town; but night arrived, I stopped in a beautiful chateau near Hagetmau. There was there a certain Lieutenant T[hurston?][1] of the 51st, a species of chicken and whippersnapper, who kicked his men in my presence to make him more important and for which I was much tempted to teach him myself how one must behave with subordinates. I had at this chateau an excellent dinner and good wine; the owner is a lovely and helpful boy, but devoted friend of his country and Buonaparte.

Mont de Marsan, Wednesday, March 2

At sunrise, I started looking for the baggage and I traversed the [River] Gabas on a boat. I soon came to Saint-Sever, a pretty town, in a charming location on the banks of the Adour. I rode down to the river by a zigzag road and I crossed it on a repaired bridge, then I took the great road that leads right to Mont de Marsan. I found the baggage one league from this town, where I dined and slept at the Boule d'Or inn.

Mont de Marsan, Thursday, March 3

I spent the morning visiting the town; I've seen the palace, the house of the prefect, the capitole and the guillotine, churches and libraries. I was seduced by this delightful town. One of the gentlemen of the Staff of Marshal Beresford, rode in the town this afternoon with a white cockade and a fleur-de-lys on his arm; everyone was looking on, but did not express either pleasure nor indignation. A few gentlemen of Bordeaux arrived today to invite the English army to enter into their city. It is assumed that they have the intention of declaring for Louis XVIII.

Mont de Marsan, Friday, March 4

The regiment left Marsan this morning by the road to Aire [sur l'Adour], and we expected a battle with the enemy. But when we had

---

[1]  It is almost impossible to know who George met here for absolute certain as there were four lieutenants in the 51st whose surnames started with a T, although two may discounted as on detached duty. This leaves Lieutenants Charles Thurston and Charles Tyndale. Of these, Thurston had only been made a lieutenant in January 1814 and he is therefore the most likely candidate to be the 'young whippersnapper'.

gone about two leagues, an order to halt arrived and we put up in farms near the city. Croker and I, who are housed together, dined and slept in the city and we intend to do the same as long as we stay here.

The troops were on the alert, wary of an attack by Florio and his followers.

Mont de Marsan, Saturday, March 5
Parade of the regiment in fatigues for the inspection of Colonel Vivian. He expressed his satisfaction. Mrs. M[orris], the wife of the lieutenant, was in the city today, on a pretty grey pony, with a beautiful saddle and a brand new bridle. She has finally persuaded her husband to buy her everything. There has surely never been a regiment more compromised by an officer, than the 18th, by the position of Mrs. M[orris].

An infantry division is quartered here; last night, we bivouacked by the bridge, the uproar from eighty men of various regiments, is a new kind of punishment. The order arrived at noon to march on Villeneuve [de-Marsan]. There, I received orders to go with twenty men to investigate the road up to Roquefort. I arrived there by the main road to Bordeaux; the mayor informed me that the French had evacuated the city two days ago. He reported their numbers, the number of the troops who had passed in one direction or the other in the last month, his evaluation of the French forces in Bordeaux, Langon and other places, and he handed me the list of supplies abandoned by the enemy. I then returned to Villeneuve, and found a suitable place, I put half of my detachment to feed their horses; the other half watched out, as I had learned from several peasants that a French officer by the name of Florio[2], at the head of twenty or thirty partisans, made a noise this morning around Roquefort. I was expecting to be attacked, but they left us alone and I came to Villeneuve at eight o'clock in the evening after doing fifteen leagues. This morning, after having seen the colonel and giving him the information that I had obtained, as my regiment is lodged several miles in advance, Vivian would have me stay for the night, but I

---

[2]  There is much confusion regarding this individual and nobody really knows who Captain Florian or Florio was. It is almost certain that he had never held an official rank in the army and appears to have been a local who brought together a small band of out of work douainiers and deserters who sought to disrupt allied supply lines and carry out espionage. His band did apparently capture Major Thornhill 7th Hussars whilst he was sleeping at Villeneuve de Marsan on the night of 9 March and Florio was later seen in Thornhill's uniform. On 13 July, the band ambushed a convoy of mules capturing an officer of the 40th Foot, taking a few men prisoner and hamstringing fifty-eight mules. Reference *The Prince's Dolls*, pages 166-7.

refused and I drove on with a guide to the small village of Perquie, where Croker was waiting for me with a good meal.

## At the advance posts, Sunday, March 6

This morning, about eleven o'clock, I received the order to go to the advance posts at Aire and send patrols to Monguilhem, Le Houga and Hontanx. I made them leave immediately upon my arrival and I have installed myself in an excellent chateau. I found a very helpful old lady who has made me as comfortable as I could desire, and what has made it even more pleasant, is that she speaks a little English. I am charmed with the local landscape; I beheld it with enthusiasm, admiring the sun which lay in a sky of bright red, reflected by the beautiful winding river and colouring the snowy peaks of the distant mountains.

## Aire [sur-l'Adour], Monday, March 7

My patrols are returned this morning: I learn that the enemy is in force at Nogaro and Manciet, nine leagues from here. Their patrols left Monguilhem when mine entered. Perquie, headquarters of the regiment, is a small village where the officers are poorly installed. There is a huge chateau, but our major, little Hughes, occupies it, and he shares this loneliness with a beautiful woman. I had dinner with my good hostess; she told me much about her family, who are Irish and who live in Dublin. She has three sons in the military, serving in the French armies opposed to the allies.

## Roquefort, Tuesday, March 8

We are now on the road to Bordeaux, where we will arrive in five or six days. When the regiment left Villeneuve, the inhabitants did not hide their joy at our departure and expressed themselves quite strongly on our account. Upon my arrival at Roquefort, where I received an order from the regiment, the first thing I saw was two men of the band of the partisan Florio hanged in the market place, by order of Marshal Beresford. I still have doubts about the justice of their punishment[3]. Russell has today placed Mr. D[olbel] under arrest for misconduct. I don't know anything of the case, but if it is

---

[3] Captain Thomas Wildman, 7th Hussars, had captured the one (it is unclear where a second man came from) member of Florio's group and had identified him positively with the help of the officer of the 40th (if he had been captured, he must have been let go very quickly) and apparently a soldier of the Brunswick Oels volunteered to perform the duties of executioner, as his comrade had been murdered by the group. *Prince's Dolls* page 168.

so serious then it suggests that Mr. D[olbel] will be driven out of the regiment and the army.

Captieux, Wednesday, March 9

Today, we had a long but very nice march through a huge pine forest. The road was as good as the most beautiful route in England. At Captieux, we had a pleasant surprise to see oxen and sheep at several butcher's stalls; they had killed them for army use. We bought everything and we all feasted, both officers and soldiers.

Langon, Thursday, March 10

Left Captieux at daybreak, we were in Bazas three hours later, which we entered with blaring trumpets. The inhabitants seemed transported with joy at our sight. They left the regiment waiting for about half an hour, formed on the square to give them time to admire the English hussars. The left squadron remained in Bazas, and we arrived at Langon after a tiring march of three hours. We have excellent accommodation in this town, and the entire body of officers dined together, all twelve for the first time, at the Hotel de l'Empereur. We were well received by the residents. The enemy occupies Saint-Macaire on the opposite bank of the Garonne. This is where all the provisions of the French army are; a large part comes from the shops in this town. The ferry boat was on the other side and our artillery attempted to destroy it this afternoon, but the enemy took possession of it. We hope tomorrow to march on Bordeaux.

The 18th were not to get the honour of marching into Bordeaux. George ended up in an affair of outposts.

Castets [-en-Dorthe], Friday, March 11

Contrary to our expectations, it is not the 18th Hussars who go to Bordeaux. We have to guard the passage of the Garonne. I was sent to Castets with a detachment of our hussars to monitor the boats and place observation posts on the banks in front of La Réole and Meilhan [sur-Garonne]. I have, since my arrival, been lodged in a beautiful and comfortable chateau. I soon received from General Lord Dalhousie[4] the secret order to prepare the way to pass a corps

---

[4]  Lieutenant General Lord George Dalhousie commanding the 7th Division.

of infantry to the other side. I immediately secured thirty-eight barges and boats; I sent the information to his lordship and I had just sat myself at the table, when news came that the enemy had attacked my detachment in front of La Réole. I rode these two leagues at a gallop, and as I was carrying out a reconaisance in front of La Réole, the enemy fired a volley of musketry at me; a ball crossed the saddle of my orderly. I judged it prudent to keep a little more distant, I went on foot and I got near the river. I saw on the opposite bank the inhabitants, but also some French officers and soldiers. The officers saw me and hailed me. I then took the opportunity to replace the videttes that the enemy fire had forced away, but they pulled back again as soon as I had left them. I then ordered my picquets to dismount, to take cover behind the trees and to fire their carbines. Immediately the French soldiers went into their houses and the residents fled; my videttes were able to resume their posts without any further trouble. I then galloped to Castets where on my arrival at the river, I found Major Winnett, of the 68th[5] with one hundred and sixty men. He quickly crossed in two boats and I sent my report to General Lord Dalhousie. Winnett must seize by surprise the town of Saint-Macaire tomorrow morning at daybreak. He bivouaqued that night on the highway and his picquets stop everything from passing.

Langon, Saturday, March 12

During last night, I received a new order from Lieutenant General Lord Dalhousie: it was to move the vessels at Castets to Langon at daybreak this morning. At four o'clock, I embarked on one of the largest, and I arrived at Langon around eight o'clock. I came to the general, who congratulated me and thanked me for my successful efforts to move Winnett and his men over the river. The attempt has been successful; Saint-Macaire was captured this morning without a shot being fired. It is the first force which has crossed the Garonne. Upon my return to Castets, I received the order to march on Beautiran with my detachment, taking the road to Bordeaux. The squadron to which I belong, having received the order to be at Beautiran by three o'clock, Mr. Dolbel came to relieve me and I went to Langon. I found good accommodation for me and my men; Deane and Chambers were having dinner; they hastened to get another bottle of Bordeaux in my honour.

---

[5]   Major James Winnett 68th Foot, he was then acting as a Brigade Major.

The British army came to Bordeaux this morning; I saw the Duc d'Angoulême pass through Langon on route to Bordeaux. I really hope that this is the last campaign of Buonaparte.

George lost part of his luggage this day, including his 'fine journal', soon after he nearly lost his freedom.

Beautiran, Sunday, March 13
I have no luck; I lost my desk[6] and part of my luggage. It is this rabble of Florio, who took them opposite Rions. I sent back my servant Sparem Joe who I then blamed for his stupidity, because he stayed to drink with the rearguard and this is the cause of everything.

It is said that the allies have entered Paris[7] and it is stated by some that the King of Naples[8] has embraced their cause. At Barsac[9], a village which is known by this name in England, the wine I bought for ten sous a bottle which would sell for 15 shillings in England. It was three years old and was delicious. At the very moment when I was sitting down at my table with Captain Russell[10], I received the order to leave immediately to reconoitre the left bank of the Garonne, between Cadaujac and Castets, to a length of eight leagues. I was very tired, but the order coming from Vivian appointing me to this service, I left immediately. My instructions were for me to seize all the boats and vessels on the right bank and to move them to the left bank. Seeing many boats on the opposite shore at Cambes, I crossed to speak to the mayor.

He invited me to stay, saying that the enemy was not there and that he would meet with the sailors and send me their response. I followed him to his chateau; where he then told me I was a prisoner. The room was full of solid, well-armed men, I sat in front of the fire with his wife; and placed my hand over my sabre. Soon all left for their homes under different pretexts. I thought that they were going to find the gandarmes to arrest me. The lady offered me refreshments which I accepted. After three hours, the mayor came to tell me that a boat was waiting for me for to take me back to the

---

6   This presumably was when George lost his 'fine copy' of his journal covering from mid-September 1813.
7   The news was a little premature, the allies entering Paris on 31 March.
8   Marshal Joachim Murat had indeed sided with the allies in an attempt to retain his crown in the Kingdom of Naples.
9   Famouse even today for its sweet sauturnes.
10  Robert Russell had become a captain in the January.

other side. It was about nine o'clock in the evening, it was raining very hard and it was very dark. The boatman landed me, and without giving an answer to any of my questions, he pushed his boat back into the current. I found myself in a wood; after several futile attempts to discover my way, and after several falls in muddy ditches, I lay down under a tree waiting for daylight. I saw then that I was very close to Isle Saint-Georges and I found my house and my orderly with my horses. I got a terrible cold and I feel very ill and am resting.

Isle-Saint-Georges, Monday, March 14
All the different picquets and observation posts between Cadaujac and Castets are installed via me; I sent my report to Colonel Vivian. Russell is lodged in the same house as me and we had dinner together. Last night I brought musicians and we danced. The mayor of the village came with his two daughters, who are charming and I danced with them.

Beautiran, Tuesday, March 15
This country is beautiful: I could live here and maybe even forget England. We danced again this night; the mayor and his wife, had entrusted to me their daughters. They were enchanted to stay. They were sitting on my knees and I lost my heart to the elder, who is delicious; but we are leaving tomorrow, and it is likely that, as with all the other loves of my life, she will not be one tomorrow. The mistress of the house sent her husband to Bordeaux and she laid siege to me; but after the departure of the mayor's girls, she stopped tempting me and I left her with old Russell and returned to my bed.

# Chapter 13

# Rapid Advance to Toulouse

Having ridden to Bordeaux, without ever entering the city, the 18th were now to catch up with the main army on their drive eastwards by undertaking forced marches.

Langon, Wednesday, March 16

We departed this morning to join the army of Lord Wellington by forced marches. It is rumoured that Soult has inflicted a defeat on us[1]; the people of the country seem to be dismayed. They fear the return of their countrymen and the punishment they will suffer for their support for us. It seems that a division of our army will remain in Bordeaux and that the 12th and 16th Light Dragoons will take the place of the 1st [German] Hussars, which follow after us tomorrow.

Bazas, Thursday, March 17, Saint Patrick's Day

It is a year ago today that the regiment was dead drunk at Luz, in Portugal. This year, it is quite different, everyone is still sober. This town will tonight be the headquarters of Marshal Beresford. A squadron of our regiment, recently arrived from England, is one day's march ahead of us; this is commanded by Captain Grant[2]. My friend Blackett, returned to the regiment[3].

---

[1]  A false rumour.
[2]  Captain Charles Grant 18th Hussars.
[3]  Blackett had previously resigned his commission in September 1813, but actually remained in the regiment and came back out to Spain again.

Roquefort, Friday, March 18
After Bazas, we moved through a pine forest to the miserable hamlet of Captieux. The day was so hot and the stage so long that we were exhausted and more than half dead of hunger.

Aire [sur-l'Adour], Saturday, March 19
The road crosses the forest to Villeneuve de Marsan and then enters an open country, when we arrived at Aire. The village is located on the left bank of the Adour. The regiment is lodged in a collection of huts, on the right bank, opposite Aire. A band of enemy partisans infests the road to St-Sever here and make things very difficult. It is believed that it is the troop of Florio. A Spanish cavalry regiment, arrived this afternoon, which I must see.

Rabastens [de-Bigorre], Sunday, March 20
Left early, we passed through Barcelonne [du-Gers], Plaisance; we arrived at Rabastens at four o'clock in the afternoon. We have heard cannon fire in the direction of Tarbes throughout the evening; the armies are engaged a league from here. The 14th Light Dragoons suffered greatly in an affair with the French cavalry, several officers are killed, wounded or prisoners[4]. Reports say that the men did not follow their leaders and fled. Some speak of a battle tomorrow morning. Soult, it seems, will occupy a position at Toulouse, which is very strongly fortified in the event of failure. Our new squadron has arrived from England, and will join us tomorrow; we will be very strong marching into battle. Today we crossed the Adour, at a ford, near Izotges[5], next to the ruins of the bridge that Soult destroyed in his retreat.

Cabanac, Monday, March 21
Left Rabastens at six o'clock, we met the new squadron two leagues beyond and we have met Captain Grant, who looked a little crazy. I was introduced to the Honourable Mr. Dawson and Mr Coote[6], two lieutenants.

My friend, Colonel Sturgeon, was killed in Tarbes yesterday[7]. Soult took up a position near this town but Lord Wellington, has

[4]   The action at Tarbes cost each in the region of 100 casualties.
[5]   At Izotges he would have actually crossed the L'Arros, a tributary of the Adour.
[6]   The Honourable Lionel Dawson was a lieutenant in the 18th Hussars, having joined from the 23rd Light Dragoons in June 1813. Robert Coote had been made a lieutenant on 22 February.
[7]   Henry Sturgeon was recorded as killed on 19 March at Vic-en-Bigorre.

obliged him to retire and start retreating on Toulouse by last night's manouevers. At two o'clock in the morning, we cut the main road that leads there. Colonel Murray is in Bordeaux and will join the regiment, to the annoyance of Hughes and others. Cabanac is a small village of approximately fifty houses; I am housed in the chateau of the mayor. The terrain is favourable for cavalry, it is an open plain. We passed today Castéra [-Lou] and Pouyastruc; none of these villages offers anything that deserves to be recalled, except a pretty girl I saw in a window. Oh! What a delicious creature! The enemy rearguard is about two leagues from us; it consists of two regiments of cavalry; it is possible that we will come up with them tomorrow. Tarbes is a very attractive town; the public buildings are beautiful. The mayor is kept under observation, he is a rabid Buonapartist.

It would seem, that Major Hughes had a bad day.

Boulogne [sur-Gesse], Tuesday, March 22
After a long march of nine hours till four o'clock, the regiment is lodged in farms around Boulogne, the village is occupied by Lord Wellington and his Staff. I'm in a miserable hole and I met with a novel thing; a derogatory host and hostess.

Lieutenant Dolbel has had a serious accident in Castets, on the Garonne; in parading before the mistress of the chateau, he wanted to jump a barrier with his horse. The animal fell and broke her neck and Mr. Dolbel received a bad blow to his side. Our major, in one of his bouts of stupidness, led the regiment, several miles out of its march today; looking for a chateau to settle in. Grant got very angry and made some well-deserved criticisms of Hughes.

Monbardon, Wednesday, March 23
We went seven leagues on the worst roads I have ever seen, hoping to catch Soult's rearguard, but without success. I'm with Croker and Ollypod [Pulsford?] in a beautiful chateau inhabited by a charming family. If ever I have the happiness to have a wife and children, heaven let me enjoy a life as these people do here!

The King of Spain, Ferdinand VII, passed through Toulouse last week, en route to Spain. He dined at a friend of our hosts and we were talking about him. He is celebrated, especially for his politeness towards the ladies. He distinguished himself, in this point of view, with a pretty girl who gave him a pear; he took it and put it to his chest, saying that he would keep it until the last day of his life and always remember her. There is no better evidence of the fall of the power of Buonaparte than the release of Ferdinand; but I fear that he returns to his kingdom with French principles, which will add nothing to the happiness and prosperity of that country[8].

The owner of this chateau is young and pretty: she has five lovely children. Her mother, a woman of Bordeaux, is perhaps in many ways even more attractive than her daughter. They asked me two thousand questions on England and appeared to be enchanted by the happy turn which the war takes. I could spend my life with this family, not just to play with the beautiful children. I like much this way of campaigning; we had an excellent dinner and a quantity of wine from Bordeaux. I hope that the war will last another year in this country.

Monblanc, Thursday, March 24
I find it hard to keep myself going; these forced marches do not suit me. We passed Lombez; during a halt, an American came to talk to us. I learned from him that Soult has no intention of destroying the beautiful bridge of Toulouse: the city is surrounded by very strong forts; it will be defended, as well as the passage over the river.

The 13th Dragoons made many prisoners from the enemy yesterday; If the 14th had charged in the same way the other day, they would not have suffered as much. We are housed in a dirty and miserable village, at the top of a hill. It is called Monblanc, why not call it Mount Black? The women, upon our arrival, hid at first and seemed very frightened; but they have gradually regained their courage and now they visit us with their impertinent questions intolerably. The Pyrenees are much steeper here than in the proximity of Bayonne.

George began to show signs of illness.

Buri [Rouaix?], near Sainte-Foy-de-Peyrolières, Friday, March 25
Colonel Vivian has today given the regiment an admirable address: he engaged the men to be firm in action and to observe good order and good relationships with the locals in ordinary times. We then finished by marching three leagues on a bad road, and I had the misfortune to receive orders to lodge my platoon in the small village

---

[8] George was correct in his general assumptions, but Ferdinand returned with anti-French ideals. Ferdinand VII returned to the Spanish king with a reactionary agenda. He quickly disowned the liberal Constitution of 1812 insisting on the Absolute power of the monarch and arresting all those who dared to speak out.

of Beaufort. We had just arrived, when we were ordered to move by Marshal Beresford, to make way for a Portuguese brigade. I then returned to Buri, where I was installed in a beautiful chateau; they gave me good wine and I spent the evening very pleasantly with the family that inhabits it. The Marshal's Brigade Major stays here, and the 4th Division is lodged and encamped nearby.

I am very sick, doctors are not enough for me. If there is a battle tomorrow, I will try to participate, but I don't know if I'll have the strength.

Leguevin, Saturday 26 March

Very wet morning; we were expecting a serious affair on our rising and we would all have preferred if this day was already over. But after marching on the road to Toulouse until two leagues from the city, the infantry was ordered to bivouac and the cavalry to take their quarters, so the bloody fight that we expected will no doubt take place tomorrow, another Sunday![9]

At Saint-Lys, which we passed, there were a quantity of pretty women they seemed charmed to see the English hussars. Leguevin is a large town of dirty appearance, with two good auberges. I am housed out of town, in the house of a priest: he and his wife are both old and ugly, they torment each other and they themselves are bored of the effect. I would like to be away from them, because I'm still very sick. The enemy is encamped on this side of the Garonne.

Colomiers, Sunday, March 27

The division on the left of the army gathered near this village on the main road to Toulouse and considerable bets have been placed on the likelihood of the army entering Toulouse tonight. We had to march to the village of St-Michel[10], which is occupied by the enemy; but we received the order from Sir Lowry Cole, who was making a reconnaissance, to retire and to re-occupy our quarters, leaving a picquet with the infantry. I feel so sick that I desire an immediate battle; I can't resist for more than a day or two and I shudder at the idea of remaining with the rearguard.

In George's absence, the 18th, led by Vivian, had driven the enemy's rearguard right into the western suburbs of Toulouse. Vivian was well

---

[9] A number of Wellington's battles occurred on a Sunday.
[10] Now a southern suburb of Toulouse.

pleased with the 18th this day.[11] George was livid, being ordered to the rear by the surgeons.

Leguevin, Monday, March 28

I am enraged; the surgeons have forced me to go with the rearguard, until the surrender of Toulouse. They will then take me into the city. The surgeons exchanged such looks, I'm sure to be seriously ill. They say that my illness is fatigue and a cold and that only rest can help me.

I learn that the regiment had an engagement with the enemy and that it behaved well; praise to God! I am happy at the praise it has received from Vivian, one of the best officers in the service. Unfortunately, several officers, including Captain B[urke], were not at their posts while their men were fighting.

Leguevin, Tuesday, March 29

I left the town to go into a beautiful uninhabited chateau. The owner abandoned it on the arrival of the English. I am now quite properly installed. Hughes sent all the horses and all the sick men to me; the veterinarian[12] accompanies them. He lives in this chateau with me, he's a lovable companion. We discovered the cellar, full with excellent Bordeaux. Chambers came to see me, I kept him for dinner and to stay overnight. The veterinarian and he were enjoying good wine and eau-de-cerise parfait, we found by forcing a closet.

Leguevin, Wednesday, March 30

I am a little better today. I have not heard from the army. The weather is rainy and it has upset the operations. The river will certainly be very high and even more difficult to cross.

Leguevin, Thursday, March 31

The weather is clear and seems to have calmed down. What a miserable life I have! Being locked up in a bedroom, unable to bear the march on a horse, and my regiment is perhaps at this time facing the enemy!

Leguevin, Friday, April 1

Thank God, I'm better! It is estimated that the enemy forces in

---

[11] *Vivian's Memoirs* page 231.
[12] Pulsford.

Toulouse number forty thousand men. Suchet and the Army of Catalonia have not yet made their junction.

Leguevin, Saturday, April 2
A part of the army of General Hill crossed the Garonne on a bridge of boats on the right; but on the other side the roads were deemed impossible for artillery, it has retired and abandoned the bridge. It is said that Lord Wellington will be passing a village on the left, named Verdun [sur-Garonne], from hence the road is excellent to Toulouse.

Chambers made me a visit and gave me hope that I could resume my service in a week and still share in the chances of the campaign. There are, in the cellars of the chateau, close to three hundred barrels of Bordeaux with a delicious bouquet; I drink a quart per day. Chambers took away a small barrel full, with two bottles of eau de cerise for Deane. The owner, who is in Toulouse, will be amazed to find his chateau so well respected.

George was clearly shocked by the excellent appearance of the Spanish troops remaining with Wellington's army, but he was not so happy with the Spanish general.

Leguevin, Sunday, April 3
A stunning Spanish army, commanded by Lieutenant General don Manuel Freire[13], arrived this evening in Leguevin, with a considerable amount of artillery. Soon after, I received the order to close up my wounded men and make as much space as possible for him. I then made an effort to ride my horse and I put my detachment in two stables; the Spanish general was still not happy and he sought in the middle of the night, an order from Lord Wellington, for me to be removed. Staff Captain Gitterick[14] came to order me to take my men to Levignac. I begged the veterinarian to get them ready, it was two o'clock in the morning when they began marching, the rain fell in torrents. As for me, I stood my ground; the mayor gave the Spaniards two hundred billets for lodgings on this chateau, but I refused to give up my apartments and all the Spaniards, officers and soldiers, ate in the kitchen.

Levignac, Monday, April 4
I got up this morning very early; I dressed and I proceeded with my

---

[13] Manuel Alberto Freire de Andrade y Armijo, commanded a Spanish division at Toulouse.
[14] Captain John Gitterick, Staff Corps Cavalry.

servants and my luggage to Levignac. The beauty of the valley in which the village is set, the majestic appearance of a beautiful chateau and gardens, a beautiful river and bridge, a church surmounted by an elegant bell tower, several beautiful houses surrounded by large gardens, make Levignac one of the most charming places I have ever seen. The mayor has conducted me into an excellent house where I have the company of two delicious young girls and their brother. The headquarters of the army is in Grenade; they say on the 18th they passed the Garonne.

Levignac, Tuesday, April 5

Despite the good accommodation and charming hostesses, I moved today into the chateau. I could not resist the temptation of living in a grand house, but I will make visits to these ladies. It is the day of the market, and the square is full of peasants who seem to contemplate my beautiful hussars with the greatest pleasure. I was able to make sure that they showed to good account. I must have the air of suffering, because I heard them say around me. 'The officer is sick'.

The battle will take place shortly, because the army has crossed the Garonne, and now Soult has to fight or flee, and I do not believe he is the man to take the latter option.

Levignac, Wednesday, April 6

I asked permission to join the regiment and I can leave as soon as Morris comes to command the detachment. People here want a resolution: fate favours one or the other, who wins matters little to them I believe, but they are tired of their lands and their homes going to ruin. We eat everything. What a pity! The ambition of one man forces two of the first nations of the world to war, when peace would make them both so happy!

# Chapter 14

# Action at Croix Daurade and Toulouse

Geoge was relieved of his duties and eagerly returned to the regiment, happy that he had not missed the expected engagement.

Levignac, Thursday April 7
Lieutenant Morris arrived with a detachment of the rearguard, I renounced my command and I am free, thank God! At three o'clock this afternoon, I rejoined the regiment.

I left Levignac and crossed the Garonne, opposite Fenouillet. I cannot go further today, I lodged with the 7th Hussars. I'm still not fully recovered, but I feel well enough to share the dangers of my brave companions.

I passed the Garonne at Beauzelle on seventeen boats that make up the bridge; I then took the route for Toulouse, but, feeling tired, I returned to Beauzelle, where the mayor very kindly lodged me. It seems that Soult was surprised by our passage; it is rumoured that he attacks us tomorrow morning. The current is so strong that the bridge has been destroyed; the army which remains on this side is under arms and will remain so all night.

Croix-Daurade, Friday, April 8
The enemy, fortunately, has not realised the situation of six thousand men being separated from the army by the breakdown of the bridge; Soult could have made them all prisoners. The first moment that the bridge was restored Lord Wellington and his Staff crossed it with the greater part of the army. We followed the main road in the direction of Toulouse in front of the village of Croix-Daurade, which we were separated from by the river L'Hers. The bridge that crosses

254

the river was occupied by a strong column of French cavalry, for the attack the 18th were at the head, supported by the 1st [German] Hussars. Lord Wellington, Marshal Beresford, Sir Stapleton Cotton and several other generals stood on a mound in rear of the brigade to observe the charge when we received the order to push on a few minutes after. The regiment was formed in columns by divisions, by the left. Colonel Vivian took command, and we proceeded in the direction of the enemy when he was unfortunately injured in the right arm. He took himself immediately to the rear, but before leaving, he ordered Captain Croker to push on with the charge, which was executed instantly. The enemy received us with a volley of musketry, but our brave hussars were not men to be intimidated by a few gunshots. In less than a minute, the enemy column was broken and we finished by making one hundred and twenty prisoners with their horses.

Our losses were only, four killed and ten wounded and two men taken prisoner[1]. Lord Wellington and his Staff raised their hats in acclaiming our hussars when they saw them in possession of the bridge. Captain R[ichard] Croker, who led this brilliant charge, was seriously wounded in the face by a sabre slash; his mare had gone a few yards in front of the men into the enemy ranks. The French dragoon who injured Croker was immediately after slashed by Sergeant Major Black[2]; almost all the men attacked this poor devil; in a few moments, his face was no longer human in appearance, he died however only several hours later. Our hussars, seeing the enemy flee, wanted to continue it through Croix Daurade, the French ranks were so tightly packed that if we had had a cannon, we would have made a horrible slaughter. But soon they made a movement to leave the road and thus unmasked the artillery that was on the walls of Toulouse and who opened fire on us. We were then forced to retreat and go back to the bridge, which we held. After half an hour we were relieved by an infantry brigade and we retired into our quarters.

Vivian is seriously wounded; it is believed that he will lose his arm[3]. Croker[4] is with him in a small house on the edge of the road, one mile behind the bridge of Croix Daurade. Soult and his Staff

---

[1]  French losses cannot be ascertained fully, but 120 Chasseurs were made prisoner.
[2]  Troop Sergeant Major William Black.
[3]  Luckily Vivian did not lose his arm, although he was still wearing a sling at Waterloo a year later.
[4]  Despite his brilliant success and severe wound, Croker failed to gain a pension on leaving the army as he did not lose a limb.

attended the action; they escaped the great rout. It is said that Soult proceeded, immediately after the charge, to arrest the cavalry general who commanded; the enemy had three regiments to defend the bridge, among others the 22nd Chasseurs[5]. It is said that as soon as Soult was aware of the construction of the pontoon bridge, he had his heavy artillery leave in the direction of Paris and his light artillery to Castelnaudary, to which he will withdraw. I hope that we will have a battle and then we will destroy his army. I feel reborn and in few days I will be quite well.

At the advance posts near Toulouse, Saturday, April 9
I am at the advance posts on the road to Toulouse: this beautiful city is before my eyes. The lower part is hidden from me by the majestic trees of the public gardens. Between us and the city passes the Languedoc canal. The bridge that crosses it, although fortified by the enemy, was captured this morning by the 1st [German] Hussars, who made prisoner hundreds of chasseurs with their horses. This announces the battle for tomorrow: Sunday is definitely our day of battle! May we be happy tomorrow in all our enterprises! The French position is immensely strong both by nature and art.

I hear ringing bells in Toulouse, I guess that the whole army and all of the residents partake and receive absolution before the battle.

Finally, the great battle arrived and sure enough this hard-fought engagement was on a Sunday. The cavalry covered the infantry attacks against the French defences lining the crest of Mont Rave. The 10th Hussars nearly charged the 18th in a case of mistaken identity, but the 18th did not suffer a single casualty this day.

Battle of Toulouse, Sunday, April 10
Day of glory for the English, Portuguese and Spanish armies, but day of carnage for all! The city of Toulouse is surrounded on three sides by the Languedoc canal and the Garonne. On the left of this river, the suburb that the enemy has seriously fortified, in front of the old wall, forms a tete de pont[6]. The French were also established at each bridge on the canal, the bridgeheads protected by the fire of musketry and cannon. From the ancient walls, beyond the canal, to the east and between it and the River l'Hers, there is an elevated

---

[5]   Two French cavalry regiments actually defended the bridge, the 5th and 22nd Chasseurs.
[6]   The suburb of St Cyprien.

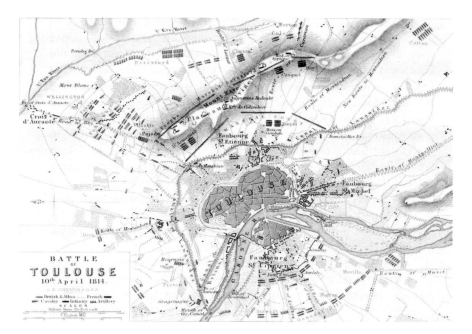

*Above: Map of the Battle of Toulouse*

height [Mont Rave] which extends to Montaudran and on which passes all the roads that pass through the region and it defends the canal and the city. The enemy have prepared five redoubts, with rows of retrenchment; all these preparations for defence were made with extraordinary diligence. On l'Hers, all the bridges to which we have access and by which the right of the French position could be turned, were cut.

However, as the roads over the Ariège below Toulouse are impassable for cavalry or artillery and almost for the infantry, there was nothing else to do than to attack. Marshal Beresford crossed l'Hers and formed his corps into three columns in the village of Croix-Daurade and immediately carried Montblanc. He then ascended the course of l'Hers over a very difficult terrain, in a direction parallel to the fortified positions of the enemy and, as soon as he arrived at the point to turn them, he formed his lines and advanced to the attack. Lieutenant General don Manuel Freire, with the Spanish army, marched along l'Hers in front of Croix-Daurade, where he arranged it in two lines with a reserve on a height in front of the left flank of the enemy. He also placed the Portuguese artillery

257

and the cavalry brigade of Major-General Ponsonby[7] in reserve. As soon as the formation was complete and Marshal Beresford could see that they were ready, Lieutenant General Freire advanced to the attack. The whole army felt there was nothing else to do, but partake in the universal joy of seeing the Spaniards attack so well. They marched in compact mass to climb the slope of the hill; about half way up, they stopped for a few minutes, then continued to advance on a strong redoubt. At pistol range, the enemy opened upon them a violent fire of musketry and artillery. The Spanish were driven back with a loss of nearly fifteen hundred killed or wounded; the affair lasted only a few minutes and the survivors fled, not immediately however, because they were so crowded that they could not unravel. One of their regiments resisted for a few minutes longer than the others, but it retired out of reach much faster than the main body.

This Spanish army is perhaps the only one which was in close contact with the enemy in Spain ever since the beginning of the war: in all cases, these poor scoundrels have suffered more than anyone else in such a short space of time. Immediately after they retired, the brave 42nd marched on the position and took this same redoubt, tomb of the Spanish. The 18th and 1st [German] Hussars faced the centre of the position, the 7th, 10th and 15th Hussars on our right. The 18th moved into a position parallel to a redoubt which our brave infantry had just taken and we stayed in that position. The 10th Hussars, who had not observed our march, took the 18th for an enemy cavalry regiment and advanced against us. They fell under a fire from one of the French redoubts, and their losses were cruel. My friend, Captain Gordon[8], was struck in the back by a cannonball. He did not survive for more than a few minutes, in him his majesty has lost one of his best cavalry officers.

On the left of the Garonne, Lieutenant General Hill drove the enemy from the fortified suburb, and General Picton, with his brave 3rd Division, won the head of the canal bridge. Therefore, the army was established on three sides of Toulouse and the cavalry was sent to cut the communications on the only road that remained to the

---

[7]  Major General the Honourable William Ponsonby, who so famously died at Waterloo.
[8]  Captain Charles Gordon 10th Hussars.
[9]  Major General Denis Pack.
[10] Apart from the 120 captured at Croix Daurade, it is unclear where the others were captured.
[11] This is actually Lieutenant Conrad Poten of 1st KGL Hussars who was returned as slightly wounded at Toulouse.

enemy. We lodged in the villages and farms and all the officers gathered in a single house.

Toulouse, Monday, April 11

The army has a day of rest; we occupy all the positions outside the city, we are absolute masters; we see the French army busy repairing the walls and preparing the defences; I believe however he will withdraw today by the road to Languedoc, the only move he can now make. Judging by the movements of the infantry, Lord Wellington will try to seize it tomorrow. If successful, the French army would fall within our power. Our losses of yesterday are very serious; estimated at four thousand men. Some regiments have lost 300 men and the brave 42nd almost all their officers. Generals Cole, Pack[9] and Brisbane are injured. We have taken only a single canon.

Since the 8th current, our brigade has made seven hundred prisoners[10]. If the other brigades of cavalry did the same, the total number must rise to several thousand. My friend Charles Poten, 1st [German] Hussars[11], was injured yesterday by a sword in the neck. He was sent on patrol and he met an enemy patrol, he attacked and made them prisoners. Captain Fitzclarence, the 10th Hussars, aide de camp to Lord Wellington, was wounded yesterday in the buttock[12]. The quantity of bodies around us is huge; it is necessary to bury the dead or leave our positions.

Toulouse, Tuesday, April 12

The enemy evacuated the city this morning around two o'clock; he retired on the lower Languedoc. So, Soult has ceded the second city of the French Empire to a force only equal to his own. Lord Wellington could have cut the retreat of the defeated army, but he wished to spare the life of many brave men. A division of our army entered Toulouse at eight o'clock by the gate of Saint-Cyprien, amongst the cheers of thousands of spectators. It crossed the city and left it by the Faubourg Saint-Michel, in pursuit of the enemy. The other divisions followed Soult by different routes.

I was sent to Toulouse to find munitions, the people welcomed me through the streets and in the squares with 'Long live the Bourbons!' The cry resounded on all sides and everyone wore the white cockade. The women were very active; they cleaned their windows and put up candles for illuminations this evening. The white flag was flying over the Capitole and all the windows were occupied by beautiful women wearing white ribbons: they expected the entrance of Lord Wellington. I could not stay to attend, but I saw the senior municipal officers and persons of distinction of Toulouse come out to meet him. I then followed the high road for about two leagues and I came to a small village called Odars. I spent the night in a beautiful chateau; a good priest gave me an excellent dinner.

---

[12] George makes this sound quite trivial but Fitzclarence was returned as 'severely wounded'.

# Chapter 15

# Peace

The news that Napoleon had abdicated finally reached Toulouse, unfortunately too late to avoid the battle. But even now Soult delayed accepting the truth of this and the cavalry trailed him as he marched further east.

Escalquens, Wednesday, April 13
Anniversary of my birth: I am today twenty-two years old, having been born in 1792. What fun, what a joy to be able to hear the news that has arrived from Paris! Buonaparte has abdicated the throne of France and a new Government is formed! It is peace!
The news has been delivered to Lord Wellington by Colonel Cooke[1], sent from Paris by the Allies with specific messages for the two armies. Napoleon will withdraw to the island of Elba in the Mediterranean, with an annual pension of eight million francs. I joined the regiment at Escalquens; the whole army has halted, and we soon expect an armistice.

Toulouse, Thursday, April 14
I visited Toulouse this morning with Luard, Hesse and Dunkin. It was necessary to go almost an hour on horseback through the streets before discovering a stable. We had almost as much trouble to get us lodgings, the hotels teeming with the world. We then visited the city. Lord Wellington remains at the prefecture. We each wear a white

---

[1] Lieutenant Colonel Henry Cooke 12th Foot had been serving with Prussian headquarters and was sent with the news by Charles Stewart along with the French Colonel St Simon, aide de Camp to Clarke, the former War Minister.

cockade, and we went to dinner at a hotel on the square where we met seven heavy cavalry officers and Kelly[2], of the Life Guards. Our dinner, accompanied by plenty of music, cost us each about 30 shillings. We then went to the theatre. The scene was well lit, but the room very badly; there was but a small chandelier in the centre of the ceiling. Lord Wellington honoured us with his presence for the presentation and the room was full of English officers. Before the piece (Henry IV) they performed a loyal song in honour of the Bourbons to which the assembly replied with the cry of 'Long live the King!'

Women of a certain type filled all the avenues leading to the theatre, their conduct would make their peers in England blush. All the military speak of the brilliant conduct of the 18th. Indeed, our men fought like lions. Lord Wellington, seeing our charge said 'Well, if the 18th do such things, I'll never complain about them again.'

Toulouse, Friday 15 April

The people are very polite and understand very well the service we have rendered them, but the shopkeepers, knowing the extent of the pockets of John Bull, have doubled their prices since our arrival. The city is full of French deserters; more than two thousand men of the army of Soult hid to await our entry. Soult, although he left Toulouse, left a general to gather the stragglers, but the people rose up against him and put him in prison.

Vivian was transported into the city; he is better, but it is still unclear whether he will retain his arm. The enemy left here Generals Harispe, Baurot, Saint-Hilaire[3] and sixteen hundred prisoners, numerous cannon and huge quantities of supplies of all kinds[4]. Here are the approximate losses of the army: English killed and wounded, 2,200; Spanish 1,800, Portuguese 600[5].

Escalquens, Saturday, April 16

The chateau of this charming village is inhabited by an old admiral who is an old dog. He paraded in the hamlet in his uniform with a

---

[2] Captain Edward Kelly 1st Life Guards was in southern France from January to April 1814, serving as a Deputy Assistant Quartermaster General (DAQMG).

[3] General Harispe lost a foot and his senior brigadier Baurot a leg. General Jean-Etienne Bartier as commander of the Haute Garonne Department, was uninjured and remained at Toulouse where he was captured.

[4] French losses amounted to around 3,300 killed and wounded.

[5] Oman numbers allied casualties at Toulouse as 2,103 British, 1922 Spaniards and 533 Portuguese killed, wounded and missing.

white cockade on his hat. It is likely that we will stay here until the signing of the peace and that we will then go to Bordeaux to embark for England. Luard and Hesse returned this evening from Toulouse, disgusted at a city where everything is so expensive.

Mourevilles [-Hautes][6], Sunday, April 17
Soult does not want to accept any of the proposals of Lord Wellington; he says that he cannot believe the abdication of his master until he has the news for himself. He brought together his Council of War last night; all have agreed to remain attached to the fortune of Napoleon until more certain information. This decision having been brought to the attention of Lord Wellington during the night, we received, at six o'clock in the morning, the order to march on Castelnaudary; the army of Soult occupied a position near the town of Saint-Félix [-Lauragais].

We met the 1st [German] Hussars and formed the brigade. I was then sent with a detachment, forming a patrol to discover the enemy. At Saint-Félix, the women came out to watch us and I saw many beautiful ones. I learned here that the enemy was at Castelnaudary. I followed the highway to Revel and Castelnaudary until a half league from the latter town and I noticed that the enemy had a strong squad of cavalry hidden behind a fold of the land. I continued in my reconaissance and I barely escaped from three enemy dragoons. Having established their position, I returned to Colonel Arentschildt[7] and I made my report to him on our respective positions and the configuration of the land. I found the brigade quartered in villages around Saint-Félix.

All believe that there will be another battle tomorrow, because Lord Wellington will not continue to parley any longer with Soult; he demands an immediate declaration in favour of the new constitution and the new government. We believe that several French regiments will desert tonight: orders are given to receive them into our lines. It is said that the French cavalry wanted a personal encounter with the English cavalry on these beautiful plains so favourable to the deployment of that arm, I don't know if it is still in their disposition, but, for my part, I am not asking for

[6] In the French account, this is identified as Maureville, but this village lies twelve miles behind headquarters at Saint Felix, whereas Mourvilles is less than two miles away to the right. I believe this is a case of mistaken identity.

[7] Lieutenant Colonel Victor Arentschildt was serving with the Portuguese Army commanded the brigade in the absence of Vivian.

any more than one thing, it is that the 18th comes to grips with two of their best regiments, and I promise they will be properly dealt with. Colonel Murray joined the regiment today; he returns from England, where he had been restoring his health, since his fall during the passage of the Esla, in Spain.

Colonel Arentschildt is in the small village of Montegut [-Lauragais], founded by some English family of this name; I'm housed in a miserable hole and I am in deadly fear, as all the peasants have scabies. The orders of the day of Vivian and Sir Stapleton Cotton about the conduct of the regiment at la Croix-Daurade are very flattering for us, here they are:

Brigade Order.
La Croix-Daurade, April 9, 1814
It is with the most sincere pleasure that Colonel Vivian congratulates Major Hughes, the officers, NCOs and soldiers of the 18th Hussars for their superb bravery and extreme strength in the affair of yesterday, which passed under the eyes of the Commander in Chief. The colonel was delighted to learn that his lordship had expressed in the warmest terms his approval of the conduct of the 18th. He regrets that his injuries prevent him for some time from sharing the honours and the dangers of his brigade, and he hopes that the regiment, will persevere in his system of firmness in their movements and energy in action, and shall reap further laurels. His dearest wish is to be at the head of the 18th.
M. von Cloudt, Brigade Major[8]

General Order
Bruguières, April 9, 1814
Lieutenant-General Sir Stapleton Cotton had the extreme satisfaction of witnessing the warlike conduct of the 18th Hussars in the undertaking of yesterday, near Toulouse, against superior enemy forces. The Lieutenant General owes his thanks to Colonel Vivian, who commanded his brigade with judgment and bravery and who was unfortunately injured at the beginning of the action. He prays that Major Hughes, commander of the 18th Hussars, officers, N.C.O.'s and soldiers of this regiment will receive his thanks for

---

[8] The French version has H.D. Clout, but his name is certain. Captain Moritz von Cloudt was appointed Brigade Major to Baron Victor Alten's cavalry brigade, which Vivian had temporarily commanded in Alten's absence. He was a permanent brigade major on the KGL Staff. Beamish reference no. 97.

their excellent conduct, strength and courage deployed by them on this occasion.
Colonel Elly. A. A. G.[9]

Mourvilles, Monday, April 18
This morning Soult concluded an armistice with Lord Wellington and we have been into the French lines to speak with their officers. We have to evacuate the village and its surroundings tomorrow; the French troops will occupy it. We will remove to the banks of the Garonne and will remain there until the signing of the peace. Across the country the white flag has been raised and declared for the Bourbons. Quincey dined with me and we talked of happy England.

Mourevilles, Tuesday, April 19
I changed lodgings to go to Monsieur Mitton; it is a good house where I am treated well. These people have a son, a prisoner in England and I promised them to send letters. Captain Croker joined us yesterday; his face bears the mark of the cut of a sabre and he will always have the scar. After the agreement with Marshal Soult, the French believed that we were to leave this morning and one of their cavalry regiments came to our cantonments to be lodged; Colonel Murray has made it clear to the French colonel that he had no orders and they did an about face.

Wednesday, April 20
We have a long march back to Toulouse, but by a different route than when we pursued the enemy. We passed through Caraman, where the heavy dragoons have their quarters. Soult went to Paris and Lord Wellington will also go there in a few days; the armistice is concluded for two months. The French troops have replaced us today. The demarcation line is the Garonne, but Toulouse will remain in the hands of the English until the peace.

Blagnac, Thursday, April 21
At eleven o'clock we found General Stewart in Toulouse, who we were not expecting; he arrived from Paris with dispatches for Lord Wellington. He inspected the regiment as it paraded near the bridge, and he expressed his high appreciation of our conduct at the battle of Toulouse. He let us know of the flattering terms in which Lord

---

[9] Brevet Colonel John Elley Royal Horse Guards, Assistant Adjutant General to the cavalry.

Wellington spoke of us. The inhabitants of Toulouse were all in the street or at their windows to see our magnificent regiment pass. Many French soldiers, having seen our charge at Croix-Daurade, knew us as well as the people of Toulouse.

We passed over the bridge on the River Garonne and we made our way into this town. I was lodged with the priest, who offered me good wine. At nine o'clock, I proceeded with Kennedy to the ball that Lord Wellington gave at the Capitole of Toulouse. There were so many people that we had much trouble getting into the hall of honour. Among the foreigners, I saw Suchet; he wore the uniform of hussars, with a huge moustache and a braid of hair hanging on each shoulder. The great Lord was covered with stars and orders. The room was beautifully decorated with coloured lanterns, laurels and flowers. There were several fine transparents. Nearly two hundred French officers attended the ball.

# Chapter 16

# Rest and Recuperation

Whilst the politicians sorted out the peace in Paris, the army settled into cantonments and then marched slowly back to Bordeaux, whilst awaiting passage back to Britain, or America, where war continued.

L'Isle-Jourdain, Friday, April 22

We traversed Colomiers and Léguevin, old quarters of the regiment; the people seemed happy to see us again: they prayed to the heavens for our safe return to England. I am lodged close to Aubiet[1], with Croker & Quincey, in the house of a lumberjack. The mayor, a very polite young man, brought wine and offered us some as he thought that might be nice; but Croker was in a very bad mood and he sent him about his business in a fairly brutal manner. In returning from the ballroom, Kennedy has fallen off his horse; he is himself seriously wounded in the side and right arm. Luard and Hesse are still in Toulouse engaging with the pretty women: I would love to be with them.

Buonaparte asked for two hundred cannon to fortify the island of Elba and a frigate to protect him and those who follow him, against the privateers. I believe that his application was rejected. He is still at Fontainebleau, but he will move in a few days.

Auch, Saturday, April 23

We are told this morning that Buonaparte departed from Fontainebleau last Wednesday for the island of Elba, together with

---

[1]  This again appears to be an error in the French version as Aubiet is nearly twenty miles west of L'Isle-Jourdain. It is possible he wrote Aurade, a small village a mile from L'Isle Jourdain.

several of his generals. After a pleasant stage, we came to this great city and we were received with great politeness by all the inhabitants. White flags and banners of the same colour float over the entire city. I am lodged in the home of a gentleman, who emigrated to England during the revolution and who served a few years in our military; he speaks English very well.

The officers all dined together, sixteen in number. As we were going to sit at the table, an aide de camp of Marshal Soult came with one of our light dragoon lieutenants, bringing orders for the French general who commanded at Bayonne. We invited them to join us. The Frenchman told us several anecdotes of Buonaparte: he was close to him, at Fontainebleau, when he signed his abdication. He told us that whenever he thought of his dear Emperor, his only friend, tears came into his eyes. He added: 'I believe that the French army will faithfully serve Louis, now that they have sworn his oath, but I'm sure that they would more readily follow Buonaparte'; this officer saw Buonaparte's farewell to his guard at Fontainebleau: 'they were all crying.' He recommended them to be faithful to the new King as France had chosen and he begged them not to forget their poor unhappy country. He added speaking with feeling: 'Do not cry about my fate, I'll be happy if I know that you are well. I cannot embrace you all, but I embrace your general.' Which he did. He then asked for the Eagle, which he kissed. 'Ah, dear Eagle! can the kisses that I give you, resound in the ears of posterity! Farewell, farewell, my heroes!' At this moment he was unable to control his emotions; he then got into his carriage. He shed a few tears and departed from his faithful Guard who were crying and offering their prayers to hea

When the offer of the pension of 8 millions was made to Buonaparte, he answered by this manly refusal; 'It is too little for an Emperor and too much for an old soldier like me'. The aide de camp and his guide are almost soul mates; they must travel at the rate of twelve leagues per day (thirty-six miles) up to Bayonne. Grant spoke strikingly good French: when the aide de camp had told us everything we wanted to know, that crazy Grant began to abuse him because of his attachment to Buonaparte, this disconcerted the poor boy.

Lavardens, Sunday April 24
Left Auch, at eight o'clock this morning, on entering Lavardens, we saw coming towards us, women and children carrying white flags and flowers, and cheering with cries of welcome. We lodged

in two chateaus, Croker and I are in one, and Luard in the other. We first all dined with the masters of my chateau, and then we went to Luard's, where we were regaled by the Mayor, in the most gorgeous way. In the evening, one of his friends came, the Mayor of Montas[2], who chatting with us, this individual was overwhelmingly anti Buonaparte, calling him names, worse than it is sensible for a Frenchman to do. He has armed his farmers, and if Auch had not declared in favour of the Bourbons, he would have attacked it. The poor devil Buonaparte, the dream of greatness is finished! He goes to wake up Elba; six months ago he negotiated to keep the borders of the Elbe; three months ago, he offered to settle on the banks of the Rhine; in the first days of March, the limits of ancient France, and now all his claims are destroyed. He now parleys to obtain some fixtures, some books, a few bottles of wine. Alas! poor Napoleon!

Condom, Monday, April 25

On the road to Condom, we passed the village of Castera [-Verduzan], renowned for its ferrous waters. The regiment is lodged here in excellent quarters. Around six o'clock, the Duke d'Angoulême[3] and the Comte de Grammont, serving in the 10th Hussars, arrived. The Prefect, the Mayor, the municipality, the regiment of the Portuguese cavalry of General Campbell[4], and an honour escort of National Guardsmen with white flags came out to meet them and followed them through the city amid cheers. In the evening, the city was brilliantly illuminated and the streets were decorated with garlands of flowers thrown as they passed. My kind host, a priest, gave me a good dinner; after soup with Russell, I went to the city to see the illuminations, in the company of several ladies I had met.

There is, two leagues from here, a small village where you can obtain a diploma for lying. The method to make yourself a knight of this order is very curious. As we expect to stay here some time, I propose to go there and to receive a knighthood. There are a few pretty women in Condom, but the Portuguese cavalry officers, who are lodged there are their favourites: two of them are getting married.

---

[2] There is no such place in the vicinity, I believe Antras may have been meant.
[3] Louis Antoine of France, Duke d'Angoulême was the king's nephew.
[4] The only General I can identify who was serving with the Portuguese Army in 1814 is Major General Alexander Campbell.

Lisse, near Nérac, Tuesday, April 26

We left Condom this morning and we found our left squadron in Nérac with the order for the Troops K and C to go to Lisse, where I am staying. Troop C, commanded by Luard, is at Casagrand[5]. I'm in a beautiful chateau, belonging to a marquis of the old nobility of the country; he came to receive me at the door and welcomed me. He has been awarded the Cross of St. Louis. His son speaks English. The wife and two lovely daughters greeted me in the kindest way.

Lisse, Wednesday, April 27

I went on horseback this morning to Casagrand, with my host's son, to see Luard, but he was absent. Upon our return to the chateau, we found three officers of the army of Suchet, who came to make a visit to the family, being sons of their neighbours. They dined with us and remained until the evening. They admired my horse Dick much. One of the officers belongs to the corps of cuirassiers, and he told me curious stories about the armies of Catalonia. The old gentleman who lives in this chateau is the Marquis de Comminges and his eldest son, my companion of this morning, the Comte de Saint-Seurin. The mother, two girls, beautiful young women, complete with twelve or fourteen domestics, forms the family.

The table is sumptuous; I take my meals with them. They drink tea or coffee in the morning and I am forced to lunch alone. The marquis and the comte, his son, are both Knights of St. Louis and always wear a red ribbon on their coat as well as a white roundel on their hats. The white flag flies over the chateau. The daughters of the marquis are charming and their elderly mother is very good to me. I give the Count English lessons and he gives me lessons in French. I was today at the headquarters in Mézin, where the roll call of the troop was held. That night we met at a Mrs. Mélignan's, all the people of the city, young or old. This is what is referred to as society. I saw several very pretty girls. Cards and conversation were the distractions of the evening; I have noticed that many men understand English. This company meets nightly and they assure me that they have something of the same kind in all the cities in the south of France. There were several knights of St. Louis and other representatives of the old nobility of the country. Most of the inhabitants of this city live in their properties.

---

[5] There is nothing similar to this name in the area, did he mean Lausseignan?

Lisse, Friday, April 29
I'm back at Lisse this morning, and I've brought Chambers, with whom I had been staying. We stay a few weeks in our current neighborhood before we embark at Bordeaux for England.

Lisse, Saturday, April 30
I have received this afternoon, an invitation from the inhabitants of Nérac to a ball and dinner they offer to the officers of the brigade of hussars, tomorrow night. The Comte has promised to accompany me.

Nerac, Sunday, May 1
I came to Nerac with the comte, to attend the ball. We first dined with Croker and then we went to the promenade on the banks of the Auzoue River. We met the most charming country girls. I thought I was close to Vauxhall.

At eight o'clock, we went to the theatre, we found all in darkness. We were enlightened at the rise of the curtain, Grant and Hesse were amused, as well as were all the assembly, by various antics, songs, etc. About nine o'clock, the presentation began: first a ballet, then a dance on a rope, songs and various dances, all for 1 shilling 10 pence, and again we saw the previous scene. Grant had certainly taken a certain amount of wine; between each act he recited comedy songs in Italian. About ten o'clock, we went to the prom. The room was not large and we had barely enough room to move. I have danced for the first time, the French country dances, with some very pretty girls, they pleased me a lot. French women have admirable lightness; they have the prettiest feet and the thinnest ankles, and not just one or two in number, but almost all without exception in this part of France. The men dance very well, some too well; I should take to a dancing master. I left the ball at seven o'clock, to return to the chateau with the comte.

Lisse, Monday, May 2
I awoke only for dinner; I have then been murdered by these ladies; they made me tell them all the details of the feast of yesterday, the name of my partners, etc. In the afternoon, the second son of the marquis arrived at the chateau with his wife, from her home at Faleyras, on the right bank of the Garonne. What a difference with life in England! A man from a good family here can for 2 or 300 pounds a year, lead a life that would cost 1,500 in England. I asked to take my troop to Lisse and Nérac, thinking that the men and horses would be better there. But the Mayor of Nérac opposes this

271

and Colonel Arentschildt did not allow it. My troopers are lodged in scattered cottages, two or three together; there are some who are three miles from me.

Lisse, Tuesday, May 3

Croker came to the chateau, but he did not dismount, which much annoyed the marquis: I apologised for the captain. I was riding with the comte and one of his sisters, a Madame Pascon, whose chateau is a little higher up the valley, on the road to Barbaste. Captain Pascon introduced me to his charming and mischievous sister. After some refreshments, we returned to Lisse, accompanied part of the way by Pascon. The main reason for our walk was to show me a small property that is for sale; it consists of a fairly nice house, good for a family of eight to ten people, with sixty acres of land surrounding it, price: 1,000 Napoleons. My Lisse friends would see me buy it. Pascon is a cuirassier officer in the army of Suchet, he told me that his regiment had beaten our 20th Light Dragoons in Catalonia during the last campaign. It is possible, although the thing appears to me very unlikely. But no matter, we're all friends now. May we stay longer! I'm weary of war.

Lisse, Wednesday, May 4

This morning, I fished in the Auzoue River with the count and we caught a few carp. The King of France, Louis XVIII, left England[6] Sunday morning, April 24. He made the crossing on the yacht *Royal Sovereign*. The Prince Regent, with all his court, took leave of his Majesty at Dover: he gave him a gift, before his departure, of a travel carriage and six grey horses. He also gave a carriage and four horses to the Duchess d'Angoulême.

Lisse, Thursday, May 5

A third son of the marquis arrived this morning; he came from Bayonne where he was visiting, he was destined for the Navy and he was a captain in the Portuguese service. He is a kind boy, the darling of the family. Terrible storm last night; the lightning was so scary that I retired early into my bedroom, where I could see it.

Lisse, Friday, May 6

The family of the marquis are very religious but not bigoted. Since

---

[6]  Louis XVIII had resided at Hartwell near Aylesbury for the last few years of his exile, from 1809-14.

I am taken in by them, the sons eat meat every day, while others refrain some days of the week.

### Lisse, Saturday, May 7

I was visiting an old chateau in the valley, beyond Mézin. The ladies accompanying me were all riding astride, in the fashion of the country; I was not able to resume my countenance until after a certain time. We were in a wood and away from sunlight. The gardens and plantations of the chateau are magnificent. After a detour to Casagrand, we returned to Lisse, adorned with roses and delighted with our ride.

### Lisse, Sunday, May 8

It is said that the partisan Florio was hanged by the populace in Pau. I find it hard to believe, and if it is true, I would have a very poor opinion of the French people. What reason is there to remove a man who has bravely fought for the government he served, and who recognised the new constitution as soon as he learned of the abdication of Buonaparte? The new constitution was burned in Bordeaux with great ceremony; everyone is unhappy. I suspect the French are already regretting losing their hero: he was the only one who can govern these people.

### Lisse, Tuesday, May 10

We give a ball tomorrow for the ladies of Mezin, the organisers are Colonel Arentschildt, Lieutenant Hesse and Comte Bobers. We talk of nothing but this feast and preparing our finest clothes. Luard came this morning at daybreak to hunt.

After lunch, we went to Mons. Pascon, who accompanied us in the woods with the son of the marquis; but we had little success, and we came back as we left, without any rabbits. My trumpeter came tonight to the castle with his instrument and he played different fashionable English dances; we danced to entertain the old marquis.

### Lisse, Thursday, May 12

I went with the comte to Nérac to attend the ball given by the officers of the brigade of hussars. We had dinner together at the Hotel de l'Etoile, where there were many officers of the 1st [German] Hussars. It was the prefect who was kind enough to lend us the rooms, they were decorated with laurel and roses in garlands, interspersed with coloured lanterns. Beautiful chandeliers complemented the lighting.

There were at least sixty young women who have come here to dance and double that simply watching. We played alternately French and English country dances; for all four dances, there was also a waltz. Refreshments were prepared of the utmost luxury. The gallery which led to the ballroom was very pretty; on each side small doors opened on to buffets. At its end, a transparency of a French lady and an hussar bending the knee before her.

Our music was at one end of the room, and a French orchestra occupied the other. Our musicians were a great success. I danced the French cotillion with a few stylish women, which I love. The French, who love the English dances, lend their attention to our instructions. I also tried to waltz, but I found myself so dizzy that I fell, to the great amusement of the company. The women, mostly beautiful, danced in a delicious way; their way of waltzing is very graceful. The men are good dancers, although none are better than the English officers, but they had the air of professionals who sought to outshine each other and gave us lessons. Among our refreshments, there was a punch that the French love to madness; unfortunately, they drank too much: a young woman was so grey that she had to give up dancing. The feast lasted for up to seven hours. The comte only danced once; my beautiful hostesses of the chateau refused to attend this ball. I suspect that the old nobility of this country to be proud to excess. No doubt my dear friends of Lisse saw this company as unworthy of the presence of the family of a marquis.

Lisse, Friday, May 13
A deluge of questions on the part of the ladies of the chateau on the feast of yesterday; they required details, conversations, gossip. We embark shortly on the Garonne to return to England.

Lisse, Saturday, May 14
I hunted a fox with the comte; we cornered one that we had pursued and killed him with my bitch Vitoria. Captain Luard switches from E Troop to K Troop, and Captain Croker to D Troop because of Captain Clements, who re-joined us and who reclaims his former troop E. Luard is not happy.

Lisse, Sunday, May 15
Marshal Suchet and his army enter Toulouse on the 17th. It is said that the British headquarters will be moved today. It seems that Marshal Soult stays in Paris: he knew, it is said of the abdication of Buonaparte and the state of affairs in Paris three days before the

Battle of Toulouse and he could have prevented it. For my part I think that, even had he known of the entry of the allies into Paris, he was entitled to fight against us or any other army that was opposed to him.

Moreover, as soon as the abdication of Buonaparte was officially known of, Soult stated for the new government. I hope that a general, as brave and capable as he is, will be justified in the eyes of France and Europe, I'd be sorry to learn that he suffered some misadventure for his bravery in defending his country against invasion.

Lisse, Monday, May 16
Yesterday, the second son of the marquis and his charming wife left for their chateau of Postiac. The chateau seems very sad without them; they made me promise to go to see them if I pass by Bordeaux to go to England. We hunted again today, but without much success. The land is so dry that the scent of the fox persists for not more than a quarter of a minute and the dogs are easily confused. Luard has come to the chateau to stay there with me; he was received very well by the good marquis and his family.

Lisse, Tuesday, May 17
We have to prepare ourselves to go to Cherbourg to embark. It is around forty-two days of marching, through the most beautiful part of France. The heavy baggage and dismounted riders return from Bordeaux.

Lisse, Wednesday, May 18
Twenty thousand English infantry men will embark at Bordeaux for America, the 14th Light Dragoons also go there. The infantry gave a ball at Condom, but there were few women. Lieutenant Crofton, of the 82nd[7] married a beautiful French girl last week in La Réole. His regiment goes to America.

Mézin, Thursday, May 19
I came to Mezin to attend the ball given by the officers of the regiment to the women of this town, in the salons of Madame Mélignan. The women jumped about and drank punch until five o'clock in the morning. Waldie was very amusing, trying to fall at

---

[7]  Lieutenant Henry Crofton, 82nd Foot.

the feet of a charming angel, unfortunately he tore his pants behind and his knees and this caused much laughter. Russell also entertained us; we had dancing after they had dimmed the lights, result, several injured legs.

## Orders arrived for all Portuguese servants to be repatriated.

Lisse, Friday, Saturday, Sunday and Monday, 20, 21, 22, 23 May
All officers were ordered to return their Portuguese servants to the various Portuguese brigades, who must receive them to repatriate them. The officers who command regiments are made responsible for the execution of this order. Therefore, I cannot take my trusty Sparem Joe, who wants to go to England. English and French headquarters are now in Toulouse, but the officers have been socialising very little. In the heart of the French, there is a deep hatred of the English; last night, several officers were insulted because they wore the white cockade and they attempted to pull their hats off.

Lisse, Tuesday, May 24
The regiment gathered before marching for roll call on the great road between Nérac and Mézin. Almost all of the French are eager to have English husbands and I truly believe that the richest of them would even accept the proposals from any hussar trooper. They dress, sing and dance in the hope of winning our hearts.

Lisse, Wednesday, May 25
I have hunted almost all day; we did find a wolf, and we forced him to a grand finish. He stood up to the dogs, but the youngest son of the marquis killed him with a rifle. It was the size of a Newfoundland dog and had eaten two sheep this morning, which made it a bit heavy. Tomorrow or the day after tomorrow, when we have a sufficient number of dogs, we hunt a boar which we heard is in the vicinity. We expect every day the order for home, but we live so happily here, the inhabitants are so kind that I would stay away from England a few more months without regret, even though I have many dear friends there.

Barbaste, Thursday, May 26
I left Lisse this morning at five o'clock with the sons of the marquis. At Barbaste, at six o'clock, we met the hunting dogs with eighteen hunters. We soon found a quantity of hares, but they were not killed

by the dogs. We did some good hunting, for up to two miles, when the dogs wanted to stop and go back. Two of the hunters had horns which they sounded often, but the dogs were still cautious; horns, cries, or whips and they would still only go where they wanted to go. Dawson and I, the only two English present, really enjoyed it. Lord Wellington who is in Madrid was pursued and stoned by Spanish troops. What trouble for such ingrates!

Lisse, Friday, May 27
I was rabbit hunting this morning very early. About ten o'clock, I proceeded to the Court Martial at Mézin. I went to see Luard with Madame Mélignan, who invited me to dinner; but this is a lean day and I had a poor meal. In the afternoon, I visited several ladies and I came back to Lisse to find Dawson here. He came to spend the night at the chateau and to hunt with us tomorrow.

Lisse, Saturday, May 28
At four o'clock this morning, the comte, his brother, Dawson and I went out with our rifles. We first woke Monsieur Pascon, who joined us and we started hunting with six pairs of greyhounds. One of the best dogs in the party that night pursued a fox which had taken refuge in the courtyard of the farm. We followed it for some time, but without success, and we came back with a hare and two rabbits. We saw no wolves in the woods; it is attributed to the invasion and to the fighting in the Pyrenees, that they were pushed out of the forests. They take one sheep per day. The order of route for the regiment arrived this evening: we march on Monday, 30 May Casteljaloux, 31 May, Bazas, 1 June Rions, 3 June Les Bons-Enfants[8]. 4 June Saint André [-de- Cubzac].

Lisse, Sunday, May 29
On the parade this morning the troop put oak leaves in their headdresses. The men were thrilled to learn that we are leaving tomorrow. Waldie had a serious accident yesterday. As he was returning from dinner at a Masonic Lodge, his mare took fright and threw him against a tree, he has broken his left arm. He was drunk, I am told.

The Comte gave me today a small coconut bowl nicely chiseled by himself in memory of him. I offered in return a small pear in

---

[8] Part of Fargues-Saint-Hilaire.

powder. As to the young ladies and their mother, I have pledged to never forget them; their goodness will never fade from my memory. Luard went to Mezin to take leave of the ladies; I prefer not go there. The women of this country have very deep feelings and I cannot bear to see a woman cry. Luard is a real tugger of hearts: he is not afraid to go say farewell to the poor creatures when he has destroyed their happiness.

Casteljaloux, Monday, May 30
I left Lisse with sadness, after an affectionate farewell.
The comte and his brother accompanied me for a mile from Casteljaloux, we are separated, but not forever, we must meet in Paris next year. I am housed with an old engineering officer who was in the service of the rebels in America and who was taken prisoner by Lord Cornwallis. He speaks a few words of English, but his wife speaks the language of the devil, because I don't understand a word of what she says. It seems that she is crazy, and having lost a son in the war, she takes me for him. A few minutes ago, she came into my room and gave me a mortal fright taking me into her arms and hugging me with all her strength. I have locked my door so that she does not come again to play one of her tricks. We have already passed through this town formerly with the army of Marshal Beresford. Captain Russell, Lieutenants Morris and Dunkin return by sea with the dismounted hussars of the regiment. The 18th will join the 2nd brigade of the left division of the English cavalry and will march across France to get to Calais and Boulogne, the ports of embarkation for England.

# Chapter 17

# The Long March Home

Because of a shortage of transports, it was decided to march the cavalry up through France to the Channel ports, where they could be easily and quickly shipped to England. Men who were without horses were to sail from Bordeaux. It was to be a long but quite pleasant forty-two-day march and the men also had the opportunity of seeing Paris on the way.

Bazas, Tuesday, May 31
Vitoria was put down yesterday and I have a small family to carry; I must at least keep the two dogs[1], which are promised. I bought a basket to put them in and I will put them on the mule. I took command of C Troop.

Loupiac, Wednesday 1 June
The regiment crossed the Garonne at Langon on boats, without accident. The river in this place is too broad and too quick to allow for the construction of a pontoon bridge. I then marched my troop to the village of Loupiac, on the right bank of the river, two miles from Rions. After changing my clothes, I mounted my Jeannette and I proceeded to Postiac; I had to cross a country where roads are unknown and I found the chateau of the second son of the marquis with great difficulty. I received great hospitality which I expected. At dinner, my host made me taste his wines, as he had promised to me; they are certainly the best

---

[1] His dog had obviously died giving birth. One of the puppies must have been named Vitoria as he appears again later.

in France and I was quite giddy when I went to bed. Went to Montarouze[2] and Faleyras, where I was the first Englishman that they had seen, I was enjoying looking around; the people marvelled at my beautiful uniform and shouted: 'Superb! Magnificent!'

Postiac, Thursday, June 2
We expected at dinner a lady who had never seen the English, but a family mourning prevented her from coming. This morning, I visited the chateau; it is one of the most beautiful I have ever seen. It is arranged in the English style, but the walls are covered with rich tapestries. The silver service is as beautiful as the Marquis'. I did the tour of the vineyards and I entered the cellar, which is so fresh that I really was chilled; I shivered for an hour afterwards. About three o'clock, after dinner, I took leave of the kind wife of my host, who accompanied me to Loupiac, where I thought I would find my troop, but the regiment had already gone. Learning that Luard had told the colonel that I was sick, I decided to go with my friend to see his brother at Saint-Macaire. We arrived there at nine o'clock in the evening, to the surprise of the family, as we were not expected. After a good supper, I retired very tired because yesterday and today I did not less than twenty-three leagues on horseback and I am yet still fifteen leagues from my regiment.

Les Bons-Enfants, Friday, June 3
This morning at four o'clock, I lunched with the two brothers, and after bidding them farewell, I took a boat to go to Rions, distant three leagues. The boatman stopped a moment at Langon, which enabled me to take leave of my other friends. At Rions, I found Ipper with my horses and we went to a town called Creon, where the mayor was walking with a white cap on his head; I took him to be a madman. I had just finished dinner when the order arrived for the regiment to go to Bons-Enfants, Carbon-Blanc and Saint-Loubès. We only got to our lodgings at midnight after a stage of three leagues. I was put into a chateau and I tried to get the owner to give me a dinner, which he seemed unwilling to make.

Bordeaux, Saturday 4 June, Anniversary of the King's birthday.
I went this morning with Duperier to visit this beautiful city. The Garonne is covered with ships and as today is the anniversary of the

2   I have been unable to identify this village with any certainty.

280

birth of the King of England, they are all covered in flags. The English warships which are in the river fired the Royal salute at one o'clock. You can see some traces of a new bridge, God knows when it will be finished![3] Visited the monuments, and especially the docks which interested me very much. The huge stores, full of all kinds of goods and especially wines, have no equal in any port in Europe, except London. Duperier was born here and he lived here once; he was rich. He knocked on the door of a beautiful house which he lived in once and he asked the people who stay there now how long they have occupied it. 'Nineteen years', they responded. 'Who lived here before you?' 'A young fool by the name of Duperier who died in England' they replied. We rejoined the regiment at Saint-André-de-Cubzac. My troop was put in a small village a mile from there; my servants and my luggage was with Captain Kennedy, in a large chateau. The owner is too polite a man to be with me; barely had I arrived, than he took me in his arms and kissed me. As revenge, tomorrow morning before leaving, I will do as much to his wife, because she is pretty.

Montlieu, Sunday, June 5

The 2nd Division of the left column is to march at seven o'clock, under the command of Colonel Arentschildt, to Montlieu, and we will be split amongst a number of small villages. Our division consists of a brigade of hussars and one of horse artillery under the orders of Colonel Dickson[4], in all fifteen hundred horses. The English cavalry allowed to cross France, consists of eighteen regiments, or sixty-six squadrons, which the most conservative calculation adds up to nine thousand horses; those of the artillery, who march with the two columns, amount to about sixteen hundred. General Vandeleur commands the left column. I am housed in a farm; farmers are very polite, but their wine is bad.

We have put together our band; Deane, the paymaster, was a few days ago in Bordeaux buying instruments and our musicians have played today during the march for the first time since our departure from Portugal, where all the instruments had been lost and the musicians put in the ranks[5]. The 1st [German] Hussars are dressed to the nines, and they are very chic!

---

[3] The famous Pont de Pierre was completed in 1822.

[4] Brevet Colonel Alexander Dickson attached officially to the Portuguese Army, but Wellington used him as his senior artilleryman in Spain.

[5] This is odd as he mentions the musicians playing a few timse in Spain, perhaps he meant to say that they were stolen when they left Spain?

Chateauneuf [-sur-Charente], Monday, June 6

The peace was signed on the 1st of the month. The Empress Josephine died on 29 May, her heart broken by the fall of Napoleon, who, the world says, treated her badly[6]. During the long stage today, by failing to take a guide, we were lost for nearly three leagues. Finally, we arrived at Roullet [-Saint-Estephe], a miserably small village where Colonel Murray remained with Croker's squadron and a part of the Staff; they were unable to continue to Châteauneuf with us.

The officers agreed to dine together at the inn and we charged the Hotel Soleil to prepare our meal. They asked us for eighteen francs per head, whereas all the people where we stayed were preparing to treat us! We knew there would be no benefit to us and we refused to pay such a ransom to the thief of an innkeeper. The people here are no longer the same as in Le Midi and we hear the Gascon language no more. The farmer's clothes resembles that of the country people in England.

I saw today the famous Spanish partisan Pujol[7], travelling to Paris. I don't know what he will do there, but from what I have heard, the French government should deliver this rascal up to his countrymen so that he receives the punishment he deserves. A French officer who speaks a little English gave me details of him that made me shudder with horror. Having committed in his country the most awful crimes, Pujol fled to France and served Napoleon during the peninsular war. He organized a band of the most wretched, the cruellest and most hardened to evil that he could find in France and Spain, and at the head of these assassins, he did not hesitate to commit the cruellest crimes; hanging, crucifixion, nailing to walls, burning people of any gender and any age, were his favourite pastimes. It is said that even part of his own family, his father and his brothers, were sacrificed by him. His memory brings icy terror to the Spanish, and his name is subject to universal execration, especially in Catalonia, where he had followed Suchet, having served under the orders of Marshals Augereau and Macdonald[8]. At Toulouse, he was in the army of Soult; his band of men had arrived a few days before the battle.

6 Josephine de Beauharnais had married Napoleon, but he had divorced her when it became apparent that she could not give him a son. She died at Malmaison.

7 Joseph Pujol, chief of the Miquelets alias Boquica was persuaded to fight for the French in Catalonia between 1808-14 and was renowned for his barbarity against his own people.

8 Marshal Charles Pierre François Augereau, 1st Duke of Castiglione and Marshal Étienne Jacques Joseph Alexandre MacDonald, 1st Duke of Taranto had both served in Catalonia.

Montignac-Charente, Tuesday, June 7

For some time now as is the case again today, we are disappointed in our efforts to be housed in large towns; it is the 1st [German] Hussars who occupy Angoulême. We are housed in the two miserable villages of Montignac and Vars; but the regiment halts here tomorrow and we intend to go to visit Angoulême. We passed Petignac, where there are large mills. The peasants have never seen the English and they stare at us. Their politeness would satisfy the most demanding. They say that we are beautiful and make us endless compliments. We had dinner today at a village inn, but we were not able to get even a knife. It seems that it is not the mode here to use a knife.[9]

Angoulême, Wednesday, June 8

We left at the start of the day, Luard and me, to visit Angoulême. The town is built on a rock that dominates the country for many leagues around. The wall and the ramparts that surround it, are planted with trees, which offer a magnificent new promenade. Almost all of the finer families have left their homes until the departure of our army. French officers have portrayed us so unfavourably that the residents really seem to be afraid of us. Their reception is quite different from that which we have received so far. After the theatre, we had to cover three leagues on horse to regain our beds in Montignac.

As they progressed northward, their reception by the locals became noticeably less friendly.

Mansle, Thursday, June 9

I'm still housed in a dirty village, composed of two streets and a small market place full of peasants. The headquarters of the brigade and regiment are here. Yesterday I was introduced to Colonel Bülow[10], of the heavy German cavalry, brother of the famous Prussian general of the same name. The roads are covered with men returning from English prisons; they insulted us as they passed, calling us in English all the names possible and screaming:"Vive l'Empereur!'

I contemplated today with admiration the ruins of a large abbey which was originally, of the same dimensions as Westminster and

---

[9] The French version makes a comment here, pointing out that Woodberry had not realised that the French peasantry always carried their own knife for such eventualities.
[10] Lieutenant Colonel John von Bulow, 1st Dragoons, King's German Legion. Beamish no. 87.

was just as magnificent. But the windows are stripped of their beautiful stained glass windows, statues are mutilated, ornaments destroyed. A large convent for monks lies nearby: now a peasant inhabits it. A sad effect of the Revolution!

Ruffec, Friday, June 10
Several officers, Major Gruben[11] and I, dined together at Ruffec; the repast cost 12 shillings per head. Hoteliers are the biggest thieves in the country; they charge the English six times more than a countryman. We have several times, in the recent past, had recourse to the magistrates to set their prices.

Couhe[12], Saturday, June 11
Almost all of the officers are tired of this cavalcade through France. I am myself very unhappy, because the residents are far less kind than around Bordeaux. They appear to be unhappy with the terms of the peace which, they say, is very hard on them. What a change within a few years! In 1812 France could have given peace to the world and maintained their supremacy over almost all of Europe. Now, by the ambition of a man which she called her Emperor, it has fallen to the lowest level and I am sure that it will never again regain its military greatness. Everyone agrees that if Buonaparte reappeared in France, after the departure of the Allies, another great revolution would still take place. It is not uncommon here still to see the tricolour cockade. Prisoners of war returning from England have treated some of our men in a most outrageous way.

Poitiers, Sunday, June 12
If this sun continues, we are going to resemble the Moors. I am a dark brown. It is impossible to sit outside in the middle of the day. We have today to march seventeen leagues. Here is the rare happiness which we enjoy: we march through France exposed to the heat of the sun for seven to eight hours a day, and arriving at the end of each stage, we are insulted by the inhabitants, of whom the largest part are Buonapartistes; they repeat that we will soon learn the news of the return of their Emperor.

I am housed in a small village called Migne [-Auxances], near Poitiers; we halt tomorrow and so I shall visit the city. The people of

---

[11] Major Otto Frederick von Gruben, 1st Dragoons, King's German Legion. Beamish no. 871.
[12] The French version identifies this as Couhe-Verac (which does not exist), Couhe is on the direct road to Poitiers.

the village have told me a curious fact; for four years, they have not made wine. The grapes are destroyed every year by small animals or insects named urbec[13]. They cannot destroy the insects. Kennedy had dinner with me. Our host has added a few trifles to our ordinary fare, he has amused us by advocating for Napoleon before us and declaring that he will soon return to amaze the world! We passed a beautiful town named Vivonne. The main street was very pleasantly decorated with garlands of flowers strewn about like a fantasy; the beautiful women there were walking out, waiting for the beginning of the festival celebrating the peace. A number of orchestras were prepared to play dances. I would have liked to stay there, but I was ordered to guard the baggage.

Poitiers, Monday, June 13

Kennedy came with me to see Poitiers; but the weather was so hot that we were forced to seek shelter in a cafe for up to three hours. We then did the tour of the city and we were struck with its ancient appearance. The public walks resemble those of Angoulême; they dominate all the surrounding country. The famous Battle of Poitiers[14] took place around this city; the inhabitants told us the details as if it had occurred during the last campaign.

We met some of our old acquaintances of the 22nd Chasseurs; they were very happy to see us, but had nothing to tell us. Here, there is a depot of cavalry and we saw detachments of several regiments. The 15th French Infantry Regiment entered the town while we were there, coming from the environs of Paris. Poitiers women are very pretty and dress very properly and even quite richly. The Cathedral was built by the English, it contains tombs of some representatives of our nobility.

Chatellerault, Tuesday, June 14

From Poitiers to Chatellerault, the way is long but enjoyable. This time the brigade is lodged together. The town of Châtellerault is not only large, but pretty. We passed [Vouneuil-sur-] Vienne; the bridge is very beautiful and recalls that of Toulouse. Manufacturers are numerous, especially those of cutlery and weaving. The women we toyed with a lot with their merchandise on offer. I took a bath in Vienne with some other officers. I am only a swimmer of medium

---

[13]  Urbec, beemare or lisette – is a blue or green weevil 5-6cm long.
[14]  Fought on 19 September 1356 between Edward the Black Prince and King John II of France.

ability and I am never safe in a river without being with a stronger swimmer than me. We are in a country of excellent beer, almost as good as English porter, and it costs about the same price.

I was very surprised to hear a man screaming in French 'Little lambs for sale, little lambs for sale, two for a sou! Little lambs for sale!' it is the air used by the hawkers in England. I noticed that this dealer is the same well known type of character I've so often seen in my own country. The dinner was attended by all our officers; our musicians played and we danced with a few young women in the city. After the champagne and the improvised ball, we found ourselves very tired. The weather is too hot and we march early every morning at four o'clock.

Caught by a terrible storm, they arrived at their quarters drenched to the skin.

Sainte-Maure [-de-Touraine], Wednesday, June 15
As soon as we had left Chatellerault, one of the most terrible storms came on which the elders of the country can ever remember. A few minutes before that nevertheless, the heat was so excessive that we could barely get into the saddle: we could only breathe with difficulty. Thunder rolled above our heads, lightning shone around our column, and threw terror into all our hearts. Finally the rain fell in torrents; the horses struggling to move forward. I thought several times that lightning would strike any one of us, but we continued despite the danger. We were soaked to the skin and we were glad to arrive at Sainte-Maure, where the brigade are lodged. This city is an important coaching stage; It is full of passengers, and there are many hostels, hotels and private houses. Very nice market in the centre of the city. They say today that Buonaparte died; I hope not, because I dream again of picquets and patrols; this life of inaction becomes tiring. Met on the road prisoners returning from England.

Tours, Thursday, June 16
We entered this beautiful city early this morning and we were received by the French garrison who were under arms in the Rue Royale. They saluted us and we returned the salute. The crowd filled the streets. Our band has had great success. The village where they sent us was happily occupied in error by the artillery, and the mayor gave me a billet for the city. The Rue Royale is the most beautiful street I've ever seen; it is very broad and built entirely of stone, exactly in the same style and if possible, more grandiose than

Portland Place in London. It is where I am located, and my hosts are very polite.

George was delighted to report that for a change it was the other cavalry column that was in some disgrace.

Tours, Friday, June 17
Several English families reside here and in the surroundings; if ever I had to leave my native country, I would choose to live at Tours or in the vicinity of Lisse. Lord Wellington, who spent this morning visiting Paris, said to General Vandeleur that he was particularly satisfied with this column; but that he bitterly deplored the lack of discipline in the right column, whose conduct gave rise to numerous complaints, they have argued and fought with the locals. Several men were even killed. The most culpable are the Life Guards. Lord Wellington gave the order to Vandeleur to allow officers of the left column to go to Paris. General Grant, the idiot who commanded us at Vitoria, is in this city. Mansfield, his aide de camp, dined with me.

Chateau-Renault, Saturday, June 18
We arrived at our quarters this morning about nine or ten o'clock; I had lunch with Colonel Murray, who allows me to go tomorrow into Paris with Captain Kennedy. One hundred and fifty of the best horses of the cavalry which march across this country must be selected and offered to the King of France; it is a gift from the Prince Regent. I do not think that they should take one from the regiment, all are exhausted. It is rumoured in the army that Princess Charlotte[15] has seen or heard a quote from a Russian prince of her charming a great person in the uniform of an aide de camp.[16]

There was great excitement when a group of officers was allowed five day's leave to visit Paris.

Vendôme, Sunday, June 19
Yesterday morning the two lieutenant colonels of the brigade exchanged acrimonious words about the march of their regiments. I don't know how it will end; by a duel, I guess. Vendôme is a great

---

[15] Daughter of Caroline of Brunswick and of George Prince of Wales, Lord Castlereagh had proposed a match between her and the Prince of Orange in 1814. However, she married in reality, in 1815, Leopold of Saxe Coburg future King of the Belgians, she died in 1816.
[16] The Prince of Orange, 'Thin Billy', was his name in the army.

and old town, rich in appearance. Murray permits Kennedy, Clements, Luard, Hughes and I to leave the regiment to spend five days in Paris. After we ate, Kennedy and I left, to make the first two stages on horseback. Halfway to Cloyes [-sur-le-Loir], we met Hughes, Clements and Luard, who travel by post. Knowing that it would be impossible to journey together, because there were not enough carriages or horses, we made them believe that we stopped in Cloyes over night. But soon after their departure, we took a carriage and we watched them until Bonneval, where they were having dinner. We could hear them laughing and making a great noise, suspecting little that we were going to play a trick on them. Indeed, convinced that we were far behind them, they had neglected to retain the post chaise; we took it and arrived in Chartres at two o'clock in the morning. We went to bed after ordering a carriage and horses to leave at six o'clock.

Paris, Monday, June 20
Chartres, which was occupied by the allies, now has several French infantry regiments in garrison. They will leave tomorrow, because the English cavalry must halt here. A regiment of Polish lancers were surprised here unexpectedly, during the preparation of their meal, by a party of cossacks and captured whole. The locals portray the cossacks as ferocious beasts; they committed great violence in the city. In some houses, they stole the silverware and all the valuables; in others, they simply required a good dinner. From Chartres we went to Rambouillet, the favourite residence of Marie-Louise[17]. She received a visit at the chateau from the Emperor Alexander and the Emperor of Austria, her father, and it was from there that she left for Germany, with her son, the King of Rome, who is said to be a very beautiful child. This village now houses the 2nd Hussar Regiment of the Imperial Guard - now Royal. It is composed of the sons of the first families. There are three regiments, but they were preserved at Leipsig and their Emperor was saved from being made a prisoner by having confidence in them.

We passed Versailles and Saint-Cloud and soon after we saw the city of Paris. Our coach took us to a hotel, in the Rue Saint-Honoré, close to the Louvre, where we obtained two bedrooms and a salon for a week, all for the trifling sum of ten pounds. After we were

---

[17] Napoleon's second wife, an Austrian princess, who replaced Josephine and gave Napoleon the son he craved.

sorted, we went in search of a tailor in the Palais-Royal: he took our measurements for civilian clothing which he promised to have for us the following morning. We then went to the Palais-Royal, where we promenaded until nearly midnight, watching the women and shopping. This is one of the main attractions of Paris; there are the most amazing variety of scenes it is possible to imagine. Shops, jewellers, tailors, booksellers, clockmakers, print dealers, china shops, cafes, baths, currency changers, gaming houses unite in a friendly rivalry to relieve the money and fleece without defiance. All we saw was shopkeepers in splendid residences. Polytechnic students told us of the prodigies of valour of the Buttes-Chaumont[18]. They had made an oath to die in their positions for the defense of Paris, and after the bloody battle of March 30, many of these brave young people were found dead next to their guns. There were six hundred in Paris; only a third have escaped death. It is said that the Emperor Alexander, seeing it better defended than other parts of the French line asked what troops were there; and when he knew that it was the Polytechnique, he ordered them to cease fire on his side, and sent a parley to give them safe passage if they wanted to return to their school. This proposal was refused immediately. The oldest of these students was eighteen years old and many were not more than 13 years old. They were the children of the first families of the country and all were destined to become officers.

Paris, Tuesday, June 21
After lunch, we saw the admirable collections of the Louvre and Place Vendome, where stands the superb column erected by order of Buonaparte in commemoration of his victories over the Austrian, Russian and Prussian armies, and made with the metal of the cannon taken from them. There was originally a beautiful bronze statue of Napoleon atop; the allies pulled it down during the occupation of Paris, and when Alexander leaves for Russia; it will for ever stand in a square in Moscow with an appropriate inscription.

At four o'clock, we went to dinner at the Café de Londres, the principal hotel of Paris; we here met a number of officers of the 1st [German] Hussars and a few Russian officers who joined us for a toast; to the great confusion of the French, to Lord Wellington and

---

[18] At the Parc des Buttes Chaumont the National Guard of Paris and the Marine Artillery fought a desperate battle against the Prussians. When the Russian uhlans captured a battery, they discovered that many of the gunners were students of the École Polytechnique, some were crying while others defiantly stood by their cannon.

the army who fought on this day last year under his command at Vitoria. We then visited the Gobelins, where they make the beautiful tapestries. The number of workers here amounted to nearly one hundred; considering their extraordinary skill and the admirable rendering of the figures, they are very poorly paid. Their magnificent works are stored without buyers, they are too expensive and today are all for gifts.

Wednesday, June 22
We have seen the Church of Notre Dame; it is very inferior to the Abbey of Westminster. Napoleon was crowned here. The letter N was placed over the high altar so that the French always had his name in their thoughts. On each side are beautiful tapestries, depicting the life of Saint Louis.

The Pantheon is under repair; we saw there the tombs of Rousseau, Voltaire, Marshal Lannes and a host of other celebrities. The Museum of the Jardin des Plantes are said to be the best of all those in Europe. From there we crossed the Seine and we saw the place where the Bastille stood. The flags captured by Buonaparte at the battle of Austerlitz were kept at the Luxembourg Palace but were taken out of Paris a few hours before the entry of the Allies and thus saved. After dinner, we went to the Opera Comique and the songs pleased me very much, but the actors remind me of Astleys in London[19]. I then proceeded to the Theatre Francais, where I stayed until the end; I continued at the Palais-Royal and I amused myself until two o'clock in the morning.

I entered this morning into the stables of the King and I saw the former stables of Napoleon, his horses and the man caring for them. This old man has accompanied Napoleon in all his campaigns, even in Russia, and not one of the horses were lost on the road back.

Paris, Thursday, June 23
At eleven o'clock, we were in the Palace of the Tuileries in full uniform to pay court to Louis XVIII. One of the gentlemen of service with his Majesty came to receive us at the door of the palace and took us into the room of the Marshals. Sunrise appears at the end of the hall, which awakes the King, we went to the chapel; the King came there at noon, accompanied by the Duchess of Angoulême and her suite! The Mass finished, we returned to the room of the

---

[19] Astley's amphitheatre was built in Lambeth in 1773 and was the home of the circus.

Marshals and we had ample opportunity to examine their portraits, because we were not presented to the King for an hour. His Majesty addressed us first in French and then in English, which he speaks remarkably well. He then dismissed us thanking us. We then visited the palace; the Duchess d'Angoulême was walking in a corridor, meditating, a book in her hand; our excellent guide presented us and she proved to be very affable. At the end of the palace, we were lead to the college of Les Invalides, an institution that rivals in the world both Chelsea and Greenwich. There are currently three thousand-nine hundred invalids accomodated. The dome is guilded and has an imposing effect. The carriage then led us to the military school, another beautiful institution for the education of the children of soldiers. Before it, extends the great plain, the Champ de Mars. This is generally where Napoleon carried out revues of thirty or forty thousand men.

In front of the military school, but on the other side of the Seine, a palace for the King of Rome has begun building; it is said that Louis XVIII is transforming it into a hospital[20]. Abandoning our carriage, we walked to the Place de la Revolution, which was where the hapless King and Queen of France were guillotined. We entered the garden of the Tuileries, which are very well maintained and filled with statues and fountains. Around the palace are posts of the Swiss Guard dressed in red, looking a bit like our soldiers, but not so well shaped.

We saw a play at the Theatre Francais called *The Jealous Husband and the Hunting of Henri IV*. This theatre is dimly lit, but the art of the actors is excellent. Before the theatre, we had seen Frascati, on the boulevards. At the end of the play, one enters through a gallery lined with ice that leads into a large square building where they bring you refreshments. At the end of one of the main avenues of the garden, small pillars stand on each side, around which the honeysuckle wraps itself. A cave opens up in the middle. The aisles are decorated with statues, which are also hand lamps. The fashionable hour is ten o'clock in the evening. A few officers of cossacks were bivouacked in this pretty place, and except a few damaged trees, no serious damage was done either here, nor on the boulevards, where several thousand Russians and Prussians are camped.

The boulevards extend around Paris for seven miles; the grand boulevards have four rows of trees that form three aisles, the middle

---

[20] In fact, the project was abandoned.

for the horsemen, the other two for pedestrians and carriages. Along these walks are spread everything that can attract and interest whilst abroad; theatres, cafes, vauxhalls, magnificent hotels and taverns are present in one continued and uninterrupted procession while music charms the ears, puppet theatres and countless jugglers entertain the eyes.

The old boulevards extend from the Observatory to the Hôtel des Invalides. They offer rides longer and broader than the others, and the trees grow better. There are very frequently public gardens, these are the New Poland and la Chaumière, where you can dance, swing, enjoy a quantity of innocent games. Here is found the modest citizen and his family: the world bright and fashionable attends the grand boulevards on the north side of Paris.

Epernon, Friday, June 24

At seven o'clock in the morning we left Paris, Kennedy and I, to go to Saint-Cloud, where we remained only a few minutes, and Versailles, where we were amazed by our visit to the château and the Trianons.

Marie-Louise is as popular here as in Rambouillet. Her memory is dear and affection for her goes as far as enthusiasm. All good wives cite her as a model of conjugal love: and that they had no doubt, her extreme youth at the time of her marriage with Napoleon must serve to support the opinion that his heart was absolutely gay at this time. He was the father of her child, and, as the poet says,

It was to be all sweetness.

Her servants regret her sincerely and speak of her as the best and the most lenient of mistresses. The elegant pavilion where Marie-Louise and the little King of Rome would make frequent visits rises like a palace of enchantment in the middle of this pastoral scene in the Trianon. The boudoir and the toilet chamber of the Empress seem to have been decorated by the hand of geniuses. It is here that the man who seemed so pleased in the middle of scenes of carnage withdrew and rested his ambition and was concerned in the charms of paternal and conjugal happiness. It can be assumed that his restless soul has tasted in these places a few moments of domestic pleasure in the quiet company of his wife and his child.

The march towards the Channel resumed.

Houdan, Saturday, June 25
Dreary marches through a species of dunes; we have to keep to the highway. I am housed in a farm outside the village of Houdan.

Mantes [-la-Jolie], Sunday 26 June
The regiment arrived at Mantes at noon after a long stage. With great difficulty, the entire brigade was housed nearby. I have been sent with my troop to the small village of Magnanville. The bridge of Mantes on the Seine is remarkable and built very level. A few days after the battle of Paris, a considerable number of corpses were seen floating in the water. They were French mostly, because the Russians and Prussians buried all their dead and threw those of the enemy for the fish. A small detachment of cossacks took possession of Mantes unopposed; they have done very little damage; they were well paid and they were given what they asked for.

Gisors, Monday, June 27
I have received the order to go and prepare the lodging for the regiment, at Abbeville, five days march.

Gournay [-en-Bray], Tuesday, June 28
After the arrival of the regiment at Gisors this morning, I went with Deane and Chambers, to visit the shops. I bought a snuff box carved in the form of a horse. This rare curiosity was found in the pocket of a cossack killed near here by the peasants. I then rode quietly on horse to Gournay. They are busy scratching the eagles and Imperial arms off public monuments and replacing them with the coat of arms of the Bourbons. I am afraid that there will be another change in a few months, so great is the fickleness of the French people. The people here look more like the English than any we have seen in this realm and are therefore, more beautiful than the generality of the French.

Neufchate [-en-Bray]l, Wednesday, June 29
I left Gournay at ten o'clock and after a march of nine hours, under a burning sun, I arrived at Neufchatel. The Sub-Prefect invited me to dinner. He is a good royalist: he spoke much of 'the good King Louis XVIII' and 'this canaille Buonaparte'. After dinner, he sent for a delightful young woman who speaks English poorly. She told me, to my great surprise, that almost the entire city is devoted to Buonaparte. She is here on a visit and she will go to England in a month. She learned her English in the convent where she was raised.

In the evening, this lady played the harp, sang and was very pleasant and very considerate. The mistress of the house, who is Italian, also sang with a very beautiful voice. I will regret, when the time comes to move on, as I almost gave my heart to this charming woman. Tomorrow the headquarters of the regiment will be at Esclavelles, two miles from the city. The 1st [German] Hussars and artillery will be accommodated in the city in turn.

Blangy [-sur-Bresle], Thursday, June 30
The Mayor of Blangy is a great fool, with whom I had a lot of trouble. I obtained lodgings for my regiment only after a lot of difficulties. He sent me to a very dirty hostel, which by the way is the best in the city. I obtained, after great difficulties, one of the worst dinners I've had for several months. All the farmers I met sing 'Vive Henri IV!'

The inhabitants seem happy with the change of government; as of all commerce, it is theirs which has suffered the most; because they manufacture lace. The Prince of Orange is known in the army under the name of 'thin Billy'. All see him as a great boy and sincerely wish he does succeed with Princess Charlotte. The cossacks were in this vicinity a few days before the abdication of Buonaparte; they looted everywhere, and strangely, there were only twenty men with an officer. It is they who are blamed for everything. The people here are never in their houses, and you would never know what becomes of them overnight.

Abbeville, Friday, July 1
I arrived at Abbeville in good time and I soon made all the necessary arrangements for the lodging of the regiment for tomorrow and Sunday. My host has told me that the amiable Sub-Prefect of Neufchatel, who I took for a true royalist, had become famous during the revolution for appointing those victims to go to the guillotine. He is, moreover, the person chosen the other day by the Department to bring an address to Louis XVIII. The poor King will do well to be very wary of him.

Abbeville, Saturday, July 2
The regiment arrived this morning at the gates of the city; and after waiting for the governor to recognise us, we were accepted in due form.

Abbeville, Sunday, July 3
I visited this morning the cathedral: the interior is beautiful, as

beautiful as Westminster Abbey. This building was built by the English when they were masters of this part of France.

Arry, Monday, July 4

Leaving Abbeville at five o'clock in the morning, we arrived here at nine o'clock. The 1st [German] Hussars are now at Auxi [-le-chateau], travelling to Brussels[21].

We crossed part of the famous forest of Crécy, in which the famous battle was won by the English in 1415. The locals tell you the details of the landing of the English at Saint-Valéry [sur-Somme] as if the event was yesterday, as well as the great battle of Agincourt.

I really am lucky; one way or another, I find a way to arrange my stay in a chateau. I'm at the Mayor's; everyone asked me a host of questions. An Italian officer came to dinner with us; my host asked a lot of questions about Madame Catalini[22], her husband was formerly a servant of this officer and Madame Catalani herself played and sang while here in a small theatre for the price of thirty-five sous for the evening.

One of the hosts of this chateau is a Polish officer of a corps of lancers, he played the violin, the mayor a clarinet, and a small black woman, teacher of the daughters of the mayor, the piano. The Italian sang in a delicious way, and then danced with the small black woman with the request 'Madamoiselle do you want to dance?' which made us laugh heartily.

Montreuil [-sur-Mer], Tuesday, July 5

Leaving the Crécy forest, we spotted the ocean which we had not seen since our stay in the Pyrenees. It is in this Department of Pas-de-Calais, at Arras, that the arch-villain, Robespierre was born[23]. When Louis XVIII received the address of the Department when going to Paris, he recalled the event, saying he would never forget the city and the Department, which had given birth to this monster. He would have done better to guard his language, because he has fewer friends here than in any other part of France. I saw here coal [on the fire] for the first time since my departure from England.

---

[21] The KGL units were all transported to Belgium in preparation for their disbanding at the end of the war. Luckily, they were still there when hostilities erupted again in 1815.

[22] Angelica Catalini, an renowned Italian operatic singer.

[23] Maximilien François Marie Isidore de Robespierre was born at Arras in 1758 and became a lawyer and politician. His name became synonymous with the 'Terror' but eventually went to the guillotine himself in 1794.

I am housed with Kennedy, in the chateau of Comte Lebrun and I was much surprised to find there my friends from Arry and the Polish officer. The count is a charming man and his brother speaks English. This family is related to the French general of the same name. Marshal Ney lived in this chateau, at the time when the French army was preparing to invade England. He gave a feast here to the members of the Legion de Honour.

Boulogne [sur-Mer], Wednesday, July 6
This town is heavily fortified to the seaward; the port and the basins are surrounded by works. The citadel commands the lower town and the port. Up town there was a beautiful view of the ocean and the chalk cliffs of Albion, which I contemplated with excited eyes. I had more than once given up hope of ever seeing my country again; but thanks be to God! I'll enjoy this happiness again. A part of the 13th Light Dragoons shipped out yesterday, but the headwind kept the transports to the coast and several are beached. The harbour master told me that they could not be got back afloat within a week, when the next high tide comes. The sea is covered with vessels and they await the wind to discover the land of liberty.

Boulogne, Thursday, July 7
I've seen this morning, the famous column erected in honour of Napoleon by Soult's Army; every man donated a day's pay for it. It was never finished, but scaffolds rise up to the height that it ought to have been[24]. It is on the summit where they built seats for Buonaparte and Marie-Louise, when the emperor sent out the prams[25] to fight the English frigates. We all had dinner together and we went to the theatre. The performance was miserable; I could have had the most beautiful actress for a Napoleon[26]. The French officers of Boulogne are the worst imaginable, there is not one that merits the name of gentleman. We sell our mules for nothing; they gave me 15 dollars for mine which cost me 150 in Lisbon and yet she is in better shape now.

We are leaving tomorrow for Calais, where we embark. I bought six shawls and a few pairs of silk stockings very cheaply; I hope that the customs officers will not visit our baggage. Napoleon lived some time at an ancient chateau in the area, he left an old bicorne hat

---

[24] The column of the Grand Armee was not completed until 1843.
[25] An open rowing boat often armed with a single cannon in the bow.
[26] Actresses at this time had a reputation little better than whores!

which the current owner retains as a rare curiosity. He has shown, Kennedy and I, and we had the honour to put it on our heads, the greasy hat of Nap.

Calais, Friday, July 8

After a long ride through the dunes, most of the time with a beautiful view of a 'good small island', we arrived at Calais, and the regiment lodged in six villages, two or three miles from the city. Calais does not abound in gay, or attractive shops and presents a rather monotonous appearance. The general appearance is quite different from that of British cities. The houses, are large and tall, built with a grey stone: the streets are fairly broad, but have no pavements. The packet boat has just arrived from England; the individuals that we saw come over were very amusing. I wish that there was a strong rule of customs on ugly people who come to France, especially on the poor of Bond-Street that dishonour their country when they are allowed to leave.[27]

As always, the delay in finally sailing for England seemed interminable.

Calais, Saturday, July 9

Sixteen small English transports, intended to ship our regiment, arrived this morning; so I hope we should be in England in two days.

There was a parade today to enable the commissioners of Louis XVIII to choose one hundred and fifty horses from the cavalry regiments. It is a present that is made to him by the Prince Regent to mount his guard of honour: but we are sure to leave with all of the best horses. They have only taken three and they are not worth 30 pounds together.

Sunday, July 10

There was a celebration in the small village where I am lodged and I was much amused. About two o'clock in the afternoon, the world began to arrive. The house of the mayor, where I live, there was a meal of twelve covers, including me. It was a feast rather than a dinner. We were there for three hours. My servant Ipper was cooking. Immediately thereafter, the violins and clarinets came into play and

---

[27] It would seem that the English abroad have hardly changed!

the dancing began; it lasted until eleven o'clock in the evening. There were a lot of pretty girls; I particularly attached myself to one of them throughout the evening. The troop all went to the houses of Hughes and Kennedy; even five officers from Calais came.

Calais, Monday, July 11
A French general has arrived in Calais; the batteries fired a twenty-one-gun salute.

Calais, Tuesday, July 12
The regiment met up at Calais to embark at five o'clock this morning, but it was night before everyone was on board. I put my troop and my horses on transport number V, but I am afraid it is too large to exit the port before several days. I have dined with Mr. Buckham[28], our old commissary, and then I went to the theatre. The pieces were vulgar and ill-chosen to be presented before the English. The actors and actresses are very immodest in their parts, and an Englishman would often find the opportunity to blush. On the other hand, those who wish to dishonour all English theatres are so well held in check by fear of the police, that an alien does not notice them in the room and they never come out until the piece is finished.

Calais, Wednesday, July 13
We expect the wind and tide will give us little chance to leave Calais within a week. Murray, Hughes and the Adjutant went last night by the packet boat. I saw today twenty cossacks, the first that I have ever met. They are General Platoff's[29] guard and arrive from England. They were here in attendance on the general, Lord Portarlington[30] and Lord Gage[31] arrived by the packet boat today. We have no other distraction than our promenading in the village, we looked at the shops and the pretty English maids. Almost all merchants of Calais have an English girl as the woman of the store. Some milliners have three or four.

---

[28]  This is a bit of a mystery and, unfortunately, we cannot check the name written in the original. One might suspect that he wrote Schaumann who had been the commissary for their time in Spain, but according to his own diary, he was at sea, sailing between Bordeaux and Portsmouth at this time. Schaumann mentions that when he took over as commissary to the 18th Hussars at Lisbon that he had taken over from a clerk named Thompson which looks nothing like Buckham. There is also no Buckham (or similar name) in any of the Army Lists of this period.

[29]  Count Matvei Ivanovich Platov was commander of the Don Cossacks.

[30]  Lieutenant Colonel John Dawson, 2nd Earl of Portarlington, commanded the 23rd Light Dragoons.

[31]  Henry Hall Gage, 4th Viscount Gage was a Conservative politician.

Calais, Thursday, July 14
Dr. Chambers left yesterday and today I received a letter from him dated from Dover. He informs me that the regiment will be directed to Lewes and Mr. D[olbel][32] is married. Ah! The poor woman, whoever it is, I pity them! The Bank of England banknotes are worth a Napoleon and half a franc. People here are generally very polite, but with what respect or interest I cannot say.

Calais, Friday, July 15
The wind is contrary to the departure of the transports; smaller ships only, may leave the port. I have been with Luard at the theatre, there I met some of my French friends of the 155th who were very polite[33].

Calais, Saturday, July 16
The wind has changed and most of the boats have left. I'm holding the hand of the only other officer of the regiment in Calais. There were disorders in the arsenal, between a few men of the 18th and people from the port. I was having dinner at that time with the commissary and I was only warned when it was all over. However, I have received from General Vandeleur, a severe letter on the subject.

Finally, the transports of the 18th sailed.

In the English Channel, transport U, Sunday, July 17
This morning, early, I found General Vandeleur and I explained to him that I was not to blame, that the disorders took place on board vessel No. 611 and I had no command there. But he told me that I was responsible for everything that concerned my men and he gave me a good lathering. I went onboard my transport and at midday we sneaked out of the port and took to sea with a fresh breeze; but, after four hours, in the middle of the passage, a calm came on and we remained motionless for several hours. One half of my troop was sick, the other is amused at their own expense. About ten o'clock in the evening, the breeze got up from the southeast and we reached the cliffs of Dover. I very much enjoy the sea; I'm never ill.

Ramsgate, Monday, July 18
Our ship has missed the port of Dover, the captain headed on to this

---

[32] It only shows the D in the French text, but he must surely refer to Dolbel.
[33] This is the only time he mentions this regiment.

one, where we arrived at noon. About four o'clock we were all
ashore and we received the order to march on Canterbury.
19 July, Ashford; 20 July, Cranbrook; 21 July, Hastings; 22 July,
Eastbourne; 23 July, Blatchington and Lewes.

Unsurprisingly, whilst garrisoned back in England, George stopped
writing in his diary and only resumed it the following year. Little of
importance occurred, the regimental history simply records that the
regimental headquarters were at Lewes until August, when it joined the
regiment in barracks at Canterbury. Whilst here, new uniforms were
issued and the peacetime establishment of only eight troops was put in
place, the superfluous officers being placed on half pay.

# Chapter 18

# Campaign of Belgium and France

Geloorge had remained at Canterbury until March 1815, but before news of the return of Napoleon could arrive, the regiment was ordered to send two squadrons to London, to police the capital, following riots over the unpopular Corn Laws, George was one of those sent.

> 6 March 1815
> The 18th Hussars are in Canterbury. Riots in London because of the Corn laws.

Despite being on a peacetime level of preparedness, the troops marched with commendable rapidity.

> 7 March
> The War Office sent orders for two squadrons of the 18th to march immediately on London. The order arrived at eleven o'clock in the evening, the officers were all at a public ball. We departed in an hour and a half.

> 8 March
> The troops passed through Dartford and arrived in London after a march of 69 miles; we are lodged in Somers Town[1] and Islington. We were jeered by the rabble.

> 9 March
> Parade in campaign dress, all is tranquil.

---

[1] Somers Town is the area just north-west of St Pancras station.

10 March
The peace continues.

11 March
I installed a picquet of sixty men at Burlington House[2]. I then put another twenty men in Tottenham Court Road.

12 March
Complete tranquillity.

13, 14 March
I ordered a picquet to Marsden's Stables, Tottenham Court Road.

March 15
Piquet at Burlington House.

March 16
My squadron moved to a riding school on City Road.

March 17
Revue in Hyde Park by Lord Uxbridge. All the cavalry were present.

18, 19 March
Piquet at Marsden's stables.

20, 21 March
Piquet at Burlington House. Buonaparte in Paris.

22 March
Piquet at Burlington House.

23, 24 March
Good Friday. Received the news that the hussars will be immediately sent to Belgium to strengthen the army of Lord Wellington.

25, 26 and 27 March
Lord Mayor's ball, I was in grand company.

---

[2] Burlington House was inherited by the Duke of Devonshire in 1753 but was really excess to requirements (Devonshire House being close by). It was later purchased by the government and is now the stunning home of the Royal Academy of Arts.

The two squadrons of the 18th were ordered back to Canterbury as the regiment was off to Belgium.

28, 29 March
The troops march to Greenwich destined for Canterbury. I'm going to a ball given by the father of Gordon[3].

30, 31 March, 1 April
Two squadrons arrived at Canterbury.

Canterbury, Wednesday, April 19, 1815
The Honourable H. Murray, our colonel, having three weeks ago received orders to hold the 18th Hussars ready for service abroad, we were daily expecting the orders to embark. They arrived yesterday evening and this morning we left Canterbury. The right wing of the regiment is headed for Dover, the left for Ramsgate. I arrived in Ramsgate and found the transports ready to receive the troops, we embarked in the afternoon in two hours, the officers only went on board at six o'clock.

We did not leave the quarterdeck until the [white] cliffs of Albion had disappeared below the vastness of the waters. I wanted to stay until the last moment of visibility and kept affectionate eyes on those shores and the inhabitants that are so dear to me. Monins[4], Luard and I, wrapped in our coats, passed the night lying on the deck. Monins was sad and wanted neither to drink nor eat with us. This young man left at Ramsgate a woman and a child; leaving so tender a companion that perhaps his thoughts must be cruel, fearing that he will never see them again.

Ostend, Department of Lys (Flanders), Thursday, April 20
Before us are the coasts of France and Belgium. We see Dunkirk very clearly with our glasses. We passed a few miles from Nieuwpoort and about ten o'clock we entered the port of Ostend. We followed the road to the right below the glacis of the fortifications. The horses were put into the water, and they had to swim for about 20 yards before landing. There were no accidents.

That evening the corps headed for the village of Ghistelles

---

[3]  Lieutenant John Rolfe Gordon had transferred in February 1815 from the 4th Dragoons.

[4]  Lieutenant William Monins only officially joined the 18th Hussars on 23 February as a cornet but became a lieutenant on 20 April 1815. He had previously served with the 52nd Foot and the 3rd Dragoons in the Peninsular, but had resigned in 1812.

[Gistel], a distance of sixteen miles, where we had excellent lodgings in private homes. The officers dined together at an auberge; with excellent wines of Reims, Burgundy and Bordeaux which were certainly not from Bordeaux, but they were preferable to a number of clarets we drink in England. All these wines cost 2 francs the bottle and dinner was 2 francs per head. The port of Ostend can receive large vessels. At the entrance was a wrecked transport of three hundred tons. The city is solidly fortified; the Duke of Wellington has recently ordered various repairs and enhancements to the works. Two Prussian infantry regiments and our 44th[5] perform the service of garrison of the place. Were the English army to suffer setbacks, it is here that it would embark to regain their native soil[6].

List of officers of the 18th Hussars who embarked with the regiment for Ostend, Wednesday, April 19, 1815, to join the army of Flanders commanded by the Duke of Wellington.

| | |
|---|---|
| Colonel | H. Murray |
| Captains | 1. Kennedy 2. Ellis 3. Croker 4. Grant 5. Luard 6. |
| Lloyd[7] | |
| Lieutenants | 1. Dunkin 2. Waldie 3. Woodberry 4. Dawson 5. French[8] 6. Coote 7. Machell[9] 8. Mc Duffie[10] 9. Rowlls 10. Gordon |
| Cornets | 1. Moller[11] 2. Monins |
| Adjutant | Duperier |
| Paymaster | W. Deane |
| Surgeon | Chambers. |
| Asst Surgeons | Pulsford and Quincey |
| Veterinarian | Pilcher |

Lieutenants who joined the corps [later]  Prior, Hesse, Blackett[12]
Major who joined                                      Clements

---

5  2nd Battalion 44th (Nottinghamshire) Regiment of Foot.
6  This view that Ostend was Wellington's line of retreat has now been debunked, if defeated Wellington planned on retiring towards Antwerp.
7  Captain James Richard Lewis Lloyd.
8  Lieutenant Martin French.
9  Lieutenant John Thomas Machell of Beverley.
10  Lieutenant Donald Mc Duffie.
11  Cornet Charles Champion Moller had joined on 16 June 1814.
12  Of these only Prior and Hesse served at Waterloo.

Oedelem, Friday, April 21

The regiment quit Ghistelles at eight o'clock and after a stage of three leagues, made our entry into Bruges, a city, surrounded by a double ditch or canal of twenty feet in width. We expected to find lodgings in this city, but they sent us to villages six miles away. Bruges is full of women and bridges; but as with all foreigners, [they] are not worth my compatriots; the latter are in considerable numbers. There are more than three hundred bridges here. The name of the city means bridge in Flemish. We remained waiting close to an hour before receiving our rations. During this time we changed our English bank notes; we were given 18 francs to one pound sterling. Oedelem is ten miles from Bruges, on the left of the road to Ghent.

I am located in the house of a widow who lost her husband six weeks ago; she lives with two daughters and two sons. The poor creature received my pity when she told me of her misfortunes. She gave me a good dinner and to reciprocate, I offered two bottles of ale and bread, the remains of my sea supply.

Eeklo, Department of the Scheldt, Saturday, April 22

After a march of four hours under a constant rain, we entered Eeklo. I could have believed myself in England, visiting one of my best friends, thanks to the cordial reception given to me by my host on my production of my billet. 'Sir', he said, 'I am glad to see you. My house is yours for the entire time you will spend in this city. I invite you to have coffee with me. Our dinner is ordered for three o'clock, you will be there?' Kennedy and the three troops which came by way of Dover arrived here, immediately after the complete regiment went on to Ghent. The officers all dined together the next day; the champagne flowed and the expenditure was only 6 francs per head.

We have just learned that three French generals, deserters from the army, arrived in Ghent, but the report does not say that one man followed them. I bet five guineas against the Frenchmen that Napoleon will still be Emperor of the French on October 6. The inhabitants of the Department of Lys are Catholics and there are more crosses in the towns and villages than I can recall having seen in Spain and Portugal. The King of Belgium and his court are in Brussels[13].

---

[13] The Congress of Vienna had recently joined Holland and Belgium together as the Kingdom of the Netherlands and had given the throne to William the Prince of Orange, (the young aide de camp's father).

The unfortunate King of France Louis XVIII is in Ghent[14] with a poor suite composed in large part of traitors. The French army concentrates its forces in Lille: they are expecting us to attack. The campaign will not open before the end of May, and even then everything will depend on the arrival of the allies. Lord Uxbridge, commander in chief of the English cavalry, will arrive in Ostend today. I received very bad reports as regards the Belgian troops, I'm afraid that they will go en masse to join the enemy at the earliest opportunity. The *Morning Chronicle*[15] is a miserable paper, it shouldn't be on sale in this country. It is found in all the cities and in all the villages, no doubt thanks to the efforts of Napoleon or his agents in England.

Ghent, Sunday, April 23
The last six miles of the route today were very pleasant especially when we enjoyed views of the beautiful city of Ghent, along one of the most beautiful canals in Europe. We saw a boat for the service of passengers, very crowded, passing on to Bruges. These boats are furnished with great taste and offer all the amenities possible. The Cathedral of Ghent is superb; I had time to dismount and put my head through the door, and I was stunned at the beautiful appearance of the interior. In my humble opinion, London excepted, Ghent is greater than all the cities I've seen; Paris is below Ghent in many ways. At the Midi Gate, many workers were busy raising fortifications, but they can only stop an army for a few days. We passed before the Royal Palace and we saluted the unfortunate Louis XVIII at his window, he stood between the Duke de Feltre[16] and Marmont[17], two great scoundrels. We we then formed square, we received rations, and we went to Swynaerde[18], two miles on the road towards Oudenarde where I lodged my troop; and I then came back to Ghent, where I bought some maps of the Department and a pipe. It seems that the King of France spends the greatest part of his

---

[14] King Louis stayed at the Hotel d'Hane-Steenhuyse, which can be visited. You have to prebook visits viaa website, as it is currently only open on Fridays and Saturdays, but it is highly recommended, it is a little gem.

[15] The *Morning Chronicle* established in 1769 was a Whig paper and pro-French.

[16] Marshal Henri-Jacques-Guillaume Clarke, 1st Count of Hunebourg, 1st Duc de Feltre, sided with the king in 1815.

[17] Marshal Auguste Frédéric Louis Viesse de Marmont, Duc de Raguse, had sided with the king on Napoleon's return.

[18] Actually Zwunaarde.

time with his priests: he would do better in the Book of the Martyrs by Fox[19].

Oudenarde, Monday, April 24

Flemish is diabolical to learn and understand. If we ask the people a question, their response is 'yo yo!' All the world detests the Prussians and praise the English, money does miracles! We passed on route the 91st, who marched towards Oudenarde (I've never seen a more beautiful body of troops); [followed] then [by] a Dutch infantry regiment. The men look good and well equipped; their uniform is French with the exception of a W instead of an N[20] and that they wear their hair up; but the last letter is perhaps still engraved in their hearts. We were much amused by a band of beggars who followed us for more than a mile doing somersaults, the funniest thing was to see women's legs in the air. In front of this city is a vast marsh, one of the main defences of the place. The heights are also fortified. It is here that the Allied armies under Marlborough were defeated[21].

At the top of the tower of the town house is a figure of an armed man with a number of weapons and taking in his hand the Orange standard. The chimes are very pretty and play every five minutes. The city was very lively all day; thousands of peasants flocked to enlist to fight against Buonaparte. The 54th and 91st[22] make up the garrison of Oudenarde, the inhabitants are not polite and appear to be disgruntled; it may be because they have to accommodate so many military.

Anzegem, Department of Lys, Tuesday, April 25

We were lost today for several miles due to a lack of knowledge of the country. We are now encamped on the banks of the Scheldt, and we intend to stay here at least a fortnight. The enemy is not more than nine leagues from us. In the last campaign, a Prussian army was camped nearby; they treated the inhabitants as the French treated them when they were here. The people of the country are very helpful to us; they fear no doubt that we might also adopt the

---

[19] John Fox, English theologian born in Boston (Lincolnshire) in 1517 and died in 1587, he embraced the Lutheran doctrine and was persecuted under Mary, but enjoyed the favour of Elizabeth, although he was non-conformist.

[20] The cause of a number of 'blue on blue' incidents during the Battle of Waterloo.

[21] He is in error, the Battle of Oudenarde, fought on 11 July 1708 was a great victory for Marlborough and his allies.

[22] The 1st Battalion 54th (West Norfolk) and 2nd Battalion 91st (Argyllshire Highlanders) Regiments of Foot.

ways of our allies towards them. The regiment occupied five villages; the headquarters is in Avelgem, with the left squadron, the rest at Kerkhove, Tiegem and Kaster. The world speaks French here and very few understand Flemish. We have two volunteers who follow the regiment; they are Captain Peter Grant, in the service of the [East] India Company[23], an officer of great merit, and Captain C. Williams[24], brother-in-law of Captain Lloyd of the West Middlesex Militia[25]. The champagne is good and at a good price; five francs the bottle. The bread is three times cheaper than in England.

Anzegem, Wednesday, April 26

Luard, Monins and I have formed a mess and it is my servant Ipper who will cook the food. We had an excellent dinner with a requisition made on the mayor of this village: there we had wine, eggs and poultry. I've been to Kerkhove to sit at a Court Martial, but my place was already taken: I saw Kennedy and French. I passed by Kaster, where you can see the bell tower for several leagues around; it is there that Lloyd, Williams, Dawson, Gordon, Rowlls and Quincey are housed. Lieutenant Prior, was placed under arrest by order of the Commander in Chief when he joined the regiment in Ostend, he arrived at Anzegem this afternoon. He belongs to the troop of Kennedy and should be in Kerkhove, but the officers do not want to associate with him; but we knew what to do. We invited him to dinner today, but we have not heard that he is part of our mess.

Kaster, Thursday, April 27

I was occupied this morning, following the orders of Colonel Murray, to draw a map of the roads around Kerkhove and roads that lead to Anzegem and Oudenarde. I have been reconciled with Lieutenant Prior; we were not talking in England. I hope that, in the future, he will change his ways and principles. Major General Vivian, who commanded the Brigade of Hussars, arrived yesterday at Harelbeke. The cantonments of the brigade are as follows:

| 7th Hussars | - | Harelbeke and surrounding areas. |
| 10th Hussars | - | Berchem and surroundings. |
| 18th Hussars | - | Avelgem and surroundings. |

---

[23] Captain Peter Grant 22nd Native Infantry Regiment HEIC.
[24] Possibly Lieutenant & Captain Charles Sawkin Williams 1st Life Guards.
[25] I can only discover a Captain John Lloyd in the West Yorkshire Militia.

In all approximately fourteen hundred[26] men and horses.

Anzegem, Friday, April 28
There was very good horse racing this afternoon on the road to Berchem and Oudenarde. The officers of the 10th threatened to get revenge for Monday.

This morning the roll call of the regiment; it consists of: 1 colonel, 6 captains, 10 lieutenants, 2 cornets, 1 surgeon, 2 assistant-surgeons, 1 adjutant, 1 paymaster, 1 veterinarian, 7 sergeant majors, [25] sergeants, corporals, trumpeters, 1 farrier, blacksmiths, [403][27] hussars and horses.

The Russian troops advance quickly; a column will arrive at Cologne on the 1st May and will be followed by others until the end of the month. There are already a large quantity of Cossacks.

Kortrijk, Saturday, April 29
Kortrijk is surrounded by a wide moat crossed by four bridges which lead to huge monumental gates. We were obliged to write our names in a register before being allowed to enter. The 35th[28] are here with the 2nd Hussars of the German Legion. The town is very pretty, with a number of excellent auberges; we had very good champagne.

We saw a band of deserters from the enemy army, an officer and 13 men. The officer blushed and appeared to be ashamed of himself and his companions. This character had good cause. As they passed in the street, a troupe of kids joined them to shout 'Vive le Roi!'

The 2nd Hussars, of the German Legion has its headquarters here. Its piquets and its patrols constantly monitor the border. The 1st [German] Hussars were brigaded with the 18th in Spain and France during the last campaign, it has it quarters at Tournai. The country which extends to Kortrijk is good cavalry country, I hope that we will one day meet here with the French cavalry. Harelbeke is the headquarters of the 7th Hussars, it is long, lined with beautiful houses, behind which there are many shacks and hovels standing in mud.

---

[26]  The French version says thousands, but that clearly cannot be correct.

[27]  The French version omits the figures after sergeant-majors, but only two days later the return shows thirty-two sergeants (sergeant major and sergeants combined) and 403 other ranks (which would include corporals, trumpeters and privates). Return dated 20 April 1815, published in Malet's *History of the 18th Hussars* page 36.

[28]  2nd Battalion 35th (Sussex) Regiment of Foot.

Anzegem, Sunday, April 30

Buonaparte has dismounted all the gendarmes and sent their horses to the army. In this way and others, it is said that he has formed a cavalry corps of thirty-five thousand men. Lord Uxbridge arrived to take overall command of the cavalry; he seems delightful.

Buonaparte has declared that Lille, Condé, Valenciennes, Boulogne, Calais, and several other cities are under siege. The inhabitants have orders to obtain provisions for six months or leave the place. I was riding at Oudenarde to examine the new fortifications, I found them to be almost finished. Several hundreds of men, paid by England, are working on them.

I have witnessed a curious spectacle: two drunks were totally incapable; they were arrested by the police, attached to one another and marched through the city with hundreds of boys and girls who pursued them with their boos. They were then whipped on the spot and sent home.

I bought a mare pony for thirteen Napoleons from Lieutenant Gordon. I named him *Cheerful*. The value of horses of all kinds has increased significantly since the arrival of the cavalry in the Netherlands and their price will soon double unless the French army marches on us, and then they will be happy to discard them at whatever price we offer for them.

The first major 'alert' was received and the regiment prepared to commence a forced march at first daylight, it was to be the last scare.

Berchem, Monday, May 1

We sent our horses to race against those of the officers of the 10th and 7th Hussars, but just as the starting signal was going to be given, Captain Gurwood arrived from Brussels in a hurry, bringing to the brigade the order to proceed immediately to the banks of the Dender. We learned that Buonaparte is at Valenciennes[29].

We went immediately to our accommodation and we quickly prepared our baggage; but ultimately, the day was too advanced to start today. We will make a forced march tomorrow.

It is impossible to have any idea of the aim pursued by the army in its movement on Brussels; to invade France or will it be to defend this country against an invasion of the enemy?

---

[29] Napoleon was actually in Paris until 12 June, but rumours of his arrival near the Belgian frontier were constant.

Edgem, Department of the Scheldt, Tuesday, May 2
The regiment came together at Kerkhove, and it left at nine o'clock. We only arrived at edgem at eight o'clock. The day was extremely hot and the distance so great that the men and horses were extremely fatigued, I was the officer of the baggage guard and I had great difficulty in following the regiment, all the roads are so bad.

We passed a dozen miserable villages, in one of them, there were more than fifty magpies. We especially noticed three sisters only four feet high, hump backed and exactly alike. The large village of Sint-Marie [-Lierde] was filled with farmers who came to see us pass; but a gloomy silence prevailed in this crowd. The population is really French at heart and the lower classes, I believe, prefer Napoleon to their current King or any member of the family of the Bourbons.

Another false alarm was caused by the Belgians practising their guns.

Edgem, Wednesday, May 3.
We were woken at six o'clock this morning by the distant sound of cannon fire. We are told that the Prussians were in possession of a large village across the border and that the enemy was withdrawing by burning the houses: but it was only the Belgian infantry which was [practising] firing a gun.

Having very bad lodgings, I was actually given another by the mayor of the village, and I am now comfortably installed in the presbytery. The cure is a fat old merry man, once confessor of a convent in the neighborhood. He is of the Order of Carmelites and he seems to love the English. edgem is a miserable little village made up of shacks; there's not another house nearly as good as the rectory. But the population is considerate and we get in it all that we desire. The women are prettier than those that we have yet seen, but they are dirty and poorly dressed! This afternoon we had an awful storm. We saw for several hours the storm clouds and I was waiting with anxiety for the effects of a storm in that country. The sky got darker and darker and the flashes that sparkled on the horizon were terrifying. The claps of thunder followed one another without interruption and appeared to shake the earth to its foundations. The tempest lasted for about an hour and during this time there were just a few showers.

Before the return of Buonaparte, in all of the cities of France, and in particular in Paris, violet was the secret symbol that designated the Emperor and was used as a sign of recognition. The faithful wore rings of the colour purple with the device they asked if someone possessed one 'Do you like violet?' and if this person answered 'Yes', they deduced that they were not a supporter. If they said, on the contrary, only 'Well?' they then recognised a brother in the possession of the secrets of the conspiracy and they added this sentence: 'They re-appear in the spring'.

Grammont[30], Thursday 4th May

General Sir Hussey Vivian spent this morning inspecting the regiment in fatigues and expressed his appreciation of both the men and horses. We are in the vicinity of a convent of Benedictine nuns, which was closed seventeen years ago; it covers an area of three quarters of a mile square. A twenty-foot wide canal and a high wall surround it. It contained thirty women, and their annual income was 180,000 francs. Its arms and its motto struck me with the words '*Hic requies mea*'[31] whilst lying down looking up at the sky. Only a peasant remains there now, and most of the cells of the nuns are transformed into stables for the cows.

The good priest, with whom I am housed, was the confessor of this religious establishment, which still retains the name of Convent of Beauprez, it about half a mile from edgem, on the Dender, in the commune of Grammont.

Iedeghem, Friday, May 5

It said now that the British army will not enter into France, but that it will form with the Belgian army a corps of observation on the border, while the Russian and Prussian armies penetrate and restore Louis XVIII on the throne. The young people of the country seem very unhappy to be called up to train to handle weapons and perform the military exercises; they believe that we will treat them as conscripts. The women cry in the village, because their husbands and sons will tomorrow go to Ghent for five days.

edgem, Saturday, May 6

This morning Lieutenant General Lord Uxbridge reviewed the regiment in full campaign dress, and said that he is pleased to express his satisfaction. General Vivian, Colonels Elley, Quentin[32],

---

[30] Now more commonly known as Geraardsbergen.
[31] Latin – Here lies peace.
[32] Colonel George Quentin commanded the 10th Hussars.

Lord Robert Manners[33], Kerrison[34] and some 20 officers of hussars followed him. After the review, I went and I watched the 1st Dragoon Guards parade and the Greys. I met Wyndham[35], who invited me to dinner; he told me the news from England.

I'm looking in vain, for an object to steal my heart who will occupy the long hours with pleasure; but this heart, is like a poor bird chased out of its nest, this heart, always returns to the centre of its affections and after vain efforts to fly, it remains there where all his memories are and all of his affections are concentrated. Nobody can travel here without a passport: a farmer cannot enter a large town without having one issued by the mayor of his municipality. A post, commanded by officers, examines them at the entrance of all who would enter.

Brussels, Sunday, May 7

I was this morning in Brussels with Chambers. We left at six o'clock, we got there at ten o'clock. Although we took a by road, the road was excellent. All the villages were filled with troops. It was one of those beautiful mornings calmed by a special serenity, everyone that lives, enjoys the countryside that surrounds him. We arrived at the small village of Broek, three miles from Brussels, where we had an enchanting spectacle from the top of an eminence; the view stretched over the whole of this beautiful city. On one side is a large city with many steeples and towers, built on the slopes of a hill nearly five miles in length; all of this gorgeous region is dotted with towns, villas and villages. We went first to the Hotel de Flandres, which was full. Then we made an attempt at the Hotel Angleterre and at the Hotel de Clarence without any more success, and we had a lot of trouble finding a place for ourselves and our horses at the Hotel d'Imperatrice.

After we were refreshed, we went to walk in the park, where thousands of people of good company gathered; and many strangers of great distinction. I met many of my old friends from England, Lord Arthur Hill, who was aide-de-camp to the Duke of Wellington, and Lord Greenock[36], who brought me a letter from Canterbury; he left that city three days ago. After dinner, we went riding on horseback and passing through the Antwerp gate, we

---

[33] Lieutenant Colonel Lord Robert Manners 10th Hussars.
[34] Colonel Sir Edward Kerrison commanded the 7th Hussars.
[35] Lieutenant Charles Wyndham Scots Greys.
[36] Lieutenant Colonel Charles Murray, Lord Greenock was a permanent Assistant Quarter Master General.

arrived at the fashionable promenade for riders. There were more than a thousand people and at least five hundred carriages of different kinds. I noticed in the number, the Royal family, the Dukes of Wellington and Richmond[37]. The King of Belgium[38] and his staff were on horseback and greeted everyone who passed. A storm came on and dispersed this beautiful meeting of people. We followed the king across the city. Oh! God! What a miserable scoundrel, he was escorted by brainless people with no shirt, who shouted: 'Vive le Roi!' and the poor king, was forced to remove his hat in salute in the rain. Her Majesty was in a state of undress and rode a beautiful grey English horse.

We then went to the opera, where we heard Ms. Catalani. She sang an Italian opera and was in great voice. The room was packed due to the presence of the king. At the entrance, he was received by the assembly among whom there were a lot of foreigners standing, with vigorous cries of 'Long live the King!' Many fugitives are arriving from Dunkirk, Calais, Valenciennes, Havre, with the saddest news of the the current state of France. They say that Buonaparte uses violent means to extort money from the population, and that part of their provisions are seized without mercy, especially in the departments of the Nord, from anyone suspected of attachment to the king. The soldiers lodge with the inhabitants and live at discretion.

Brussels, Monday, May 8

This morning we went to the museum of the Department of the Dyle, on the main square. We saw some beautiful paintings by Van Dyck, Rubens and many other famous masters, contained in 15 rooms. In others, there were some excellent paintings by modern masters, arranged in the same way as the exhibition at Somerset House.

As soldiers we don't pay anything to enter. The habit of the country is that the soldier goes for free everywhere, except in the theatre, and again they do not pay in the stalls. The square is located in the upper town. The courthouse is across the main street that leads from the lower town: it's a beautiful monument. Nearby are the Hotel de Flandres and the Hotel Bellevue and several other

---

[37] General Charles Lennox, the 4th Duke of Richmond. His wife famously gave the ball on 15 June.
[38] King William I of the Netherlands, the ex-Sovereign Prince of Orange (Belgium and Holland having just been declared one kingdom by the Congress of Vienna).

notable buildings. On the other side is the museum of which I have spoken. The park is near this place: it is beautifully laid out, all the walks are shaded by majestic trees. Fountains and statues are distributed with taste in the middle of the flower beds with great care.

Around the park, there are a few large houses occupied by the representatives of the foreign powers and the first characters of the state. The Duke of Wellington resides in one of them. In the same park is a theatre; the stage is in the wood. The Jardin des plantes, in the lower town, deserves the attention of all visitors, as well as the cathedral. There is a lovely horse ride to do around the city walls, around the park were frequent traders. But in all the walks, in all the theatres, I haven't seen a pretty face. Women here are remarkably ugly, but well decorated, with all the bright impotence of the toilette.

The magnificent Belgian Carabinier Regiment, formerly in the service of France under Napoleon, is in the barracks here. These elite men have a very fine uniform; most were six feet tall. It is said that those particularly devoted to Buonaparte assume that they will pass to his side at the first opportunity. Last week, their musicians played on horseback, followed by some of the men.

At Nevers, one of the favourite cavalry generals of Napoleon, commands. He is in this city and seems to enjoy the favour of the king. It is said that Buonaparte wrote to him to travel to Paris to take command of a division of his army and that the general immediately handed the letter to the king. As for me, I would not trust him and I would have neither him nor his regiment in the capital of the kingdom. The Saxons, who are part of the Prussian army, were disarmed a few days ago and sent to the rear. They refused to serve alongside the Prussians and take an oath of obedience to his Majesty the King of Prussia[39]. They came as a body to kill General Blùcher, who escaped their great scheme. They destroyed his house with all it contained, then they paraded in the streets of Lille shouting 'Long live the King of Saxony! Long live the Emperor Napoleon!'

Op Hasselt, Département de L'Escaut, Wednesday, May 10

---

[39] The 'Saxon Mutiny' was actually caused by the heavy-handed approach of the Prussian generals to a difficult issue. Part of Saxony had become Prussian after the war and the Prussians insisted that the Saxon troops were divided, with those from the Prussian area passing into the Prussian army. The revolt was harshly put down and these experienced troops were lost to the allies during the subsequent campaign.

**BRITISH ARMY**

**Brigades of Cavalry (on 1st May 1815)[40]**

**1st Brigade**
7th Hussars[41]
10th Hussars              Major General Vivian
18th Hussars

**2nd Brigade**
11th Light Dragoons
12th Light Dragoons    Major General Vandeleur
16th Light Dragoons

**3rd Brigade**
1st Dragoon Guards
2nd Dragoons (Scots Greys)   General Ponsonby
6th Dragoons

**4th Brigade**
13th Light Dragoons
23rd Light Dragoons
15th Hussars

**5th Brigade**
1st Life Guards
2nd Life Guards        General Somerset
Royal Horse Guards (Blues)

**German Contingent**
**King's German Legion**

---

[40] This organisation was changed again on 29 May following the arrival of more troops and therefore bears little relation to the organisation used at the Battle of Waterloo.

[41] On 29 May, they were formed into two Hussar Brigades:
**1st Brigade**
7th Hussars
15th Hussars          General Grant
2nd Hussars KGL
**2nd Brigade**
10th Hussars
18th Hussars          General Vivian
1st Hussars KGL

**1st Brigade**
1st Dragoons
2nd Dragoons       Major General Dornberg
2nd Hussars KGL

**2nd Brigade**
1st Hussars KGL      Colonel Arentschildt
3rd Hussars KGL

**3rd Brigade**
Hussars of the Prince Regent
Hussars of Breme     Colonel Estorff
Hussars of Verden
1st Royal Dragoons

**Infantry Brigades (At 1st May 1815)**

**1st Brigade**
1st Foot Guards      Major General Maitland
2nd & 3rd Battalions

**2nd Brigade**
2nd Battalion Coldstream Guards
2nd Battalion 3rd Foot Guards

**3rd Brigade**
1st Battalion 71st Foot
1st Battalion 52nd Foot    Major General Adams
9 companies 3rd Batt 95th

**4th Brigade**
3rd Battalion 14th Foot
1st Battalion 23rd Foot    Colonel Mitchell
1st Battalion 51st Foot

**5th Brigade**
2nd Battalion 30th Foot
33rd Foot       Major General Halkett
2nd Battalion 69th Foot
2nd Battalion 73rd Foot

**6th Brigade**
2nd Battalion 35th Foot
1st Battalion 54th Foot          Major General Johnstone
2nd Battalion 59th Foot
1st Battalion 91st Foot

**German Contingent**

**King's German Legion**

**1st Brigade**
1st Battalion KGL
2nd Battalion KGL               Colonel Halkett
3rd Battalion KGL
4th Battalion KGL

**2nd Brigade**
5th Battalion KGL
8th Battalion KGL               Colonel Ompteda
1st Light Battalion KGL
2nd Light Battalion KGL

**British Army**
**Divisions**

**1st Division**                **Major General Cooke**
1st English Brigade
2nd English Brigade
Artillery Brigade               Captain Sandham

**2nd Division**                **Major General Sir Henry Clinton**
3rd English Brigade
1st KGL Brigade
3rd Hanoverian Brigade
Artillery Brigade               Captain Napier

**3rd Division**                **Lieutenant General Charles Alten**
5th English Brigade
2nd KGL Brigade
4th Hanoverian Brigade
Artillery Brigade KGL           Captain Cleves

**4th Division**     **Major General Sir Henry Hinuber**
**(then Colville)**
4th English Brigade
6th English Brigade
6th Hanoverian Brigade
Horse Artillery Troop KGL  Major Sympher

I know neither the strength nor the number of brigades of the Hanoverians, nor those of the Belgian army, but I am assured that all the forces under the command of the Duke of Wellington do not exceed 48,000 men. We expect every day 10,000 Portuguese soldiers[42] and the Scottish brigade, 42nd, 71st and 79th regiments. I received this morning at five o'clock the order to attend Ophasselt, a remote village two miles from Iedeghem, to prepare the lodgings of the 7th Hussars, who's quarters near Ninove are assigned to the Life Guards and the Blues. The headquarters of the brigade are moved to Grammont.

Ophasselt, is a small village on the main road to Grammont and Ghent, it consists of six or eight suitable houses and a few hovels in the mud; nothing in Ireland can give you an idea of this misery. We learnt today of the works of fortification at Montmartre. The workers were set to work last Thursday. They will build a line of entrenchments and on the heights a great number of batteries at Montmartre and Buttes-Chaumont. They will mount two hundred and fifty cannon. The French Army of the Rhine occupies the lines of Wissembourg: I do not know exactly its strength.

Ophasselt, Thursday, May 11

I went this morning to Grammont with Lieutenant Monins, and rode on horseback to the top of the mountain which dominates the town which is built on the slopes of a steep hill. There is a small chapel and a semaphore station; we saw from thence with the naked eye, Brussels, Enghien, Nivelles, Genappe, Soignies, Ath, countless other villages and part of France. A division of the Belgian Army passed Ophasselt. It seems that they are good troops: they did twelve leagues yesterday, five this morning, and have yet to make another

---

[42] The Duke of Wellington had written to the government to consider asking Portugal to supply troops, but paid by Britain. The government rejected the idea, as even if the Portuguese government had agreed, they would take far too long to arrive and German troops would be cheaper to obtain.

five before the night's halt. A good march, but I fear that they are not much good for anything else. The reason for their movement, is that Buonaparte concentrates his army at Lille and we cannot rely on the troops there as an advance-guard. The French cavalry gathers at Valenciennes. I saw this morning Prince Frederick [of] Orange[43]; he is a fine figure of a man, he commands a division of the army under Lord Hill, who was with him.

Ophasselt, Friday, May 12
Order for all officers staying in Brussels to return immediately to their regiments; no officer will have the right to go to Brussels any longer without permission of the commanding general. We are installing hospitals in Ostend and Brussels; we send all our patients there. We have only a few there at the moment and these are men of bad conduct. General Vivian expects to see the enemy enter this country by this road[44], that is why he has pushed back the Belgian army.

Ophasselt, Saturday, May 13
The surrounding countryside is covered with wheat and rapeseed. All the crops promise a year of abundance for the farmers. I rode to Grammont to buy sugar, I paid 2 francs a pound. This is a pretty nice town, which boasts three churches, which is remarkable, a stately town house with four small pinnacles, a clock and a carillon, two fountains, on the one of which is a naked love who pours water, the source coming from the top of the mountain. Some of its streets are very steep and difficult to ride in. Last Thursday I went on horseback, climbing to the top of the mountain, which surprised the entire town. The Dender which crosses the lower town, passes under six or eight bridges. The wine is cheap; here are the prices: Bordeaux, 3 francs; Hock, 3 francs 50; Champagne, 5 francs. Any kind of meat, 5 stivers[45] the pound; poultry, 2 francs a pair; eggs, 20 for 1 franc. The greater part of the currency of copper in circulation in this country consists of old English halfpence. There are 5 pence and 4 pence coins minted under the Revolution and made of the metal of the bells. All gold and silver coins have the effigy of Napoleon.

Grammont, Sunday, May 14
The 4th English Infantry Brigade (14th, 23rd and 51st Regiments)

---

[43] Prince Frederick of Orange was the king's second son.
[44] This would indicate that he expected to be attacked from the direction of Tournai.
[45] The stiver was worth about 10 centimes. It was the currency of Holland.

are camped at Grammont. I dined there with my friends and most of the officers. We entered into the large church, which is in the place, during the service, but the military have privileges and so this did not prevent us walking by, examining everything. In each confessional stood a priest ready to confess the women. We saw many beautiful paintings.

The Holland Schnapps is good and not expensive: a quart for 10 stivers, approximately 10 English pence. Napoleon has the art of governing the French, but not to rule the world. He can rule over these people, he deserves this scourge! I wish with all my heart that we could grant him this favour, but it is impossible; because although Buonaparte knows how to lead the French to their satisfaction, which the Bourbons ignore, the rest of Europe requires that we finish him.

Ophasselt, Monday, May 15
The Hussar Brigade executed several manouevres under the orders of Vivian. The depot of the regiment departed Canterbury for Romford on Wednesday, April 26. The 10th has theirs in Brighton, the 7th in Hounslow. The weather is as hot as in Spain or Portugal, and it is almost impossible to ride or walk in the middle of the day.

Ophasselt, Tuesday 16 May
The heat was so strong today that it prevented me from going to the races at Ninove. Luard was told that they were very successful. B[acon][46], of the 10th, won several races himself. This young buck has this last week removed a woman who lived with Captain S[wetenham], of the 16th Light Dragoons. The story, as told, does not honour Mr. B[acon]. This woman, a widow, was maintained for several years by Lieutenant S[wetenham] and B[acon] recently offered her £200 per year if she wanted to come to live with him and leave her lover, which she accepted. Captain S[wetenham] sent an envoy to thank Mr. B[acon] but that he did not wish to get rid of this woman, adding that if he did, moreover, he would do so in a manner more worthy of a gentleman. There are those who say that Mr. S[wetenham] should call out Mr. B[acon]. For me, I find that he acted very correctly.

---

[46] Lieutenant Anthony Bacon had previously served with Swetenham in the 16th Light Dragoons; he had a reputation for high living and spending his father's money.

Ophasselt, Wednesday, May 17
Buonaparte seems to concentrate his efforts on Belgium. There are in the camps and cantonments along the border a well-equipped army of at least eighty thousand men which he can collect in a few days, not to mention the garrisons. If he succeeds in forcing the Anglo-Prussians lines, I am told we are poorly covered by fortified places, Belgium is open. He relies on the moral support of the inhabitants and forced loans and requisitions to give him what he needs, while in case of defeat, fortresses cover his retreat. It is always the audacious with him and with the skillful tactician Carnot[47], his Guard and all the violent men that France possesses, who will fight with the strength of despair and who know as well as their leader the old adage 'The first battle is worth ten others.' It is possible that the violent hatred held by the French for the Prussians will lead the first attack to be on their positions, but it is far more likely that the enemy will strike in the direction of Ghent, between Lille and Dunkirk and it will seek to evict our army on the Meuse to cut our communications with England, and if it is possible, with Antwerp where we have concentrated all our supplies. Buonaparte hopes no doubt, that this operation will be favoured by the questionable loyalty of the Belgian army. If he takes Belgium, it also ensures France, and he can extend his plans to the left bank of the Rhine. It is assumed that he is currently at the border and that he will soon attack. As for the future, no man can predict with any certainty. The Prussian forces are on the banks of the Meuse.

A number of races and reviews were organised to pass the time.

Ophasselt, Thursday, May 18
The brigade was reviewed by Vivian, who then directed it on Grammont, where Lord Hill inspected it; all those who have seen the Hussar Brigade say that it is the most beautiful brigade in Europe. The Austrian armies were successful and it seems that they have defeated Murat in Italy in several battles and finally, at Forlì[48]. He was completely beaten and the latest news from Italy, is that his retreat has turned into rout, the debris of his army has fled towards Ancona.

---

[47] Lazare Nicolas Marguerite, Count Carnot, known as the 'Organiser of Victory' in the Revolutionary Wars, was now serving Napoleon as Minister of the Interior.

[48] The Battle of Ronco on 21 April 1815 was fought just south of Forli. The Neapolitan army, retreating following the disaster of the Battle of Occhiobello, was pursued by an Austrian corps under the command of General von Neipperg. Murat's troops turned to hold the Austrians at the Ronco river. The Neapolitans rear guard was defeated by a smaller advanced Austrian force, compelling Murat to retreat further.

Ophasselt, Friday, May 19
I rode to Zottegem, to see the review of eight thousand Dutch and Belgian troops by Lord Hill. The impression they made was good and the manoeuvres were executed with the utmost precision.

The weather is highly variable; one day it is so hot it is hard to bear the sun! The next day, it rains; warm the next day, the next day it can be so cold that one is forced to wear overcoats and jackets, it is the case today. Several men have caught fevers.

The Duke of Wellington is appointed Marshal of the Army of the Netherlands.

Ophasselt, Saturday, May 20
I was riding to Sint-Maria to see Deane; I met the Brigade Major Harris[49] and several others who dined with him. I took my place in the middle of them and I left them at ten o'clock. During the meal, a peasant brought a letter to the adjutant who opened it and read to his surprise and ours that Captain Kennedy had been detained as a spy by the Mayor of Lewuwergem. He requested him to write or to go there to secure his release. Kennedy loves to reconoitre the country and enquires of the inhabitants on the provisions and of the people's views towards their government. It seems he entered into the cantonments of the Belgian troops and that he began to question the men on their strengths and their attachment to their country. He was then arrested and imprisoned as a spy.

Lord Uxbridge will review all of the English cavalry next Wednesday. His lordship believes that there will be no battle, but I still doubt this.

Ophasselt, Sunday, May 21
Riding this morning my chestnut horse *Varment* I met on the race course B[acon] and his woman; she watched him exercise his horses; she wore cossack pants. My horse is up against *Diddler*, of Lieutenant Rowlls in a race of a mile next Tuesday: at stake, 20 Napoleons.

An English vidette was killed at the advance posts; commencement of hostilities.

Ophasselt, Monday, May 22
I went to Sint-Maria to sit on a Court Martial. The Prussian army of the Rhine are not expected before the 15th of next month and its

---

[49] Captain Thomas Noel Harris, unattached half pay, was Vivian's Brigade Major.

strength is not half of that indicated in the English newspapers. The Duke of Wellington gave the order to establish a hospital for fifteen hundred men in Antwerp. I see no probability of the opening of the campaign for some time: to all appearances the enemy waits for our declaration of war to descend on us.

Ophasselt, Tuesday, May 23
All the officers of the cavalry of the army met this morning in a small field two miles from Grammont to see the races organised by the Brigade of Hussars. Most of the officers of the brigade had entered their horses. The first race was as perfect as a race in England. Ten others succeeded it; we then retired into a small grove in the shade of which the officers of the 10th Hussars had prepared refreshments at the expense of the brigade, with a great abundance of champagne and hock. I mounted my chestnut baggage horse, but I was easily beaten by Mr. Rowlls' *Diddler*. The cavalry will be reviewed on Monday next by the Duke of Wellington and Prince Blücher. The French have cut all the bridges along the border from Douai to Gravelines.

Ophasselt, Wednesday, May 24
This morning I went to Iedeghem to see the review of the two brigades of heavy cavalry by the Prince of Orange. He arrived around noon and was received by Lord Uxbridge, General Vivian, Lord Edward Somerset, Ponsonby, Hill, Vandeleur and a number of generals who I do not know the names of, who were brought to meet him by a road on the right. The procession moved to the centre at the gallop and he received the salute; then he moved along all the lines. The different regiments then marched by his Royal Highness by half squadrons and then returned to their quarters. The Duc de Berry[50] came after the revue with Marshal Marmont. The Duke is a small individual who looks like a hunchback. I've seen now three leading representatives of the male branch of the Bourbons, the King, the Duke de Angoulême and the Duke de Berry, and, God help us! If I were French, I would not serve under a race of such a despicable appearance.

Marshal Marmont is a fine old man who remains constant; he wore the uniform of a Marshal of France. Prince Blücher was invited to take the revue with the Prince of Orange, but learning that the hussars were not there, he replied that he himself was an old hussar, as he had been for seventeen years, and that he would not take a

---

[50] A nephew of the king.

step to see any other English troops than the hussars, which he considered to be the finest soldiers in Europe. My faith! Mr. Blucher is right and I admire his very good taste. The women of this country are the most shameless creatures; I am absolutely disgusted. I've seen such scenes in public, in full view, that I am left stunned. As are the women of my country in seeing them do it!

Ophasselt, Thursday, May 25
It is said that the brigade will soon be moved to the advance guard, due to the desertion of several men of the 1st Hussars, of the German Legion, which is now on the service of outposts around Tournai.

Dunkin is sick in Brussels; Moller is sick in the neighbourhood. Ellis is also ill, he will not be able to serve for a few days. I myself had pains in my limbs and back, but tobacco and grog have improved my health without the assistance of the doctor.

Ophasselt, Friday, May 26
The brigade left this morning in full uniform for the banks of the Dender, near Schendelbeke; there we met with the 2nd Cavalry Brigade commanded by Brigadier Vandeleur. Soon after Lord Uxbridge arrived and we executed different manoeuvres in two brigades.

It is said that the part of the French army which is near Valenciennes received orders to march on the Meuse in the direction of Givet. The Prussian army of the Meuse has been strengthened to oppose them. Buonaparte is said to be very busy in Paris in the work of government and they do not talk of his arrival at the border.

Ophasselt, Saturday, May 27
There are more beggars here than in the south of France, England, Spain and Portugal together. I counted them today; I am housed outside the village in an isolated farmhouse and in came twenty-nine since this morning. None leave without receiving a large slice of bread buttered by my good hostess and her daughter. Some, who were too noisy with their pleas, have received a few pots of water from me. Lord Wellington and Prince Blücher meet at Grammont tomorrow night. An officer came to prepare their lodgings and those of their Staffs; the requisition is for one hundred houses.

Ophasselt, Sunday, May 28
The desertions from the 1st Regiment of Hussars, German Legion, have been serious. Since the return of Buonaparte to France, the

regiment has lost forty men; last week twenty-three of them left the hussar regiment and arrived with the enemy at Lille.

The 15th Hussars arrived at their quarters near here. Tomorrow two brigades of hussars will form; the 7th and 15th English Hussars, and the 2nd German Hussars form the 1st Brigade. The 10th, the 18th English Hussars, with the 1st German Hussars form the second. The first will be commanded by Major General Grant; the second by our dear General Vivian.

The enemy have brought considerable forces forward to defend the passage of the Ardennes. The entrenchments at Givet are completed. At Valenciennes everything is prepared for receiving us, if we tackle these formidable fortifications. Thousands of workers are said to be busy completing it. A large entrenched camp is formed at Famars.

Finally, there was a great cavalry review of all the British cavalry at Schendelbeke.

Ophasselt, Monday, May 29

At eight o'clock this morning, the cavalry gathered in a meadow on the banks of the Dender, near Schendelbeke. At eleven o'clock, it formed in three lines, the first comprising of four regiments of hussars formed in twenty-four half squadrons, with two batteries of artillery lying on the flanks; the second, two regiments of Life Guards and the Blues, the 2nd, 1st and 6th Dragoon Guards with three brigades of artillery on the flanks and centre; the third, 11th, 12th, 13th, 16th and 23rd, Light Dragoons with two brigades of artillery.

At midday the Duke of Wellington arrived with Prince Blücher and was received by Lord Uxbridge. We fired a twenty-one-gun salute and he reviewed the three lines. His Grace took almost three hours to traverse the lines, each of them being nearly three quarters of a mile in length. There followed a parade by half squadrons. The day was beautiful and the curious were countless.

During the passage of the lines, the Duke with Lord Uxbridge on his right and Prince Blücher on his left. I was very eager to see this brave veteran; he praised all the hussar officers. Behind them came the Prince of Orange, the Duke of Brunswick, the Duc de Berry, Duke of Feltre, the Duke of Richmond, all our general officers and a large number of Russian, Prussian and Saxon generals. I have never seen such a deployment. Some were so covered with stars, orders, gold lace and beautiful plumes that I would almost like to be at war with them in the hope to ransom one of the less important ones.

I learned today that, for unknown reasons, Napoleon suddenly cancelled a review that he was to be at on Sunday the 21st of this month, and that some of the troops had already assembled at the Tuileries when the order was given. In addition, that war is currently declared and there has already been a naval combat[51]. The first British troops arriving from America disembarked at Ostend on the 23rd[52]. They consist of two infantry regiments.

The day of the Assembly of the Champs de Mai in Paris, there will be a big fete. In the morning the Imperial Guard and the National Guard will be under arms. Entertainment provided and food will be issued in the Champs Elysées and in the evening there will be a general illumination, a concert in the Tuileries, illumination of fireworks on the Place de la Concorde and free performances in all the theatres.

Ophasselt, Tuesday, May 30

Todays races were very beautiful, despite the adverse weather conditions. We were expecting the Duke of Wellington and Prince Blücher, but rain prevented them from coming. Vivian, Lord Robert Manners, General and Colonel Hill were Commissioners. It began with a race of thoroughbreds; only nine horses left at the signal, eight arrived together, the winner by half a neck. The next was also good and won by the same horse. Then came a race of half-bloods for five guinea stakes; it greatly amused us as the owners rode themselves and some were bad riders. Luard rode his *Dick*, but he lost. There were a few races, but barely half the races could take place, because of the weather. The rain drove us away. The field was enclosed on all sides: we had built a platform and 20 mounted hussars guarded the track. Among the riders we noticed the Prince of Orange and his brother, Lords Uxbridge, Somerset, Hill, Bradford[53], Arthur Hill, Manners and Portarlington. Vivian, Vandeleur, Ponsonby and several infantry generals. At one time there were nearly two thousand riders, almost all officers. I dined with Lloyd, Quincey and Gordon; I was so drunk that I came off my horse several times in returning home. It is the first and last time that I get myself in such state during my stay in this country.

---

[51] On 30 April 1815 off the coast of Italy, the French frigate *Melpomenne* of 40 guns was captured in an unequal contest with the 74-gun *HMS Rivoli*.

[52] The war with America had ended and the troops were hurried back to Europe, some actually arriving in time to fight at Waterloo.

[53] Lieutenant Colonel Sir Henry Hollis Bradford, 1st Foot Guards, Assistant Quarter Master General.

The Champ de Mai that was to be held in Paris last Sunday has delayed, if not definitively abandoned.

Ophasselt, Wednesday, May 31.
The 1st [German] Hussars are definitely brigaded with us (2nd Brigade). They have about five hundred men and horses and are in very good condition. From the moment when they left us in Abbeville, last July, they have been in barracks in Charleroi until the return of Buonaparte to France. They then went to Tournai, where they are currently. I don't know if it is us who will go to join them in Tournai, or if they will come to us here.

Ophasselt, Thursday, June 1.
The headquarters of the enemy is at Avesne. They watch the passes between Champagne, French Flanders and Picardy. They strengthen Laon, Château de Guise and various other places; the farmers are ordered to leave with their provisions at the beginning of the invasion and to arm themselves with their farm tools: but the poor people will be too happy to see us move forward and greet us, upon our arrival, as the liberators. Woe to the nation ruled by a military leader! He will always be at war or seek pretexts for hostilities.

Ophasselt, Friday, June 2.
The brigade was out this morning in the meadow near Schendelbeke in campaign order, and General Vivian has taught the videttes the way to operate on the ground. I am appointed to the scouts of the advance guard and Waldie lieutenant of the reserve. These are positions of honour and I have confidence that I will do my duty when needed, so as to deserve the praise of my seniors. I spent the evening at Grammont and I learned that several French regiments left Valenciennes by car[riage] to be transported to the Vendée, where a major insurrection[54] has erupted. Marseille is put under siege[55].

Ophasselt, Saturday, June 3.
Lord Uxbridge offers a gold cup with a value of 50 guineas, it will

---

[54] The latest uprising in the Vendée did not last long, but did cause the loss of a number of veteran troops from Napoleon's army at Waterloo.
[55] Marseilles had declared for the king.

be contested for next Tuesday by the officer's war horses ridden by their owners. The distance is four times seventy yards

Two pickets will be planted seventy yards from each other and the horses will go round each twice. Each officer carries their sabre unsheathed and if it touches the reins of the right hand during the race, he will be disqualified. The bulk of the French army appears to be confined to the vicinity of the Sambre and the Meuse. The flower of the army is encamped in front of us. Napoleon believes that it will carve the English into pieces; what a farce!

Ophasselt, Sunday, June 4.
Anniversary of the king's birthday. Assured that the artillery of the allied armies counts some seven hundred cannons, all in perfect condition. Napoleon has ordered everything which is not necessary for the defence of the places to retire into France and this measure has been executed with extraordinary precipitation.

According to authentic news, Murât is in a very bad situation: he is squeezed by the Austrian armies. His communications with Naples by road are completely cut and he withdraws to Lesi hoping to fight their way through the mountains.

I just learned that a French frigate was captured in the Bay of Naples by one of ours after a stubborn fight.

Ophasselt, Monday, June 5.
The regiment rode this morning to Schendelbeke as if on campaign under the command of Vivian. The 7th was on the ground under the orders of General Grant for two hours, it did not stop raining. Almost all the officers of the brigade train their horses for Lord Uxbridge's cup. It is said that Napoleon recently left Paris, but we know nothing for sure. General Order. After today everyone in the army will be be paid regularly each month, all are happy, because the English exchange rate is very high for a bill of 100 francs from England: we lose 20 francs discount, and the Bank of England one pound notes are worth 15 shillings or 17 francs.

The races continued, but so did the training for war. But their drunken antics did not please the locals.

Grammont, Tuesday, June 6.
Saw today the roads leading to the race course, I imagine that the entire population of the department was there. All cars were put in requisition and a part of the 'beautiful set' of Brussels honoured

us with their presence. Lord Edward Somerset and Colonel Howard[56] were Commissioners. It began around noon with a race between stakes for half-breed horses, then by another for thoroughbreds, both very interesting. Eleven horses raced in the first and thirteen in the second. There were several matches between ponies and mules by which we were well entertained. In the middle of the feast, it began to rain violently and the weather did not clear up until late in the evening. We took refuge in an old chateau, where they had been prepared refreshments. We partook, seventy in number of an excellent cold dinner, and copiously supplied with champagne. Everything had been done under the direction of the Mayor of Ninove, who has twice been the organiser of festivities.

Within two hours, the troop had time to eat and we got drunk together. I seem to remember a bad boy of the 10th Hussars, standing on one of the tables, he began to break with a big stick all the bottles and glasses; the rest of the company took part in this mischievous entertainment, and then darting on horses we went to the race field, half falling on the road and many horses galloping to the stables without their riders. The most mad launched into a race across the fields to the bell tower, in the night, and gave the farmers an idea of the independence of the English hussars shouting in the streets of the villages: '*Vive Napoleon*' – and I must not forget to mention this, because the thing either happened or I dreamt it, they overthrew two cars and so agitated the women that were there as to give them a fright, by charging their husbands or their protectors in true cossack fashion. Well I injured my horse *Dick* who ran the steeplechase; although I left the saddle three times, so I did not suffer the lesser evil.

Ophasselt, Wednesday, June 7.
Here is a copy of the total of the expenses for all the wines used in yesterday's celebration: total wines: 979 francs; total for dishes: 730; port 40 francs; cooks, boys, etc., 50 francs; final total 1,800 francs, or 50 francs per officer of the brigade. There were a number of complaints brought to the general; I guess we will also have to pay for all the damages caused in the vicinity. The Mayor of Ninove declares that he wants nothing further to do with a band of English

---

[56] This almost certainly refers to Major the Honourable Frederick Howard, 10th Hussars, but he was not a lieutenant colonel.

cossacks. It is believed that the Assembly of the Champ de Mai took place in Paris last Friday[57].

Ophasselt, Thursday, June 8.
I was in Grammont tonight and I heard the news. Murât is completely defeated and gives up his kingdom. It is said that he landed in Toulon and is in Paris: if it is so, Buonaparte will have him in his army as he is the first general of cavalry in the world. Tonight, Captain Ellis was struck by an attack of apoplexy and is now in bed, without knowing anything and his left side is pulled in a hideous way[58]. Surgeons attribute this to a cold caught the day of the racing. If he recovers, he must, they say, be immediately sent back to England. Lieutenant Hesse, arrived this afternoon at the general headquarters from England in good health and a good disposition. He is there, just in time to take command of the squadron of Captain Ellis. At the time he left England, Captain B[urke] was serving in the regiment, doing his service, and I strongly suspect this fellow may want to try to stay in the regiment. The officers gathered the other day and have sent a letter to Colonel Hughes, urging him to inform Captain B[urke], that, if he does not immediately exchange, that his conduct will be revealed to the Duke of York.

Ophasselt, Friday, June 9.
Ellis is still very sick. The surgeons of the brigade, after a consultation, stated that if he recovers, he will no longer resume service in the army. These last few days we have received many deserters from Cambrai and Valenciennes. Today, I have seen two cavalry officers who arrived from Cambrai. There were three in the party, but a few miles from the border, they were discovered by a patrol of French lancers; one of them was caught and killed on the spot by them, the other two put their salvation down to the speed of their horses. I had dinner with Moller, who is recovering and he will soon be able to resume his service in the regiment.

Ophasselt, Saturday, June 10.
Today, brigade manoeuvers under the orders of the Earl of Uxbridge. Our brigade is known by the name of 'Glory Boys' or 'Wellington's Darlings'. Some officers of the regiment believe they will not fight us, that the French people will put an end to the war by removing

---

[57] This great meeting designed to seal Napoleon's new constitution was more famous for Napoleon reissuing the sacred eagles to his regiments.
[58] It is quite likely that Ellis suffered a stroke.

Napoleon. But I expect that all the brave people who have stood up against the tyrant will be crushed before we can relieve them. The French reports say that the insurgents are defeated everywhere.

Ophasselt, Sunday, June 11.
The Belgian troops desert in large numbers to the enemy. They are unhappy with the merging of their country with Holland; I am afraid that all that remain will follow this example at their earliest opportunity. I received from the Ministry of War, the following letter dated 2 June 1815:

To Lieutenant George Woodberry, 18th Hussars in Flanders.
Sir,
I am required by the Secretary of State at the Department of War, to inform you that a mandate was sent to the Treasury of the army to deliver the sum of 164 pounds sterling 5s. 0d., i.e. one year's pay for a lieutenant of cavalry[59]. His Royal Highness the Prince Regent has the pleasure to grant this to you, in the name and on behalf of his Majesty, because of the severity of the injury you received at Mendionde and the expenses incurred for the care required to recover. I am, Sir, your very obedient and honoured servant. W. Merry.

We now know why the people rejoiced twice last week: it is that Napoleon took the Champ de Mai, and the new Constitution has been recognised. The Paris newspapers say that Napoleon will leave for the army and that he will establish his headquarters in Laon. This is where the army of reserve is.

The rumours of action soon were now rife.

Ophasselt, Monday, June 12.
Buonaparte is certainly at the border, inspecting the lines: he moves on the Rhine. Now that he is with the army, there is no doubt that events will move quickly. We expect to march Thursday or Friday[60]. Nearly half of the items usually worn by the hussars have been returned to the stores. It is believed that we will hand in our pistols to further alleviate the workload of the horses. Lord Uxbridge expects an energetic action.

---

[59] Worth about seven thousand pound in modern terms.
[60] Amazingly they were sent orders that very Thursday night to march on Quatre Bras on the Friday.

Ophasselt, Tuesday, June 13,
The regiment was sent out in combat dress with Murray. Ellis, still paralyzed, will be sent tomorrow to Ostend and from there to England. Marshal Soult sent a beautiful declaration to the French army; It ends as well: 'To arms! The signal will be given for every man to be at his post. The enemy is numerous, but our victorious columns will gain more than glory. Soldiers! Napoleon may guide our steps or not; but we are fighting for the independence of our beautiful homeland: we are invincible!'

Ophasselt, Wednesday, June 14.
We enjoyed our races today, although the clay soil was unfavourable. The plain of Schendelbeke served as a racetrack. The Lord Uxbridge Cup was won by Captain Fraser, of the 7th Hussars[61]. The speech, delivered by the Emperor Napoleon at the Champ de Mai assembly, published in full in French, is in the hands of thousands of the inhabitants of this country. These copies were printed by order of the French government and distributed by its agents or its spies in this Kingdom. The Emperor's speech was beautiful and satisfies everyone:

Numbers voting for the Acte Additional of the Constitution and for
Napoleon                      1,288,357
Number of voters against      4,207

The Army gives 222,000 votes for and 320 against. As for the Navy, 22,000 votes for, there are 275 opposing.
In the Department of Côtes-du-Nord, 6,000 votes for, and 1,058 against. Eleven departments have not yet sent their results; it is the same for a few regiments.

Ophasselt, Thursday, June 15, 1815.
The enemy is said to be advancing with Buonaparte towards Charleroi[62]. Lord Wellington gives this evening a grand ball in Brussels: I was invited by Lord Arthur Hill, but I think it's too far.[63]

---

[61] Captain James Fraser who served as an extra aide de camp to the Earl of Uxbridge.
[62] An interesting statement, given that he was unknowingly stating exactly what was then happening.
[63] George was not on the official invitations, but Lieutenant the Honourable Lionel Dawson of the 18th was invited, although it is unclear whether he actually attended.

# Chapter 19

# The Battle of Waterloo

General Order

Soldiers: This day is the anniversary of Marengo and Friedland, which twice decided the destiny of Europe. Then, as after the battles of Austerlitz and Wagram, we were too generous. We believed in the protestations and oaths of princes to whom we left their thrones. Now, however, leagued together, they strike at the independence and sacred rights of France. They have committed unjust aggressions. Let us march forward and meet them; are we not still the same men? Soldier: At Jena, these Prussians, now so arrogant, were three to one; at Montmirail six to one. Let those who have been captive to the English describe the nature of their prison ships, and the sufferings they endured. The Saxons, the Belgians, the Hanoverians, the soldiers of the Confederation of the Rhine, lament that they are obliged to use their arms in the cause of princes who are the enemies of justice, and the destroyers of the rights of nations. They well know the coalition to be insatiable. After having swallowed up twelve millions of Poles, twelve millions of Italians, one million Saxons, and six millions of Belgians, they now wish to devour the States of the second order among the Germans. Madmen! One moment of prosperity has bewildered them. To oppress and humble the people of France is out of their power; once entering our territory, there they will find their doom. Soldiers: We have forced marches before us, battles to fight, and dangers to encounter; but if firm in resolution, victory must be ours. The honour and happiness of our country are at stake! and, in short, Frenchmen, the moment is arrived when we must conquer or die!
signed: Napoleon.
A true copy: Marshal Duke of Dalmatia, Major-General.

Napoleon invaded Belgium at dawn on the 15 June, rapidly driving the Prussian defenders out of Charleroi and advancing in two wings, the left under Marshal Ney driving directly up the Brussels road and the Right under Marshal Grouchy driving the Prussians to the east. Wellington had only finally been disabused of his belief that Napoleon would attack his western flank late on the evening of the 15th and he now ordered his troops to march immediately for the army's pre-arranged point of concentration at Nivelles. Only later were the troops ordered on to Quatre Bras.

Nivelles, Friday, June 16.
We received this morning the order to march immediately on Enghien: we arrived in this town, where a new order sent us on to Braine le Comte and General Vivian dispatched me to Tournai to order the 1st [German] Hussars to join the brigade at Nivelles.

The distance is twelve leagues, and I was commanded to proceed with the greatest diligence. I conformed and I arrived at Tournai at two o'clock, very tired. However, as I thought my regiment was engaged, I refreshed myself and I quickly retraced my steps. Going, I had passed through Ath, a large town well-fortified, but completely controlled by the heights surrounding it: it could not withstand a siege; then Leuze, which is a beautiful town but almost abandoned by its inhabitants. Ath and Leuze have the highest towers I ever saw: they can be seen several miles away. Upon returning, I took another road and I passed through the villages of Calonne, where the beautiful convent makes a wonderful effect in the valley; and of Chièvres, whose church is superb.

At Soignies, on the main road from Brussels to Paris, I found the population very alarmed: they were waiting for the arrival of the enemy. I intended to find my regiment at Braine-le-Comte, but a hurried order had made them advance at the trot to Nivelles, it is therefore likely that the enemy has advanced. A party of Belgian infantry arrived in this town after a march; the men had no other idea than to plunder and their officers watched them do it; they probably had a share of the spoils. I have never seen a more shameful scene. It was four o'clock when I arrived in Nivelles: I entered the first house and by chance, I was well received by the owners. The town was full of English casualties. Buonaparte is four miles from here with his army and tomorrow we need to fight or retreat.

The cavalry had only arrived in the vicinity of Quatre Bras at nightfall, where they discovered that the British and Belgian infantry had been involved in a very bloody contest. The cavalry immediately sent out picquets and the remainder tried to rest, ready for the expected renewal of battle the next day.

Discovering in the morning that Blücher had been defeated and forced to retire to Wavre, Wellington ordered a retreat to another planned position at Mont St Jean in front of Waterloo. The infantry and artillery marched off immediately, whilst the cavalry provided a screen, preventing the French discovering the movement. Finally, in the middle of the afternoon, when the infantry had safely passed the narrow defile at Genappe, the cavalry was ordered to retire in three columns. The 18th formed part of the column retiring to the right (east) of Genappe and although followed closely were not brought to serious action, before they arrived in the early evening safely at the position of the army. Captain Lloyd's bat man had been killed by a cannon ball and two men were wounded during the retreat.

Saturday, June 17.
I got up at five o'clock and after an hour-long horse race, I joined my regiment. My troop was immediately sent to reconnoitre, but I did not follow them. I went on *Dick* and traversed the field of battle, where I met Lord Arthur Hill. He told me that Lord Wellington was intending to withdraw immediately on a strong position close to Brussels. I took this news to the regiment, but none of my colleagues believed me. An hour after, the artillery withdrew, followed by the baggage carts and infantry. The cavalry formed into lines and remained in position for nearly three hours.

The enemy was placed on a superior point and its line made a superb and imposing appearance. Ten minutes after our movement began of retiring, one of the most horrific storms which I ever remember came on. In an instant, we were all soaked to the skin. The enemy cavalry marched after us under the orders of the ex-King Murât[1]. Buonaparte and his staff were there.

Our brigade retired on a path way to the right of the Brussels highway, passing through the villages of Ways-la-Hütte [Ways], Glabais and Maransart, up to a small hamlet of twenty huts named Couture [Saint-Germain]. We then found ourselves in our new position on the far left [of the battle line]: it was still raining very

---

[1] The rumours that Joachim Murat had joined the army and commanded the cavalry were rife, but completely untrue. Napoleon had snubbed Murat and had refused to utilise his services with the army, a costly error.

heavily and the brigade received orders to bivouac in a small wood. The French lancers followed our rearguard throughout the day, but never attacked. Our men wanted to charge several times, but the rogues continued to advance. The 7th who retired by the great road, attempted to charge the lancers at Genappe but it was repulsed with considerable losses and I regret having lost my friend their commander Hodge.[2] The Life Guards have behaved very well: after the 7th had been repulsed by the lancers, they were formed in line and they charged and immediately broke the enemy column. Throughout the evening, there was terrible fighting, and we expected every moment to be called. I believe that if the enemy had pressed this evening, nothing could have prevented them being in Brussels tomorrow morning.

Yesterday the Prussians were defeated at Ligny: their losses are great. Ligny is a small village of thatched cottages, on a stream that flows through flat plains. It contains several farms surrounded by walls and pierced by gates: the Prussians had converted each of these into a fortress and the French attempted to force the entrance to the village with their superior numbers. They were four times repulsed, finally they set fire to the main farm with a battery of howitzers and surrounded the village. The Prussians then abandoned the position. Their losses are stated at fourteen thousand men and they are gone, God knows where, as Smith[3], of the 10th was sent on a patrol without being able to find them.

While Buonaparte defeated the Prussians, another French column advanced on Brussels by the main road from Charleroi to Quatre Bras. The Duke of Brunswick and the Prince of Orange were there with their corps. The battle was as hot as Ligny; the Duke [of Brunswick], carried away by his eagerness got too near the musketry and was shot, a ball passed through him arm at the wrist and penetrated the stomach, he took his last breath at the end of ten minutes. His sufferings were short.

It is in a hostel, near the junction of the Quatre Bras, where the fight was the most contested where shelter was sought by the poor wounded in the courtyard.

It was near here that one sees the bodies of hundreds of cuirassiers which charging our infantry came under their fire and

---

[2] Hodge was believed at this time to have been injured and captured, this is an indication that George brought his diary up to date after the battle of the 18th, by which time it was becoming more evident that Hodge had died. His detailed knowledge of the fighting at Ligny also confirms this.

[3] Lieutenant William Slayter Smith, 10th Hussars.

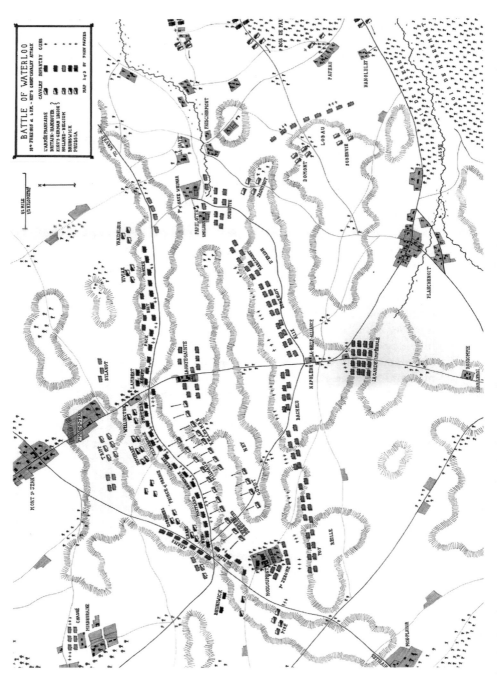

*Above: Map of the Battle of Waterloo*

fell without being able to avoid their fate. I hope that our poor wounded have been relieved prior to our retirement[4].

George was now about to take part in the great battle he had always dreamt of. The 18th spent much of the battle forming the extreme left wing, supporting the Nassau troops in Papelotte, but more importantly sending out patrols to establish and then maintain communications with the Prussians who were marching to join Wellington. Later, around 18.00 hours, towards the final crisis of the battle, the cavalry brigades of Vivian and Vandeleur along with Vincke's Hanoverian Brigade of infantry were ordered to march to the centre of the line, just above La Haye Sainte farm, to bolster the buckling line. Here the cavalrymen suffered heavily from both musketry and cannon fire, but they doggedly maintained their position and even pushed up on the wavering allied infantry in this area to prevent their flight.

Finally, the Imperial Guard were defeated and the light cavalry, including Vivian's and Vandeleur's Hussars charged across the shallow valley and launched a series of devastating attacks on the crumbling French line. The cavalry took heavy casualties, but their efforts rapidly turned a relatively orderly retreat into a chaotic rout. This charge made up for all their failures in Spain in 1813.

> Battle of Mont-Saint-Jean or of Waterloo, Sunday, June 18, 1815.
>
> We remained at our bivouac for up to ten hours; we left it at the call of the trumpet. We thought that the army would advance in concert with Blucher's Prussians, but you can deem our surprise when having arrived in our position (our place being on the extreme left), we saw several strong enemy columns marching to attack and we found our picquets attacked by French cavalry and repulsed by it some distance.
>
> The skirmish lasted until nearly eleven o'clock, when the battle began, which continued for up to eight hours in the middle of the most horrible carnage.
>
> The position of the armies was as follows:
>
> Right of our position, a little in front of our line, was a country house [Hougoumont] which the Duke of Wellington immediately understood the importance of, as should they prevail, they could attack us on this side. It was the key to the right. This crucial point was given to the Guards under the command of Lord Saltoun. They

---

[4] Most of the allied wounded at Quatre Bras were successfully evacuated to Brussels.

worked all night to fortify it to their best ability: the gardens and a wood which served as a park was held by the troops of Nassau and sharp shooters.

A half past ten there was a movement in the enemy line and a coming and going of many officers around a certain place where stood a considerable body of infantry that we later knew to be the Imperial Guard. There was Buonaparte in person and it is from this point that all orders left. During this time the enemy masses formed and everything announced the fight which began at half past eleven. The enemy attacked with one of its corps and pushing on with his usual cries, on the house on our right. The troops of Nassau soon fled[5], but the enemy was received by the part of the Guards who were occupying the house with such resistance that he was forced to give up his attempt, leaving many killed and wounded in the place. Wellington then sent fresh troops who recaptured the wood and garden, and the combat ceased for the time being on this side.

We saw the enemy columns advancing towards the centre of our line. A deathly silence ensued; not a shot was heard for nearly an hour. We observed anxiously the enemy's movements; the French cavalry, formed in place next to the infantry, that marched on our centre. At that same time, about 2 o'clock a Prussian A.D.C. of Blucher's arrived from the left, he enquired for Wellington and told us that 30,000 Prussians were advancing to our assistance. Soon afterwards we saw them coming but at a great distance. Nothing could equal the grandeur of the sight of the attack on our centre, the enemy opposed a horrible fire of artillery from more than 200 pieces[6] under cover of the smoke of which Buonaparte made a general attack with cavalry & infantry in such numbers that it required all the skill of Wellington to post his troops & all the good qualities of the latter to resist the attack. General Picton who was on the road from Brussels to Charleroi advanced with the bayonet to receive them but was unfortunately killed at the moment when the enemy appalled by the attitude of the division forced & fled, thus fell one of the finest characters in the British army – Picton.

---

[5]  This is a constant claim of the time but has now been largely refuted, many Nassauers fighting all day alongside the Guards within the chateau complex.

[6]  This describes the massive assault undertaken by d'Erlon's corps. It is interesting as George could clearly see the French preparations, that although he describes a very heavy preliminary bombardment, he does not mention a 'mass battery'. This is because there was no such thing, the guns being stationed between the infantry columns as normal.

The Life Guards & Blues then charged with the greatest vigour and the 49th[7] and 105th French regiments lost their eagles in this charge together with from 2 to 3,000 prisoners. A column of French cavalry at whose head were the cuirassiers, charged but were not successful. After this the Prussians came up & commenced skirmishing & getting in the rear of the enemy. The French cavalry charged them in style but nothing could save the fateful day. The French army was defeated. The French cavalry, the admiration of all, due to the bravery shown by the cuirassiers, with their bullet-resistant armour[8], who repeatedly charged our squares, with their cannon in the gaps. Our infantry, which decreased, decreased, remained immovable until the last moment.

About an hour before the end, an aide de camp came to the Duke of Wellington and told him that the 5th Division was reduced from four thousand to five hundred men and that it could no longer hold 'I have no one to send, said the Duke, but they must keep their position as I do, to the last man'. 'God bring me night or Blücher' the Duke had responded in the morning to Lord Uxbridge, who had expressed the fear that the English could not resist the desperate attacks of Napoleon. 'It will take several hours to kill them all and I know that they will not move!'

Command of the 95th was passed to Volunteer Kellet after all the officers of this brave regiment were killed or wounded[9].

An hour later, the English heard the shooting behind the right flank of the enemy: they sounded the charge and then began the most terrible carnage. June 18 ended in the most glorious victories for our arms.

The brigade of General Sir Hussey Vivian was all day on the extreme left of the army; it was not engaged before half past seven when the Prussians arrived. We were moved to the right and we charged the Imperial Guard, cuirassiers, lancers and gunners, we drove a passage into the middle of the mass until we had reached the farm of the Belle-Alliance, where we were commanded to halt! And here we gave three cheers, the enemy was fleeing.

Immediately afterwards, we went to the bivouac; I had a good dinner with Luard and I slept deeply after the fatigues of the day.

---

[7] This is an error for the 45th who lost its eagle to Sergeant Ewart of the Scots Greys and which can now be seen at Edinburgh Castle.

[8] This is an error; the British infantry was delighted to discover that the cuirass was no defence against a musket ball fired at close distance.

[9] This was false.

Houtain-le-Val, Monday, June 19.

Daybreak we were under arms and soon we went to the small village of [Blank- Maison du Roi?] one mile away, where Major-General Vivian spent the night. We had a light breakfast and we wrote letters that Sir Hussey promised to send for us with the dispatches of the Duke of Wellington. About ten o'clock, I was sent onto the battlefield to pick up our wounded and bury our dead[10]. This chore was for me very painful, because I found a large number of brave men of my troop, many of whom were injured and had spent the night without relief, while we rested in the camp. I am surprised that I was able to forget these poor boys even without orders, and neglected the fulfilment of this duty.

I obtained two carriages, and after installing them in them, I sent them to hospital in Brussels, where I am sure that they will receive all possible care. I gave my purse to these poor devils; money is scarce, but they have even more need than me. I buried 27[11]. All the French artillery which remained after the battle fell into the hands of the Prussians during the night, as well as the baggage. A column of about ten thousand Prussian's today follows the main road. The Greys took an Eagle yesterday: it was a sergeant who took it from a French officer after a hard fight. Colonel [Blank][12] who commanded the Cumberland Hussars, one of the most handsome units at the battle, took his regiment away from the action to Brussels, without any order. En route these deserters spread the news that our army was defeated; this resulted in the most outrageous scenes; almost all the baggage of the English officers was looted. On my return from the field of battle, the regiment had left for Nivelles, where I followed, I did not catch them until Houtain le Val. Nivelles is one of the most romantic cities that I have seen; from a distance it resembles a Chinese city.

Lord Uxbridge suffered this morning the amputation of his right leg above the knee; Captain Harris, our Brigade Major, lost his left arm almost at the same time. Moreover, poor Harris is seriously injured with a bullet in the stomach and they cannot remove it.[13]

---

[10] Each regiment sent detachments to the battlefield to help their own, they generally appear to have ignored the plight of soldiers from other regiments.

[11] An interesting statement, and initially confusing given that the regiment suffered seventy-two wounded, seventeen missing and only thirteen dead at Waterloo! Most of the missing may well have been dead however. Indeed, no less than thirty-four men are recorded on the Prize Roll Register as having been 'discharged dead' although some of those will be men who died of their wounds at a later date.

[12] Colonel Hake.

[13] Harris did survive.

Ipper arrived with my luggage; but he lost my favorite dog, Vitoria. The village of Plancenoit, which was occupied by the [French] guard during the battle, is no more than a heap of ruins. The chateau was in flames when the rout of the French began and it lit up all the surrounding country. There are thousands of wounded and dead in the most horrible spectacle imaginable.

Colonel Howard, of 10th who was killed in the charge: he fell surrounded by the infantry, but the rogues immediately blew his brains out. Lieutenant Gunning, of the 10th, falling from a ball he received in this charge cried out; 'Oh God!' Lieutenant Hesse was injured when our regiment engaged the leading square of the Imperial Guard, he fell from his horse and the two squadrons which followed him passed over the body[14]. The first was commanded by Luard, I was on the left and Hesse on the right. Lieutenant Duperier, our adjutant, received a shot in the head; he is in Brussels with Hesse, both will recover. Hesse was shot through his right arm. My favourite little horse Dick received two wounds from shards of shrapnel. It is believed that Gordon is dead[15]: he had two horses killed under him. Machell and Rowlls have each lost a horse in the charge.

---

[14] Hesse did survive, but he died in 1819 in a duel with Count Leon, a natural son of Napoleon.
[15] Gordon was not even wounded as will be seen shortly.

# Chapter 20

# The March on Paris

Having defeated the French army so dramatically, the necessity was to march into France without delay, to push their advantage and maintain the confusion. Blucher and Wellington therefore drove hard for Paris, largely ignoring the French fortresses on their route or leaving reserve forces to deal with them. The light cavalry led the advance.

> Merbes-le-Château, Tuesday, June 20.
> We went this morning from Houtain to Nivelles and thence by the chaussee to Binche. This was a terribly long march; and throughout the day we did not have much to distract our attention, the country being absolutely flat with ditches and not a hedge visible. I slept half the way, and I have avoided being suffocated by the dust and heat. The road was filled by English, Belgian, Prussian and Hanoverian troops. Lieutenant G[ordon] who had been 'absent assumed killed', his horse being killed under him: during the battle of the 18th, returned today. He mounted another and left for Brussels. Colonel Grant is so angry regarding the case that he has removed him from his command of his troop and he has put McDuffie in his place. If we can admit, like Hudibras[1] , that:
>> He who fights and runs away
>> May live to fight another day
> We do not think so in the 18th Hussars. He also wants the officers to meet and consider whether to request G[ordon] to leave the

---

[1]  Hudibras, is sort of imitation of Don Quixote, by Samuel Butler, born in 1612 in Strensham (Worcester), died in 1680.

regiment immediately. General Vivian said that if Lieutenant G[ordon] does not leave the corps of hussars, he will have him Court Martialed[2]. The town of Binche is very curious: its walls seems to be very ancient. This village is near the Sambre, but we did not see it. The population claims to be delighted with our success, but it also welcomed the arrival of the French. I suspect them to be French at the bottom of their heart.

It would seem that all of the troops were guilty of pillage, including the British, but they were less guilty of wanton destruction.

Maubeuge camp, Wednesday, June 21.
We entered into France this morning: it is now that the French nation will undergo all the horrors of the war. The town of Maubeuge is very strong and is seen as one of the keys to France. Its garrison consists of National Guards; they fired on several of our staff officers who approached it. We summoned them to surrender, but they stated that they will fight to the last. If all strongholds do the same, we will have plenty to do before reaching Paris.

Vivian was wounded in the ankle by a stray bullet and today he followed the brigade in a closed wagon. We saw Mons at a great distance in a valley to our right. In this camp, which is near the village of Malplaquet, there is a large farm that has been set aside for housing the officers of the regiment.

We have looted everything. The inhabitants are very scared: however one of these individuals had the audacity to tell us that they expected to be protected by the British army and found us instead worse than the cossacks, whom they had a visit from during the last war. If we continue like today, I'm sure the whole country will declare for Napoleon to be rid of us and in the long run we will find an enemy in every cottage. I've seen today such scenes after we had crossed the border that my heart was bleeding for these poor farmers; their harvests, which offered such beautiful promise, were destroyed at pleasure by the Prussians, Hanoverians, the Belgians, and I am sorry to say, by the English. We have received complaints, but we have responded by saying that they needed to thank their Emperor for all of their ills. They say no, it's the fault of the army; that Napoleon would have never left the island of Elba if the army

---

[2]  Lieutenant Gordon did resign from the army in early 1816.

had not insisted on him coming back. Oh! the poor devils! What illusions!

At this farm there were beautiful lambs and we paid 1 franc for them to the farmer, who demanded 12 francs. We paid nothing for the poultry and pigeons, no more than for the beer, we drank to the regiment. The men had made today a very long march; they were tired and thirsty, they had three barrels of beer. This country is just like the south of the France; It is a plain without a hedge: we see everywhere the corn, wheat, and barley. Eight hundred and thirty English officers have been killed or wounded on the 16th, 17th and 18th of this month. This is a wonderful butcher's bill for John Bull. The French deserters marched on Arras, Douai, Cambrai and Valenciennes, followed closely by the Prussians. On the 18th we had before us, between us and the enemy, the two regiments from Nassau and who had passed over to the English at Bayonne in December 1813[3] Since then, they have always been part of our army. On the 18th, they skirmished bravely, and the enemy recognised them perfectly, because they fired on them continually with his artillery and too successfully. Many have fallen.

Le Cateau-Cambrésis camp, Thursday, June 22.
We left this morning at four o'clock, after taking leave of the poor farm people who have cursed us heartily. We soon entered the Forest of Mormal[4], where it is assumed that hundreds of fugitives of the Grande Armée of Napoleon are hidden, pending an opportunity to escape and return home or to the army. The remains of the 2nd Guards Brigade[5] are accommodated in a miserable village in the middle of the forest. The officers say that they do not like this situation.

Today there was much irrational news; I was told that the [French] government had declared against Napoleon and that an envoy had delivered a proposal to the Duke of Wellington to deliver himself up, provided that France can make the choice of its own government; then, that several strongholds would be made over to us. The village of Montay, on the banks of the Selle, is one of the nine villages burned and rebuilt by the Allies during the last campaign. We saw the city of Landrecies on our left; where the Sambre can be crossed, but we have not seen this river.

---

[3] Three battalions of German troops had marched from the French lines into the British lines on 11 December 1813 including two battalions of Nassau troops.
[4] The Forest of Mormal stretches from Bavay to Landrecies.
[5] Byng's Brigade consisting the Coldstream Guards and 3rd Foot Guards.

The city of Cateau-Cambrésis is pleasantly situated on a slight eminence: the Selle stream runs before it in the bottom of a ravine. The Duke of Wellington is in a beautiful house at the entrance to the city. On the18th a captain of the Scots Greys by the name of [Blank - Payne?[6]] fled the field of battle and took most of his troop with him. Captain Gardiner's cannon[7] were taken four times and finally captured by our infantry. The cavalry was halted for two hours awaiting orders near the town of Bavay; it is the first city which we took possession of in France. Very few people remain, most homes are abandoned. The white flag flies over the churches, but it is not respected.

The Prussians arrived here yesterday and looted a little; a Hanoverian column (infantry) will be camped tonight in the vicinity: they won't take what the others have left. In a few days maybe, the Belgian troops, these fellows who fled during the battle and are therefore in our rear, will pass, and, finding everything removed, attack, insult and slaughter half of the residents who no longer have anything to satisfy their greed. Oh! I hate these Belgian scoundrels! There was in this vicinity a serious fight between the French and the English commanded by the Duke of York[8]. The last battle will be called the Battle of La Belle Alliance[9]. It is a curious fact that the English cavalry had abandoned the pursuit of the enemy after the battle in a small village called the Belle Alliance. It's there that we gave our three hurrahs! The Duke of Wellington sent from Malplaquet a proclamation to the French nation on the 21st of this month. He said that he entered France with a victorious army, not an enemy, but to aid the French to shake off the yoke that oppresses them. The property of those who have followed Napoleon will be sequestered.

Picquet near Le Cateau-Cambresis, Friday, June 23.
Buonaparte has gathered his army at Laon, but it is believed that it will not offer battle, although the fortified lines are stunning, in the

---

[6] Captain Edward Payne quit the army within months of the battle, is this why? There is some evidence that Payne's squadron suffered a very much lower number of casualties than the other squadrons, this linked with Payne's rapid departure from the army would seem to confirm that he, just like Lieutenant Gordon of the 18th had been 'persuaded' to leave the army rather than the embarrassment of a court martial.

[7] Lieutenant Colonel Sir Robert Gardiner's Troop of Royal Horse Artillery.

[8] He refers to the Duke of York's victory at the Battle of Beaumont-en-Cambresis (also known as Coteau or Troisvilles) on 26 April 1794.

[9] Such it is called to this day in Germany.

words of the French. I went out this morning at daybreak to Damon [Le Verte Donjon?], where it was believed that the French had a picquet: but upon my arrival I found that they had left the village. Yesterday at ten o'clock their force there was of four hundred and fifty cuirassiers under the command of General Count Mitot[10], who had lunch with the mayor before leaving. I imitated his example. I found the white flag flying over all the churches. In the pretty town of Bohain [-en-Vermandois], there was one in every window.

I picked up several deserters or individuals joining the army, and I brought them with me to the general for inspection. I have moved my patrol to Busigny, Malmaison, Premont, etc. The brigade halted today to rest; the army does the same. We are now on the same line as the Prussian army, which covers our left. We hear the sound of cannon to our right it probably comes from Cambrai. I guess that our troops prepare their approaches before they invest it. Cambrai, which is five leagues, has a garrison of National Guards. Valenciennes, is nine leagues, in the same direction.

Since the battle General Vandeleur has command of the cavalry of the army, he is the oldest cavalry general present. Colonel Quentin was wounded in the foot on the 18th. I saw him several times during the day and I can say that he is a truly brave and excellent officer.

Picquet in Escaufort, near the chateau, Saturday, June 24.
The enemy's army is at Laon with Buonaparte: we do not know his strength, but everyone agrees that they will fight with the energy of despair under the orders of the Emperor who seems

So tired of disasters resulting from his fortune
He would gamble his life for any chance
To improve the situation or die.

Cambrai was attacked the other night; our losses were only one officer and thirteen men. The garrison has withdrawn into the citadel which is strong by nature and art. We need to maintain our communications with Belgium and the Duke of Wellington will certainly sacrifice men to take it. I wrote to Duperier who is in his bed in Brussels, seriously injured; I've included a bill of exchange for 10 pounds sterling. This brave boy is regarded as dangerously

---

[10] I assume that he means General Comte Edouard Milhaud who commanded the IV Cavalry Corps at Waterloo.

wounded; I hope sincerely that he returns. My friend Hesse is better. Louis XVIII and his entourage arrived at Le Cateau this afternoon and the city is illuminated tonight. Avesnes was taken the 22nd of this month with forty-five pieces of canon and large amounts of supplies.

General Rey, former aide de camp of Buonaparte, commands in Valenciennes: this is the same that defended San Sebastian in Spain so stubbornly when the place was besieged and assaulted by General Graham.

Morcourt, near Omissy, Saint-Quentin, June 25, 1815.

At eight o'clock in the morning we received the order to leave Escaufort and go to join the brigade on the great road to Saint-Quentin. We could not find them and we made our way to Morcourt with some difficulty because the roads were so congested with troops and in a sad state. We passed through several villages built of mud; I have no memory seeing such miserable hovels in any of my travels. Near Morcourt is a canal[11], there is perhaps not one like it in the world: the bridges that cross it are very well constructed and all made of stone. Many boats loaded with wheat for the French army fell within our power.

Omissy, a poor hamlet a few scattered shacks, it contains only two or three good houses, of which the best is occupied by General Vivian and his staff. When we came to billet ourselves we found all the other troops already occupying all the houses. I then led mine to Morcourt where I obtained all possible help for my tired hussars. There is a marsh near this village which contains a quantity of fish and on which you can see many wild birds. Napoleon abdicated again; he declares to the French people:

At the Elysée Palace.

22 June 1815

Declaration to the French people.

In starting war to maintain national independence, I was counting on all efforts and wills coming together and on the support of the national authorities. I had reason to hope for success and braved all the declarations of the Allied powers lined up against me.

Circumstances appear to have changed. I offer myself in sacrifice to the hatred of the enemies of France. May they be sincere in their

---

[11] Canal de St Quentin.

declarations and really only hold a grudge against my person. My political life is over and I declare my son Emperor of the French, under the title Napoleon II. The current ministers will form a provisional governing council. The interest I take in my son leads me to invite the Chambers [of Peers and of Representatives] to organise the regency by law without delay. You should all unite for public safety and in order to remain an independent nation.

Ever since the famous day of Poitiers[12], the pride of France has been completely humiliated by British arms. May this last victory serve to ensure the peace of the world for centuries! Poor Buonaparte had to be in a terrible state after the battle of the 18th, as the French newspapers say that he remained for forty hours without speaking or eating. An hour before the rout at Waterloo, he said to those that surrounded him: 'It is a pity to destroy such brave troops.'

Germaine, near Ham, Monday, June 26.
Another long march; I am surprised that our horses can endure the fatigues which they endure. All the villages in this region are similar and a single description can be used for all the houses: they are made of wood and mud, and the inhabitants seem very poor. Everyone shouts: 'Long live the King!' and the white flag flies from all sides, but their sincerity seems dubious. The citadel of Cambrai was assailed this morning who had declared: 'They would cut us to pieces', but surrendered whilst we were preparing to attack, our losses are light. The Prussians besiege Ham, which is poorly fortified and which, I hope, will soon capitulate. I cannot see anything to oppose our entry into Paris and I hope to be there in a few days. I hear the cannon in the direction of Péronne.

Amy, Tuesday, June 27.
We left this morning at ten o'clock with a very long march ahead. We passed through Nesle and Roye. This town is pretty, it has a beautiful old cathedral. The fortifications were repaired and were put in a state of defence, but the citizens had left before we arrived. We crossed the Somme on a small bridge that the enemy has forgotten to destroy. Some say that Buonaparte is a prisoner in Paris, others that he was rescued last Saturday. The town of Nesle seems

---

[12] The Battle of Poitiers occurred on 19 September 1356 where an army under the Black Prince defeated a much larger French force.

very hostlile to us and to the cause of the Bourbons. Nobody opened their mouths to shout: 'Long live the King!' and no trace of a white flag or white cockade.

Ressons [-sur-Matz], left of the road to Compiègne, Wednesday, June 28.

It is reported that Buonaparte and two of his brothers have embarked at Le Havre for England[13], we marched today five leagues on the road to Paris. We passed through several villages where the Prussians were housed last night, and we found them deserted and looted houses filled the background. The unfortunate inhabitants now feel the effects of the war and can get some idea of the miseries that their own armies caused when they were victorious. The servant of Lord Robert Manners was flogged before the brigade this afternoon for stealing a horse. General Vivian then delivered a speech to the brigade. It camped around three farms which were all looted by the Prussians; they took all the cows and horses and we have almost nothing left. Today we passed near a beautiful chateau; seeing the doors and windows open, I visited with many of my comrades and I found the greatest disorder. All the cabinets had been forced. Our curiosity and compassion both being excited, we went inside and after searching in the different rooms, found ourselves in a room with an elderly gentleman and two beautiful young girls. What was our horror and our indignation upon learning from the old man, who was crying, that his two daughters had been raped before his eyes and that the Prussians had beaten him and nailed him to the window while committing this outrage! Poor wretches! I pity this unhappy country! May the Prussians suffer cruelly! I hope my prayer is answered and the Prussians who have committed this terrible crime will fall in the first skirmish!

Senlis, Thursday, June 29.

This morning, the brigade assembled and marched for two hours on the main road, in the direction of Paris. We passed through Marquéglise, the most romantic little village I have ever seen, and Monchy [-Humieres], which is completely plundered: there is not a house that still has a piece of furniture; then Grandfresnoy which is in an equally sad state. The people will not hesitate to take up arms against the Prussians, these villains. Pont-Sainte-Maxence town is

[13] Another false rumour.

large and beautiful: the bridge on the Oise was destroyed last year to halt the march of the Allies: it was a remarkable work, the repair will require two years. Beyond the bridge, lies a very strong natural position to defend the river. The French army of Paris, commanded by Soult, worked on the passage of the Oise, to hold it, but the Prussians have prevented him by making a crossing with a part of their army before his arrival. They then fought a battle with the French, who they defeated. Certainly, the enemy did not expect to see this happen as quickly.

The headquarters of Lord Wellington are in a large chateau near Pont-Sainte-Maxence, named Plessis-Longeau[14]. We had, to our left, the famous forest of Compiègne. Buonaparte's hunting lodge is quite ruined now, I am told, thanks to the Prussians.

For the regularity of its buildings and its cleanliness, the town of Senlis surpasses all those we have seen. All the shops were closed and you couldn't see anyone in the streets: it was a good reception for the hussars. General Vivian went to find the mayor and told him that everything would be respected in the city if the mayor immediately beat the drum, and the town crier proclaimed for everyone to welcome us. Soon after, the city seemed very cheerful; we all got good billets, and the brave people provided us with a good dinner with all desirable ease. The Prussians abused this city badly and looted whatever they found that may have value. A deputation from Paris met us this morning; They were trying to find Lord Wellington; an aide de camp of Blucher's accompanied them; the famous Lafayette[15] was one of these.

Blücher's army is ahead of us by a few miles and it is believed that tomorrow it will be at Saint-Denis, which is only six miles from Paris. It will halt there to wait for our army.

Camp of Roissy [-en-France], Friday, June 30.
We left the delightful city of Senlis this morning with great regret, deploring the situation of its brave people which will be looted by the next brigade which will enter. We marched six leagues and we now camp near the rear of the Prussian army. Its outposts are less than two leagues from Paris. This small town is ruined, like all those that we have passed. The large village of Louvres is the most abused

---

[14] Now known as Saint-Martin-Longeau.
[15] Marie-Joseph Paul Yves Roch Gilbert du Motier, Marquis de Lafayette, the same man whom Americans remember for his close friendship with George Washington during the American War of Independence.

of all. Buonaparle is still in Paris, and it is understood that he still commands the army. The Prussians and the French were engaged throughout the morning; I've seen many carts, full of wounded, pass the village, as well as a band of one hundred and fifty French prisoners. We distinctly see Paris from the tops of the hills. All talk is of a battle tomorrow morning, but I do not think that it will occur before Sunday. It may even be prevented by an armistice, and the surrender of Napoleon and the army. We hunted for poultry and rabbits, the only beings left in this village. A mile from here, is a large town: named Gonesse, where Lord Wellington put sentries to protect the properties: you can purchase foodstuffs here; everywhere else there is nothing left, thanks to the rapacity of the Prussians, our brave allies!

Camp of Roissy, 1 Saturday: July.
We are waiting for the order to march as the enemy has fortified Paris and Buonaparte commands; Blücher has requested the assistance of Lord Wellington. It will take us to do the thing once again, or all will be lost. No fighting this morning (eight o'clock), but the general opinion is that we will attack Paris tomorrow; if this is so, we will enter and then pillage. For the moment, all our thoughts and all conversations are on this subject. The army marched all night to this village and we have rested a while. The day preceding a battle is more annoying than the battle itself. I'd rather take part in a dozen battles than stay waiting the same number of days. I rode to Gonesse, and thanks to the sentries placed by Lord Wellington as protection, I could buy wine, chocolate, bread, butter and ham. The whole army is very unhappy with the dispatch of the Duke about the Battle of Waterloo, especially the cavalry[16].

There was expectation of another battle before Paris would fall.

Le Bourget camp, Sunday, July 2.
Yesterday evening, about ten o'clock, when everyone was in their tents taking some rest, came an order from the Duke of Wellington who ordered our brigade to proceed immediately in advance. So off we went in haste to Le Bourget, where we are now one post from Paris. After having been smothered in road dust, we encamped in a field to the right of the town.

---

[16] Very few if any, were pleased by Wellington's sparse despatch.

At six o'clock this morning, we moved our bivouac to the banks of a small stream that flows to the right of the city, opposite Saint-Denis. All the houses are abandoned and looted. In the church there are several Prussian wounded; I discovered three dead among them who I had removed. Luard and I travelled the streets to find a house where we could sleep, but all were in the most horrible state. In one of them, we saw two men and a child murdered. I say murdered, because they all had the look of peasants. The Prussians have joined the right and act against the enemy in that direction. The Bavarian army arrived near Paris, to our left; they defeated General Rapp[17].

The Prussian forces do not amount to sixty thousand men. We heard a violent cannonade and we believe that it may have been an attack. Today from the side of the enemy, many flags of truce came, and many went from our side and were received by them.

We have the most wonderful bivouac in the garden of a large chateau surrounded by moats filled with water and also filled with carp and tench; I spent part of the day fishing. Prince Blücher, promised his army, that if the French defend Paris, he will allow them the looting of the two suburbs of Saint-Germain and Saint-Antoine. We all look forward to the pillage of Paris rather than the danger of taking Paris. The enemy has now twelve thousand cavalry men; I don't know exactly the number of infantrymen, but it is, apparently considerable.

I lost my favourite little horse Dick; stolen from the camp by a few Belgian soldiers who were hanging around us. Several detachments seek him for me (by permission of Colonel Murray) and I hope to find him.

Péronne was taken by storm; it is a very old town, and at one time was thought to be impregnable because it had never been taken. It now loses its nickname of 'la Pucelle', which had been given to it.

A Provisional Government, composed of Fouché, Carnot, Caulaincourt, Grenier and Quinette[18], who will act in the name and on behalf of Napoleon II was established in Paris. Marshal Grouchy[19]

---

[17] George is in error here. General Jean Rapp had won the battle of La Suffel against the Austrians under the Crown Prince of Wurttemberg on 28 June 1815. The Bavarians commanded by General Wrede did not encounter any French troops on their march to Paris.

[18] The members of the French commission set up on 22 June 1815 were indeed Joseph Fouché (President), Lazare Carnot, Paul Grenier, Armand Augustin Louis de Caulaincourt and Nicolas Marie Quinette.

[19] Marshal Emmanuel de Grouchy, 2ème Marquis de Grouchy, had led 30,000 troops which had been detached by Napoleon from the main army in Belgium to prevent Blücher meeting up with Wellington. His failure to do so has been heavily criticised (especially by Napoleon), but his retreat with his corps intact into France after the terrible defeat of Waterloo, has been roundly described as brilliant.

arrived in Paris; he has rallied a large number of fugitives which he has incorporated into his army. When he arrived, it is estimated his forces to be 50,000 men. Soult has 60,000: Paris must have more than 100,000 troops in all.

Camp of Le Bourget, Monday, July 3.
A suspension of hostilities was signed between the Allies and the French this morning. We hope that everything is settled and that we will immediately start to enter Paris. God be praised! May it really be true and the war is over! We are now desperately hungry.

We cannot get anything for gold or silver, and we do not even receive our rations. The men, naturally, suffer even more so than the officers. I was now at the advance guard. The First Brigade of the Guards are with us in this village and are on duty on the road to Paris. On this road we have a picquet of two squadrons. The position of the enemy is considered by all our engineering officers, as one of the strongest in Europe, almost impregnable.

We will soon know what became of Buonaparte: It is believed that he has escaped. Some say he went to Cherbourg. We were tonight at Aubervilliers, a large village between the road to Le Bourget in Paris and Saint-Denis. There are two large houses here occupied by French soldiers. They are firmly entrenched there and it will prove very costly to dislodge them. Our picquets are in the city and occupy several large well-defended houses. An officer led us to the top of a roof, where we saw the position and the works of Montmartre.

The capitulation of Paris was announced, but the hand over was sure to be difficult.

Camp of the Bourget, Tuesday, July 4.
I received this morning the details of the agreement with the French nation:
'The Field Marshal has the great satisfaction to announce to the troops under his command that, together with Marshal Prince Blücher, he has concluded a military convention with the Commander-in-Chief of the French army in Paris, under the terms of which the enemy undertakes to evacuate Saint-Denis, Saint-Ouen, Clichy and Neuilly today at noon, and Paris tomorrow. The French army will withdraw behind the Loire'.

I killed a peacock this morning that I had seen in a small grove of my garden. I found it after much trouble.

My poor Dick is back, a Belgian soldier had offered him for sale, to an orderly of an officer of the 1st [German] Hussars who recognised him and brought me back my favourite horse. In the evening, I rode with Major Grant and Luard, to Saint-Denis, to see if this town was delivered to our army. The roads that give access have been cut. We found ourselves with a passage of some difficulty and we waited for them to bridge the gap to allow us to enter the town. The tricolour flag was flying on the Church of Saint-Denis, and on the town hall; all the National Guards had the national cockade in their hats. We were probably the first Englishmen to enter the town, and the population, which appears devoted to Buonaparte, threw us some very black looks. We asked a Guard officer at the town hall why they had not lowered the national colours to replace it with the white flag: he replied that it had not yet been decided on who would be given the crown. If it is Louis XVIII, they will change the flags; if it is the Duke of Orléans, they will keep the tricolour.

Fifty yards from the gate of Paris was posted a French piquet. An officer came to let us know this was the line of demarcation until tomorrow at noon when Montmartre will be delivered up. A sergeant of the Guards who was trying to enter the city by the gate of Paris, which was to pass near the French lines, heard their fire, which made him almost die of fright.

Then there was a very funny scene which ended with Major Grant administering a thrashing to a French civilian and by whom insults were directed at all the French present. There was a sortie this morning from Saint-Denis of about ten thousand men; every inhabitant able to bear arms wore the National Guard costume.

The King of Spain re-establishes the Jesuit order in his kingdom; it is the first time they have been there since the time of their expulsion. It is amazing to see them brought back, especially by a king, it is a fearsome religion for all princes because of their regicidal doctrines.

Here is what is given as the exact description of the steam frigate recently launched in New York, length of bridge, three hundred feet; width, two hundred feet; thickness of the hull, thirteen feet, alternating oak and cork boards. It has forty-four guns, four of which are 100 pound guns, the guns of the maindeck are 60; those in the rear and the foc'sle of 42. In the event of an attempt to board, the mechanism is able to unload one hundred tons of boiling water per minute onto the deck of the opponent. At the same time, it operates on its gunwales three hundred cutlasses with the greatest regularity and an equal number of iron pikes of great length that it darts out of its sides and retracts with a prodigious force all in a quarter of a minute.[20]

Saint-Denis near Paris, Wednesday, July 5.
I rode today to Saint-Denis with Grant and Luard; we went first to the church hoping to see the tombs of the Kings of France, but to our disappointment we found the church empty. At least it seemed such, because we could not discover a tomb or even a trace of a burial up until the point where our guide showed us a few slabs under which is the Royal mausoleum. The church is beautiful, but there is nothing particularly striking within: it cannot compete with certain English cathedrals.

We then went to the Hotel de Ville, but we saw nothing there to merit the slightest mention except the extreme rudeness of some National Guardsmen. We then rode on horseback around the city to examine the works of defence. One of our officers of the engineers informed us that if the French had not accepted the convention, it would have required great sacrifice, the most moderate plan calculated on the loss of two thousand men to make us masters of it. The guns hoisted on these works are twenty and thirty pounders and belong to warships.

Montmartre as seen from Saint-Denis, has a very nice effect: the spires on the many churches in Paris that one sees on each side and the picturesque frame of the hills that surround it form a whole charming view. While we were at Saint-Denis, Lord Wellington passed through the town, going to Saint-Ouen, where the headquarters of the army are currently. The stable of Louis XVIII and the Duke of Berry arrived at Saint-Denis with an officer to bring them to the place: immediately after the entire city was decked with white flags. Saint-Denis, I am assured, certainly favoured Buonaparte and however treacherously these act, I hope that the poor old King will puncture their present malevolence.

Picton – Original Poetry

They are sacred bare twigs which sway
With a bleak solemnity on the Tomb
Where sleeps the brave fallen warrior
Who once commanded the battle.

---

[20] This was a steam-powered battery designed by Robert Fulton to protect New York harbour named *Demologos* (renamed the *Fulton* on his death). The design took steam-powered warships down a blind alley and was never fully completed.

Fame devotes the grass that grows,
The humble small flower which blossoms,
The dew which falls at the end of the day,
Lays on the soldier.

I saw him in the heat of battle:
His indomintable eye challenged destiny.
I contemplated the noble front of a veteran
In the middle of the terrible melee.

But before the Sun had reached the West,
That eye was closed, this generous chest,
This Warrior figure had fallen to sleep
On foreign land!

La Villette and Montmartre, Thursday, July 6.
This morning we got all up early and we have prepared our hair
with leaves of laurel and queues for our entry into Paris. But at four
o'clock in the afternoon no order had yet arrived. We then went to
dinner at La Villette, and while they prepared our meal we made a
tour of the fortifications of Montmartre. This exceptional position
could be defended with fifteen thousand men against either the city,
or against a besieging army. The view of Paris from these heights is
magnificent, no description can give an idea. You command a view
from there of the city, the Seine and the beautiful hills that surround
it.

Montmartre is a small town that looks like Gibraltar. The streets
are too narrow. The Church is in ruins and almost all the houses,
especially those bordering the fortifications, are in the same state.
All the works are now delivered to our troops and are currently
occupied by a Dutch corps; it could destroy Paris in a few hours
from Montmartre.

The first view of Paris from the side of La Villette and Saint-Denis
is held from a wide and beautiful paved road, lined with two rows
of trees on each side. But we seek in vain those pretty country
houses, the charming and varied housing to be seen in England, the
fruits of commerce and the opulence of the merchants. Returning by
La Villette, we were bombarded by a bunch of scoundrels,
supporters of Buonaparte, who threw stones at us for some time to
force us to remove the laurel from our hair. But we maintained our
composure and they left us to return in peace. I must admit that I
was angry and at some point I had to restrain myself very strongly

from not slashing at someone who had launched a piece of brick at me, shouting: 'Remove the laurel leaves'! If we wear the laurel and oak in accordance with general orders to enter tomorrow into Paris, I expect a far different reception than what we had hoped for. The First Brigade of the Guards were on duty at La Villette and the gate of Paris with the National Guard. Back at the bivouac, we found that the aide de camp to General Vivian had us destroy some of the works of the small entrenched camp which amused us to do:

The house of General Vivian is loved by everyone; There is no man in the service of his Majesty who deserves better.

Today was the triumphal entry into Paris, but the 18th were not given the privilege of attending.

Suresnes[21], Friday, July 7.
We received the order for us to march this morning at three o'clock; We were convinced that it was to go to Paris, but we were very disappointed. We learnt that the brigade was to move to Suresnes. The march took us through the middle of a delicious country covered with vines, the first I have seen since I left the south of France. We passed through Courbevoie and, from this moment, we had a wonderful view of Paris. The Seine is as beautiful as the Thames at Richmond. The bridge that crosses it is particularly striking to the eye of an Englishman; because all our bridges are built differently. It is flat and the great road of Saint-Germain and Paris passes.

Suresnes is a pretty little village consisting of three or four streets, with many summer houses. The palace of the Princess de Vaudémont, allied to the family of the Bourbons, is immediately above Suresnes. Nothing in its exterior or interior appearance can give an Englishman the idea of a palace for a moment; everything is extremely simple, but very suitable. The aviary contains beautiful pheasants and birds of every species. The menagerie is not so well stocked: we saw a beautiful Newfoundland dog with his bitch and a black pig. It was formerly the residence of the famous Barras; this is same place where Buonaparte met Josephine for the first time, then mistress of Barras. It was an old servant of the palace who told me this fact: he was then serving in the house. He led me around the rooms and the apartments. The princess is a small woman of

---

[21] Suresnes lies near St Cloud.

forty-five years, with the swivel eye; she is a girl, and Kennedy, who is always seeking women, addressed to his Highness a polite note informing her that her property was under good care and that is what had prompted him to leave Paris for Suresnes.

The construction which crowns the Mont Valérien was intended for a convent, according to the desire of Empress Marie-Louise; but since the return of the Bourbons, it is a military school. It is a building of brick, two-winged: it commands a very extensive view. On the opposite bank is Bagatelle, the castle of the Duke of Berry. the park which surrounds it, with its escape routes to the river, is the most picturesque. Suresnes' gardens are filled with flowers and ripe fruit which we did not deprive it of. The Prussians extorted the other day for fifteen thousand bottles of wine.

The 10th Hussars and the artillery go to Sontaputeaux [Puteaux?]; the English and Hanoverian infantry are confined to the Champs Elysees and Bois de Boulogne. The two Chambers, fully expecting to be dissolved upon the arrival of Louis XVIII have moved their session to Orléans, and the majority of the members have gone there.

Carnot seems to have followed the army and seems willing to keep the government together. Davout[22] sent a circular to the absent officers to join their corps. The negotiations for the surrender of Paris and the cessation of hostilities have ended at the Palais de Saint Cloud, favourite residence of Buonaparte, and in the same room where he held his Council of State. Yesterday, in accordance with the conventions, all the barriers were delivered up.

---

[22] Marshal Louis-Nicolas Davout, Prince of Eckmuhl.

# Chapter 21

# Visiting Paris

Paris, Saturday, July 8.

General Vivian gave permission at ten o'clock this morning for one-third of the officers of each regiment to go to Paris, I was appointed and off we went five in number, Murray, Lloyd, Luard, Dunkin and me.

We left our horses at the Hote d'Autriche and we went on foot to the Palais-Royal, where we promenaded for up to three hours. We then went to Very's[1] very near to the Tuileries Gardens and we took a prime place at a window, from where we saw Louis XVIII enter into Paris.

I know that some have found this a magnificent spectacle; for me, I've never seen a dirtier set of ragamuffins than those that preceded the King and which are his army. The old man seemed pleased; he smiled and greeted everyone. But there was not the twentieth part of the crowd that we expected to see. When we arrived this morning, the tricolour floated on the Vendôme column and all public buildings; all the National Guardsmen wore the tricolour cockade. As soon as Louis was at the gate of Paris, the white flag flew everywhere, and you saw nothing but white cockades. After dinner at Very's, we walked in the garden of the Tuileries; we saw the king showing himself to his supporters at one of the windows of the palace. The populace responded to his waving by shouts of 'Vive le Roi'. If his rival Napoleon showed himself at the same time and had uttered a few words standing on top of a bench, the people would have quickly shouted: 'Long live the Emperor!'

---

[1] Very's was a very chic restaurant of the time.

The greater part of the Parisians seemed absolutely indifferent to the arrival of His Majesty and I have the firm conviction that Buonaparte will still launch that unhappy country into a war with Europe, if he manages to reach America where it is believed that he wants to take refuge. The whole of the world have told me: 'The King, that you have given us will remain on the throne as long as the Allies remain there.'

We travelled along the boulevards with Luard for up to nine hours. The promenade on a delicious evening, was covered with people who were enjoying in peace the fine evening. The air was so calm that it barely stirred the leaves of the trees or the flames of the candles of wax that had been attached to the facade of the houses to celebrate the return of the King. I must say that the illuminations were petty and would have disgraced a provincial town. Troops of individuals who are I suspect paid by some agents of the government, roamed the streets shouting: 'Long live the King!' and forced the inhabitants to illuminate. We will prevent the return of Napoleon and occupying this country for a few years and will demand the dismissal of the army. General Rey[2], who commands at Valenciennes, evicts all the inhabitants who haven't enough supplies. He sent the garrison a violent order of the day: he declares that he will never give up the tricolour flag.

Suresnes, Sunday, July 9.
When the Allies entered Paris last year, flags taken at different times by the French from the Austrians and Prussians and which were exposed for some time in the Luxembourg Palace, were removed and hidden with care, lest they were claimed by their original owners. After the departure of the Allies was reported, I saw them in the House of Peers. They made them disappear again. I hope that this time the Allies claim that they will no longer maintain the insatiable vanity of the corrupt Parisians. If some English banner is located in the number, I intend that it will be peremptorily claimed, due to unmerited gentleness which is currently used to deal with the French people.

Saint-Gloud and Sèvres, Monday, July 10.
I went with Luard to visit this chateau and I found it inhabited by Blucher and his staff. We had unimpeded access to all parts of the chateau, except in the bedroom of Marie-Louise, which is reserved by

---

[2] General Luis-Emmanuel Rey had famously resisted the British siege of San Sebastian in 1813; he was now governor of Valenciennes.

Blücher! The chapel is very simple and without a single golden ornament. Buonaparte rarely bothered his priests; never, I believe, except for public ceremonies. The first room contains a superb painting, representing General Desaix at the moment when wounded, he falls from his horse into the arms of General Junot, during the famous battle of Marengo, which he won, thanks to the rapid march of his reserves. This beautiful painting is by David, and the characters are life-size. Over the fireplace of another room, hung the painting of Buonaparte crossing the Alps; but the Prussians took it. I saw it in the passage that leads to the grand staircase. They want to destroy it without doubt, or remove it. The interior of this palace is so magnificent that we were dazzled on leaving. The gardens are in a shameful state, as a Prussian division are encamped there. The cascades play, and most of the fountains: I have no hesitation to say that St Cloud is a paradise compared to some of the other palaces and other parks I've seen.

The Emperors of Russia and Austria, and the King of Prussia arrive tonight in Paris. The Château de Vincennes continues to refuse submission to the King. The entrance to Paris by the bridge of Neuilly to the eye offers a very majestic perspective. The barrier consists of two imposing military constructions having all faces of the porticoes supported by beautiful Doric columns. These buildings are separated by iron grids. In front of the barrier is a magnificent triumphal arch, started by Buonaparte and called the Arc de l'Etoile[3].

Paris, Tuesday, July 11.
I am angry to see the state in which the museums are. Those of the Jardin des Plantes are already shamefully plundered, especially the museum and the Amphitheatre of surgery and anatomy. Hundreds of bottles have been removed; I saw an individual holding two and who drank the spirits contained therein, which had been used to retain a few shreds of human flesh or curious anatomical debris. The Louvre will be stripped of half of its paintings, and among these are some of the most beautiful; the Prussians have stated that they would return all those that were stolen from Berlin. If the Emperor of Austria, the King of Belgium, the Emperor of Russia act similarly in what was taken from them, then little will remain. The Prussians had sentries at the Louvre and other museums.

In the evening, after dinner at Very's I went to the Opera, to see *Castor and Pollux*[4]. The room was full of English and Prussian

[3] Or to give it its full name the Arc de Triomph de l'Etoile it was not completed until 1836.
[4] This opera by Jean-Philippe Rameau was first performed in 1737.

officers: included among them Prince William of Prussia[5], Lord Hill, General Alten, Vandeleur, Lord Combermere and his wife[6]. News of the most various circulating on Buonaparte's whereabouts, some say he is with the army of the Loire – others that he was taken at sea by one of our cruisers which seems most likely.

We receive at this moment from England the news of a death of Mr. Whitbread[7]; he killed himself by cutting his throat. I am comfortable with that, and I wish that his friend Whitman[8] and others would follow his example. The depot of the regiment is moved from Romford to Brighton, they left Romford the 6th of this month. The Prussians have taken Orléans. The bridge over the Loire is intact, but the French have raised strong entrenchments on the left bank of the river.

Versailles, Wednesday, July 12.
I came here on horseback with Chambers and I visited the palace for the second time; I gained even more amusement than the first time. Louis XVIII is going to make many repairs over the years and when finished, Versailles will surpass all palaces in the universe.

After visiting the town which has suffered a lot by the Prussians, we had lunch at the Hotel de France and we returned for dinner. The main army of Buonaparte, which retreated beyond the Loire, has entered the service of Louis XVIII. But the staff and the commanders who control some of the fortifications are opposed to our army and the supporters of the Bourbons, they appear committed to a desperate resistance. In the north, they ordered the fortresses to surrender to the king, but they refuse to do so. The people of this unhappy country are prey to all the horrors of the sieges or are forced to abandon their homes and wander in the woods. The same acts of violence, threaten desolation to the cities in the east, west and south and to end it will require that France suffers in all of its parts including those still free of the inseparable miseries of the passage and residence of large armies. A huge number of free corps, which are associations of bandits, roam the countryside and commit all kinds of depredations.

Since the British army entered into France, it has maintained its food and fodder from the country that it has passed through by

---

[5] Prince William, the fourth son of the King of Prussia had commanded the cavalry reserve during the campaign of 1815.
[6] Lieutenant General Sir Stapleton Cotton, had become the 1st Lord Combermere in 1814.
[7] The reforming politician Samuel Whitbread, son of the brewer, had committed suicide on 6 July 1815.
[8] He probably refers to the Whitmans who were fellow brewers.

regular requisitions. Our commissaries made no payment, and the English government will never pay what we took, but regular receipts were provided so that owners can subsequently give the French government proof of the quantities of food that they have provided to us.

Paris, Thursday, July 13.
I visited the Luxembourg Palace today. This evening after we dined at Beauvilliers[9], Lloyd and I went to the Théâtre des Variétés on the boulevards. We had an altercation that nearly ended up in a duel with a French cavalry officer. Yesterday, an officer of the 1st Light Dragoons of the German Legion made an example of a French officer who insulted him in the evening. They fought in the Champs-Elysées and the French officer was shot through the lung. The Parisians are very busy overthrowing the busts of Buonaparte and erasing his initials on the public monuments. The Château de Vincennes still refuses to submit to Louis XVIII and the tricolour flag still flies on its walls.

Malmaison, Friday, July 14.
Major Clements is en route with a detachment of remounts to repair the gaps in the regiment: we expect them shortly. I rode to Malmaison; I went for dinner, I dressed and I was in Paris at the opera with Luard, Lloyd and Pulsford. The King of France was there with Monsieur and the Duke de Berry. All three were in a dressing room and appeared surrounded by several marshals and officers covered with decorations. Every five minutes, a few individuals of the gallery hollered: 'Vive le Roi'! And of course, the whole room imitated them. The loss of the Prussians from June 15 to July 3 is killed, 5,770; wounded, 16.350, prisoners and missing, 11,000. General total: 33,120 also includes four general officers wounded at Ligny and two others at Waterloo

Paris, Saturday, July 15.
I dined at Beauvilliers with Lloyd and Hamilton of the 10th Hussars and we then went to l'Opera-Comique, where we stayed until ten o'clock. We then went to Doctor Quincey's buffet, but finding the house full, we have been at Monsieur Laperrière's, where we walked in the garden for a few hours, and then we took a cabriolet to return.

---

[9] Antoine Beauvilliers had opened the first grand restaurant in Paris.

Paris, Sunday, July 16.

After having dined at Suresnes, I was in Paris in a cabriolet with Croker, Luard and Deane. We visited the Tuileries and in the Marshal's room we saw portraits of Murât, Lefèvre, Soult, Massena, Davout, Jourdan, Ney, Brune, Victor and Macdonald. The view of the gardens from the windows of the palace is very beautiful. They are always open to the public and form the main promenade of Paris. 'Les beaux et les belles' were gathered by the thousands, and we saw several companies who were dancing in the air in the fashion: 'Vive Henri IV!' which they sang accompanied by others. Several groves of majestic chestnut trees provide a delicious shade. Under their shelter, thousands of people walk or sit down to talk. A carriageway that extends throughout the length of the garden, is decorated with two admirable rows of large orange trees in boxes. Between them are a great number of beautiful statues and vases of marble, after seeing the garden and the crowd from the top of the gallery, we went into the Council Chamber where we saw a beautiful column made at the manufactory of Sèvres porcelain in honour of the French army, after the campaigns of 1805 and 1806. In another room is a statue worth two hundred and fifty pounds offered by the city of Paris to posterity in honour of Napoleon.

We left the palace to go to the Opéra-Comique. An hour later, we left and we went to Tivoli, where we remained until two o'clock in the morning. The establishment at night resembles the Vaux-Hall in London, but is not so well lit. On the other hand, the gardens are arranged with more taste than any public garden in England. At nine o'clock the entertainment begins. Here we see the Grand Turk, sitting on a kind of throne, and telling tales of great adventure to the women; there, a magician with astonishing dexterity; in another corner, a young woman plays the harp and charms the ears by its agreeable sounds. Elsewhere there are orchestras and people who indulge in the pleasure of dance, wooden horses and several swings. A pool of water with three boats filled with the world, long retained us. At half past eleven, very nice fireworks. During this a young girl danced and performing, climbed on a rope attached to the top of a structure; when she was almost at the top, rockets and firecrackers went off all around her and she appeared as if surrounded by fire. This show was magnificent, and all of the company seemed to be enchanted at the amusements of the evening.

Finis

Chapter 22

# Aftermath

The journal does seem to end abruptly and it may be that the French editor chose to remove further entries regarding France after the end of the war; however, it is just as likely that George simply lost interest in recording further events in the journal. Either way, it can be assumed that little of real value will have been lost.

The regiment moved to Beauvais in Picardy on 3 August 1815 to relieve the problem of obtaining sufficient forage for the horses. On 11 December, the regiment marched to Neufchatel-en-Bray in Normandy and to Gournay-en-Bray the following day.

George and the 18th Hussars were destined to remain in France until the end of 1818, serving with the Army of Occupation, set up under the terms of the Second Treaty of Paris, signed on the 20 November 1815. Under this treaty, a multinational force, numbering in total 150,000 men and commanded by the Duke of Wellington, was to be stationed in northern France, holding a number of key fortresses. The French were liable for the costs of supplying this army which was initially designed to stay for five years, but was eventually disbanded after only three years in November 1818, when the French paid all of their outstanding indemnities of some seven hundred million francs to the allies early, via a very large bank loan from Barings & Co. During this period the 18th was brigaded with the 12th Light Dragoons, with its cantonments around Montreuil-sur-Mer and Boulogne, and its headquarters at Etaples. The regiment was to remain there for the next two and a half years.

We know nothing concrete about George during this period, except that he chose to resign his commission in early 1818 because of ill health, before the Army of Occupation finally withdrew that November. Colin

Yorke has recently discovered a copy of a letter George wrote at this time from London to William Deane.

Mr Deane Esq.
18th Hussars,
British Army,
France.

1 January 1818

My Dear Deane,
Owing to my ill state of health, I have not been able to arrange my affairs yet, but hope to do so in a week or two from my continual bad state; worse if possible than when at Boulogne. But on by so little impudence, fancying I was better than I really was, going to the theatre I was in a hour, [I had a] relapse and am now mending very slowly. I have sent in my resignation, it being dangerous to trust myself to the chance of recovery, if I get another relapse. I sent Greenwoods an order to pay you the amount of the value of my Lieutenancy £265.10, when it is sold and I will pay into their hands for you £300 in a week or fortnight. I have requested Luard to send my things for sale and I have quarters, and the value of them and my horses to be paid to you. If I, by chance should continue to mend, I am to go to the south [of France] and make Boulogne in my way, perhaps in 2 months or so, and then I will see you and in the meanwhile believe me my dear Deane, your sincere friend.
G Woodberry.

Remember me to my old friends.

My address is:
John Usher Esq.,
No 19 Change Alley[1],
London.

His reasons for resigning are clearly stated by him to be on health grounds, but whether this was the complete truth, we cannot be certain, because we do know that he did go back to France and later attested

---

[1] Change Alley lies directly south of the Royal Exchange in the heart of the City of London.

that he had become a Roman Catholic in 1818 whilst in France; and the reason for this was most certainly because of a woman. However, for whatever reason, no wedding seems to have gone ahead in France and perhaps the thought of remaining in a boring garrison in the same vicinity for the foreseeable future was then unbearable to him. What is certain is that he resigned from the Army on 19 March 1818 and that Robert Norris finally gained his lieutenancy by his departure.

He then, in the same year, appeared on the island of Trinidad & Tobago in the West Indies, ostensibly to help with the arthritis he was then reputedly suffering from, or was it simply a broken heart? There is however, an intriguing little piece which appeared in the *Blackwood's Magazine* published in Edinburgh in the August 1815 edition. An article set as a parody on *The Beggar's Opera* by John Gay, introduces a character by the name of no less than Sir George Woodberry and which describes the hero's attempts to save a young lady from her unkind parents. Was this our George involved in a scandal regarding affairs of the heart? Was he rejected by Amelia Perkin's parents? Did this cause his swift removal to Trinidad? We cannot be sure, but there is certainly an underlying theme here of unrequited love.

However, in Trinidad, George appears to have met and quickly become friendly with a Sir William White who owned large estates in Trinidad, St Kitts and Nevis[2]. White wrote to General Simon Bolivar, who wished to gain the independence of Venezuela from Spain; and was in search of experienced soldiers with which to strengthen his army, he recommended George Woodberry to him. Bolivar replied in a letter dated 29 September 1818, stating that George would be very well received and that he should come to Venezuela and attend his headquarters at Angostura[3]. George was given the rank of lieutenant colonel and served with the artillery; then, in November 1819, George was made Chief of Staff to General Juan Bautista Arismendi who commanded the 'British Legion'[4].

A Captain Adam met him in March 1819 stating that 'Marino, General of the army of the East, and to whom we had letters of introduction, was at Coriaco, near Cumana: but, upon my introduction to Colonel

---

[2] Some of this information comes from the excellent work undertaken by Peter Hicks for his reprint of the French version, but has been added to with further research undertaken since by the editor and Colin Yorke.

[3] Now known as Ciudad Bolivar in Venezuela.

[4] A corps of ex British and European soldiers, often known as the 'Albion Legion' hired effectively as mercenaries to support the Wars of Independence in Colombia, Venezuela, Ecuador and Peru, they were mostly recruited in London by a Colonel Uzlar.

Woodberry, Adjutant-General of the British Legion, he, with that pleasing manner and address for which he is eminently conspicuous, took charge of them, and promised to have them forwarded immediately to the general. The kindness of this gentleman did not rest here, he provided us with comfortable quarters, those lately occupied by Colonel Low, and gave us an invitation to dine at the Field Officers' Mess, an invitation which we thankfully accepted'.[5]

He later served with the 3rd Division commanded by General Ambrosio Plaza at the Battle of Carabobo on 24 June 1821, where General Bolivar's army defeated that of Spanish Field Marshal Miguel de la Torre, effectively establishing Venezuelan Independence.

I must however, correct one error that has recently been propagated. Desmond Gregory published a book in 1992 called *The Rediscovery of Latin America in the Early Nineteenth Century*. In it he refers to accounts written by the participants of the Wars of Independence, the best of which he claims is *Recollections of a Service of Three Years, During the War of Extermination in the Republic of Venezuela and Columbia*. This was written anonymously, and published in London in 1828, but he has stated that he believes that it was written by our George Woodberry. The anonymous author states that he was originally in the 15th Hussars, which of course could be a typographical error, but his service in South America was with the Navy, a service in which we can confidently state that George never served. This account cannot therefore be by George.

Lieutenant Colonel George Woodberry is however the author of a journal that runs from 25 November 1820 to 14 June 1821 and this was published within Arturo Santana's *La Campana de Carabobo (1821); Relacion Historica Militar,* in 1921. This does not cover the Battle of Carabobo and cannot be included within this present publication both because of its size and because it is unrelated to his service in the British Army.

George was formally recognised as one of the heroes of Venezuelan Independence and his name accordingly appears on the Monument of the Heroes in front of the Capitol or Federal Palace at Caracas.

We know that in 1823, George Woodberry, who was by then Chief of Staff to General Paez, is mentioned in documents as one of the founder members of a lodge of freemasons, the first in Venezuela. Records also show that in August 1824, George planned to marry a Miss Anna Ascanio, and supplied documents and witnesses to the Archbishopric of Valencia, attesting to his date of birth, that he was a Catholic (he

---

[5] Captain Adam Page 70.

claimed to have converted whilst in France in 1818) and that he was single. The wedding apparently went ahead on 20 September 1824 and was officiated by Don Francisco Javier Narvarte, priest.

He was granted Venezuelan nationality on 17 February 1825 in La Gran Colombia and was also granted a pension. He is mentioned as working in Valencia (capital of the State of Carabobo) on 24 August 1826 in a letter received by Sir Robert Ker Porter who was then a British Consul, written by a Mr O'Leary, who refers to Woodberry as now in the 'Colonial Service'. At that time, George used his own letterhead showing his place of residence as Valencia. Records also reveal that from 1832 he was still receiving a pension of one-third of his salary at 559 pesos and 92 reales.

After the War of Independence, George appears to have wanted to settle down with Anna[6], a native of the region and reputedly the daughter of a local chieftain. She apparently brought a dowry of land in a place called El Terronal, Güigüe, near the city of Valencia, in Carabobo State. On first seeing the land, George is reputed, according to family tradition, to have described it as 'Paradise' and he began cultivating cocoa and, later, coffee there[7].

The Pedernales Hacienda was land given as an inheritance. This hacienda was thirty-nine kilometers from Guigue, but it was later expropriated by Juan Vicente Gómez[8] early last century when he saw, and fell in love, with it. He apparently sent a cheque and simply gave seven days' notice of eviction to the family. The descendants of George Woodberry therefore lost their lands.

George and Anna, it seems, had three children; Jorge (George), Miguel (Michael) and Georgiana. All three married and had many children.

Just as this book was going to print, George Woodberry's death certificate was discovered (incorrectly written as Jorge Wolvery) although we do not have his actual gravestone. George died on 14 July 1833 at Puerto Cabello a port city on the north coast of Carabobo State, Venezuela, (was he trying to sail home?), his widow Anna was allowed to remarry in church to her cousin, one Juan Jose Liendo, in December 1833.

---

[6] Family tradition seems to believe that his wife was called Mercedes. The name certainly appears in later generations and it is quite possible that Anna also held the name of Mercedes, but this cannot be proven.

[7] This area was then rich agricultural land and many large landowners held estates here; but aparently there is nothing there today beyond abject poverty.

[8] He became dictator of Venezuela in the early Twentieth Century.

It is known that the family deposited his military effects, including his sword, with the State Museum many years ago, but given the current problems in Venezuela it has proven impossible to locate them.

Had he survived until 1848, George could have applied for the Military General Service Medal (which Queen Victoria had just ordered to be issued, post-dating its issue for any major battle since 1800) with five bars for the battles of Vitoria, Nivelle, Nive, Orthes and Toulouse. The location of his Waterloo Medal, which he did receive, is also unfortunately not known.

# Bibliography

Anon., *Army Lists*, various years.

Anon, *Recollections of a Service of Three Years During the War of Extermination in the Republics of Venezuela and Colombia, by an Officer in the Colombian Navy* (London, 1828).

Adam, Capt. William J., *Journal of Voyages to Marguaritta, Trinidad & Maturin* (Dublin, 1824).

Adkin, Mark, *The Waterloo Companion* (London, 2001).

Barrios, Hector, *Los Heroes de Carabobo* (Caracas, 2004).

Beamish N. Ludlow, *History of the King's German Legion 2 Vols.* (London, 1832).

Bromley J. & D., *Wellington's Men Remembered*, 2 Vols. (Barnsley, 2012 & 15).

Bryant, A., *The Great Duke* (Glasgow, 1971).

Burnham, R., & McGuigan, R., *The British Army Against Napoleon* (Barnsley, 2010).

Chandler, D., *Dictionary of The Napoleonic Wars* (London, 1979).

Cochrane Capt. C., *Journal of a Residence and Travels in Colombia During the years 1823 and 1824* (London, 1825).

Cole, M., & Gwynne, S., *Memoirs of Sir Lowry Cole* (London, 1934).

Dalton, C., *The Waterloo Roll Call* (London, 1904).

Dawson, Paul L., *Au Pas de Charge! Napoleon's Cavalry at Waterloo* (Stockton on Tees, 2015).

Glover, G., *From Corunna to Waterloo, The Letters and Journals of Two Napoleonic Hussars 1801-16* (London, 2007).

Glover, G., *The American Sharpe, The adventures of an American Officer of the 95th Rifles in the Peninsular and Waterloo Campaigns* (Barnsley, 2016).

Gregory, D., *The Rediscovery of Latin America in the Early Nineteenth Century* (London, 1992).

Gurwood, J. *Duke of Wellington Despatches 1799-1815* (London, 1837-8).

Hall, John, *A History of the Peninsular War Vol. VIII, The Biographical Dictionary of British Officers Killed and Wounded 1808-14* (London, 1998).

Helie, G., *Journal du George Woodberry Campagnes Du Portugal et d'Espagne de France de Belgique et de France (1813-15)* (Paris 1896).

Hicks, Peter., *Lieutenant Woodberry Journal de Guerre (1813-1815)* (Paris, 2013).

Hunt, Eric, *Charging Against Napoleon, Diaries & Letters Of Three Hussars* (Barnsley, 2001).

Ludovici, A., *On the Road with Wellington, the Diary of a War Commissary in the Peninsular Campaigns By August Ludolf Friedrich Schaumann* (New York, 1925).

Malet, H.E., *Historical Records of the Eighteenth Hussars* (London, 1869).

Malet H.E., *The Historical Memoirs of the Eighteenth (Prince of Wales' Own) Hussars* (London, 1907).

Mollo, John, *The Prince's Dolls, Scandals, Skirmishes and Splendours of the Hussars 1739-1815* (Barnsley, 1997).

Mullen, A.T., *The Military General Service Roll 1799-1814* (London, 1990).

Park, S.J & Nafziger, G.F., *The British Military, Its System and Organization 1803-1815* (Ontario, 1983).

Porter, Robert Ker, *Sir Robert Ker Porter's Caracas diary, 1825-1842: A British diplomat in a newborn nation* (London, 1966).

Oman, C., *A History of the Peninsular War* (London, 1930).

Oman C., *Wellington's Army 1809-1814* (London, 1913).

Veve, Thomas, *The Duke of Wellington and the British Army of Occupation in France 1815-18* (Westport,1992).

Vivian, C., *Richard Hussey Vivian, First Baron Vivian, A Memoir* (London, 1897).

# Index